SUPRALAPSARIANISM RECONSIDERED

T&T Clark Studies in Systematic Theology

Edited by

Ian A. McFarland
Ivor Davidson
Philip G. Ziegler
John Webster†

Volume 43

SUPRALAPSARIANISM RECONSIDERED

Jonathan Edwards and the Reformed Tradition

Phillip A. Hussey

LONDON • NEW YORK • OXFORD • NEW DELHI • SYDNEY

T&T CLARK
Bloomsbury Publishing Plc, 50 Bedford Square, London, WC1B 3DP, UK
Bloomsbury Publishing Inc, 1359 Broadway, New York, NY 10018, USA
Bloomsbury Publishing Ireland, 29 Earlsfort Terrace, Dublin 2, D02 AY28, Ireland

BLOOMSBURY, T&T CLARK and the T&T Clark logo are trademarks of
Bloomsbury Publishing Plc

First published in Great Britain 2024
Paperback edition published 2026

Copyright © Phillip A. Hussey, 2024

Phillip A. Hussey has asserted his right under the Copyright, Designs and Patents Act, 1988, to
be identified as Author of this work.

For legal purposes the Acknowledgments on pp. x–xi constitute an extension of this
copyright page.

All rights reserved. No part of this publication may be: i) reproduced or transmitted in any form, electronic or mechanical, including photocopying, recording or by means of any information storage or retrieval system without prior permission in writing from the publishers; or ii) used or reproduced in any way for the training, development or operation of artificial intelligence (AI) technologies, including generative AI technologies. The rights holders expressly reserve this publication from the text and data mining exception as per Article 4(3) of the Digital Single Market Directive (EU) 2019/790.

Bloomsbury Publishing Plc does not have any control over, or responsibility for, any
third-party websites referred to or in this book. All internet addresses given in this book were
correct at the time of going to press. The author and publisher regret any inconvenience caused if
addresses have changed or sites have ceased to exist,
but can accept no responsibility for any such changes.

A catalogue record for this book is available from the British Library.

Library of Congress Cataloging-in-Publication Data
Names: Hussey, Phillip A., author.
Title: Supralapsarianism reconsidered : Jonathan Edwards and the
Reformed tradition / Phillip A. Hussey.
Other titles: Jesus Christ as the "Sum of God's decrees"
Description: London ; New York : T&T Clark, 2024. | Series: T&T Clark studies in systematic
theology | Revision of the author's thesis (doctoral)–Saint Louis University, 2021, under the title:
Jesus Christ as the "Sum of God's decrees":
an engagement with the theology of Jonathan Edwards. |
Includes bibliographical references.
Identifiers: LCCN 2023051124 (print) | LCCN 2023051125 (ebook) |
ISBN 9780567714787 (hardback) | ISBN 9780567714824 (paperback) |
ISBN 9780567714794 (pdf) | ISBN 9780567714800 (ebook)
Subjects: LCSH: Edwards, Jonathan, 1703–1758. | Jesus Christ–Person and offices. |
Reformed Church–Doctrines.
Classification: LCC BX7260.E3 H87 2024 (print) | LCC BX7260.E3 (ebook) |
DDC 232/.8–dc23/eng/20240126
LC record available at https://lccn.loc.gov/2023051124
LC ebook record available at https://lccn.loc.gov/2023051125

ISBN: HB: 978-0-5677-1478-7
PB: 978-0-5677-1482-4
ePDF: 978-0-5677-1479-4
ePub: 978-0-5677-1480-0

Series: T&T Clark Studies in Systematic Theology, volume 43

Typeset by Newgen KnowledgeWorks Pvt. Ltd., Chennai, India

For product safety related questions contact productsafety@bloomsbury.com.

To find out more about our authors and books visit www.bloomsbury.com
and sign up for our newsletters.

For Oliver Stewart Hussey

Blessed are the pure in heart, for they shall see God.

Mt. 5:8

CONTENTS

Acknowledgments	x
List of Abbreviations	xii
INTRODUCTION	1
Theological Retrieval	1
The Dogmatic Concern	4
The Interlocutor	8
The Structure of the Argument	10

Part I
THE REFORMED CONTEXT

Chapter 1	
THE CONTOURS OF LAPSARIANISM: DIVERSITY IN SEVENTEENTH-CENTURY REFORMED THEOLOGY	15
Francis Turretin (1623–87): Infralapsarianism Exemplified	18
The Object of Predestination	19
Christ and the Cause of Election	22
The Order of the Decrees	24
Petrus van Mastricht (1630–1706): Lapsarianism Mediated	27
Acts and Objects of Predestination	28
The Acts of Election	32
The Acts of Reprobation	33
Order of Predestination	37
Rigid and Mediated Supralapsarianism Compared	38
Thomas Goodwin (1600–1680): Supralapsarianism Modified	42
Super-Creation Grace	43
Supralapsarian Christology	45
Individual Election and Reprobation Compared	49
Some Lapsarian Conclusions	51
Chapter 2	
LAPSARIANISM PROBLEMATIZED AND PURIFIED: HERMAN BAVINCK AND KARL BARTH	57
Herman Bavinck on the Inadequacy of the Infra- and Supralapsarian Distinction	57
Preliminary Problems with Infralapsarianism	58

Preliminary Problems with Supralapsarianism	60
The Deeper Problem with Infra- and Supralapsarianism	62
The Election of Christ	66
Karl Barth and Purified Supralapsarianism	68
The Lapsarian Excursus of *Church Dogmatics* §33.1	70
The Common Presuppositions	70
The Advantages and Deeper Problems of Infralapsarianism	74
Purified Supralapsarianism	76
Supralapsarianism, Covenant, and *das Nichtige*	78
Theological Summary	84

Part II
JONATHAN EDWARDS AND LAPSARIANISM

Chapter 3
CREATION, CHRIST, AND THE DECREES — 91

The Relationship between God and the World	93
The Election of the Son of God *ad intra*: The Father's Election of the Son	97
The Election of the Son of God *ad extra*: Election as Creative Communication	99
The Election of Christ and Supralapsarian Christology	108
"Miscellanies" no. 1245	109
The End of the Incarnation	113
Summary	117

Chapter 4
COVENANT, CHRIST, AND THE DECREES — 121

The Covenant of Works	125
Adam's Reward and the Covenant of Works	129
The Angelic Covenant and Reward	132
The Covenant of Redemption	134
Relation to the Covenant of Works	138
Relation to the Covenant of Grace	140
The Marriage Covenant and the Election of Jesus Christ	147
A Covenantal Synthesis	148
The Remainder	154

Chapter 5
PARTICULAR PREDESTINATION, CHRIST, AND THE DECREES — 155

The Order of the Decrees	156
The Harmony of the Decrees	156
Harmony and Christ	159
"Miscellanies" nos 700 and 704	161
Original and Hypothetical Ends	162

Priority and Posteriority in "Miscellanies" nos 700 and 704   164
The Decree Concerning the Permission of Sin, *Felix Culpa*, and
    Redemption   173
   The Image of God and the Holy Spirit   173
   Permission of Sin and the *Felix Culpa*   174
   Felix Culpa and the Work of Redemption   178
Particular Election and Reprobation   180
   Christ, the Holy Spirit, and the Elect   182
   The Beatific Vision   184
   Hell and the Reprobate   189
   Christ and the Reprobate   193
Conclusion   195

Part III
SUPRALAPSARIANISM RECONSIDERED

Chapter 6
A MODEST THEOLOGICAL SKETCH   203
   Theological Summary   203
   The Problems in Edwards's Account   207
      The Motive for the Incarnation   208
      Vindictive Justice   211
   The Promise of Edwards's Account   213
   Desiderata for Supralapsarianism   216
   Thinking Creation, Incarnation, and Fittingness   219
   Thinking Supralapsarianism and the *Felix Culpa*   223
   Concluding Theological Postscript   225

Bibliography   227
Index   241

ACKNOWLEDGMENTS

This monograph stands as a revision of my PhD dissertation. Many individuals along the way have, each in their own way, helped me think through— and at times strongly challenged—the ideas presented in this book, as well as provided much needed encouragement along the way. Accordingly, a debt of gratitude is in order. My PhD advisor, Michael McClymond, both challenged me to articulate my arguments with stringent clarity and gave me ample space to pursue the topic as I saw fit. Such is rare, and I am grateful. For the friends and colleagues, both past and present, at Beeson Divinity School and Saint Louis University—some of whom read the entire manuscript—I am immensely thankful. I hope this work serves as a testimony to the academic rigor and devotion to the Lord Jesus Christ that was impressed upon me so long ago at Beeson. To the women and men of the churches that I have belonged to in Birmingham, AL, and Saint Louis, MO, thank you for constantly reminding me that theology is best undertaken in service of the church's confession of the triune God. Many thanks to Ken Minkema, Director of the Jonathan Edwards Center at Yale, who graciously provided invaluable transcriptions of a few of Edwards's unpublished sermon manuscripts, thereby allowing my untrained eye to make sense of Edwards's otherwise indecipherable handwriting. I also want to thank the editors of this series for their enthusiastic support of the project. The overall production and editorial team at T&T Clark, who work behind the scenes and so often go unacknowledged, were also a delight to work with. And, finally, I must express thanks to my family, of whom words fail. My wife, Claire, bore with much (too much!) patience many years of my mind being occupied with thoughts of Jonathan Edwards and supralapsarianism; my son, Peter, too young to care about such things, happily reminds me not to take myself too seriously. This book is dedicated to our son, Oliver: *credo in carnis resurrectionem, vitam aeternam.*

Portions of chapters three and five appear elsewhere. They are kindly reproduced here in expanded and revised form and, when appropriate, by permission.

In chapter three:

Hussey, Phillip, and Michael McClymond. "Creation and Predestination." In *The Oxford Handbook of Jonathan Edwards*, edited by Douglas A. Sweeney and Jan Stievermann, 199–214. Oxford: Oxford University Press, 2021. Reproduced by permission of Oxford University Press. (https://global.oup.com/academic/product/the-oxford-handbook-of-jonathan-edwards-9780198754060?cc=us&lang=en&#).

Hussey, Phillip. "Jesus Christ as the 'Sum of God's Decrees': Christological Supralapsarianism in the Theology of Jonathan Edwards." *Jonathan Edwards Studies* 6, no. 2 (2016): 107–19.

In chapter five:

Hussey, Phillip. "Jonathan Edwards on Divine Justice and Anger." In *Righteous Indignation: Christian Philosophical and Theological Perspectives on Anger*, edited by Gregory Bock and Court Lewis, 98–113. Lanham, MD: Lexington Books/Fortress Academic, 2021. All rights reserved. Reproduced by permission of Rowman & Littlefield.

All English translations appear here by permission:

Excerpt from *Reformed Dogmatics, Volume 1* by Herman Bavinck, copyright © 2003. Used by permission of Baker Academic, a division of Baker Publishing Group.

Excerpt from *Reformed Dogmatics, Volume 2* by Herman Bavinck, copyright © 2004. Used by permission of Baker Academic, a division of Baker Publishing Group.

Excerpt from *Reformed Dogmatics, Volume 3* by Herman Bavinck, copyright © 2006. Used by permission of Baker Academic, a division of Baker Publishing Group.

Excerpt from *Institutes of Elenctic Theology* by Francis Turretin (ISBN 978-0-87552-456-6). Used with permission from P&R Publishing, PO Box 817 Phillipsburg, NJ 08865 www.prpbooks.com.

ABBREVIATIONS

CD	Barth, Karl. *Church Dogmatics*. Edited by G. W. Bromiley and T. F. Torrance. 4 vols in 13 pts. Edinburgh: T&T Clark, 1936–77.
Inst.	Turretin, Francis. *Institutio theologiae elencticae*. 2nd edn. Geneva: Samuel de Tournes, 1688.
RD	Bavinck, Herman. *Reformed Dogmatics*. Edited by John Bolt. Translated by John Vriend. 4 vols. Grand Rapids, MI: Baker Academic, 2003–8.
TPT	Mastricht, Petrus van. *Theoretico-practica theologia: qua, per singular capita theologica, pars exegetica, dogmatica, elenchtica et practica, perpetua successione conjugantur*. Ed. nova, priori multo emendatior et plus quam tertia parte auctior. Utrecht: Thomae Appels, 1699.
Works	Goodwin, Thomas. *The Works of Thomas Goodwin*. 12 vols. Edinburgh: James Nichol, 1861–6. Reprint, Lafayette, IN: Sovereign Grace Publishers, 2000.
WJE	Edwards, Jonathan. *The Works of Jonathan Edwards*. 26 vols. New Haven, NJ: Yale University Press, 1957–2008.
WJEO	Edwards, Jonathan. *The Works of Jonathan Edwards Online*. 73 vols. New Haven, NJ: Jonathan Edwards Center at Yale University. http://edwards.yale.edu/.

INTRODUCTION

Schemes in theology which reject the doctrine of the divine decree necessarily present a fractional and disconnected view of God, man, and nature.[1]

—William G. T. Shedd

Theological Retrieval

What follows is a dogmatic sketch and reconceptualization of supralapsarianism in the mode of theological retrieval. It remains only a sketch because the dogmatic portion only appears in the final chapter after many chapters of stage-setting, and only at that point proffers a modest theological construction. Two matters are of note before proceeding to an introduction and outline of the subject matter proper. The first concerns the nature and task of dogmatics. Dogmatics is "the knowledge that God has revealed in his Word to the church concerning himself and all creatures as they stand in relation to him."[2] In this sense, dogmatics lies at the intersection of divine revelation and ecclesial confession. Dogmatics is a "function of the Christian Church" as it submits itself to the tutelage of prophets and apostles in the laying out and ordering of *dogmata*, or articles of faith.[3] So conceived, "dogmatic reasoning produces a conceptual representation of what reason has learned from its exegetical following of the scriptural text."[4] In dogmatics the theologian often employs extra-scriptural terms (e.g., *homoousias*, supralapsarianism) in order to reproduce as precisely and faithfully as possible the content of revelation. So, John Owen comments

---

1. William G. T. Shedd, *Dogmatic Theology*, vol. 1 (New York: Charles Scribner's Sons, 1888), 398–9.
2. Bavinck, *RD* 1:38.
3. Barth, *CD* I.1, 17.
4. John Webster, "Biblical Reasoning," in *Domain of the Word: Scripture and Theological Reasoning* (New York: Bloomsbury T&T Clark, 2012), 130.

Use is to be made of words and expressions as, it may be, are not literally and formally contained in the Scripture; but only are, unto our conceptions and apprehensions, expository of what is so contained. And to deny the liberty, yea, the necessity hereof, is to deny all interpretation of the Scripture,—all endeavours to express the sense of the words of it unto the understandings of one another; which is, in a word, to render the Scripture itself useless.[5]

Put another way, "dogmatics … just is exegesis carried out in an elaborative manner."[6]

Dogmatics is also an activity of faith,[7] and so its labors remain caught up between old life in Adam and new life in Christ. As an activity of faith, dogmatics concerns itself with the reproduction of the words of scripture into ecclesial confession, and, by extension, concerns itself with *dogmata* already "incorporated in the consciousness of the church and confessed by it in its own language."[8] Of course, dogma is not absolutely identical with the truth of God itself, nor is it to be conflated with pronouncements of Holy Scripture. "The prophets and apostles are appointed by God, dogmaticians are not."[9] Nevertheless, dogmatics takes confessional realities seriously because the confirmation, recognition, and refinement of the truths inherent in the evangelical pronouncements are part and parcel of the church's ongoing mission. The distinction between systematic and dogmatic theology appears at this junction, although only relatively. Whereas dogmatic theology is more explicitly concerned to further elucidate, even critique, the existing *dogmata* laid down by the church, systematic theology exercises a greater liberty regarding ecclesial confessions.[10]

The second matter of note concerns the method of theological retrieval. Although the primary material for constructing a dogmatic theology is Holy Scripture, theological retrieval facilitates the production of dogmatic theology because it attends to the deposit of faith entrusted to and reflected upon by the communion of saints throughout time. Reflecting on this matter, Michael Allen and Scott Swain refer to the Christian tradition as the elicitive principle of theology such that the posture of retrieval stands as its ethical handmaiden.[11] Karl Barth, in his own way, said the same: "there is no past in the Church, so there is no past

---

5. John Owen, *Brief Declaration and Vindication of the Doctrine of the Trinity*, 379, as quoted in Steven Duby, *Divine Simplicity: A Dogmatic Account* (New York: Bloomsbury, T&T Clark, 2016), 56.

6. Duby, *Divine Simplicity*, 56.

7. Cf. Barth, *CD* I.1, 17–24.

8. Bavinck, *RD* 1:30.

9. Webster, "Biblical Reasoning," 131.

10. Cf. Robert Jenson, *Systematic Theology, Vol. 1: The Triune God* (New York: Oxford University Press, 1997), 22.

11. Michael Allen and Scott Swain, *Reformed Catholicity: The Promise of Retrieval for Theology and Biblical Interpretation* (Grand Rapids, MI: Baker Academic, 2015), 36.

in theology."[12] The basis of these claims is rigidly christological: Jesus Christ is the *living* Lord of the church and, as such, shines the light of his wisdom into the communion of saints united to him throughout history.[13] Such an understanding of tradition informs both the prospect and ethics of retrieval. The present is not privileged; neither is the past pristine. The task of retrieval is critical, not nostalgic, exercising confidence and discernment as the theologian listens to the great cloud of witnesses as they listened to Christ. Through this act of listening, theologies of retrieval often "decenter" the critical judgments of modern sensibilities "by trying to stand with the Christian past which, precisely because it is foreign to contemporary conventions, can function as an instrument for the enlargement of vision."[14]

Procedurally there exist different sorts of retrieval projects, whether Roman Catholic, Protestant, or Orthodox.[15] Despite these different confessional approaches, Darren Sarisky has helpfully outlined a sort of "family resemblance" between them. I will simply summarize these resemblances here to indicate the manner of retrieval undertaken in the pages that follow.[16]

1. Theologies of retrieval deny a progressive view of history that holds past ideas as scientifically outmoded.
2. Theologies of retrieval are not concerned to repristinate the past in rigid conformity; retrieval is not mere repetition.
3. Most importantly, the aim of retrieval is to "think *with* rather than *about* historical texts"; it is, in this sense, a thinking with and beyond them for the sake of the present.

---

12. Karl Barth, *Protestant Theology in the Nineteenth Century*, as quoted in John Webster, *Barth's Earlier Theology: Four Studies* (New York: T&T Clark, 2005), 112.

13. Cf. Michael Allen, "Reformed Retrieval," in *Theologies of Retrieval: An Exploration and Appraisal*, ed. Darren Sarisky (New York: T&T Clark, 2017), 76–9.

14. John Webster, "Theologies of Retrieval," in *Oxford Handbook of Systematic Theology*, ed. John Webster, Kathryn Tanner, and Ian Torrance (New York: Oxford University Press, 2007), 590.

15. One prominent example of theology in the mode of retrieval is *ressourcement*—a movement associated with Roman Catholic theologians in the middle third of the twentieth century. Immersion in the texts of the church fathers provided a "rediscovery of the inseparability of exegesis, theology, and spirituality" for theologians such as de Lubac, Chenu, and Congar, which in turn provided a much-needed liberation from the self-imposed constraints (and false dilemmas) of modern theological methods. Webster, "Theologies of Retrieval," 590. See also the collection of essays edited by Darren Sarisky: *Theologies of Retrieval: An Exploration and Appraisal* (New York: T&T Clark, 2017).

16. Darren Sarisky, "Tradition II: Thinking with Historical Texts—Reflections on Theologies of Retrieval," in *Theologies of Retrieval: An Exploration and Appraisal*, ed. Darren Sarisky (New York: T&T Clark, 2017), 198–205.

4. The theologian of retrieval becomes an active participant in a conversation with the text; in other words, there is no such thing as a purely disengaged reading.
5. Theologians of retrieval relate to the text (and its author) as pupils before a teacher, and, only after listening, appropriate the material in their own speech and idiom.
6. Theologies of retrieval involve "selectivity and discrimination." Quite obviously, certain texts and authors are deemed more appropriate than others depending on the theological topic under consideration; there also exist texts not worthy of retrieval at all. In this sense, evaluative judgments about texts and their validity are inevitable.

Overall, it must also be noted that retrieval is not historical theology, even though the work of historical theology is indispensable to the task. Historians—rightly so—are wary of normative judgments for fear of misrepresenting the past anachronistically. Retrieval, on the other hand, is not simply concerned with getting past figures and texts "right" contextually (even though that is a concern), but with a larger question: are they right theologically, and, if so, what can we learn from them? Both concerns—the historical and the dogmatic—animate this project, though the latter is ultimate and the former penultimate.

The Dogmatic Concern

The dogmatic topics under consideration in this study are creation, predestination, and Christology, specifically their supralapsarian form and entanglement. Because I take on this task in a self-consciously Reformed mode, it is proper to call it a work in *Reformed* dogmatics.[17] For many, the doctrine of predestination appears to be

---

17. Any definition of what constitutes *Reformed* remains somewhat elusive, especially since—unlike Lutheranism for example—"that which is Reformed has not been laid down in a single confession but found expression in numerous creeds." Bavinck, *RD* 1:177. Although the definition could be pursued genealogically with respect to Zwingli and Bullinger, Bucer and Calvin, and others, I employ the term theologically to signal my commitment to the expression of doctrine as laid down across the various Reformed confessions and catechisms. Bavinck captures the overlapping, though not exclusive, emphasis well: "The Reformed person does not rest until he has traced all things retrospectively to the divine decree, tracking down the "wherefore" of things, and has prospectively made all things subservient to the glory of God." Bavinck, *RD* 1:177. Richard Muller's comments are also salient: "Reformed theology appears not as a monolithic structure—not, in short, as "Calvinism"—but as a form of Augustinian theology and piety capable of considerable variation in its form of presentation, and capable also of clarification and augmentation on fine points of doctrine." Richard Muller, *Christ and the Decree: Christology and Predestination in Reformed Theology from Calvin to Perkins* (Grand Rapids, MI: Baker Academic, 2008), 176.

a peculiar Reformed obsession.[18] When the topic of predestination is mentioned in the context of Reformed theology, the immediate thought-form is often that of individual "double" predestination, wherein God elects some to eternal life and consigns others (reprobates) to hell. The *Westminster Confession of Faith*, for example, outlines the contours of this approach to the decree of predestination, wherein "by the decree of God, for the manifestation of his glory, some men and Angels are predestinated unto everlasting life, and others fore-ordained to everlasting death. These Angels and men thus predestinated and fore-ordained, are particularly, and unchangeably designed, and their number is so certain, and definite, that it cannot be either increased, or diminished."[19] To some, this type of formulation leads to "colored readings of the biblical text";[20] for others, such formulations are indeed despotic.[21] I, at least, find certain premises at work in Reformed theology to be correct, precisely because sovereign election—despite protestations to the contrary—is woven into the biblical text.[22]

Despite the individualized (i.e., "double") approach mentioned above, such an articulation of predestination has neither been exclusive nor exhaustive. It has taken on various permutations in, for instance, Friedrich Schleiermacher, Herman Bavinck, Karl Barth, and, more recently, Suzanne McDonald.[23] A most impressive reformulation occurs in the hands of Barth, wherein predestination "comes to refer, not to a decision of God in which the human race is divided into the elect and

---

18. B. B. Warfield goes so far as to say that the "doctrine of Predestination was … the central doctrine of the Reformation." According to Warfield, the central concern for the "absolute dependence on the God of grace for salvation" was purified in Reformed thought so as to find its proper "theological expression in the complete doctrine of the *praedestinatio duplex*." Benjamin Warfield, "Predestination in the Reformed Confessions," in *The Works of Benjamin B. Warfield, Vol. IX: Studies in Theology* (Grand Rapids, MI: Baker Books, 2003), 117–20.

19. John R. Bower, *The Westminster Confession of Faith: A Critical Text and Introduction* (Grand Rapids, MI: Reformation Heritage Books, 2020), III.3–4, 200.

20. Peter J. Thuesen, *Predestination: The American Career of a Contentious Debate* (New York: Oxford University Press, 2009), 217.

21. David Bentley Hart, *Beauty of the Infinite: The Aesthetics of Christian Truth* (Grand Rapids, MI: Wm. B. Eerdmans, 2003), 134.

22. Even though the fundamental reality of predestination is both biblical and catholic, this does not mean that (significant) disagreements do not remain with regard to the particularities of the dogmatic presentation. Cf. Matthew Levering, *Predestination: Biblical and Theological Paths* (New York: Oxford University Press, 2011), 177–201; Mark R. Lindsay, *God Has Chosen: The Doctrine of Election through Christian History* (Downers Grove, IL: IVP Academic, 2020).

23. Barth and Bavinck will be explored in Chapter 2. For Schleiermacher and McDonald, see Friedrich Schleiermacher, *On the Doctrine of Election, with Special Reference to the Aphorisms of Dr. Bretschneider*, trans. Iain G. Nicol and Allen G. Jorgensen (Louisville, KY: WJK, 2012); and Suzanne McDonald, *Re-Imaging Election: Divine Election as Representing God to Others and Others to God* (Grand Rapids, MI: Wm. B. Eerdmans, 2010).

the reprobate, but to God's self-election and the election of humanity, both actual in Jesus Christ."[24] Ingredient to Barth's account of election is his christological purification of "supralapsarianism." The language of supralapsarianism and infralapsarianism most often refers to an intra-Reformed dispute on the order, objects, and end(s) of predestination. Barth fixated on the debate because he recognized in it the integration of a host of theological questions and concerns, especially those of nature and grace. As such, an understanding of the lapsarian debate in the seventeenth century will prove instructive for this study, as well as the pointed and dogmatic questions Barth raises in his analysis of it. So too will the theological critiques of the debate by Herman Bavinck. Each in their own way helps frame dogmatic questions that need answering, even if I do not find their final answers theologically viable (Barth) or sufficiently worked out (Bavinck). To be sure, the contemporary discussion on election (and rejection) has been shaped to a large extent by Barth's and his interpreters' theological reconstruction of the doctrine of God around the doctrine of election. But rather than pursue a defensive or polemical path, I plan on presenting an alternative way forward through the retrieval of another Reformed theologian's "purification" of supralapsarianism. In this sense, I will attempt to answer Barth's and Bavinck's dogmatic questions using the theological insights of Jonathan Edwards.

So, much like Barth's fixation, this study reconsiders the relation between Christ, creation, and predestination through the lens of infra- and supralapsarian debate. My proximate concern, however, will not be the relation between divine sovereignty and human freedom, a concern which so often animates the debates surrounding predestination. Neither, strange as it may sound, will it expressly be the eternal destinies of human creatures. Similar to Matthew Levering's recent project, my main focus will be on God's eternal plan.[25] Unlike Levering, my focus centers on the integration of creation, predestination, and Christology in the divine plan; or, in a different idiom, I will explore the positive relation that exists between the good pleasure of God's will in creation and the predestination of Jesus Christ (cf. Eph. 1). To pick up Barth's forceful query with relation to the decree of predestination as articulated in the Reformed tradition: Where is the picture of God in Jesus Christ?

In fixating on the relation between the decree of creation and the predestination of Christ, I am also seeking to examine the interrelation between two theological questions: *Cur mundus?* and *Cur Deus homo?* Regarding the latter question, the language of supralapsarianism has been employed with reference to the motive of the incarnation of the Son of God vis-à-vis the Fall.[26] This is often referred to as

---

24. John Webster, *Karl Barth*, 2nd edn (New York: Continuum, 2004), 91.

25. Levering's work is also a project of retrieval, which fixes upon the thought of Catherine of Siena and Francis de Sales after offering up, more or less, a selective survey of predestination. See Levering, *Predestination*, 192–201.

26. Most recently, see Edwin Chr. van Driel, *Incarnation Anyway: Arguments for a Supralapsarian Christology* (Oxford: Oxford University Press, 2008).

supralapsarian Christology because it discusses the logical place of the incarnation in the decree. Is the incarnation decreed *supra lapsum* or *infra lapsum*? For the sake of redemption or not? Such questions on the contingency of the incarnation have a long history, becoming particularly lively in the disagreements between Thomists and Scotists.[27] Close to hand—quite obviously given the "lapsarian" nomenclature—is God's deeper purpose in permitting the fall of human creatures and (im)propriety of speaking of a *felix culpa*, with the term *felix culpa* itself coming from the Latin Easter Vigil (*Exsultet*):

O certe necessarium Adae peccatum, quod Christi morte deletum est!
O felix culpa, quae talem ac tantum meruit habere Redemptorem!
O truly necessary sin of Adam, which was blotted out by the death of Christ!
O happy fault, that merited to possess such and so great a Redeemer!

Discussions involving supralapsarianism forms of predestination and supralapsarian Christology—though closely related in terms of their concerns on the logical order of the decrees, God's end in creation, and God's purpose in permitting sin—have not been brought together in a dogmatically cogent manner. In dogmatically reconsidering the relationship between Christ, creation, and predestination, I aim to show that this is both necessary and desirable given the scriptural emphasis that God predestined human creatures for adoption through Jesus Christ according to the purpose of God's will (cf. Eph. 1:5). Although a discussion of the election and rejection of individual creatures within the larger architectonic of supralapsarianism is certainly important, that concern remains secondary for the present study. The dogmatic sketch offered in the final chapter sets forth the integration of creation, predestination, and Christology, while slightly gesturing toward implications for individual election and reprobation, along with attendant concerns of divine and human causality. The latter question,

---

27. See Justus H. Hunter, *If Adam Had Not Sinned: The Reason for the Incarnation from Anselm to Scotus* (Washington, DC: The Catholic University of America Press, 2020); Dylan Schrader, *A Thomistic Christocentrism: Recovering the Carmelites of Salamanca on the Logic of the Incarnation* (Washington, DC: The Catholic University of America Press, 2021); and Dylan Schrader, introduction to *On the Motive of the Incarnation*, by The Salmanticenses (Discalced Carmelites of Salamanca), trans. Dylan Schrader (Washington, DC: The Catholic University of America Press, 2019), xiii–xlix. Another important discussion is that of Marilyn McCord Adams, *Christ and Horrors: The Coherence of Christology* (Cambridge: Cambridge University Press, 2006), 174–91. For Adams, the incarnation is conditionally necessary upon God's decision to create *this* world, which, because it is material—and therefore mutable—inevitably entails human-horror participation. God accepts such horrors as part of the cosmic package in creating. Even still, God's assimilative and unitive aims in creation necessitate (upon the condition of creating) the incarnation in order to accomplish various stages of horror-defeat, which ultimately leads to universal restoration (pp. 66, 189–91).

as Matthew Levering rightly notes, is not illegitimate and in fact arises "every time one contemplates God's love and saving power."[28] As Levering further suggests, the question of God's rejection cannot be suppressed at length and, when taken up, must be approached with humility and patience before the God whose judgments are unsearchable and ways inscrutable (cf. Rom. 11:33).[29] My aim is not to suppress at length, but to dogmatically prioritize the end of predestination before any consideration of the contours of individual election and rejection.

The Interlocutor

As a work of theological retrieval, this study attends to the theological reasoning of Jonathan Edwards to provide a coherent theological account of supralapsarianism after the manner mentioned above. He has been chosen as the primary interlocutor because, as a transatlantic Reformed thinker and polymath, Edwards worked within the Reformed tradition and sought to advance that tradition in the face of perceived Enlightenment, Deist, and Arminian threats. In so doing, he bequeathed to those after him a promising and provocative—at times problematic—theological oeuvre. Edwards, not surprisingly, defended double predestination in the vein of the *Westminster Confession*. More shockingly, however, Edwards coupled this defense with a rich trinitarian and christological approach to creation and predestination few have rivaled in the tradition, and he did so in ways that resonate with the thought of the likes of Herman Bavinck and Karl Barth. As Edwards wrote in "Miscellanies," no. 1245, "in that grand decree of predestination, or the sum of God's decrees ... the appointment of Christ, or the decree respecting his person ... must be considered first."[30] The fuller logic of his reasoning makes him an ideal conversation partner for the constructive task. And, as mentioned above, Edwards's theological reasoning also helps mitigate a contemporary instinct to restructure the doctrine of God in terms of election. By attending to the full compass of Edwards's thought, another path forward appears with regard to Christology, creation, and election.

In taking up Edwards as an interlocutor, I will also provide an extended interpretation of Edwards's thoughts on these matters. This is closer to the work of

---

28. Levering, *Predestination*, 199.

29. For a recent overview of various Thomistic positions on individual predestination, see Taylor Patrick O'Neill, *Grace, Predestination, and the Permission of Sin: A Thomistic Analysis* (Washington, DC: The Catholic University of America Press, 2019). O'Neill argues the best Thomistic presentations (in keeping with Thomas himself) foreground absolute and conditional necessity, and therefore the radical contingency of created being with its attendant noncompetitive and mixed relation. This undergirds the permissive nature of God's decree of reprobation and the subsequent fact that human creatures become the proximate causes of sin, which, in turn, causes the actual reprobating act by God.

30. *WJE* 23:180.

historical theology. In this narrower and penultimate sense, I provide an appropriate interpretation of Edwards's thought by examining the various discussions of "decrees," "predestination," "election," and "reprobation" across his corpus. Strangely enough, the vast secondary literature on the theology of Jonathan Edwards reveals relatively little sustained treatment of Edwards's intellections and reflections on the divine decrees. Although much ink has been spilled over Edwards's understanding of the will, and by proxy liberty, necessity, and original sin, this interest has not significantly carried over into his thoughts on predestination as it relates to the divine decrees, creation, and Christology. The same can be said of the recent renaissance of Edwards's trinitarian theology. Recent theologians and historians have placed significant emphasis on Edwards's trinitarianism for understanding his entire theological project, but such an emphasis remains underdeveloped with regard to how it actually comports with the specificities of predestination. Edwards's precise position needs, in this sense, significant elucidation and (re)interpretation.

As will be brought out with greater clarity throughout my interpretation of Edwards's theology, discussions within the secondary literature have had difficulty characterizing Edwards's lapsarianism, as well as the integration of his thoughts on God's self-glorification, Christology, the work of redemption, and individual election and rejection. Almost all interpreters, in one sense or another, highlight the disjunctive nature of election and reprobation in Edwards's theology. While some place this in a metaphysical and deterministic framework,[31] others also see a theological problem associated with his articulations of the trinitarian work of creation and redemption.[32] This disjunction has led to strong critiques of his account of reprobation, primarily on christological and trinitarian grounds, as opposed to a critique based on a determinist theological system as such. Based on this interpretive landscape, a few issues need clarification.

First, no interpreter seems to be able to put together an accurate account of Edwards's lapsarianism. For some, he is an infralapsarian;[33] to others, a

---

31. See, for example, Thomas A. Schafer, "Jonathan Edwards' Conception of the Church," *Church History* 24, no. 1 (March 1955): 52-4; John Newton Thomas, "Determinism in the Theological System of Jonathan Edwards" (PhD Diss., University of Edinburgh, 1937), 108-42; John Stafford Weeks, "A Comparison of Calvin and Edwards on the Doctrine of Election" (PhD Diss., University of Chicago, 1962), 195-256; and Oliver Crisp, *Jonathan Edwards and the Metaphysics of Sin* (Burlington, VT: Ashgate, 2005), 5-24.

32. See, for example, Amy Plantinga Pauw, *The Supreme Harmony of All: The Trinitarian Theology of Jonathan Edwards* (Grand Rapids, MI: Eerdmans, 2002), 119-50; and Stephen Holmes, *God of Grace and God of Glory: An Account of the Theology of Jonathan Edwards* (Grand Rapids, MI: W. B. Eerdmans, 2000), 125-67.

33. The infralapsarian position is the minority report. Cf. John Gerstner, *The Rational Biblical Theology of Jonathan Edwards*, vol. 2 (Powhatan, VA: Berea Publications, 1992), 161; Michael McClymond and Gerry McDermott, *The Theology of Jonathan Edwards* (New York: Oxford University Press, 2012), 334; and Sam Storms, *Tragedy in Eden: Original Sin in the Theology of Jonathan Edwards* (Lanham, MD: University Press of America, 1985), 275, n. 162.

supralapsarian;[34] to others still, a strange blend of both;[35] or, quite possibly, he eludes the categories.[36] Apart from declaring Edwards incoherent, something appears to be missing from this interpretive picture. In the very least, no interpreter sets the lapsarian quandary within Edwards's larger theological vision with any cogency. It remains, as such, an unresolved issue. Second, and directly related to the first point, Edwards's Christology and trinitarianism remain underdeveloped as they relate to his articulation of the decrees. It is relatively clear that Edwards desires to make Christ the object of election in a larger communicative sense, but it is not so clear how Jesus Christ, as the sum of God's decrees, concretely relates to the individual creatures—both elect and reprobate—in the communicative matrix of creaturely existence, nor is it immediately evident how this impacts larger decretal realities. In a similar sense, how God's triunity is significant for material content and telos of the divine decrees remains opaque. If the world was created with the ultimate end of communicating God's triune glory in and through Jesus Christ, as Edwards makes clear in *End of Creation* (*WJE* 8:399–536), then the relationship between the decree of predestination and the end of creation should exhibit a trinitarian and christological structure given his overall thought. I argue, in fact, that it does, taking shape around the election of Jesus Christ *ad intra* and *ad extra*.

The Structure of the Argument

To reiterate, my primary aim in this study is to dogmatically think, with Edwards as my conversation partner, through the connection between the decrees of creation and election in their christological form. This study also contains a secondary aim. In this secondary sense, I work through Edwards's sprawling and unsystematic discussions of decrees, election, rejection, predestination, and Christology to critically examine his actual position, as well as the cogency of it. Building upon this, the primary aim does ask whether Edwards's understanding can answer certain critical and dogmatic questions posed in modern theology

---

34. Cf. Frank Foster, *A Genetic History of the New England Theology* (Chicago: The University of Chicago Press, 1907), 79; George Fisher, *History of Christian Doctrine* (Edinburgh: T&T Clark, 1896), 401; and Holmes, *God of Grace and God of Glory*, 131. For both Foster and Fisher, Edwards's supralapsarianism is rooted in Edwards's—on their reading—adherence to a form of philosophical determinism.

35. Cf. Crisp, *Metaphysics of Sin*, 5–24; Joe Ben Irby, "Changing Concepts of the Doctrine of Predestination in American Reformed Theology" (ThD Diss., Union Theological Seminary in Virginia, 1975), 90; Schafer, "Jonathan Edwards' Conception of the Church," 52; Thomas, "Determinism in the Theological System of Jonathan Edwards," 130.

36. Cf. Michael Allen, "Jonathan Edwards and the Lapsarian Debate," *Scottish Journal of Theology* 62, no. 3 (2009): 313–15; and Brian Scholl, "The Excellency of Minds: Jonathan Edwards's Theological Style" (PhD Diss., University of Virginia, 2008), 191.

and, in light of the prior interpretation, set forth a modest theological sketch of supralapsarianism.

The argument proceeds in three parts. In Part I, I explore the discussions of infra- and supralapsarianism in the periods of Reformed scholasticism (Chapter 1) and twentieth-century theology (Chapter 2). Chapter 1 sets the stage by attending to the nuances and specificities of the lapsarian debate within its seventeenth-century context after the Synod of Dordt. In particular, I focus on the lapsarian presentations of Francis Turretin, Petrus van Mastricht, and Thomas Goodwin. These theologians are chosen on three suppositions: (1) Edwards himself considers these thinkers to be the foremost masters of theology and employs their reasoning in his own argumentation; (2) as representatives of the high orthodox period in Reformed theology, these thinkers provide a highly developed terminological and theological framework for conceptualizing the divine decrees; and (3) each figure articulates a different species of lapsarianism. By approaching the interpretation of Edwards in this manner, I am able to adjudicate the finer points of his lapsarian reasoning in a theologically and historically sensitive manner, as well as articulate with clarity what is unique in Edwards's account within the framework of Reformed theology. One major finding of this chapter is the recognition that the infra- and supralapsarian debate is not simply about the so-called objects of predestination, but more so about how one integrates the spheres of creation and redemption, nature and grace.

Chapter 2 turns to the theological critiques of the seventeenth-century lapsarian debate as found in the dogmatic works of Herman Bavinck and Karl Barth. The purpose of the second chapter is to trace the contours of Bavinck's and Barth's critiques to lay bare pressing dogmatic concerns and questions with regard to predestination. That said, this study is neither a comparison of Barth/Bavinck and Edwards on the decrees, nor a comparison of Barth/Bavinck and the Reformed tradition. Nor I am overly concerned as to whether or not their critical stances toward Reformed tradition accurately portray the material content of the tradition, at least in terms of the historiography. Furthermore, I will not be concerned with providing an exhaustive interpretation of the positive contributions of Bavinck and Barth on election and reprobation. I will only attend to those matters insofar as they prove instructive for elucidating their dogmatic concerns. Overall, their dogmatic questions take shape around three realities: (1) the construal of the end of the decree predestination; (2) the christological center of God's decrees; and (3) the (causal) interaction of the decrees.

In Part II, I analyze Jonathan Edwards's lapsarianism across three chapters. Chapter 3 parses Edwards's thoughts on the election of Jesus Christ, as well as the implications of such an election for the origin and end of creation. In particular, Edwards views creation as a "condecent" necessity in order that God the Father might show forth and share the Father's love for the Son (and vice versa). Bound up with this discussion is Edwards's endorsement of a species of the supralapsarian Christology. Chapter 4 turns to consider the impact of Edwards's intellections on the election of Jesus Christ for his covenant theology. Here, I show how the election of Jesus Christ provides the interpretive key for understanding

Edwards's remarks that all of God's decrees are reducible to or contained in the covenant of redemption. The election of Jesus Christ, in this sense, also proves to be the key for mapping the relationship between the covenant of redemption, covenant of works, and covenant of grace within Edwards's theology. In Chapter 5, I adjudicate the remaining matters within Edwards's lapsarian vision, especially the tensions created by his understanding of the election of Jesus Christ as they pertain to the permission of the Fall and reprobation. It is in this chapter that I situate Edwards within the traditional infra- and supralapsarian debate. Given Edwards's theological position that all of God's decrees find their harmonious integration around the election of Jesus Christ, I argue that he is best classified (given the rationale of Chapter 1) as a supralapsarian, even though the objects of predestination are clearly fallen human creatures for Edwards.

In the final chapter, I succinctly synthesize the theological importance of the findings of Chapters 3 through 5. I also address counterarguments to my interpretation, as well as address unresolved tensions within Edwards's theology. This is especially true for the case I present for understanding Edwards on the relation between the incarnation and the occasion of the Fall and the work of redemption. After adjudicating a few interpretive issues, I then set forth the promise of Edwards's lapsarian vision, which in turn leads to the laying out of several desiderata for constructing a supralapsarian vision today. This sets the stage for the modest dogmatic appropriation of Edwards's supralapsarian vision. Of particular importance is Edwards's contention that the positive content of God's will in the predestination of Jesus Christ entails trinitarian communication and adoptive union. Again, the question that concerns this study is not whether Edwards was in basic continuity or discontinuity with the Reformed orthodox; nor is it to portray the development of Edwards's thought. While these are certainly important areas of historical research, the question at hand is ultimately dogmatic. Thus, in Chapter 6, I develop the implications of Edwards's theological reasoning so as to reconsider supralapsarianism.

Part I

THE REFORMED CONTEXT

Chapter 1

THE CONTOURS OF LAPSARIANISM: DIVERSITY IN SEVENTEENTH-CENTURY REFORMED THEOLOGY

Discussions of the divine decree have a long history in theological discourse as theologians have sought to make sense of the intention and execution of God's will *ad extra*. The decrees are, as it were, the "bridge" between intrinsic and transient acts in God; they are the immanent acts of God *ad extra*.[1] Put more precisely, the decrees of God are immanent acts that necessarily connote a relation to something external to God and, through God's free activity and power, terminate on those things outside of God.[2] Such decrees are often broken down into general (e.g., creation and providence) and particular (e.g., predestination) categories. As Reformed theology developed after the Reformation—through codification and, most often, internal and external debates—there arose a debate

---

1. Cf. Turretin, *Inst.* 5.1.1. English Translation (ET): *Institutes of Elenctic Theology*, ed. James T. Dennison, Jr., trans. George Musgrave Giger, vol. 1 (Phillipsburg, NJ: P&R Publishing, 1992), 431. Hereafter, all references to Turretin's work will be to the 1688 Latin edition with the English volume and pagination following in parentheses (e.g., Turretin, *Inst.* 5.1.1 [ET: 1:431].). I have followed Giger's translation, though any augmentation I make to it will be noted in the citation.

2. According to the majority of Reformed orthodox divines, God is not bound by an absolute necessity, whether internal or external, to actualize such decrees. Johannes Maccovius's statement here may be taken as exemplary: "There is a distinction between absolute necessity and necessity on the presupposition of the divine will. Absolute necessity regards God's internal works. Necessity on the presupposition of the divine will regards his external works. This distinction occurs in almost all scholastics. It can easily correct the error of those who think that freedom is not compatible with necessity. For all things God works outside of Him, He does with the necessity on the presupposition of his decree, and yet He does them freely." *Scholastic Discourse: Johannes Maccovius (1588–1644) on Theological and Philosophical Distinctions and Rules*, ed. Willem J. van Asselt, Michael D. Bell, Gert van den Brink, and Rein Ferwerda (Apeldoorn: Instituut voor Reformatieonderzoek, 2009), 169.

over how one should conceive the manner and order of God's particular decree of predestination, which is commonly referred to as the infralapsarian and supralapsarian controversy. The theological seedbed of this controversy reaches as far back as Augustine's engagement with Pelagius over the will, although, historically speaking, any designation of a theologian or theological school as infralapsarian or supralapsarian remains somewhat anachronistic before the period of confessionalization leading to the Synod of Dordrecht (1618–19). At the Synod of Dordrecht, certain Reformed orthodox theologians were strongly engaged in a debate with the theology of Jacob Arminius (1560–1609) and that of his followers, also known as the Remonstrants.[3] Arminius had developed a doctrine of predestination in contradistinction from, in his view, the overly deterministic systems of Theodore Beza and William Perkins; as a result, a conflict arose between Franciscus Gomarus and Arminius at Leiden University, where both were serving as professors in the first decade of the seventeenth century. The individual conflict spilled over into a national conflict, which came to a head at the Synod of Dordrecht and ended with a rejection of the Remonstrant (i.e., Arminian) position on predestination as unorthodox.[4]

---

3. For a basic introduction to the Remonstrant Controversy at the Synod of Dordrecht, see Herman Selderhuis, "Die Dordrechter Canones, 1619," in *Reformierte Bekenntnisschriften*, Bd. 3/2, 1605–75, ed. Ebehard Busch, Torrance Kirby, Andreas Mühling, and Herman Selderhuis (Neukirchen-Vluyn: Neukirchener Theologie, 2015), 87–93; Herman Selderhuis, "Introduction to the Synod of Dordt (1618–1619)," in *Acta et Documenta Syndodi Nationalis Dordrechtanae (1618–1619)*, vol. 1, Acta of the Synod of Dordt, ed. Donald Sinnema, Christian Moser, and Herman Selderhuis (Göttingen: Vandenhoeck & Ruprecht, 2015), xv–xxxii; and Donald Sinnema, "Introduction," in *Acta et Documenta Syndodi Nationalis Dordrechtanae (1618–1619)*, vol. II/2, Early Sessions of the Synod of Dordt, ed. Donald Sinnema, Christian Moser, Johanna Roelevin, and Herman Selderhuis (Göttingen: Vandenhoeck & Ruprecht, 2018), xxi–xxviii. For a more detailed discussion, see the following: Aza Goudriaan and Fred van Lieburg, eds., *Revisiting the Synod of Dordt (1618–1619)* (Leiden: Brill, 2011); and Donald Sinnema, "The Issue of Reprobation at the Synod of Dordt (1618–1619) in Light of the History of the Doctrine" (PhD Diss., University of St. Michael's College, Toronto, 1985).

4. For an overview of the theology of, and recent scholarship on, Jacob Arminius and Arminianism, see William den Boer, *God's Twofold Love: The Theology of Jacob Arminius (1559–1609)* (Göttingen: Vandenhoeck & Ruprecht, 2010); Marijke Tolsma, Keith D. Stanglin, and Theodoor Marius van Leeuwen, eds., *Arminius, Arminianism, and Europe: Jacobus Arminius (1559/60–1609)* (Leiden: Brill, 2009); Richard Muller, *God, Creation, and Providence in the Thought of Jacob Arminius: Sources and Directions of Scholastic Protestantism in the Era of Early Orthodoxy* (Grand Rapids, MI: Baker Book House, 1991); Keith D. Stanglin and Thomas H. McCall, *Jacob Arminius: Theologian of Grace* (New York: Oxford University Press, 2012); and Keith D. Stanglin, *Arminius on the Assurance of Salvation: The Context, Roots, and Shape of the Leiden Debate, 1603–1609* (Leiden: Brill, 2007).

1. Contours of Lapsarianism

Though the Canons of Dordrecht remain historically important for understanding the confessional boundaries of the doctrine of predestination within Reformed theology, the Canons by no means settled the question.[5] While Reformed orthodox theologians after Dordrecht maintained a univocal rejection of Remonstrant and Socinian schemes vis-à-vis the divine decrees, those same theologians by no means maintained a theological univocity among themselves. Some were "infralapsarian," others "supralapsarian," and others still offered modified lapsarian pictures. Unfortunately, the scant scholarship that is available on the lapsarian controversy often reduces the debate into general categories concerning the individual objects of predestination *tout court*.[6] Or, at the very least, it tends to interpret the debate through a preconceived theological grid that distorts the nuance. In a typical picture, the lapsarian debate revolves around the question of whether the object of election and reprobation is the human being not yet created and not yet fallen (supralapsarian), or whether the object of election and reprobation is the human being created and fallen (infralapsarian).[7] Such a conclusion is not entirely false, although a reduction of the debate to merely this question proves most unhelpful, both historically and theologically. The debate is layered and, although it does certainly focus on the individual objects of predestination, the overall purpose of creation and fall, as well as the intersection of Christology, covenant, and election, also falls within the theological purview, either explicitly or implicitly.[8] In a larger sense, the lapsarian debate within

---

5. As Selderhuis notes regarding the lapsarian debate at the Synod of Dordrecht, "Die Dordrechter Lehrsätze gegeben übrigens eine infralapsarische Position wieder, ohne die Supralapsarier zu verurteilen." ["Incidentally, the Dordrecht doctrines describe an infralapsarian position without condemning supralapsarianism as well."] "Die Dordrechter Canones, 1619," 88. See also Klas Dijk, *De strijd over Infra- en Supralapsarisme in de Gereformeerde Kerken van Nederland* (Kampen: J.H. Kok, 1912), 217–19.

6. On the infralapsarian and supralapsarian debate, see the following: J. V. Fesko, *Diversity within the Reformed Tradition: Supra- and Infralapsarianism in Calvin, Dort, and Westminster* (Greenville, SC: Reformed Academic Press, 2001); Pieter Rouwendal, "The Doctrine of Predestination in Reformed Orthodoxy," in *A Companion to Reformed Orthodoxy*, ed. Herman Selderhuis (Boston: Brill, 2013), 553–90; Dijk, *De strijd over Infra- en Supralapsarisme*; and Heinrich Heppe, *Reformed Dogmatics*, trans. G. T. Thomson, ed. Ernst Bizer (London: George Allen and Unwin, 1950), 133–89. A discussion of the controversy can also be found in major systemic works. See, for example, G. C. Berkouwer, *Divine Election*, trans. Hugo Bekker (Grand Rapids, MI: Wm. B. Eerdmans, 1960), 254–77.

7. This is the conclusion, for example, reached by J. V. Fesko: "One of the main points of this essay has demonstrated that the debate was not over the *ordo decretorum*. Rather, the debate has largely centered on the material cause, the object of predestination." *Diversity within the Reformed Tradition*, 303.

8. These larger focuses will be more thoroughly examined in Chapter 2, wherein they are brought into sharp relief through the theological critiques of Karl Barth and Herman Bavinck.

Reformed orthodoxy foregrounds a central theological question: What is the relationship between God and the world, and what is God's purpose in creating therein?

This chapter explores the contours of lapsarianism as articulated by Francis Turretin, Petrus van Mastricht, and Thomas Goodwin. The choice of these figures is not arbitrary, even if highly selective. These theologians, broadly speaking, represent a diversity of lapsarian opinions within Reformed orthodoxy, and they are particularly helpful for their clarity and robustness of thought. My goal in this chapter is to provide an exemplary—not exhaustive—account of the diversity prevalent in the lapsarian controversy; in particular, I aim to show that more is at stake in the debate than the *objectum praedestinationis* (object of predestination), simply considered. Furthermore, these various lapsarian positions provide a helpful interpretive grid for conceptually assessing the lapsarianism of Jonathan Edwards, especially considering that Edwards was intimately acquainted with the thought of each theologian. The broad contours of these lapsarian schemes, therefore, set the conceptual stage for not only understanding Edwards's unique theological positions (Part II), but also for my own constructive engagement with the lapsarian question through a retrieval of Edwards's theology (Part III).

Francis Turretin (1623–87): Infralapsarianism Exemplified

Francis Turretin (or François/Francesco Turrettini) was a towering figure in the period of Reformed high orthodoxy (*c.* 1620–1725). Turretin, like his father before him and son after him, was a professor of theology at the academy of Geneva, a post he held from 1653 until his death. The major theological achievement of his life was his three-volume *Institutio theologiae elencticae* (*Institutes of Elenctic Theology*), a work published only a few years before his death. The work is a magisterial example of polemical theology, both representing and countering the views of his opponents (Roman Catholic, Lutheran, Socinian, Remonstrant, atheist, and even other Reformed divines). In terms of content, Turretin's *Institutes* contains highly technical and substantive discussions of various theological loci arranged according to a synthetic method, which generally follows the *quaestio* method.[9] And it was its thoroughness, not its novelty, which secured Turretin's theological influence. As Pieter Rouwendal well notes, "Turretin was not so much a renewer of reformed theology as he was a conservator."[10] It is in this way—both in his precision and conservation—that Turretin well exemplifies the infralapsarian position within Reformed high orthodoxy. Turretin's lapsarian discussion can be found within the larger framework of the divine decrees, which is the "Fourth Topic" of his *Institutes of Elenctic Theology*. In order to chart out his lapsarian

---

9. Willem J. van Asselt, *Introduction to Reformed Scholasticism*, trans. Albert Gootjes (Grand Rapids, MI: Reformation Heritage Books, 2011), 157–9.

10. Rouwendal, "Doctrine of Predestination," 585.

position, I shall focus on three areas: (1) the object of predestination; (2) Christ and the cause of election; and (3) the order of the decrees.

The Object of Predestination

According to Turretin, the question concerning the object of predestination is not simply about the "whatness" of the rational object (man, angel, etc.); rather, the question pertains to the "quality" (*quale*) of the human object: "of what kind" of creature is the object of God's predestinating decree.[11] The particular "quality" Turretin has in mind corresponds to the state of the human creature vis-à-vis creation and the Fall. The opinions of orthodox divines, according to Turretin, vary on this issue and can be reduced to three camps: (1) those ascending beyond the Fall (*supra lapsum*); (2) those descending below the Fall (*infra lapsum*); and (3) those stopping in the Fall (*in lapsu*). The first maintain that the object of predestination is "man either not yet created or at least not yet fallen."[12] The second group view "man not only as fallen, but also redeemed through Christ" as the object of predestination, while those holding a middle ground (i.e., *in lapsu*) maintain "man only as fallen was considered by God predestinating."[13] Turretin adheres to the third (*in lapsu*). In terms of Turretin's technical exposition, he suggests those descending below the Fall (i.e., *infra lapsum*) are semi-Pelagians and Arminians because they maintain that faith is the preceding condition (i.e., impulsive cause) of election.[14] Despite this confusion in nomenclature, the exposition will make clear that Turretin's "in-lapsarian" position is what we call infralapsarianism today.

In order to render the state of question regarding the object of predestination more precise, Turretin observes three distinctions. First, the question concerns whether creation of man and the permission of the Fall "stand in the relation as means (*habeant ad modum medii*) with respect to the decree of salvation and damnation, and whether God in the sign of reason is to be considered as having thought about the salvation and destruction of men before he thought of their creation and fall."[15] As evidenced here, the question does not concern temporal order but rather the logical order *in signo rationis* (in the sign of reason). Whether one is supralapsarian or infralapsarian, the temporal execution of the decrees

---

11. Turretin, *Inst.* 4.9.2 (ET: 1:341).
12. Turretin, *Inst.* 4.9.3 (ET: 1:341).
13. Turretin, *Inst.* 4.9.3 (ET: 1:341).
14. An impulsive cause (*causa impulsiva*) is a cause that goes before, moving or preparing the way for an efficient cause. See Richard A. Muller, *A Dictionary of Latin and Greek Theological Terms: Drawn Principally from Protestant Scholastic Sources*, 2nd edn (Grand Rapids, MI: Baker Academic, 2017), s.v. "*causa impulsiva*." In this context, faith, as foreknown by God, impels God to elect.
15. Turretin, *Inst.* 4.9.6 (ET: 1:342). Translation slightly altered. Though I have removed it, Giger adds "*in signo rationis*" as an editorial gloss after "*habeant ad modum medii*" in order to specify that this is not a discussion that involves temporal steps.

is not up for debate. The lapsarian question pertains to logical distinctions or structural instants in the order of the divine decrees. These distinctions correspond to rational analysis (*in signo rationis*), although they are not simply a product of reason reasoning (*ratio ratiocinans*); according to Turretin and other Reformed divines, these logical distinctions have a foundation in the object (i.e., the divine mind).[16] Second, Turretin maintains the question concerns "whether sin holds itself antecedently to predestination as to its being foreseen (*praevisum*)."[17] The third distinguishing feature of the question is similar to the previous one: whether the fall into sin has the "relation of quality or preceding condition in the requisite object."[18] According to Turretin, "learned" supralapsarians deny this, while he affirms it.

As a polemical piece, Turretin sifts through several reasons "learned" supralapsarians who view the object as *creatable or created but not fallen* are misguided.[19] Foremost, Turretin reasons that a nonentity (i.e., *homo creabilis et labilis*) cannot be the object of predestination because this conflates and confuses the order of creation with the order of redemption.[20] In making a nonentity an object of predestination, supralapsarianism dissolves the integrity of the creation. Following this line of thought, Turretin regards creation and the Fall, not as means of predestination, but as means of the natural order and dispensation of providence.[21] The fall into sin and actual sin, therefore, must serve as the logically requisite conditions for predestination and not the means of it. Turretin employs an analogy here: "Disease in the sick is the previous condition without which he is not cured, but it is not the means by which he is cured."[22] Creation, the Fall, and sin, in other words, are not means within the supernatural order of predestination; they are means in the natural order of providence. Finally, Turretin suggests that the supralapsarian position is easily twisted to suggest that God determines to create in order that God might destroy; or, said another way, God permits sin in order to punish sinners. The conclusion, for Turretin, must be that the end of predestination with respect to human beings (in particular) "supposes necessarily creation and fall in the object."[23]

But why is such a supposition theologically necessary for Turretin? Turretin's answer goes to the heart of his infralapsarian logic. As Turretin makes clear, *in-lapsarianism* (i.e., what we now call infralapsarianism) properly distinguishes

---

16. On these scholastic terms, see Muller, *Dictionary of Latin and Greek*, s.v. "*distinctio*" and "*in signo rationis*."

17. Turretin, *Inst.* 4.9.7 (ET: 1:342).

18. Turretin, *Inst.* 4.9.8 (ET: 1:343).

19. It is not necessary to work through the entirety of Turretin's critiques here since the theological rationale is equally apparent in his own *in-lapsarian* solution.

20. Turretin, *Inst.* 4.9.9 (ET: 1:343).

21. Turretin, *Inst.* 4.9.12 (ET: 1:344).

22. Turretin, *Inst.* 4.9.13 (ET: 1:344).

23. Turretin, *Inst.* 4.9.20 (ET: 1:347).

between the orders of creation and redemption, nature and grace.²⁴ When considering the decrees associated with providence in general and predestination in particular, one must take into account different ends. For Turretin, the order of creation (nature) and the order of redemption (grace) pertain to discrete ends. In the order of creation and *in signo rationis*, God's end is the manifestation of his glory in the exercise of certain attributes apart from mercy and justice.²⁵ According to Turretin, "it was the communication and (as it were) the spreading out of the power (*velut* ἔκστασις *potentiae*), wisdom and goodness of the Creator which shone forth"²⁶ in both the creation and fall of man, albeit in different ways. Indeed, the Fall is the last work within the bounds of nature before the work of redemption, which pertains to the "higher and supernatural order of grace."²⁷

Turretin's emphasis on the distinction between the order of nature and grace explains his disagreement over and qualification of an important maxim: *Quod ultimum est in executione, debet esse primum in intentione*, that which is last in execution, ought to be first in intention.²⁸ For Turretin, the maxim is applied differently within each order. When speaking of the order of nature, God's ultimate end is the "manifestation of God's glory in common by the creation and fall of man."²⁹ This entails the display of God's glory in the form of goodness and wisdom in general, though nothing of mercy and justice per se. Turretin formulates the disjunction between the orders of nature and grace sharply: "There is no necessary connection and subordination between creation, fall, and redemption."³⁰ There exists a "great chasm" (μέγα χάσμα) between creation and redemption; it is the chasm of sin, and sin is against nature (*peccatum est contra naturum*).³¹ Sin is the means to the end neither with respect to salvation nor with respect to damnation; it is most properly the occasion for the work of redemption and judgment. For Turretin, then, different "ends" imply different "means" therein. The "economies of providence and predestination" cannot and should not be confounded. The decree of creation and the Fall belong to providence, whereas predestination belongs to grace. God's execution of mercy and justice applies only within the order predestination because it supposes sinful man as its object (*homo creatus et lapsus*). Michael Bell summarizes well the operative principle here: "Probably

---

24. In other Reformed and infralapsarian dogmaticians, this will be referred to as general (i.e., creation) and special (i.e., grace) decrees. See Heppe, *Reformed Dogmatics*, 145–6.

25. Turretin, *Inst.* 4.9.22 (ET: 1:347).

26. Turretin, *Inst.* 4.9.22 (ET: 1:347).

27. Turretin, *Inst.* 4.9.22 (ET: 1:348).

28. Here, Turretin takes a rather jocular jab at the supralapsarianism of William Twisse: "and [with this maxim] Twisse makes himself hoarse and on which alone he seems to build up the artfully constructed fabric of his disputation on this argument." Turretin, *Inst.* 4.9.23 (ET: 1:348).

29. Turretin, *Inst.* 4.9.23 (ET: 1:348).

30. Turretin, *Inst.* 4.9.23 (ET: 1:348). Translation mine.

31. Turretin, *Inst.* 4.9.23 (ET: 1:348).

the single most important factor in the development of [Turretin's] teaching on the *objectum* was his usage of the distinction between the orders of providence and predestination, nature and grace, and creation and redemption. Most of his arguments, both for infralapsarianism and against supralapsarianism, can be either directly or indirectly attributed to his usage of this crucial distinction."[32]

Christ and the Cause of Election

Apart from the opinions mentioned above regarding the object of predestination, Turretin discusses the opinion of those "who maintain that not only man as fallen and corrupted by sin, but men also as redeemed by Christ (and either believing or disbelieving in him) was considered by God predestinating."[33] This is the position Turretin idiosyncratically refers to as infralapsarian.[34] It is held, according to Turretin, by semi-Pelagians and Arminians and "all those who maintain that Christ is the foundation of election, and foreseen faith its cause."[35] In order to combat this "unorthodox" view, Turretin explores a christological question: "Did Christ enter into the decree antecedently as the impulsive and meritorious cause, on account of which is was destined to us?"[36] Turretin says no.

The simplest explanation Turretin offers for denying Christ as the antecedent foundation of particular election is that "election was made from God's mere good pleasure."[37] God's good pleasure is, in fact, the root cause of all of God's decrees for Turretin, apart from which another cause "cannot and ought not" (*non potest nec debet*) be sought.[38] Given this fact, how does Turretin understand the relation and distinction between Christ and the decree of election then? The distinction rests upon the difference between election as such and redemption of the elect. Christ, in this way, was ordained as mediator as a result of God's election. The preordination of Christ as Savior and head of the elect follows as an effect from the efficient cause, which is simply God's good pleasure. Put another way, God's good pleasure is the efficient cause of election and salvation, wherein Christ is the

---

32. Bell goes on to note that this distinction gives Turretin's lapsarianism a "Thomistic appearance." Michael Daniel Bell, "*PROPTER POTESTATEM, SCIENTIAM, AC BENEPLACITUM DEI*: The Doctrine of the Object of Predestination in the Theology of Johannes Maccovius" (PhD Diss., Westminster Theological Seminary, 1986), 240. This discussion, as Bell highlights, is intimately related to those involving the subordination and coordination of means and ends in God's decrees, especially with regard to things of the same kind.

33. Turretin, *Inst.* 4.9.31 (ET: 1:350).

34. Again, this is not how one typically classifies infralapsarianism in textbook theology today.

35. Turretin, *Inst.* 4.9.31 (ET: 1:350).

36. Turretin, *Inst.* 4.10.2 (ET: 1:351).

37. Turretin, *Inst.* 4.10.5 (ET: 1:351).

38. Turretin, *Inst.* 4.10.5 (ET: 1:352).

means to obtain the end. Christ, in scholastic parlance, is the instrumental cause of election, namely, the decreed means (instrument) used to bring about the desired effect.[39]

Turretin unpacks this difference exegetically from Eph. 1:4, wherein it states that individuals are "elected in Christ." According to Turretin, this does not mean that elect human beings already exist in Christ; rather, Christians are said to be elected "as about to be in Christ (*in Christos futuros*) and to be redeemed by Christ."[40] Turretin's gloss is key: "so that the infinitive *einai* is to be supplied to denote that Christ is the primary means of election to be executed and the cause of salvation destined to us through him, not as the cause of the decree by which it is decreed (*decernitur*)."[41] Election in Christ pertains to predestination to salvation *in* or *by* Christ. In this way, election is not founded *on* Christ as to efficient cause, but rather founded *in* Christ as to means. Importantly, however, Turretin indicates that the blessing flowing from election could not be executed in creation apart from Christ as mediator. Blessings are "founded in Christ as the meritorious and efficient cause because without him nothing can be communicated to the creature."[42] The communication of blessings, therefore, is destined in Christ because every blessing from God is to be conferred by Christ. Jesus Christ is, according to Turretin, the only means of God's obtaining God's end in electing.

The overriding concerns for Turretin as they pertain to Christ and the cause of election remain twofold: the order of the decrees and the universality of grace. These twin concerns are not unrelated and in fact reduce to his overall polemic against Arminianism and Amyraldianism. The election of Christ and the election of human beings must be so understood as to be a "priority of order, not of causality."[43] The Arminians, according to Turretin, want to make Christ the prior

---

39. See Muller, *Dictionary of Latin and Greek*, s.v. "*causa instrumentalis*."

40. Turretin, *Inst*. 4.10.10 (ET: 1:353). Turretin italicizes *futuros*.

41. Turretin, *Inst*. 4.10.10 (ET: 1:353).

42. Turretin, *Inst*. 4.10.11 (ET: 1:353). This also has ramifications for interpreting Turretin's federalism. It seems to me that it is not entirely correct to posit, as J. Mark Beach does, that "since there was no alienation or estrangement existing between God and man in the covenant of nature, a Mediator was not needed." *Christ and the Covenant: Francis Turretin's Federal Theology as a Defense of the Doctrine of Grace* (Göttingen: Vandenhoeck & Ruprecht, 2007), 165. Beach's remarks conflate mediator with redeemer. John Calvin, for example, acknowledged this difference: "Even if man had remained free from all stain, his condition would have been too lowly for him to reach God without a mediator"; *Instituiones*, 2.12.1; ET; John Calvin, *Institutes of the Christian Religion*, vol. 1, ed. John T. McNeill, trans. Ford Lewis Battles (Louisville, KY: Westminster John Knox Press, 2006), 465. See also Edwin Chr. van Driel, "'Too Lowly to Reach God without a Mediator': John Calvin's Supralapsarian Eschatological Narrative," *Modern Theology* 33, no. 2 (April 2017): 275–92. Thus, and in a similar vein to John Calvin, the relationship between Christ's mediatorial role and the covenant of nature in Turretin's theology might be underdeveloped and vague, but it is nevertheless there.

43. Turretin, *Inst*. 4.10.19 (ET: 1:354).

cause of election in order to extend grace in a universal manner, so that Christ would be destined and sent for more than those particularly elect (understood in Turretin's sense).[44] For Turretin, however, election in Christ must be understood in keeping with such particularity: Christ is the instrument of execution in obtaining God's election, an election already logically determined in the decree by the sole good pleasure of God.

Once again, it is important to note the larger context of the theological discussion. As before, Turretin sees election of Christ to belong to the order of grace, which is distinct from the order of creation. The ordering of the decrees is heavily dependent upon the twofold order of God's transient works: nature and redemption. Although Turretin does not put it so bluntly, his theological reasoning indicates that articulating election as founded *on* Christ disastrously confuses the twofold order of the works of God as understood in Holy Scripture. Whether pushing back against Arminian, Amyraldian, or supralapsarian positions then, how one maps the decrees vis-à-vis the proper order remains a primary point of disagreement for Turretin, although for different reasons and with differing degrees of theological impropriety.

The Order of the Decrees

In truth, the divine decrees admit of no real distinctions because God decrees in one simple and unified act. This does not mean, as explained earlier, that logical distinctions are excluded according to the mode of the knower, distinctions which have a foundation in the object. A priority and posteriority, even dependency, is recognized among the various decrees based on the manner in which human beings come to know these divine realities. For Turretin, the chief mode of knowledge is Holy Scripture. Based on his interpretation of Scripture, Turretin recognizes, as we have seen, two principal works of God: creation and nature on one hand, and redemption and grace on the other. Between the two works (orders)—and strictly as a means—comes the decree concerning the fall of the human race. Oddly enough, according to Turretin, the decree of the Fall pertains to neither order.[45] But within the two discrete orders themselves—creation and grace—a manifold number of moments are recognized according to their diversity (e.g., the mission of Christ or glorification). Given this diversity, the order of the decrees admits of various interpretations, which may be summarized under four types already mentioned: supralapsarian, Arminian, Amyraldian, and Turretin's own position (in-lapsarian).

The supralapsarian position, according to Turretin, logically arranges the decree of predestination before the decrees of creation and permission of the

---

44. Turretin, *Inst.* 4.10.19 (ET: 1:355).

45. Even though Turretin had intimated previously that the Fall belonged within the order of creation/providence, his more technical discussion confusedly places the decree of the Fall as a logical bridge between the two orders.

Fall. In this schema, the decrees of creation and permission of the Fall have the "reason of means (*rationem medii*) to the manifestation of [God's] mercy and justice as the end."[46] Turretin summarizes the supralapsarian order as follows: (1) God decrees, in his good pleasure, the manifestation of his glory in the exercise of mercy and justice through the salvation and damnation of human creatures; (2) God decrees to create; (3) God decrees to permit the Fall; and (4) God decrees to send Christ to redeem the elect. Such an order for Turretin, although it contains nothing "absolutely repugnant" to salvation and the analogy of faith, seems overtly harsh and unsuitable to the order as found in Holy Writ.[47] Apart from the objections already considered above concerning the object of predestination, Turretin offers several further theological criticisms. The most trenchant of these concerns the order of creation, fall, election, and reprobation. For Turretin, creation and fall cannot be considered the antecedent means of election and rejection. If this were so, then sin would be on account of damnation and not the other way around. Sin must be present in a real object, not a *non ens* (nonbeing), in order to "warrant the decree of rejection."[48] Logically and morally then, supralapsarianism misses the mark on Turretin's interpretation.

The next opinion Turretin rejects is the one proposed by Arminius and his followers. Although Turretin spends some time unpacking his polemic, the finer details would lead us astray from the more salient points. What remains important is the division Turretin recognizes (and rejects) in the Arminian order of the decrees. For Turretin, the school of Arminius wrongly adheres to a twofold order in the decrees: "one general, indefinite, incomplete, conditional and revocable; the other complete, peremptory, definite and irrevocable."[49] The "peremptory" decrees correspond to the "salvation and destruction of individuals as [God] foresaw they would or would not believe,"[50] whereas the more general decrees apply to God's general beneficence to mankind in Christ, who makes possible salvation by removing the obstacle of divine justice.[51] Turretin believes this makes election and rejection dependent on foreknowledge instead of God's sovereign will, which in turn makes God dependent on the human will. As such, Turretin opposes this order as a theological defect, which "not even in word" touches "upon the true nature of election."[52]

---

46. Turretin, *Inst.* 4.18.4 (ET: 1:418). Translation mine.
47. Turretin, *Inst.* 4.18.5 (ET: 1:418).
48. Joel Beeke, *Debated Issues in Sovereign Predestination: Early Lutheran Predestination, Calvinian Reprobation, and Variations in Genevan Lapsarianism* (Göttingen: Vandenhoeck & Ruprecht, 2017), 203.
49. Turretin, *Inst.* 4.18.10 (ET: 1:421).
50. Turretin, *Inst.* 4.18.6 (ET: 1:419).
51. Turretin, *Inst.* 4.18.11 (ET: 1:422).
52. Turretin, *Inst.* 4.18.8 (ET: 1:420).

Similar to the Arminian order—and more important for understanding Turretin's own position—is the Amyraldian order of the decrees.[53] Amyraldianism maintains a distinction between hypothetical and particular decrees. God's hypothetical decrees are founded upon God's universal love and mercy by which he gives Christ so as to open a way of salvation for each and every person. This is, in fact, the exact position of the Remonstrants. Wherein they differ is with reference to God's foreknowledge. According to Turretin's interpretation of Amyraldianism, God foresaw that, given human depravity, all would reject the good news offered in Christ. As such, God then issues a particular decree determining the salvation of some. Thus, there first exists within the order of grace a decree that offers Christ "hypothetically" to all, though not faith; next, there exists the special decree giving faith to some.[54] Turretin rejects the Amyraldian position for multiple reasons: (1) God cannot love people with one decree (hypothetical), and zealously hate in another (special); (2) God does not consider the means (Christ) before the end (redemption); (3) it questions the efficacy of the atonement; (4) it places calling prior to election, which again confuses means and the ends; and (5) it emphasizes a preposterous distinction between God as lawgiver and God as Father. The second of the reasons listed above proves most pertinent. In the same manner as his rejection of Christ as the efficient cause of election, Turretin argues that God does not will a general (hypothetical) and particular Christ for mankind. The mission of Christ, according to Turretin, procures something definite, namely salvation. It does not procure a possible salvation by removing the obstacle of divine justice through satisfaction. Without elaborating any further, the overall critique should be clear: In the order of grace, God does not have a twofold intention—one hypothetical (sending Christ for all) and one particular (applying the death of Christ to some). Such a bifurcation is, for Turretin, repugnant to the witness of Scripture.

Finally, after several long sections, Turretin comes at last to explicate the opinion he believes to be the "common one among the Reformed," an opinion lying in between supralapsarian and Amyraldian fringes. The order of the decrees, in the human manner of reasoning, must be broken down according to the twofold order of the works of God: providence (nature) and predestination (grace). "In the former," Turretin argues, "God is conceived to have thought first about the manifestation of his glory in the creation of man, then in the permission of the fall."[55] In the latter, God first thought about "the manifestation of his glory in the exercise of mercy and justice by the election of some and the reprobation of

---

53. For a confessionalization (of sorts) of the rejection of the species of Calvinism emanating from the school of Saumar, see the *Formula Consensus Helvitica*, which was composed in 1675 by John Henry Heidegger, with the assistance of Francis Turretin and Lucas Gernler. On Saumar and Amyraldianism, see Van Asselt, *Introduction to Reformed Scholasticism*, 150–3.

54. Turretin, *Inst.* 4.18.13 (ET: 1:423).

55. Turretin, *Inst.* 4.18.21 (ET: 1:428).

others," and only afterward—in the logical order of the decrees—about the means necessary for procuring the stated end.[56] Within this latter order of grace, God's decrees should be ordered as follows: (1) God elects to save some individuals from an actual fallen race, therein leaving others in their native corruption; (2) God elects Christ as the means of redemption, wherein he is the head and surety of the elect alone; and (3) God effectually and irrevocably calls the elect by "preaching of the gospel and the grace of the Holy Spirit, giving them faith, justifying, sanctifying and at last glorifying them."[57]

According to Turretin, this lapsarian order proves to be most suitable in three ways. First, it corresponds most properly to the order espoused in Scripture, which "subordinates the mission of Christ and redemption to election."[58] Second, it maintains an appropriate relation between the intention of an end and the intention of the means, such that "in the execution the means should first be used before the end is arrived at."[59] Although this sounds similar to the maxim endorsed by Turretin's supralapsarian brethren, Turretin's differentiation between God's twofold works signals the divergence. The end attended to in the covenant of grace, according to Turretin, is the "salvation of the elect, but the means to procure it are Christ and the call to the individual by word and Spirit."[60] The christological movement is unambiguous: "Christ would never be sent into the world unless the elect were to be redeemed."[61] There is a clear order of intention: first election and only then redemption in Christ. Third and finally, the in(fra)lapsarian order follows the economic operations of the triune persons in salvation: elected by the Father, redeemed by the Son, and regenerated by the Spirit.

Petrus van Mastricht (1630–1706): Lapsarianism Mediated

Unlike his predecessors Williams Ames, Gisbertus Voetius, and Johannes Cocceius, the life and work of Dutch orthodox divine Petrus van Mastricht remains relatively little known.[62] Despite such contemporary unfamiliarity, Mastricht exercised a considerable influence upon the Dutch and New England theological landscape during and after his tenure as professor of theology and Hebrew at Utrecht,[63] and this in large part due to his style of theology. Unlike Turretin's *Institutio theologiae elencticae*, Mastricht's magnum opus—*Theoretico-practica theologia*—entailed,

---

56. Turretin, *Inst.* 4.18.21 (ET: 1:428).
57. Turretin, *Inst.* 4.18.22 (ET: 1:429).
58. Turretin, *Inst.* 4.18.23 (ET: 1:429).
59. Turretin, *Inst.* 4.18.23 (ET: 1:429).
60. Turretin, *Inst.* 4.18.23 (ET: 1:429).
61. Turretin, *Inst.* 4.18.23 (ET: 1:429).
62. For a biographical sketch, see Adriaan C. Neele, *Petrus van Mastricht (1630–1706): Reformed Orthodoxy: Method and Piety* (Leiden: Brill, 2009), 27–61.
63. Cf. Neele, *Petrus van Mastricht*, 2–14.

according to Richard Muller, a "perfect balance" of "exegetical, dogmatic, historico-polemical, and practical" theology.[64] This unique blend of the rigor of the scholastic system with *praxis pietatis* most likely set Mastricht apart in the minds of those—like Jonathan Edwards—commending his work.

In this section, I will focus on Mastricht's lapsarian discussions found across various headings in *Theoretico-practica theologia*, especially the positive presentations found in each *pars dogmatica*. Locating Mastricht's exact form of lapsarianism, whether supra- or infra-, has proved difficult. Some identify him as an infralapsarian,[65] others a supralapsarian,[66] and others still as a mediator between the two.[67] As I will demonstrate, Mastricht is best conceived of as a supralapsarian because of the way he teleologically prioritizes the display of God's glory as mercy and justice,[68] even as he attempts to mediate the lapsarian debate by distinguishing between the objects of predestination and the objects of election/reprobation. Because much of the material covered in Mastricht's discussion of the divine decrees and predestination overlaps with Turretin, I will only attend to the portions that signal the theological divergence and lapsarian mediation. In order to situate Mastricht's lapsarianism, I will isolate two areas: (1) the acts and objects of predestination, which also include the corresponding acts of election and reprobation; and (2) the order of predestination. At the end, I will also note how Mastricht's position differs from, as he calls them, the "rigid" supralapsarian position(s).

Acts and Objects of Predestination

As has been noted with Turretin and will be again noted with Thomas Goodwin, fundamental to this debate is the distinction between intended ends and means. In this regard, Mastricht's framing of ends and means, as well as the order of their relation, prove integral for understanding his complex breakdown of the acts and objects of predestination. Prior to his discussion of predestination and under the subheading "*De Decretis Dei*," Mastricht notes how the divine decree includes (*connotare*) three realities: (1) the intended end (i.e., God's glory); (2) the concept of means and their selection and arrangement to that end; and (3) the intention of the will qua chosen means.[69] This threefold breakdown conceptually sets the stage

---

64. Richard Muller, "Giving Direction to Theology: The Scholastic Dimension," *Journal of Evangelical Theological Society* 28, no. 2 (1985): 191.

65. Dijk, *De strijd over Infra- en Supralapsarisme*, 43. Despite listing Mastricht among the infralapsarians, Dijk goes on a few pages later to list Mastricht among those who sought a settlement between the two positions (48).

66. Cf. Herman Bavinck, *RD* 2:388.

67. Cf. Karl Barth, *CD* II.2, 132–3; Heppe, *Reformed Dogmatics*, 162.

68. Recall, Turretin views the manifestation of God's glory in this way as strictly a post-Fall telos.

69. Cf. Mastricht, *TPT* 3.1.16. Since the preparation of this book, the third volume of Mastricht's *TPT* has been translated into English. That translation is published as

for how Mastricht will work through the particular decree of predestination. In this way, Mastricht's subsequent discussion of predestination demonstrates how the singular decree of predestination also observes three conceptual realities (i.e., end, means, and intention), though he fills it out with far greater specificity based on the fact that the genus of predestination concerns specifically the "eternal state of the rational creatures."[70]

First, the decree of predestination entails the proposed end of the declaration of God's glory, not generally, but in three particular ways: (1) as divine power and dominion; (2) as the glory of grace and mercy; and (3) as the glory of vindicatory justice (*gloriam justitiae vindicativae*).[71] In making this first point about power and dominion, Mastricht leans heavily into the biblical text of Romans 9:21. Regardless of the freedom of the creature, God may destine out of the same mass (*ex eâdem massa*) of humanity some as vessels of wrath and others as vessels of glory according to God's pure, unmixed good pleasure (*pro puro puto beneplacito*).[72] For Mastricht, God's good pleasure remains the sole impulsive cause of predestination, along with its adjuncts election and reprobation.[73] The most important feature of this discussion is the proposed end: God's glory in the form of the power and dominion as channeled through grace and justice. By setting up the end in this way and prioritizing it in his lapsarian discussion, Mastricht's position displays its supralapsarian superstructure.

The second moment observed in the decree fixes upon the conceptualization of means within the larger divine plan of predestination.[74] As before—and in good scholastic fashion—Mastricht breaks down this second observation concerning means into three further points: (1) gracious salvation and just condemnation are established as means by God to manifest the glory of his grace and justice; (2) the means of predestination also includes the creation of a general humanity with whom God establishes a covenant of works and allows its neglect (*derelictio*) "so that God might have an object, in whose gracious salvation and just condemnation,

---

follows: *Theoretical-Practical Theology*, vol. 3, ed. Joel Beeke and trans. Todd Rester (Grand Rapids, MI: Reformation Heritage Books, 2021). For those interested, *TPT* 3.1.16 corresponds to *TPT* 3.1.XVI in the English translation. All translations of Mastricht's work are mine.

70. Mastricht, *TPT* 3.2.3; Cf. Mastricht, *TPT* 3.2.1, 6–7.

71. Mastricht, *TPT* 3.2.8. On *justitia*, especially *justitia vindicativa*, as an essential divine attribute, see Mastricht, *TPT* 2.18.7. I have chosen here and throughout this chapter to translate *justitia vindicativa* as "vindicatory justice" instead of "avenging/punitive righteousness." On the use of this term in Protestant scholasticism, see Muller, *Dictionary of Latin and Greek*, s.v. "*iustitia Dei*."

72. Mastricht, *TPT* 3.2.8.

73. Cf. Mastricht, *TPT* 3.3.11.

74. Mastricht, *TPT* 3.2.9.

God might make known the glory of mercy and wrath";[75] and (3) these proposed means also include the selection of singular persons "from all creatures" in whom "mercy and wrath might be revealed."[76] The third observation concerning the decree of predestination then follows, namely the "intention and designation of means, from which the gracious salvation and just condemnation of others might be procured."[77] Mastricht highlights, in particular, the restitution of some through the Son as Mediator and dereliction of others in their sin. That is, God wills the means of salvation as the complete work of Jesus Christ and faith in him, and God wills the means of condemnation as a passing over creatures in their sin. Overall, Mastricht is drawing a distinction between general means (salvation and condemnation) and particular means unto salvation and condemnation (Christ and preterition).

Functionally, these three structural and broad observations within God's predestining decree preface Mastricht's further discussion of predestination in "four acts." The four logical acts of predestination specify in far greater detail the logical structure of the decree, especially as it touches upon the so-called objects. In this way, the four logical acts prove to be Mastricht's most technical breakdown of the different aspects of the decree *in signo rationis*.

The first logical "act" in the decree of predestination "proposes the manifestation of the glory of mercy and vindicating justice."[78] As is evident, this corresponds to the intended end of God's decree (i.e., the first observation mentioned previously). After articulating the ultimate end in the first logical act, Mastricht moves to the conceptualization of means as manifest in the second and third acts. The second act entails the decision by God to create and permit the fall of all human creatures in their common beginning (*principio*). From those created and fallen creatures, God elects in the third act some (in which consists the glory of mercy) and rejects others (in which the glory of vindicatory justice obtains). In the fourth and final act, Mastricht isolates God's "intention of preparing and directing the means analogous to election and reprobation."[79] Only in this fourth act does Mastricht specify the concrete means as either put in (election) or found in (reprobation) the object. The fourth act, therefore, refers to particular means.

---

75. Mastricht, TPT 3.2.9: "quo nim. *objectum* haberet, in cujus gratiosâ *salute* & justâ *condemnatione*, gloriam manifestaret, misericordiae & irae." NB: I have chosen to maintain Mastricht's original italics in the footnotes.

76. Mastricht, TPT, 3.2.9: "Ex creatis *omnibus*, delectus singularum *personarum* ... *misericordia & ira* patefieret."

77. Mastricht, TPT 3.2.10: "*Intentio* & destinatio *mediorum*, quibis gratuita *salus* quorundam, & justa *condemnatio* aliorum, procuraretur."

78. Mastricht, TPT 3.2.12: "*Propositum manifestandi* gloriam, *misericordiae & justitiae vindicantis*."

79. Mastricht, TPT 3.2.12: "Intentio *praeparandi* ac dirigendi *media*, electioni & reprobationi analoga."

After discriminating between the four logical acts in the singular decree, Mastricht maps "objects" to each logical act. "By reason of the first act of predestination," Mastricht argues, "the object could not have been, except a human able to be created (*creabilis*) and fall (*labilis*), for nothing is presupposed, at the point the decree happened, concerning the creation and the fall."[80] By reason of the second act, it is properly "the human being fit to be created and fall" (*homo creandus* and *lapsurus*), while in the third act the object is considered "having been created and fallen" (*creatus* and *lapsus*).[81] In the fourth and final act, the object is the human being "elected and rejected" (*electus* and *reprobus*). Of consequence here is the distinction Mastricht makes between the general objects of predestination on the one hand, and the particular objects of election and reprobation on the other. According to Mastricht, the first two acts in God's decree pertain to human beings "*creabilem* & *labilem*; *creandum* & lapsurum" (creatable and fallible; fit to be created and fall), while the latter acts correspond to the objects of election and reprobation as "*homo creatus* & *lapsus*" (having been created and fallen).[82]

By maintaining these conceptual distinctions between the various acts and their corresponding objects, Mastricht believes he has charted a middle ground between rigid supralapsarianism and infralapsarianism in such a manner that the relative correctness of each lapsarian position can be recognized and despairing opinions conceded. This middle ground rests upon a careful clarification of means and attending objects. According to Mastricht, the second act in particular need not entail the specification of definite means as found in the object. Mastricht's lapsarian mediation, therefore, focuses on the distinction between the objects of predestination and the objects of election/reprobation, wherein the former is universal and indefinite, while the latter is particular and definite.

Despite the clarifications involving acts and objects, Mastricht has not broached directly the relation between the four acts and sin itself. Recall that Turretin charges supralapsarianism as putting sin in the decree as a means of reprobation, making it seem like God permits the Fall in order to damn sinners, with the implication that damnation is God's first thought prior to sin. On Turretin's interpretation, reprobation and damnation function coordinately in the supralapsarian system. Mastricht emphatically denies this equivocation. In order to understand this better, Mastricht's parallel discussions under the headings "*De Electione*" and "*De Reprobatione*" need to be considered. What becomes increasingly clear in these loci is Mastricht's emphasis on the asymmetry between election and reprobation such that the end of particular election corresponds to the glorious

---

80. Mastricht, *TPT* 3.2.12: "Ratione *primi* actus praedestinationis, objectum non potuit fuisse, nisi homo *creabilis* & *labilis*, quoniam praesupponitur, nullum adhucdum decretum factum, de creatione & lapsu."
81. Mastricht, *TPT* 3.2.12.
82. Mastricht, *TPT* 3.2.12.

end of predestination, while no such correspondence can be found in the act of reprobation.

The Acts of Election Under the heading on election, Mastricht indicates how the one and most simple decree of election can be once again conceived—in the human mode of conception—in four logical acts, with each act mapping onto a logical act of predestination articulated above. It is important to keep in mind here the distinction Mastricht has already made between predestination proper (the first two acts) and election and reprobation proper (acts three and four). Accordingly, the first two acts in Mastricht's breakdown of election (and rejection) should always be understood in a general and indefinite sense.

The first logical act of election, according to Mastricht, is the plan to manifest the glory of mercy "in the gracious beatification of the human creature (at that point) creatable and fallible."[83] As Mastricht specifies elsewhere, such beatitude cuts with a christological edge. In this first act of election, "Christ is involved as the means of gracious beatification; with regard to the final [act], the principal cause of the beatitude of the elect."[84] To be clear, Mastricht denies that Christ is the impulsive cause of election as the God-man.[85] Christ is, strictly speaking, the instrumental, and therefore meritorious, cause of election as the Mediator (i.e., God-man),[86] with the sole, impulsive cause of election being the pure, unmixed good pleasure (*purum putum beneplacitum*) of the Father, Son, and Spirit.[87] It is certainly peculiar, however, that Mastricht has articulated a specific christological means within the first act, which, ostensibly, is only reserved for articulating an end without consideration of means. As far as I can tell, Mastricht does not clarify this point. In his *pars elenchtica*, when addressing the question of whether Christ is the *fundamentum* of election, Mastricht simply reiterates the standard Reformed orthodox opinion (contra the Arminians) that Christ as God-man is "the effect of election, and instrument of God, through whom God establishes to save the elect."[88]

In attending to the second act of election, Mastricht reiterates without further qualification that God creates and permits the Fall so that a common (indefinite) object—*homo creandus & lapsurus*—would be available for the manifestation

---

83. Mastricht, *TPT* 3.3.6: "*primus* est *propositum* manifestandi gloriam misercordiae, in gratuita hominum (adhucdum) creabilium & *labilium beatificatione*."

84. Mastricht, *TPT* 3.3.9: "Itaque *primo* electionis actu … Christus involvitur *ut medium* beatificationis gratuitae; in *postremo*, ut causa principalis beatitudinis electorum."

85. Mastricht, *TPT* 3.3.10. A meritorious cause (*causa meritoria*) is "an instrumental cause that contributes to a desired effect by rendering the effect worthy of taking place." Muller, *A Dictionary of Latin and Greek*, s.v. "*causa meritoria*."

86. Mastricht, *TPT* 3.3.9.

87. Mastricht, *TPT* 3.3.11.

88. Mastricht *TPT* 3.3.18: "Christus sit *effectus* electionis, & *instrumentum* Dei, *per* quod constituit electos servare."

of mercy, namely as vessels of mercy prepared for glory.[89] After listing several scriptural references corresponding to this second act, Mastricht turns swiftly to the third act. It is precisely at this juncture that the particularity of election takes shape.[90] According to Mastricht, the third act entails a "designation and separation of a certain number of human creatures in whose beatification the glory of mercy might be revealed."[91] Such an act specifies the *propria ratio* of election.[92] Because the third act is the crux of the difference between particular election and rejection, Mastricht painstakingly makes three further distinctions regarding God's election within the third act itself: (1) God's election is an act of love (*delectionem*), which distinguishes it from the separation of the reprobate; (2) this act of elective love is "in order to the greatest and supernatural good";[93] and (3) God's elective love, as seen in comparison with reprobation, maintains the virtual intention (*virtualis intentio*) of conferring this greatest and supernatural good from beginning to end.[94] Overall, the point Mastricht is attempting to emphasize foregrounds the positive nature of election as opposed to the privative nature of reprobation. As will be evidenced in the next section, Mastricht understands reprobation as communicating nothing to the human object, whereas in election, God directly communicates the good leading unto beatitude, which, as Mastricht indicates, is God's virtual intention from the beginning. Finally, there is the fourth act of election which involves the intention of preparing and directing the means of election. In bringing the elect to their proper end, Mastricht highlights in particular the means of redemption through Christ, as well as the application of redemption through faith.[95] Overall, Mastricht's discussion of the acts of election foregrounds a key point about election itself: the end of election corresponds to the end of creation, namely the manifestation of God's glory in the form of merciful beatification. This intended end highlights the supralapsarian bent of Mastricht's lapsarianism; the orders of nature and grace contain one and the same overarching telos.

The Acts of Reprobation Although Mastricht's discussions of both election and reprobation map onto the logical acts of predestination, they do so in an asymmetrical manner. In order to fully see the depth of this asymmetry, it is prudent to begin with Mastricht's definition of reprobation. Definitionally, reprobation is the "predestination of a certain number of human creatures, so that, through their

---

89. Mastricht, *TPT* 3.3.6.
90. The Reformed orthodox typically refer to this as the *comparative* act.
91. Mastricht, *TPT* 3.3.6: "*Tertius* designatio & segregatio *certorum* quorundam hominum, in quorum *beatificatione*, gloria *misericordiae* patefieret."
92. Mastricht, *TPT* 3.3.6.
93. Mastricht, *TPT* 3.3.6: "(2) Dilectionem in ordine ad *summum & supernaturale bonum.*"
94. Mastricht, *TPT* 3.3.6.
95. Mastricht, *TPT* 3.3.6.

own just condemnation, the glory of vindicatory justice might be manifested."[96] Given the difficulty in this statement, Mastricht further specifies that God does not predestine creatures "to destruction, as to an end, nor delight in the death of the sinner per se; but to the glory of his justice, whose *medium* is, not any whatsoever, but just condemnation."[97] In discriminating between reprobation and damnation, Mastricht isolates the central feature in the asymmetrical relationship between election and reprobation. This point is brought out with great clarity within his discussion of the acts of reprobation, especially since Mastricht pauses along the way to note the key divergences between election and reprobation.

In the first logical act of reprobation, God plans (*propositum*) to make known the "glory of vindicatory justice (Rom. 9:22), not however of the damnation and destruction of man, which does not have any reason of good (and therefore no end), neither by reason of God, nor by reason of man."[98] According to Mastricht, the damnation of the human creature cannot include a good end unto itself based on its lack of direct participation in the supernatural good. This signals the first key (asymmetrical) difference between election and reprobation for Mastricht:

> In this first place is a difference between election and reprobation, that election is not only the glory of mercy, but it also considers the salvation of the elect, according to the end having been proposed in Rom. 9:23, while reprobation intends only the manifestation of justice as the end; neither has it considered the just damnation of the reprobate, except as a means.[99]

Tellingly, Mastricht refers elsewhere to the gracious salvation of the elect as a "subordinate end" under the supreme end of the glory of grace and mercy.[100] Within this line of reasoning, Mastricht believes the general means of enacting election follows naturally from the supreme end of predestination precisely because it positively participates in God's glorious grace. In this sense, salvation stands as a subordinate end and good in itself. Within reprobation, however, no

---

96. Mastricht, *TPT* 3.4.5: "Est autem *reprobatio, certorum quorundam hominum praedestinatio, ut per eorum justam condemnationem, manifestetur gloria justitiae vindicis.*"

97. Mastricht, *TPT* 3.4.5: "Deum non *praedestinasse* hominem ad *exitium,* tanquam ad *finem,* aut *morte peccatoris delectari* per se; sed ad *gloriam justitiae suae,* cujus *medium* sit, non qualiscunque; sed *justa condemnatio.*"

98. Mastricht, *TPT* 3.4.6: "*Propositum* manifestandi *gloriam justitiae* vindicativae Rom. IX. 22. non autem damnandi & *perdendi hominem,* quod ullam *rationem boni* (adeoque nec *finis*) non habet, nec, ratione *Dei,* nec ratione *hominis.*"

99. Mastricht, *TPT* 3.4.6: "Et in hoc *primum* est electionis & reprobationis *discrimen,* quod election non *gloriam* tantum misercordiae; *salutem* etiam electorum, pro *fine* sibi propositam habeat Rom. IX.23. dum reprobatio, *solam justitiae* manifestationem, velut *finem* intendit; nec *justam* reprobi *damnationem* considerat, nisi ut *medium.*"

100. Mastricht, *TPT* 3.3.11.

such subordinate end may be located. Damnation, following upon reprobation, is never such a good.

Moving to the second act of reprobation, Mastricht again isolates God's plan (*propositum*) to create and permit the Fall. As with the second act of predestination and election, the emphasis lies on the indefiniteness and commonality of human beings fit to be created and fall (*creandi* and *permittendi lapsum*). For Mastricht, God both reprobates and elects from a common lot (*commune*) without positively "inserting wrong" (*injuriam inserat*) to anyone. The shift from indefiniteness to definiteness occurs in the third act of reprobation. In a parallel manner to the third act of election, the third act of reprobation involves a designation of particular human creatures (e.g., to designate Judas) in whom justice might be revealed. "And in this [third] act strictly and most properly consists reprobation."[101] Because reprobation is not "from love, nor from the communication of any good, but only privation"[102] it cannot be confused with election. Whereas in election there is "love with separation" (*dilectio cum secretione*), reprobation is "the negation of love with separation" (*dilectionis negatio cum secretione*).[103] In this negative act, God "wills to leave some without eternal life, and according to sin justly condemn."[104] The overall lack of (immediate) communication of the good signals the second divergence between election and reprobation. Unlike the act of election, "the curse of reprobation merely denies the good, and does not bring in evil, except by the intervening merit of the creature."[105] The "just merit" being, of course, the will of the creature that enacts sin.

In the fourth and final act of reprobation, Mastricht turns to the intention and preparation of the specific means, which includes the permission to actual sin, the dereliction in sin, and just condemnation on account of sin.[106] In making this point, Mastricht notes the final two divergences between election and reprobation. While election is the proper cause of all its specific means, reprobation is only the antecedent cause of damnation and actual sin.[107] That is, all of the means that follow from God's election are given directly by God, whereas God's reprobative act is entirely negative. God does not put in sin, as it were. The final divergence between election and reprobation follows from this: reprobation does not have the reason of cause and effect between the means themselves because the permission of sin is not the cause of dereliction but sin itself. The means of reprobation are

---

101. Mastricht, *TPT* 3.4.6: "Et in hoc actu, strictius & maximè propriè consistit *reprobatio*."

102. Mastricht, *TPT* 3.4.6: "quia non est *ex dilectione*, nec *boni* alicujus *communicatio*; sed tantum utriusque *privatio*."

103. Mastricht, *TPT* 3.4.6.

104. Mastricht, *TPT* 3.4.6: "quo Deus *vult* quosdam vita aeterna *destitui*, & *propter peccata* justè condemnari Rom. IX.13."

105. Mastricht, *TPT* 3.4.6: "quando reprobationis *odium*, bonum tantum *negat*, nec malum *infert*, nisi *merito* creaturae interveniente."

106. Mastricht, *TPT* 3.4.6.

107. Mastricht, *TPT* 3.4.6.

strictly negative and not directly the cause of the next means. This is different from election wherein "calling is the cause of justification and justification of glorification."[108] Thus, Mastricht reasons, the means of reprobation are negative all the way down: not redemption, not calling, not granting faith, not prevention from sinning and dereliction in it, and not remission of sins.[109] Even here, though, Mastricht makes sure to close the door on any possible Arminian or Pelagian threats by rooting everything in the divine will instead of foreknowledge. "All means, whether negative or positive, are ordered to their own end through a positive act of the divine will."[110]

Central to Mastricht's discussion of the four acts of reprobation is the distinction between reprobation and damnation. When speaking of reprobation, Mastricht maintains that the principal and impulsive cause is solely God's good pleasure,[111] with the implication being that the human being is not *reprobatable* by means of sin (*non tamen per peccatum sit reprobabilis*).[112] Sin is not an external necessity compelling God to reprobate this or that creature. God reprobates based upon God's absolute dominion, which, for Mastricht at least, follows only upon the supposition of God's permission of the fall of human creatures into a common beginning. Even still, reprobation is vastly different from damnation and punishment, which "justly presupposes blame." Because of sin (*propter peccatum*), therefore, the human creature is "damnable and fit to be damned" (*damnabilus* and *damnandus*).[113] Sin exists as the meritorious cause of punishment, "though not the cause of the destination," which is independent and eternal in the decree.[114] In other words, the wages of sin are damnation but, given God's antecedent decree of reprobation, a place has already been prepared by God for those fit to be damned.

But all of this, then, raises thorny questions with regard to the relation between sin, reprobation, and damnation in the decree. Mastricht addresses these difficulties by further clarifying the distinction between the decree of reprobation and the decree of damnation. As he does throughout the discussion of predestination, Mastricht makes use of the four logical acts of reprobation in order to specify the precise relation of sin to God's decree. According to Mastricht, the first act of reprobation presupposes sin as strictly possible.[115] The second act sets the "futurition of sin" (*peccati futuritionem*). In speaking of futurition, Mastricht

---

108. Mastricht, *TPT* 3.4.6: "dum in electione, *vocatio*, est *causa* justificationis, justificatio *glorificationis*."

109. Mastricht, *TPT* 3.4.6.

110. Mastricht, *TPT* 3.4.6: "*Omnia* tamen ista *media*, seu *negativa* sint, seu *positiva*, per actum divinae voluntatis *positivum*, diriguntur in suum *finem*."

111. Mastricht, *TPT* 3.4.8.

112. Mastricht, *TPT* 3.4.8.

113. Mastricht, *TPT* 3.4.8.

114. Mastricht, *TPT* 3.4.8.

115. Mastricht, *TPT* 3.4.13. According to Mastricht, the "root and foundation of possibility and impossibility is not in things but in the power of God." *TPT* 2.20.12. On the nature of possibility, futurition, and actuality in Reformed orthodoxy, see Richard

draws a philosophical distinction between *futuritio* and *futurum*. "*Futuritio* exists from eternity" as an immanent act in God concerning things *ad extra*, whereas "*futurum* originates in time."[116] This does not mean, however, that future things (*futurum*) do not follow from the decree. Concerning futurity, God's decree is the proper cause of all things, whether they are necessary, contingent, free, good, or evil. Futurity in this sense expresses an infallible eventuation and coming to be. From these infallible futuritions, God produces in time future things (*futurum*) through God's will, either effectively (if it is good) or permissively (if it is evil).[117] Based on this distinction, God's decree is the cause of the futurition of sin, though not of the future sin itself (*ipsius peccati futuri*), whose proximate cause arises from the free will of the sinner (*liberum arbitrium peccantis*).[118] It follows for Mastricht that sin enters the picture within the third act as that which merits condemnation (i.e., the meritorious cause). After which, according to the fourth act, sin enters "at the same time with condemnation as the means to the glorification of vindicatory justice."[119] Nevertheless, as Mastricht makes clear, sin "does not enter in any manner as the impulsive cause itself of the act of reprobation."[120] The impulsive cause of reprobation is strictly God's good pleasure.

Order of Predestination

To reiterate once again, like Turretin, Mastricht too holds that while God's decree occurs singularly and most simply, one may speak of an order within the decree. This is admitted not only "according to our mode of conceiving" (*pro nostro concipiendi modo*) but in the divine counsel according to its own mode (*suo modo*).[121] When conceiving the order of the divine decree, one recognizes that "God wills the end first, then the means to that [end]."[122] Yet, so Mastricht reasons, this must be conceived in such a manner that there exists a most wise coordination (*sapientissima coordinatio*) "of the prior and posterior thing, especially of the means and end."[123] Not without reason, then, Mastricht intentionally explicates the order

---

A. Muller, *Divine Will and Human Choice: Freedom, Contingency, and Necessity in Early Modern Reformed Thought* (Grand Rapids, MI: Baker Academic, 2017), 181–289.

116. Mastricht, *TPT* 3.1.16.

117. Mastricht, *TPT* 3.1.17.

118. Mastricht, *TPT* 3.1.17.

119. Mastricht, *TPT* 3.4.13: "peccatum ingreditur unà cum condemnatione, velut *medium* ad glorificationem justitiae vindicativae."

120. Mastricht, *TPT* 3.4.13: "sed ut *causa impulsiva* ipsius reprobandi actus, nullo modo ingreditur."

121. Mastricht, *TPT* 3.1.26.

122. Mastricht, *TPT* 3.1.26: "Per *ordinem* istum decretorum divinorum, rectè concipimus ac dicimus, Deus *prius velle finem*, quam *media* ad illum."

123. Mastricht, *TPT* 3.1.26: "Quod tamen non statim, de diversis in Deo *volitionibus* est capiendum, acsi alia ibi sit *prior*, alia *posterior* una item alterius *causa*: sed de *re decretâ*

of predestination under the category of God's wisdom.[124] The wisdom of this order is understood along the common maxim regarding the end and means: *quicquid est primum in intentione; illud ultimum est, in exsecutione: & vice versa, quicquid est ultimum in exsecutione; hoc primum fuit in intentione.*[125]

In accordance with this maxim and his previous discussion regarding the distinction between the end and means in predestination, as well as the logical acts, Mastricht's ordering of predestination may now be fully outlined, an order he believes "Scripture teaches and evidence clearly confirms."[126]

1. God proposes to himself to manifest the glory of grace (*gratiae*) and justice (*justitiae*).
2. God creates mankind in his image, stipulates with his creatures a covenant of works, and permits them to fall (*in lapsus*).
3. From those created and fallen (*ex creatis* and *lapsis*), God elects this one by name, and rejects that one.
4. God confers (*conferre*) the means of salvation for the elect ones, namely redemption through the Son as Mediator and the application of redemption in the administration of faith; against the reprobate, God negates (*negare*) the means of salvation, and hands them over in their sin.
5. God eternally saves the elect through faith (*per fidem*) on account of Christ (*propter Christum*); God eternally condemns the reprobate on account of sin (*propter peccatum*).
6. God obtains, by consequence (of #5), the glory of mercy in the salvation of the elect, and the glory of avenging justice (*justitiae vindicis*) in the condemnation of the reprobate.[127]

Rigid and Mediated Supralapsarianism Compared

After working through the various dimensions of Mastricht's species of lapsarianism, it is now time to draw out the nuance by briefly comparing Mastricht to those falling under the label "rigid" supralapsarians, in particular William Perkins, Johannes Maccovius, and William Twisse.[128] Let me first highlight the

ac volita, ut apud Deum, volitio & *sapientissima coordinatio* sit, prioris & posterioris rei, praecipuè mediorum & finis."

124. Mastricht, *TPT* 3.2.21: "Unde *sapientissimus* ille resultat, praedestinationis *ordo*..."

125. Mastricht, *TPT* 3.2.21.

126. Mastricht, *TPT* 3.2.21: "Hunc ordinem Scriptura docet, & experientia liquido confirmat."

127. For nos 1–6, see Mastricht *TPT* 3.2.21.

128. Cf. William Perkins, *The Manner and Order of Predestination*, in *The Works of William Perkins*, vol. 6, ed. Joel R. Beeke and Greg A. Salazar (Grand Rapids, MI: Reformation Heritage Books, 2018), 273–384; Asselt, et al., *Scholastic Discourse*, 154–65; William Twisse, *Vindiciae gratiae, potestatis ac providentiae Dei: hoc est Ad examen libelli Perkinsiani de praedestinationis modo et ordine, institutum a Jacobo Arminio, responsio scholastica, tribus*

most important overlaps between Mastricht and what he refers to as "rigid" supralapsarianism. Like the supralapsarian William Perkins, Mastricht holds the opinion that the "supreme end of predestination is the manifestation of God's glory, partly in His mercy and partly in His justice,"[129] and this without consideration of the Fall. This is also the position of William Twisse, who regards the end of predestination as "the manifestation of God's glory in a way of mercy mixt with justice."[130] The supralapsarian position, as seen generally in these descriptions, prioritizes not only divine purpose, but this particular purpose, namely God's glory as manifested specially in mercy and justice. Most importantly, supralapsarianism integrates this purpose across the orders of creation and redemption.

In keeping with this specified end, Mastricht likewise agrees with the rigid supralapsarians that the "common means of accomplishing this counsel is twofold: the creation and the permission of the fall."[131] Turretin, recall, strongly denies this point precisely because creation and fall cannot be means—even common and indefinite ones—leading to the end of God's glory in the form of mercy and justice. For Turretin, this would be a category error. Mastricht believes he attenuates the force of this criticism by proposing four acts of predestination, and, as a result, ultimately draws a distinction between the general objects of predestination (*creabilis and labilis*) and the particular objects of election/ reprobation (*creatus and lapsus*). Interestingly enough, Mastricht's mediating position bears similarity to that of Johannes Maccovius. Typically considered a rigid supralapsarian, Maccovius attempted to cede some ground to the infralapsarian position by drawing a fine distinction between the order of intention and the order of execution in the decree. The former corresponds to the realm of God's absolute power (*potentia absoluta*) and what is possible, while the latter corresponds to God's ordained power (*potentia ordinata*) and what is actualized in creation with regard to God's intelligence and will (i.e., the decree to achieve God's ordained end).[132] Maccovius could thus argue: "Regarding the goal, with respect to the

---

libris absoluta, 2nd edn (Amsterdam: Joannes Janssonius, 1648), 49–117; William Twisse, *A Treatise of Mr. Cottons, Clearing Certaine Doubts Concerning Predestination. Together with an Examination Thereof* (London: J. D. for Samuel Creek, 1648). On Perkin's lapsarianism, see Richard A. Muller, *Christ and the Decree: Christology and Predestination in Reformed Theology from Calvin to Perkins* (Grand Rapids, MI: Baker Academic, 2008, 160–71; on the supralapsarianism of Maccovius and Twisse, see Bell, "*PROPTER POTESTATEM, SCIENTIAM, AC BENEPLACITUM DEI*," 130–213. For a helpful overview of the context of Twisse's response to John Cotton, see David Como, "Puritans, Predestination, and the Construction of Orthodoxy in Early Seventeenth-Century England," in *Conformity and Orthodoxy in the English Church, c. 1560-1660*, corr. edn, ed. Peter Lake and Michael Questier (Woodbridge: Boydell Press, 2000), 64–87.

129. Perkins, *Manner and Order of Predestination*, 305.
130. Twisse, *Treatise of Mr. Cottons*, 3–4.
131. Perkins, *Manner and Order of Predestination*, 305.
132. Cf. Bell, "*PROPTER POTESTATEM*," 144–57, 202–5.

intention, the human object of predestination is creatable man (*homo creabilis*). Regarding the goal with respect to execution, the human object of predestination is man to be created and created, man being permitted to fall and fallen (*est homo condendus, conditus, permittendus in lapsum, lapsus*)."[133] Although not identical with Maccovius's lapsarian position, Mastricht viewed the human objects under distinct aspects as well, loosely that of the intended end (act one), general means (act two), and particular means (acts three–four).

The distinction between the general objects of predestination and particular objects of election/reprobation, while somewhat overlapping with Maccovius, also proves to be a point of divergence with someone like William Twisse.[134] According to Twisse, the object of predestination, which includes particular election and reprobation, is strictly "*massa nondum condita*" (mass not yet formed)[135] Twisse's reasoning, although logically rigorous and thorough to excess in its overall presentation, may be boiled down to four points: (1) the intention of the end is always logically prior to the intention of the means; (2) the decree of predestination only concerns one intended end and the means to that end; (3) the sole intended end in the genus of predestination is the manifestation of God's glory in a way of "mercy mixt with justice"; and (4) everything else following in the decree of predestination concerns coordinated means. On this last point, Twisse maintains "the decrees of creating, permitting sin, and damning are not to be subordinated to each other, but are rather to be coordinated, and in the sole decree to be reduced to the end intended by God with regard to that whole *medium* having been adapted."[136] When this fourfold reasoning is consistently worked through, there can only be one logical object across the board for Twisse: human beings having not yet been made (i.e., possible human beings). To say otherwise would be to confuse the end with the means, and eventually, at least for Twisse, introduce logical contradictions based on his rigorous adherence to the principle that intention has logical priority over execution.[137]

Twisse's hard-nosed emphasis on the coordination of intended means and the logical priority of the intended end reveals the deeper divergence at work between his and Mastricht's version of supralapsarianism. Granted, however, this difference is difficult to see based on Mastricht's rather dense—and, in truth, cumbersome—discussion. But it is nonetheless there, manifesting itself most clearly in Mastricht's discussion of election. Within Twisse's supralapsarian logic, the decree of the end

---

133. *Scholastic Discourse*, 157.

134. Bell states that Twisse "represents supralapsarianism in both its purest and maturest forms." "*PROPTER POTESTATEM*," 170.

135. Twisse, *A Treatise of Mr. Cottons*, 41.

136. Twisse, *Vindiciae gratiae*, 71: "Quare non subordinanda sunt inter se decreta creandi, peccatum permittendi & damnandi; sed coordinanda potius, & in unum decretum redigenda de medio illo integro ad finem à Deo intentum accommodato." Cf. Twisse, *Vindiciae gratiae*, 108, 392. Cf. Twisse, *Treatise of Mr. Cottons*, 3.

137. Cf. Twisse, *Vindiciae gratiae*, 53–4; 108; Twisse, *Treatise of Mr. Cottons*, 3.

1. Contours of Lapsarianism 41

of predestination does not incorporate subordinate ends, either in the form of election or reprobation. Salvation and damnation are coordinate means of working out God's intended end of manifesting God's glory as mercy mixed with justice.[138] Twisse, then, draws the closest analogy possible between election and reprobation, salvation and damnation, as means within the decree of predestination.[139] Mastricht, in contradistinction, believes the gracious salvation of the elect should be inserted as a subordinate end in the decree in keeping with God's overall virtual intention to the end. The implied subordination of ends at work in the "first act" of election for Mastricht signals a dissonance between election and reprobation that does not exist for Twisse. This point requires nuance, especially since Mastricht indicates in his discussion of the "acts" of predestination that salvation enters into the decree under the aspect of means. For Mastricht, salvation positively coordinates with the end of predestination (i.e., the glory of mercy) such that it may be considered a subordinate end unto itself. Damnation, on the other hand, bears a negative relation to the end of predestination (i.e., the glory of vindicatory justice) such that it cannot be considered an end at all.

Overall, the heart of Mastricht's mediation rests on his willingness to countenance the salvation and beatification of the creature as part and parcel of the end of predestination, whereas damnation remains strictly a negative means. In this way, election proves to be, in some sense, a part of the final goal of creation in a way that reprobation is not. The logic of such a position indicates that God creates in order to elect and save, but not to reprobate and damn. But one must question—as Twisse himself did with others holding a similar position—Mastricht's logical consistency on this point if, as he states, God's ultimate end in predestination is the manifestation of glory via mercy and justice. What Mastricht's lapsarianism actually entails, or so it seems, is that God creates in order to elect and reprobate in general, though not to reprobate and damn in particular. This leaves Mastricht with a somewhat unique and, quite frankly, confusing position. Mastricht wants to have his cake and eat it too. Unlike Turretin, Mastricht does not separate the orders of creation and redemption in such a manner as to foster different ends. Mastricht desires, like Twisse, the integration of the orders of nature and grace around the ultimate end of God's glory in the form of mercy and justice, even though he shrinks from making election and reprobation coordinate. This leads Mastricht to propose a cumbersome four-act schema, wherein the second act allows for indefinite objects fit to be created and fall in order that they may elected and reprobated for the purpose of manifesting God's glory in mercy and vindicatory justice. It is not clear, though, what this actually solves. In the end, Mastricht attempts a mediation wherein he is supralapsarian on the general objects of predestination and infralapsarian on the particular objects of election/reprobation, even as election in his scheme has a supralapsarian resonance. In all of this, however, the question must be asked: Is this the appropriate end? Is

---

138. Twisse, *Treatise of Mr. Cottons*, 56, 113, 144.
139. Twisse, *Treatise of Mr. Cottons*, 144.

the major premise concerning mercy and justice correct? Do any Reformed orthodox divines of a supralapsarian persuasion modify this picture? The answer is yes: Thomas Goodwin.

Thomas Goodwin (1600–1680): Supralapsarianism Modified

Independent minister, Westminster divine, and Reformed orthodox theologian Thomas Goodwin left behind a vast oeuvre, covering theological loci ranging from predestination to ecclesiology.[140] Commenting on Goodwin's theological output and depth of thought, Mark Jones recently claimed—and not without good reason—that Goodwin represents the "very best Reformed theology of the seventeenth century."[141] Strangely, however, Goodwin's theology has been the subject of little scholarly attention.[142] This is especially true with reference to the lapsarian question.[143]

Toward the beginning of his *Discourse of Election*, Goodwin observes, with regard to the lapsarian question, that a "distinction to the end and to the means, in the decrees of God, is so generally acknowledged, that I need not insist upon it."[144] Yet, as he immediately qualifies, exactly what one understands as the end and

---

140. In the "Preface to the Reader" in the first publication of Goodwin's works (1681), the editors noted this: "He had a genius to dive into the bottom of points, to 'study them down,' as he used to express it, not contenting himself with superficial knowledge, without wading into the depth of things. His way was to consult the weightiest, if not all the authors that had written upon the subject." Reprinted as "The Preface to the Reader," in *The Works of Thomas Goodwin*, vol. 1 (Lafayette, IN: Sovereign Grace Publishers, 2000), xxix.

141. Mark Jones, *Why Heaven Kissed Earth: The Christology of the Puritan Reformed Orthodox Theologian, Thomas Goodwin (1600–1680)* (Göttingen: Vandenhoeck & Ruprecht, 2010), 35.

142. Maybe this neglect can be attributed to, as B. Hoon Woo recently noted, the "difficulty of reading Goodwin—his sentences are long and complex, and his exegetical work is intricate and thorough to the point of excess." *The Promise of the Trinity: The Covenant of Redemption in the Theologies of Witsius, Owen, Dickson, Goodwin, and Cocceius* (Göttingen: Vandenhoeck & Ruprecht, 2018), 189.

143. For the relevant scholarship on Goodwin and this topic, see the following: Paul Edwards Brown, "The Principle of the Covenant in the Theology of Thomas Goodwin" (PhD Diss., Drew University, 1950); J. R. Fry, "The Grace of Election in the Writings of Thomas Goodwin" (PhD Diss., University of Durham, 1971); Michael S. Horton, "Thomas Goodwin and the Puritan Doctrine of Assurance: Continuity and Discontinuity in the Reformed Tradition, 1600–1680" (PhD Diss., University of Coventry, 1998); Jones, *Why Heaven Kissed Earth*; Mark Jones, "Thomas Goodwin's Supralapsarian Christology," in *A Puritan Theology: Doctrine for Life*, ed. Joel R. Beeke and Mark Jones (Grand Rapids, MI: Reformation Heritage Books, 2012), 149–59; and B. Hoon Woo, *Promise of the Trinity*, 187–234.

144. Goodwin, *Works* 9:84.

the means in the decrees "needs some explication."[145] It is such an "explication" that positions Goodwin as a modified supralapsarian.[146] In order to understand the nuances of Goodwin's "explication" more fully, I will organize his lapsarian theology around three different, albeit interconnected, realities: (1) super-creation grace; (2) supralapsarian Christology; and (3) individual election and reprobation.

Super-Creation Grace

According the Goodwin, any proper understanding of the logical order of the divine decrees hinges upon the distinction between the end and the means.[147] In terms of the lapsarian question and its object, Goodwin states the matter simply: "God had a respect unto man considered as unfallen, in his election of him unto the end, and also man as fallen into sin in his decrees to the means."[148] The end that Goodwin has in mind here—which he consistently emphasizes across his various writings on election and Christology—is a "supercreation and supernatural grace through Christ as mediator of union,"[149] which indeed is that "fullness of glory that God designed to bring his elect into."[150] The means to bring about this end, however, all suppose man "as fallen as the object of them." Goodwin distinguishes his position from the "pure supralapsarian" in that pure supralapsarianism brings the means (e.g., the Fall) into the decree to the ultimate end.[151] Even still, Goodwin is not technically infralapsarian insofar as the order of grace is not contingent on the Fall. Put more precisely, pre-Fall human beings were not bound for the ultimate end of creation by virtue of their natural (and holy) state, even as law-keepers. As Goodwin explains, "Holiness in Adam by creation, whilst he stood, and in which he was created, was not a means at all … of that election glory."[152] Election glory is a "super-creation" grace within the created, not simply redemptive, order.

145. Goodwin, *Works* 9:84.
146. Given that Horton claims Goodwin is "an infralapsarian Calvinist" and Trueman insists he is "vigorously supralapsarian," Jones's remark is salient: "The problem may be that the usual taxonomies of infra- and supralapsarianism may need to be revised since Goodwin does not appear to fit nicely into either position." *Why Heaven Kissed Earth*, 128, n. 31. See Horton, "Thomas Goodwin and the Puritan Doctrine of Assurance," 66; Carl Trueman, *The Claims of Truth: John Owen's Trinitarian Theology* (Carlisle: Paternoster Press, 1998), 138. I agree with Jones's point here, and I hope this section serves as a "revision" of sorts.
147. As with Turretin and Mastricht, however, this should not be considered a real distinction on the part of God, which would vitiate divine simplicity. Goodwin puts it this way: "I readily grant that the decree of the end and that of means were both in God's mind at once, and in it neither had a priority or posteriority." *Works* 9:87.
148. Goodwin, *Works* 9:84.
149. Goodwin, *Works* 9:85. For the Christology associated with this statement, see the next section.
150. Goodwin, *Works* 9:84.
151. Goodwin, *Works* 9:84.
152. Goodwin, *Works* 9:84–5.

In order to clarify his position, Goodwin attends to the controversy concerning the object(s) of predestination. Without adjudicating the finer details of the debate, Goodwin simply underscores his point that God's decrees are neither wholly pitched upon a mass of "creability" before the Fall, nor a mass of mankind considered and viewed first as fallen into sin.[153] Instead, the divine decree proceeds from a twofold respect. Foremost, God decrees qua end "upon their unfallen and creable condition," and makes that "estate or condition the *terminus à quo*" of the decree.[154] In conjunction, God decrees qua means upon the fallen condition of humankind. As Mark Jones comments here, the issue for Goodwin is "not whether election has reference to the means."[155] For Goodwin that answer is obviously yes. The issue, rather, involves a careful distinction between the end and the means such that a differentiation between election (love) and predestination (mercy) is properly recognized. Strictly speaking, election flows from God's communicative love, which grants a "super-creation" grace apart from the Fall. Mercy, however, entails the condition of fallenness and only "respecteth misery."[156]

At this point, one might reasonably ask what exactly does Goodwin mean by "super-creation" grace apart from the Fall? Given the mutability of humanity's original state, Goodwin posits that "super-creation" grace was necessary to become fixed immutably unto God. Super-creation grace, therefore, only results from God's election.[157] This is part and parcel of the reality that God's ultimate end in creation and election is communication and union. In other words, super-creation grace is the grace of union with God in beatitude. Goodwin reasons as follows:

> That God ... did by that election also ordain those whom he so singled forth unto a super-creation union with himself and communication of himself, as the highest and utmost end (as to what concerned us) he elected them unto; so as the height and top of our salvation is consummated, and that union with himself which is far above that oneness we had by the law or dues of our creation.[158]

Such "super-creation" communication and union, moreover, is structured around a species of supralapsarian Christology for Goodwin. The ultimate end of election, and by extension creation, is the communication of God's self—whether in God's attributes or the fullness of God's life as Trinity—through supernatural union with the God-man, Jesus Christ.[159] Super-creation grace is christological through

153. Goodwin, *Works* 9:86.
154. Goodwin, *Works* 9:87.
155. Jones, "Thomas Goodwin's Supralapsarian Christology," 156.
156. Goodwin, *Works* 2:145.
157. Goodwin, *Works* 9:99.
158. Goodwin, *Works* 9:99.
159. Goodwin, *Works* 9:94–104. On the importance of union with Christ in Goodwin's theology, see especially Jonathan M. Carter, *Thomas Goodwin on Union with Christ: The Indwelling of the Spirit, Participation in Christ and the Defence of Reformed Soteriology* (London: T&T Clark, 2022). Carter recognizes that Goodwin's supralapsarian emphasis on

and through: "That the communication of [God's] self is founded upon union, is eminently seen in the man Jesus, whose predestination is the pattern of ours."[160]

Supralapsarian Christology

Goodwin's articulation of communion through union is best characterized under the umbrella of supralapsarian Christology. The language of supralapsarianism as applied to Christology technically refers to the incarnation, and it is often encountered in counterfactual form: would the Son of God have assumed human form apart from sin? However, in the medieval discussion of this subject, the question is layered, involving not only hypotheticals, but also general questions pertaining to purpose: Is the redemption from sin the primary reason for the incarnation? Or, whether and how can we determine divine reasons for divine operations *ad extra*?[161] This manner of framing the question demarcates Goodwin's supralapsarianism from its counterfactual counterpart. In this way, Goodwin advances a form of supralapsarianism that groups all of God's decrees around the God-man, Jesus Christ.[162] In his exposition of 1 Cor. 8:6, Goodwin notes the following:

> God's eternal purposes concerning all things were made in Christ, as God-man. God's eternal purposes concerning the creatures, or his works that are out of or without himself, are immanent acts of God's, remaining in himself. And God yet so honoured this our one Lord, as not to purpose any thing which was to be out of himself, *ad extra*, without the contemplation of his being God-man, on whom (as such) all things should depend.[163]

the glory of the God-man undergirded Goodwin's entire theological project such that it grounded and shaped his soteriology (see pp. 204–8).

160. Goodwin, *Works* 9:105. Goodwin's distinction between creation and super-creation has direct consequences for his articulation of *foedus naturae* and Adam's "natural" reward. Cf. Goodwin *Works* 7:7–53. On the question of Adam's reward within Reformed orthodoxy, especially for Goodwin and Turretin, see Mark A. Herzer, "Adam's Reward: Heaven or Earth?" in *Drawn into Controversie: Reformed Theological Diversity and Debates within Seventeenth-Century British Puritanism*, ed. Michael A. G. Haykin and Mark Jones (Göttingen: Vandenhoeck & Ruprecht, 2011), 162–82. While Herzer's essay is helpful on the level of general description, the christological convictions undergirding Goodwin's position, as well as the theological ramifications of it for thinking through the covenant of nature, remain muted. See Chapter 4 for my discussion of Adam's reward in Jonathan Edwards's theology, wherein something akin to Goodwin's reasoning is at work.

161. For a helpful discussion of the medieval period and the development of this question, see Hunter, *If Adam Had Not Sinned*; and Schrader, introduction to *On the Motive of the Incarnation*, xiii–xlix.

162. Cf. Jones, "Thomas Goodwin's Supralapsarian Christology," 149–59.

163. Goodwin, *Works* 4:531.

As Goodwin's comments indicate, the decrees of God find their beginning and end in the Son as the God-man. Jesus Christ—in the entirety of God's works *ad extra*—is the "end and perfection of all,"[164] so much so that creation only comes into existence as a result of God's immanent willed movement and foreknowledge toward the God-man.

> Now in the beginning of these ways, and the first thoughts of them, did God possess Christ God-man in his foreknowledge, as the richest treasure of all his glory to be manifested in his creation, *without which he would not have proceeded* to any other work, or have walked forth in any creature way, but rested in the blessed society of the Three without them.[165]

Jesus Christ is the "final cause or end for whom all things were made."[166] In the order of the decrees, Jesus Christ stands first in intention; he is the intention *ad finem*, under whom the remainder of God's external works remains subordinate. Even still, it is not the case for Goodwin that God's ordination of the Son as God-man is a natural necessity for God, at least in the sense that for God to be God the Son must be the God-man. "It cannot be said to have been a natural due to the second person," argues Goodwin, "to be made man."[167] However, given the supposition of God's decree for the Son to "subsist in a human form," it then becomes the necessary due of Christ, as God-man, to be "set up by God in those decrees, as the end of all those things."[168] Put in scholastic parlance, the making of Christ as the end in God's decrees "was a natural necessary consequent" of God's decreeing the Son into union with mankind.[169] In the designed union of the Son with the man Jesus, therefore, God "hath and doth make the highest manifestation of his glory, and communication of himself, such as by no created ways or means else could have been obtained."[170]

The incarnation of the Son of God, according to Goodwin, entails a twofold end: (1) the manifestation of God's perfections to creatures, and (2) the communication of God's love and goodness to creatures. For Goodwin, God wills to not only reveal God's perfections and communicate himself to "creatures reasonable," but wills to do so in the highest manner possible. Given Goodwin's prior arguments regarding God's decrees in creation, such a revelation and communication can only proceed as ordered to and from the God-man. The "highest manner possible" is necessarily by means of the God-man. According to Goodwin, all communication depends upon union; even

---

164. Goodwin, *Works* 4:470.
165. Goodwin, *Works* 4:471.
166. Goodwin, *Works* 4:471.
167. Goodwin, *Works* 4:471.
168. Goodwin, *Works* 4:471.
169. Goodwin, *Works* 4:474.
170. Goodwin, *Works* 4:477.

further, and by extension of the same premise, the "nearer the union the nearer communication."[171] Therefore, the highest communication depends upon the highest union, and this occurs by no other means than the "personal union of a creature with one who was God."[172] The mere fact (or law/covenant) of creation stands as a shadow compared to the reality of the communication of God through union with Christ. In this way, the predestination of the Son as God-man underscores the central movement of God toward human creatures: the grace of adoption, which is "super-creation" grace, a grace that only flows from the saints' union with Christ.

This grace of adoption is the principal glory that God designs to himself in election. Indeed, the grace of election is first and foremost the grace of adopted union; as such, the foremost object of God's electing grace is the God-man. Jesus Christ is the pattern and example of all election, and the predestination of Jesus Christ "transcends all that grace which was or could have been cast upon all his elect, any way considered."[173] Goodwin casts this in a strongly supralapsarian light:

> From the pattern and example of whose election it is evident, that grace is not to be limited, or only to be understood of favour towards creatures that have sinned, and are delivered out of sin and misery; for the highest grace (which divines style *gratia unionis*, the grace of the personal union in the man Jesus), above all other elevations or demonstration of grace whatsoever, was found in the instance of him, who could have no sin ... wherefore grace, and the election of grace ... imports not solely in opposition to, or exclusion only of, works since the fall, but of all sorts of works, in what state soever.[174]

As it pertains to God's relation to human creatures, the election of Jesus Christ involves a double ordination: (1) the relation of a head, or spouse to a husband; and (2) the relation of a Savior and redeemer, which is a "super-addition to that of headship."[175] According to Goodwin, these relations correspond to differing aspects or conditions in the human creature. The former corresponds to persons apart from the Fall, "*in massa pura*, in the pure lump of creatureship, or as to be created."[176] The latter pertains to persons considered by God as fallen, "and so as objects to be saved."[177] Both reveal the glory of God's grace in distinct manners, although they should not be construed disjunctively. The connection between them is the centrality of the God-man in the decrees, even if the object of grace

---

171. Goodwin, *Works* 4:480.
172. Goodwin, *Works* 4:481.
173. Goodwin, *Works* 9:95.
174. Goodwin, *Works* 9:95.
175. Goodwin, *Works* 9:96.
176. Goodwin, *Works* 9:97.
177. Goodwin, *Works* 9:97.

is considered under different aspects: one before the Fall and one after.[178] Here, even the original objects of super-creation grace were "permissively ordained" to fall into sin so that the grace of God in Christ might be further amplified and illustrated. The Fall, accordingly, becomes an occasion for the grace of adoptive love to the elect to be extended as the grace of saving mercy.[179]

This seems to leave Goodwin in a tricky theological spot with regard to the incarnation. How does one construe the christological movement in such a way as to take account of God's election pre- and post-Fall? Goodwin is adamant that the predestination of Christ was "not simply or only founded upon the supposition or foresight of the fall, as if only occasioned thereupon."[180] To bring Christ into the world only on account of sin, so Goodwin reasons, would be to make God subject to the creature and to make humans "the end of that union."[181] Furthermore, this would only reduce the gift of Jesus Christ to his benefits (e.g., redemption or heaven). Goodwin insists that the benefits of Christ (e.g., salvation) are "far inferior to the gift of his person unto us, and much more to the glory of his person itself." Goodwin continues: "His person is of infinite more worth than [all his benefits] can be."[182]

Even still, Goodwin remains wary of explicating God's predestination of Christ along counterfactual lines. "Neither yet, on the other side, do I, nor dare I," Goodwin argues, "affirm that Christ should have been incarnate, and assumed our nature, though man had never fallen."[183] Any attempt to articulate the reality of the incarnation without consideration of the Fall engenders, in Goodwin's mind, a great theological "chimera."[184] Two ends appear to be at work in the decree for Goodwin: adoption and redemption. Nevertheless, Goodwin's main point—which indeed reveals the centerpiece of his supralapsarian Christology—is that of the two, adoption and redemption, "the glory of Christ's person, in and through that union, had the greatest sway, and that so as even redemption itself was subordinated to, and ordained for the glory of his person, as the end of all first and chiefly intended."[185] Christ and the glory of his person remain the primary content of God's decretive will for the world: "God's chief end was not to bring Christ into the world for us, but us for Christ. He is worth all creatures. And God contrived all things that do fall out, and even redemption itself, for the setting forth of Christ's

---

178. Goodwin maintains a distinction between the "primary" election of Christ as God-man and the "relative" election of Christ, which corresponds to Christ's relation to human creatures as head (before and after the Fall) and redeemer (only after the Fall).
179. Goodwin, Works 9:97–8.
180. Goodwin, Works 1:99.
181. Goodwin, Works 1:99.
182. Goodwin, Works 1:99. Cf. Goodwin, Works 4:481.
183. Goodwin, Works 1:99.
184. Goodwin, Works 1:99.
185. Goodwin, Works 1:99–100.

glory, more than our salvation."[186] In the order of human understanding, therefore, the relation of Christ to elect human persons as "head" has priority over the relation of Christ to elect human persons as "redeemer." But this raises the question, what relation does Christ bear to the rejected? Asked differently, how does Goodwin's supralapsarian Christology reframe for him the infralapsarian and supralapsarian question with regard to the individual objects of election and rejection?

Individual Election and Reprobation Compared

The uniqueness of Goodwin's articulation of super-creation grace and supralapsarian Christology is brought into sharp relief in his comparison of individual election and rejection. Within his comparative analysis, Goodwin stresses that the acts of election and reprobation are not equals in God's intention, especially toward the creature as sinner. There is, in fact, an "infinite difference."[187] At the outset of his comparative discussion in the *Discourse on Election*—and in keeping with his overall decretal framework already outlined in that work—Goodwin once again maintains a strong distinction between the end and the means. To be sure, the decrees of election and rejection pertain both to the end and means, although they must be considered, according to Goodwin, in different "acts" (or "parts") and in vastly disparate ways.

The first act of election and rejection is *ad finem* (to the end) and considers creatures before the Fall.[188] In the pre-Fall state, God ordains a communication of himself to creatures that takes them above the natural state of creation. This also entails a non-ordaining of a certain portion of creatures, whom God denies "super-creation" grace. God has exercised a "pure absolute act of dominion" in electing some creatures to union with the God-man and in rejecting others

---

186. Goodwin, *Works* 1:100. Cf. Goodwin, *Works* 9:98–9. Overall, this raises serious concerns for Jones's central thesis in *Why Heaven Kissed Earth*, namely, that "Goodwin's Christology is contingent upon his doctrine of the covenant of redemption." *Why Heaven Kissed Earth*, 145. To be fair, Jones himself recognizes this in his later essay on Goodwin's christologically inflected supralapsarianism: "I address the issue of Christ's glory in [*Why Heaven Kissed Earth*], but on further reflection I would have made more of Goodwin's christological supralapsarianism." "Thomas Goodwin's Supralapsarian Christology," 154, n. 35. This "making more," or so it seems to me, actually entails a reversal of the entire thesis: Goodwin's doctrine of the *pactum salutis* is contingent upon his Christology.

187. Goodwin, *Works* 9:157.

188. Such an understanding of the acts of reprobation should not be confused with the positive and negative acts of reprobation, as is standard for both infralapsarians and supralapsarians. In the standard model, the negative act includes desertion, while the positive includes damnation on account of sin. This is also referred to as the comparative (negative) and absolute (positive) acts of reprobation. See, for example, Turretin, *Inst.* 4.14.1-22 (ET: 1:380–6); and Perkins, *Manner and Order of Predestination*, 315–17.

to a sustained existence in their natural state.[189] This should not be construed as judgment from God, as it were, because sin is not present in the creature. Goodwin relies here on a distinction between the "first" and "second" act of reprobation, wherein the creature is unfallen in act one and fallen in act two. "And thus did God without consideration of the fall," writes Goodwin, "ordain his chosen to that super-creation glory, though he denied the rest that great good."[190] This denial to the rest is the "first act" of reprobation. It is an act of pure dominion and not an act of justice—which will become central to the "second act" and thus reveal the great disparity between election and reprobation. Goodwin further clarifies the "first act" of election and rejection with regard to pure creation:

> He did yet purpose to ordain them to other good things of an excellent nature and kind, as that creation perfect holiness which was God's image and the dominion over all the works of his hands, which Adam, and in him we all, were appointed unto by the law of his and our creation, which condition we all predicate as a complete happiness; but still this was not that good we speak of, not that glory in which God becomes all and in all.[191]

The decree of election in the "first act," according to Goodwin, underscores the infinite distance between God and man, such that man—even by his natural (and holy) state—could not and would not partake of God's heavenly glory. So conceived, God's elective grace remains the "supremest end in the decrees"; it is an end "simply and for itself desired" by God.[192] Rejection in the form of damnation (i.e., the "second act"), however, was "never intended by [God] for itself, as an end which he delights in."[193] This remains true even if, in God's permissive decree, both the elect and non-elect were allowed to fall together. So enters Goodwin's speculation on the purpose of God's permission of the Fall:

> But it pleased God to permissively decree those elect to fall together with the rest, as for many other holy ends, so for this one especially that respect the matter at hand, that we might discern the difference of immutable holiness running along with glory, which election brings us unto, Eph. i.4, from that of created holiness; which, if we suppose man had not fallen from, but stood by his free-will, grace had not been so manifestly discerned, but the glory of it would

---

189. Goodwin, *Works* 9:155. Goodwin, in fact, quotes Bāñez to solidify his point about the freedom of the divine will in election: *Est manifestatio maxime libertatis, quam habet divina voluntas circa dispensationem bonorum supernaturalium, quae maxima est perfectio divina.*
190. Goodwin, *Works* 9:155.
191. Goodwin, *Works* 9:155-6.
192. Goodwin, *Works* 9:157.
193. Goodwin, *Works* 9:157.

have been obscured and attributed unto man's free will, and not the grace of election.[194]

Given the reality of the Fall, Goodwin reasons that in the "second acts" of election and rejection God takes into account new means for the elect. In election, these new means are Christ as redeemer, faith in the redeemer, and repentance from sin.[195] Of course, these new means remain ordered toward the same end for the elect: communion with God through union with the God-man. This is not the case with reprobation, however: "Together with this new act ordaining to these means, there was a denial of giving the same unto the *rest*, to whom [God] had also denied glory afore in the first act of preterition."[196] The difference between the first and second "acts" of reprobation hinges upon the reality of sin. God's denial of means to the reprobate, "after man is considered as fallen, is not as then an act of pure dominion, sovereign dominion, but has a *jus ordinatum* in it, which justly may move [God] thereunto."[197] Goodwin recognizes that this distinction sets him apart from pure supralapsarianism, which cannot but make reprobation an "act of pure dominion" in the second act akin to election. Nevertheless, Goodwin maintains that, in the second act, "though sin is not *causa reprobationis* [the cause of reprobation] take the act, *est tamen causa reprobabilitatis* [it is nevertheless a cause to have been reprobated]."[198] This was not so in the first act of reprobation. God reprobates in the "second act" according to the rule of justice; God elects in the "second act" according to new interposition of the same sovereign grace and absolute dominion.

Some Lapsarian Conclusions

This extended analysis of the lapsarian positions of Turretin, Mastricht, and Goodwin has revealed a key interpretive point for adjudicating the lapsarian question: one cannot and should not construe the infralapsarian and supralapsarian debate within Reformed orthodoxy simply in terms of the objects of predestination; the controversy, in fact, hinges upon a larger discussion of the end(s) of creation and redemption.[199] Although the controversy surely includes a detailed discussion of the objects of predestination, how one even approaches

---

194. Goodwin, *Works* 9:158.
195. Goodwin, *Works* 9:158.
196. Goodwin, *Works* 9:159.
197. Goodwin, *Works* 9:160.
198. Goodwin, *Works* 9:160.
199. This is Mark Jones's precise point with regard to Thomas Goodwin's theology and the lapsarian question: "the infra/supralapsarian debate cannot have in view only predestination, where man is considered fallen or unfallen." "Thomas Goodwin's Christological Supralapsarianism," 156.

that discussion is already colored by the prior construal of God's intended end, as well as the relationship between the order of nature (pre-Fall) and the order of redemption/grace (post-Fall).

In Francis Turretin's infralapsarianism, the distinction between the twofold works of God *ad extra*—nature and grace—remains the preeminent theological dividing line. In the works of nature, the intended end is "the communication and (as it were) the spreading out of the power, wisdom and goodness of the Creator which shone forth."[200] The sin of the creature disrupts and deludes this natural order and end therein, which brings about another supernatural end: the grace and mercy of election and the display of justice in the reprobate. The advent of Christ, as such, remains completely tied to redemption (i.e., the order of grace), and only then as an instrumental means of redeeming the elect.[201] For Turretin, the person and work of the incarnate Christ always remains subordinate to the decree of election.[202] Confusedly, however, Turretin fails to locate the decree of the Fall within the order of either nature or grace. It exists as a sort of logically necessary bridge between creation and grace. Such a logical bridge, in the end, raises questions of the consistency of God's intended end(s) in creating and redeeming. Can God's intended end(s) really be divided up in this manner?

Petrus van Mastricht's lapsarian scheme attempts a mediation between supralapsarianism and infralapsarianism. Ingredient to Mastricht's proposal is the ability to distinguish between the indefinite objects of predestination and the definite objects of election/rejection. This distinction, more or less, enables Mastricht to maintain the priority of divine purpose, all the while taking seriously (as infralapsarianism desires) the execution of means vis-à-vis sin. Even with this concession, Mastricht's scheme is still best characterized as a species of supralapsarianism based on integration of the end of predestination across the orders of nature and grace. This end—without consideration of the Fall—is the manifestation of God's glory in the form of mercy and vindicatory justice. This is exactly what infralapsarianism denies.

In terms of the later interpretation of Jonathan Edwards's theology, two points are worthy of note. First, Mastricht's species of supralapsarian showcases that one of the most pressing issues within the framework of supralapsarianism is the teleological integration of nature and grace. Only then can one proceed to the discuss the so-called objects of predestination. Second, and following from the first, election functions within Mastricht's lapsarianism in a more general and

---

200. Turretin, *Inst.* 4.9.21 (ET: 1:347).

201. To be fair, Christ remains the only, and as such necessary, means of accomplishing the grace of election toward sinful creature.

202. On the subordination of Christ to the decree of election in Turretin's infralapsarian scheme, see Brannon Ellis, "The Eternal Decree in the Incarnate Son: Robert Rollock on the Relationship between Christ and Election," in *Reformed Orthodoxy in Scotland: Essays on Scottish Theology 1560–1775*, ed. Aaron Clay Denlinger (New York: Bloomsbury T&T Clark, 2016), 59–63.

architectonic sense than reprobation. Precisely in this way, Mastricht proves to be supralapsarian on general election and reprobation, and infralapsarian on particular election and reprobation. Just because the "objects" of particular election and rejection are "created and fallen" does not automatically imply that one is an infralapsarian full stop. Overall, though, Mastricht's proposed supralapsarian integration and its attendant distinction between the objects of predestination and the objects of election/reprobation yields a confused solution. On this score, Karl Barth's comments seem appropriate: Mastricht proved both parties were, in a sense, right, "only by telling them that in their most important convictions they were wrong. He did not simplify the issue for himself or the two schools."[203]

Different from the opinions of both Mastricht and Turretin is that of Thomas Goodwin. Goodwin's lapsarianism, like Turretin, seeks a logical distinction between nature (creation) and grace (super-creation). However, where Turretin sees radical discontinuity, Goodwin sees christological continuity. Such continuity, in the end, bears greater similarity to the tendency within supralapsarianism to foreground teleology and integration, albeit with a totally different end in view. Within Goodwin's supralapsarianism, the continuity that extends across the Fall centers on communion with God through union with the God-man. Goodwin calls this the predestination of Jesus Christ. God's gracious election does not simply correspond to the eternal state of creatures upon the supposition of the Fall. It is foremost christological and entails an election of human creatures to a "super-creation" adoptive union. The main design of election—or the "quintessence of our union with God"—consists in a "possession and enjoyment of all this is mutually God's or Christ's."[204] This sharing of all that is mutually God's through union with Christ reflects the trinitarian moorings of Goodwin's supralapsarianism. That is, within the oneness of essence that the Father, Son, and Spirit have in their common enjoyment, as well as the "mutual intercourse" and "sweet converse" that the persons have in their "circumcession," one discovers the *motus primo primus* of creation and election. According to Goodwin, the foundational motive for God's creating the world in, by, and for Christ is a "counsel of the heart of God among the Holy Three from everlasting," a *Sacratissimus Consensus Trinitatis*, most sacred consensus of the Trinity.[205] "Higher than this we cannot go."[206]

The consequences of all of this for classifying Goodwin's lapsarianism are extremely important and undergird my specification of him as a modified supralapsarian instead of mediating lapsarian. Goodwin's lapsarianism is best

---

203. Barth, *CD* II.2, 133.
204. Goodwin, *Works* 9:136.
205. Goodwin, *Works* 9:144.
206. Goodwin, *Works* 9:144. Even still, Goodwin indicates that there is something "natural" in God that disposes his will to create and elect: "Only what [God] should do for us, being matter of will in him, he might do it, or not do it as he pleased, and to whom, or whom not, as he pleased, because it was a matter of will, yet something that was natural was the inducer of his will thereunto." *Works* 9:148.

conceived of as modified supralapsarianism because the ultimate end in creation and predestination is not the manifestation of God's glory as power and dominion in the special form of mercy and justice. The end of creation and the end of election are union with Christ and the enjoyment of his person, and, by extension, the other persons of the Trinity. Significantly then, Goodwin's supralapsarianism integrates two questions: *Cur Deus homo?* and *Cur mundus?* Although usually separated in the formal discussion of the lapsarian question within Reformed orthodoxy, Goodwin's discussion reveals their necessary correlation.[207]

Finally, Goodwin's modified supralapsarianism also places him—in a much clearer sense than Mastricht—in a situation wherein he is supralapsarian on election and rejection in the "first act" before the Fall, and infralapsarian on election and rejection in the "second act" after the Fall. In this picture, election structures the entire framework of creation such that creation always remains subordinate to election in the decree because the end of creation is communicative union with God only in and through Christ's election.[208] Although the *esse actuale* of elect human creatures takes into account their fallen state for Goodwin, the *esse notionale* (or creable) of elect human creatures was always ordered to the christological end apart from the Fall.[209]

All in all, this vignette of seventeenth-century Reformed orthodoxy presents a diversity of lapsarian opinions with varying degrees of theological complexity and nuance. Such theological nuance proves valuable and necessary in mapping the multifarious nature of Jonathan Edwards's lapsarian position (Part II). That said, interpreting the theology of Jonathan Edwards vis-à-vis the lapsarian question is a penultimate goal of the present work. The primary task is itself theological: to engage the fundamental questions at the heart of the debate, and, in turn, provide

---

207. Matthias Scheeben—the nineteenth-century Roman Catholic dogmatician—frames the matter like this: "The answer to the question *Cur Deus homo?* is then also an answer to the question *Cur mundus?* Or *Ad quid mundus?* What direction is given to the world by the Incarnation? This question, although ordinarily too little noted in theological science, is as much in place as the first question." Matthias Joseph Scheeben, *The Mysteries of Christianity*, trans. Cyril Vollert, S.J. (St. Louis, MO: B. Herder Book Co., 1946), 429. Overall, Scheeben's species of supralapsarianism bears a remarkable similarity to that of Goodwin and, as we shall see, Jonathan Edwards.

208. The prepositions *in* and *through* are significant. The fact that Goodwin locates election both *in* and *through* Christ tempers the fear (Barthian fear!) that Christ remains too often subordinate to predestination in Reformed theology. Turretin, by way of contrast, refuses to consider Christ as the foundation of election (i.e., in Christ) because it reeks of Arminian synergism to him (cf. Article I of the *Remonstrantia* of 1610). In this sense, polemics might have forced Turretin's theological hand and clouded his ability to countenance an alternative theological formulation of the "in Christ." As an aside, Goodwin's lapsarian position also bears some similarities to that of Scottish theologian Robert Rollock. See Ellis, "Eternal Decree in the Incarnate Son."

209. Goodwin, *Works* 9:164–6.

a constructive, though modest, dogmatic account integrating God's decree concerning Christ's predestination, God's decree concerning creation, and human predestination. In order to further facilitate this larger task, it will prove helpful to analyze two modern critiques of infra- and supralapsarianism. By approaching the constructive task through this heuristic setup, the theological concerns and presuppositions at work in the lapsarian debate will be foregrounded and further probed for theological propriety. Furthermore, such a heuristic method will also allow me to bring to light the theological work that remains to be done. To that end, I now turn to the theological critiques of two twentieth-century Reformed theologians: Herman Bavinck and Karl Barth.

Chapter 2

LAPSARIANISM PROBLEMATIZED AND PURIFIED: HERMAN BAVINCK AND KARL BARTH

This chapter turns from seventeenth-century analysis to the more recent theological critiques of Herman Bavinck (1854–1921) and Karl Barth (1886–1968). Bavinck and Barth, each in their own way, problematized the manner in which the seventeenth-century lapsarian debate was framed. Bavinck's critique was largely formal, while Barth's was material; yet both were christological, even though in strikingly different manners and with vastly different theological implications. In critiquing the debate, they attempted to think with and beyond—though not apart from—the Reformed tradition. Their theological projects were, in this sense, self-consciously works of dogmatics. As such, the questions that Bavinck and Barth raise in critiquing the tradition are themselves theologically instructive. By attending to the way Bavinck and Barth critically engage the seventeenth-century debate, the theological concerns and presuppositions at work in the debate will be further illuminated. This will, in turn, produce a set of interrelated theological questions and insights that require careful attention. The aim of this chapter, therefore, is to excavate these questions—and desired insights therein—through an interpretation of the salient points of Bavinck and Barth's lapsarian discussions.

Herman Bavinck on the Inadequacy of the Infra- and Supralapsarian Distinction

The heart of Herman Bavinck's critique of the lapsarian question resides in the second volume of his *Reformed Dogmatics*.[1] In order to understand the nature of his critique, it is profitable first to articulate his explanation of the contours of debate and the various distinctions being drawn. According to Bavinck, the difference between infralapsarianism and supralapsarianism trades on a narrow

---

1. For a larger overview of Bavinck on election and God's decrees, see Cornelis P. Venema, "Covenant and Election in the Theology of Herman Bavinck," *Mid-America Journal of Theology* 19 (2008): 69–115, especially 74–8.

or broad definition of predestination.² In the restricted sense, the order of God's decrees has the decree of predestination following that of creation and the Fall, which closely mirrors the infralapsarian order. Supralapsarians, by contrast, broaden the definition of predestination to include the decrees of creation and fall within it, such that creation and fall are taken as means to the ultimate end of God's glorification in the eternal state of human creatures.³ In terms of God's foreknowledge, both infra- and supralapsarians affirm that reprobation proceeds from determination of the divine will, thus rendering the difference between them more formal than material. Both parties recognize that God, in some sense, includes the fall into sin and eternal punishment in the decree.⁴ Bavinck understands both as rejecting Pelagian free will, as well as rejecting faith and sin as the respective grounds for election and rejection. That is, both infralapsarians and supralapsarians default, in the end, to the good pleasure of God's will.⁵

So where does the difference lie? According to Bavinck, the difference rests in the order of the decrees.⁶ Infralapsarianism prefers to emphasize the historical and causal order (with an emphasis on plurality), whereas supralapsarianism prefers the ideal and teleological order (with an emphasis on unity).⁷ Put another way, infralapsarians desire to stress the significance, to some degree, of each decree in its own right; for supralapsarians, every decree remains subordinate to the ultimate decree.⁸

Preliminary Problems with Infralapsarianism

With this preliminary understanding in place, it is now possible to chart out more fully Bavinck's critique, which is contained, more or less, within his own positive dogmatic construal of the decrees. In his positive discussion, Bavinck helpfully pinpoints where he believes both infra- and supralapsarians generally fall foul. Bavinck thinks each of the two camps suffers from a one-sided and somewhat myopic perspective. Let me begin with the mistakes of infralapsarianism as Bavinck sees them.

Even though infralapsarianism should be praised for ostensibly sticking to the historical order and attempting to think through the demands of pastoral practice, it ultimately does not "satisfy the mind."⁹ Foremost, Bavinck criticizes the infralapsarian position on reprobation as containing a nascent Arminian

---

2. Bavinck, *RD* 2:383.
3. Bavinck, *RD* 2:384.
4. Bavinck, *RD* 2:384.
5. Bavinck, *RD* 2:384.
6. Interestingly enough, Bavinck does not believe the main difference rests on the object of predestination as such. See Chapter 1 for a historical recognition of this very point.
7. Bavinck, *RD* 2:384–5.
8. Bavinck, *RD* 2:385.
9. Bavinck, *RD* 2:385.

understanding of foreknowledge.[10] Just as faith and good works are not the cause of election, sin too is not ultimately the cause of reprobation. Both follow from God's sovereign good pleasure.[11] That is, the decree of reprobation—in some sense—always comes before the decree of sin.[12] According to Bavinck, if this is false, then two questions inevitably arise: Does God's permission of sin consist in bare foreknowledge after all? Did the Fall thwart God's design?[13] The answer for the Reformed, on Bavinck's reading, is decidedly no.[14] A Reformed-minded theologian must, in one way or another, include the Fall in God's decree as foreordained. This leads to another and deeper question: Why did God (even if the decree is construed as permissive) foreordain the Fall? An infralapsarian has no answer other than God's good pleasure. And this, says Bavinck, simply falls back into an articulation similar to that of supralapsarianism.

But this is not the only dilemma for the infralapsarian viewpoint. If the decree of reprobation follows the decree of the Fall, where does one logically place it exactly? Was it after Adam's first sin, and therefore only original sin? This might lead to the exclusion of all actual sins committed after Adam. Why not, Bavinck asks, just place the decree after the actualization of individual sins and so reprobate each person for that reason?[15] Such an order might correspond well to reprobation as rooted in God's justice as it meets the historical circumstance and execution of the decree. However, no Reformed orthodox divine would dare say this because it is the straightforward teaching of Arminius. Again, the specter of foreknowledge looms large. According to Bavinck, infralapsarianism rather haphazardly places the decree of reprobation after the Fall (unspecified with regard to original sin), though it certainly comes before actual sins.[16] Once again, the infralapsarian has wandered into supralapsarian territory.

---

10. Dijk points out, in fact, that Turretin himself cannot escape the doctrine of the *praevisio*: "Here too it appears that, although Turretin wants to include the fall of man in the decree of God, he cannot escape from the doctrine of the *praevisio* and does not dare speak of a *praedestinatio lapsus* in the real sense." ["Ook hier blijkt dat, al wil Turretin den val des menschen in het decreet Gods opnemen, hij zich niet ontworstelen kan aan de leer der praevisio en van eene praedestinatio lapsus in eigenlijken zin niet durft spreken."] Dijk, *De strijd over Infra- en Supralapsarisme*, 42.

11. Bavinck, *RD* 2:385.

12. It might be helpful on the front end to note Bavinck's consistent use of the qualifying phrase "in a sense" (or "in some sense") in his discussion of election and especially reprobation. This qualification shows Bavinck's reluctance to ascend higher than the *voluntatem Dei*. The will of God is not without *ratio*, even though it remains unfathomable for the human creature. Such language of reservation mirrors, as will be evident in later chapters, Jonathan Edwards's use of "as it were."

13. Bavinck, *RD* 2:385.

14. Bavinck, *RD* 2:385.

15. Bavinck, *RD* 2:385.

16. Bavinck, *RD* 2:386.

Preliminary Problems with Supralapsarianism

Although Bavinck's initial criticism of infralapsarianism sounds damning, his evaluation of supralapsarianism cuts deeper. After acknowledging that supralapsarians at least refrain from futile attempts at theodicy and ground the decrees in God's holy and wise, although inscrutable, will, Bavinck appraises supralapsarianism as in fact offering no solution, only hand-waving. The first mistake Bavinck isolates in the supralapsarian position is the specification within God's ultimate decree of the manner in which God's glory unfolds in the eternal state of rational creatures. Reformed theology specifies, correctly according to Bavinck, that the promulgation of God's glory is the ultimate end of God's work *ad extra*; however, the supralapsarianism goes further in specifying the manner of promulgation, a manner which suggests that God reveals God's justice exclusively in the eternal state of the reprobate and, in the eternal state of the elect, exclusively reveals mercy.[17] This criticism relates to another issue, namely that the objects of the divine will in election and reprobation stand as equals. Within supralapsarianism, according to Bavinck, eternal perdition and eternal salvation are often seen as eschatologically symmetrical; sin and salvation become the identical means of God's glorification.[18] For Bavinck, this cannot possibly be true, as Scripture—on Bavinck's reading—nowhere isolates the eternal double state of human creatures as the crown and climax of God's glory.[19] Most properly, Bavinck levels this critique against both infra- and supralapsarians, at least in the sense that both gravitate toward the manifestation of God's justice among the reprobate in their eternal state. Bavinck registers an important point:

> It is not true that God's justice can only be manifested in the wretched state of the lost and his mercy only in the blessedness of the elect, for in heaven, too, his justice and holiness are radiantly present, and even in hell there is still some evidence of his mercy and goodness.[20]

Here, Bavinck contends that it is utterly incorrect to represent hell as the goal of predestination.[21] A profound asymmetry exists between election and rejection; one must consistently recognize that election is categorically different from reprobation.[22] Election pertains to a goal (i.e., an optimal end), while reprobation

---

17. Bavinck, *RD* 2:386.
18. Bavinck, *RD* 2:387. Historically speaking, no supralapsarian—as far as I am aware—would ever phrase it exactly like this. Election and reprobation might be closely analogous (e.g., Twisse), but never symmetrical in "the same sense."
19. Bavinck, *RD* 2:389.
20. Bavinck, *RD* 2:389.
21. Bavinck, *RD* 2:389. As with the previous point, this critique also has purchase with regard to infralapsarianism for Bavinck.
22. Bavinck, *RD* 2:389. Recall from Chapter 1 that Petrus van Mastricht too registered this point.

remains an imperfection in the created order. Reprobation cannot be willed by God in and for itself.²³

The final mistake that Bavinck isolates pertains to the objects of predestination, namely that the objects of election and reprobation are possible humans.²⁴ Bavinck notices here how supralapsarianism quickly moves into the infralapsarian order because the provisional decrees must be followed by the decree to create possible humans and then permit them to fall.²⁵ Bavinck goes so far as to say that the supralapsarian order differs from infralapsarianism only in an Amyraldian sense (i.e., in the sense of abstract possibilities).²⁶ Many supralapsarians, according to Bavinck, begin with generalities concerning the decree to reveal God's perfections (e.g., mercy and justice) to possible human beings, only to then decree their actualization, permission to sin, and punishment (on account of their sin). Nowhere, Bavinck recognizes, do Reformed theologians of the supralapsarian persuasion speak of a predestination to sin.²⁷ Reprobation is never the efficient cause of sin. So, the question remains: why does God willingly permit the Fall?²⁸ Bavinck believes supralapsarianism often provides an inconsistent answer. Despite such inconsistency (on both sides), Bavinck notes an important overlap between the two camps:

> All agree also that sin, though not outside of the power of God's will, is and nevertheless remains contrary to his will, that it is not a means to the ultimate goal but a serious disruption of God's creation, and therefore that Adam's fall was not a step forward but most certainly a fall.²⁹

In other words, the fall into sin is not a *felix culpa* in a step-wise sort of manner.³⁰

---

23. For a discussion of Bavinck (and Berkouwer) on the asymmetry of election and reprobation, see also Eduardo J. Echeverria, *Divine Election: A Catholic Orientation in Dogmatic and Ecumenical Perspective* (Eugene, OR: Pickwick Publications, 2016), 171–99.

24. As mentioned in the previous chapter, this is the most common objection against supralapsarianism and often viewed as the primary point of division. More problematically, perhaps, this sometimes includes a "possible Christ."

25. Bavinck, *RD* 2:387.

26. Bavinck, *RD* 2:389.

27. Bavinck, *RD* 2:387–8.

28. Bavinck, like Calvin, says the language of permission is unhelpful overall if by permission we attempt to sidestep the efficacy of God's will (cf. *RD* 2:387). Cf. Calvin, *Institutes of the Christian Religion*, 956.

29. Bavinck, *RD* 2:387. Berkouwer's commentary on the lapsarian debate is instructive here: "Perhaps it is precisely at this point that the deepest motifs of supra and infra touch each other without conflict. They are the motifs of the simplicity (unity) of God's almighty counsel on the one hand, and of the rebellion *contra*, but not *praeter*, *voluntatem Dei* on the other." Berkouwer, *Divine Election*, 276.

30. Bavinck does, however, venture into something reminiscent of a *felix culpa* later in his discussion of possibility of sin in God's will: "[God] willed [sin] so that in it and against

The Deeper Problem with Infra- and Supralapsarianism

Before proceeding directly to the deeper problem inherent in the two lapsarian positions, perhaps it is best to note, on Bavinck's theological interpretation, the truth inherent in each. The truth at work in supralapsarianism concerns the unity of God's decrees and that all things remain subordinate to God's end in creation.

> The entrance of sin into the world was not something that took God by surprise, but in a sense willed and determined by him; that from the very beginning the creation was designed to make re-creation possible; and that even before the fall, in the creation of Adam, things were structured with a view toward Christ.[31]

On the other hand, the truth inherent in infralapsarianism corresponds to the differentiation, or diversity, of the decrees. The purpose at work in creation and the Fall are more than means to a final end. According to Bavinck, in the infralapsarian position one sees glimmers of both a teleological and causal order.[32] Sin, which is acutely registered within infralapsarian schemes, is therefore never positively willed by God, and must be understood as an incursion into the good of creation.[33]

This concern for unity in diversity and diversity in unity moves into the heart of Bavinck's formal critique and the theological concerns which it raises. To wit, Bavinck criticizes one-sided perspectives on order: on the one hand historical and linearly causal (infralapsarian), and on the other teleological (supralapsarian). In other words, Bavinck criticizes the manner in which infralapsarianism places final causation in the background, and the manner in which supralapsarianism places it in the foreground. Neither orientation, says Bavinck, satisfies theologically because such one-sidedness cannot account for the rich, complex, and interconnected fullness of the scriptural presentation.[34] So conceived, Bavinck enfolds both the causal and teleological order within something larger: an organic order.[35] At the heart of Bavinck's formal critique and problematization of the lapsarian debate, therefore, lies his organicism.

---

it he might bring to light his divine attributes. If he had not allowed it to exist, there would always have been a rationale for the idea that he was not in all his attributes superior to a power whose possibility was inherent in creation itself." *RD* 3:64. Even still, Bavinck never portrays God as the efficient cause of sin; God is, at most, the deficient cause (cf. *RD* 3:62). The notion of the *felix culpa* will loom large in my interpretation of Edwards's lapsarian picture (see Chapter 5).

31. Bavinck, *RD* 2:391.
32. Bavinck, *RD* 2:391.
33. Bavinck, *RD* 2:391. Note, however, that Bavinck believes sin could be willed for a greater and wise purpose. Again, Bavinck appears—despite his protestations—to countenance some form of a *felix culpa*.
34. Bavinck, *RD* 2:391–2.
35. Bavinck, *RD* 2:391.

The main features of Bavinck's philosophy of the organic appear in his 1904 work, *The Christian Worldview*.[36] In contrast to an atheistic and mechanistic construal of the world, Bavinck posits God's triunity as the ground and fount of the world's unity in diversity. James Eglinton describes Bavinck's portrait of reality as "triniform."[37] The world's organic form, on Bavinck's account, exists analogously to God's absolute unity in diversity.[38] As Eglinton argues, Bavinck desires a "trinitarian appropriation of reality ... a theology of Trinity *ad intra* requires a cosmology of organicism *ad extra*."[39] Given organicism's triniformity, the first salient feature of the organic motif is the precedence of unity over diversity.[40] Accordingly, there exists an overarching unity that provides the intelligibility for diversity without destroying diversity or sacrificing unity. Diversity, instead, unfolds the beauty of unity.[41] In this relation between unity and diversity, Bavinck also attempts, as Bruce Pass argues, to overcome the separation between the real and the ideal, the epistemological and the metaphysical in the wake of Kant.[42] Out of the first feature flows a second: the organism is bound by a common idea.[43] The rich diversity at

---

36. Herman Bavinck, *Christian Worldview*, trans. and ed. Nathaniel Gray Sutanto, James Eglinton, and Cory C. Brock (Wheaton: Crossway, 2019). My account of Bavinck's organic motif follows and is indebted to the scholarship of James Eglinton and Nathaniel Gray Sutanto. See James Eglinton, *Trinity and Organism: Towards a New Reading of Herman Bavinck's Organic Motif* (London: Bloomsbury T&T Clark, 2012); and Nathaniel Gray Sutanto, "Organic Knowing: The Theological Epistemology of Herman Bavinck" (PhD Diss., The University of Edinburgh, 2017). The latter has now been published as Nathaniel Gray Sutanto, *God and Knowledge: Herman Bavinck's Theological Epistemology* (London: Bloomsbury T&T Clark, 2020).

37. Eglinton, *Trinity and Organism*, 67.

38. Bavinck, *RD* 2:331.

39. Eglinton, *Trinity and Organism*, 68. Rather importantly, this is a one-way theological street. The unity in diversity perceived in the world should not drive our understanding of God's triunity. Nor is this indicative of a "Hegelian" becoming in God. See Eglinton, *Trinity and Organism*, 51–80. Sutanto's comments are also appropriate: "The theological assertion here involves the realistic claim that the nature of God *requires* that God's creation would bear his marks ... creation is seen to be marked by unities and diversities precisely because the Christian views the world in light of the revelation of the triune God." Sutanto, "Organic Knowing," 34.

40. Bavinck, *Christian Worldview*, 74; Eglinton, *Trinity and Organism*, 68; Sutanto, "Organic Knowing," 32–3.

41. Bavinck, *RD* 2:436. Cf. *RD* 2:422.

42. Bruce Pass, *The Heart of Dogmatics: Christology and Christocentrism in Herman Bavinck* (Göttingen: Vandenhoeck & Ruprecht, 2020), 29–30. Overall, Pass argues that the formal properties at work in Bavinck's organic philosophy are indirectly derived from Schelling, even as Bavinck maintains—unlike Schelling—a key distinction between the world-ideal relation and the God-world relation. In other words, Bavinck finds "organicism" to be a serviceable philosophical tool for theological use post-Kant.

43. Eglinton, *Trinity and Organism*, 69; Sutanto, "Organic Knowing," 33.

work in the world and its history finds its exemplary cause in the divine ideas, which, more profoundly, take root in the divine Logos.[44] As Nathaniel Gray Sutanto explains, "The divine ideas are the archetype for the things exemplified in creation, and because God is one, a single idea orchestrates and organizes the cosmos into a single central locus."[45] At the center of these divine ideas resides Jesus Christ. "In Christ, in the middle of history," Bavinck argues, "God created an organic center; from this center, in an ever widening sphere, God drew the circles within which the light of revelation shines."[46] Finally, organicism articulates a non-reductionistic, non-monistic telos, namely the honor of the triune God.[47] Bavinck's teleological understanding of the organism strongly pushes back against a mechanistic worldview, or, better still, a thoroughgoing metaphysical (and methodological) naturalism. Bavinck, according to Pass, employs the concept of organism in order to signal the proper "correspondence of mechanical and teleological explanation."[48]

Overall, Bavinck makes use of the organic motif to specify the proper relation between the divine counsel and the history of the world. Bavinck's use of the organic motif pushes back against Hegelian Idealism, wherein God is pan(en)theistically part of the world's organism; it also ultimately rejects Idealism precisely because Bavinck's organicism roots itself in a fundamentally Christian doctrine: *creatio ex nihilo*.[49] God and the world are not in the same genus.[50] Utilizing the organic idiom, Eglinton registers the same point: "The deliberate intent of Bavinck's system … is to consistently describe the creation as organic and the Creator as Triune."[51] The telos of creation, in all its unity and diversity, is the God made known in Jesus Christ. No ontological blurring exists, only a good creation called good precisely because it is serviceable to the revelation of God's triune perfection in Jesus Christ.[52]

How, we may now ask, does Bavinck's organicism concretely inform his theological critique of the lapsarian debate? Preliminarily, it means that both parties were mistaken in placing the decrees prior to the ultimate end as "means in subordinate relation" to one another.[53] It is certainly true that everything is

---

44. Bavinck, *Christian Worldview*, 79.
45. Sutanto, "Organic Knowing," 33.
46. Bavinck, *RD* 1:383.
47. Bavinck, *RD* 2:433-4; Bavinck, *Christian Worldview*, 89.
48. Pass, *Heart of Dogmatics*, 31.
49. This does not mean, however, that Bavinck's use of organism is not dependent on German Idealist conceptualizations of organism, especially the notions of a constitutive principle and development. See Pass, *Heart of Dogmatics*, 27-37.
50. On this type of mixed relation between God and creation, see John Webster, "*Non Ex Aequo*: God's Relation to Creatures," in *God without Measure: Working Papers in Christian Theology, Vol. 1: God and the Works of God* (New York: T&T Clark, 2016), 116-26.
51. Eglinton, *Trinity and Organism*, 70.
52. Bavinck, *RD* 2:439.
53. Bavinck, *RD* 2:390.

subordinate to the ultimate goal (i.e., God's triune glory), but Bavinck resists drawing the conclusion that this entails subordination of means to each other in a causally linear manner. Bavinck's organicism yields a coordination of decrees that unfolds its riches in eternity.[54] Realities such as creation, the Fall, faith, and unbelief occur not simply as mechanistic causes, mere means to be dispensed with at consummation. In terms of election and rejection, then, Bavinck's reasoning indicates that they cannot and do not run along parallel tracks toward eternal states *tout court*. To render the ultimate goal of the created order as the revelation of God's will in the form of justice to the reprobate and mercy to the elect is too austere.[55] Predestination to eternal death and predestination to eternal life should not be taken as ultimate goals in the same sense.

Against such austerity, Bavinck argues for an interconnected pattern working in harmony or concert.[56] God makes harmonious connections when decreeing, as when God decrees prayers and answers to prayer.[57] For Bavinck, God's decrees remain unconditional (i.e., acts of pure sovereignty) even though secondary causes exist and maintain an integrity within the world. An exact and duplicate harmony exists between the decrees in the eternal counsel of God and creaturely time.[58] God's decree corresponds to reality as it historically appears to the creature; it is not an illusion. From the human perspective, the decree replicates creaturely reality, even as God's idea of reality precedes the actual experience of reality.[59]

Given the limitations of human capacities, the splendor of the organic structure is difficult to comprehend. The human mind defaults to either the causal (infralapsarian) or teleological (supralapsarian) order, which often results in clash and confusion. But for God the structure is both causally and teleologically connected as an ever-present, single organism. According to Bavinck,

> the whole picture is marked by immensely varied omnilateral interaction … . In short, the counsel of God and the cosmic history that corresponds to it must not be pictured exclusively … as a single straight line describing relations before and after, cause and effect, means and end.[60]

---

54. Bavinck, *RD* 2:390. Bavinck finds such a coordination already at work in the Reformed tradition itself. On this point, Bavinck quotes, really paraphrases, William Twisse: "These elements are not just subordinated to each other, but are also related coordinately." In Twisse, *Vindiciae gratiae*, 71.

55. Bavinck, *RD* 2:391.

56. Bavinck, *RD* 2:391.

57. Bavinck, *RD* 2:400. Bavinck uses the example of rain in the time of a drought.

58. Bavinck, *RD* 2:400. Significantly, at least for this project, Bavinck references Jonathan Edwards on this exact point. Bavinck's footnote refers to the reprinted Worcester edition: *The Works of President Edwards*, vol. II (New York: Leavitt & Allen, 1857), 514. As found in the Yale critical edition, this citation references Edwards's discussion of the decrees in "Miscellanies," no. 29, *WJE* 13:216.

59. Bavinck, *RD* 2:397.

60. Bavinck, *RD* 2:392.

Bavinck views the organic whole as a nexus of coordinating relations, wherein the whole is not directly reducible to its aggregate parts or relations. To be sure, the parts are interconnected and reciprocally determinative, but never reductively and mechanistically linear. The world, according to Bavinck, reflects a divine and artful tapestry in which all of the parts are organically connected so as to showcase the eternal design of God's unified counsel.[61] God's divine counsel—that is, the unified decree—functions as the constitutive principle of the world's organism. Even still, as we saw earlier, the organic connection present in the world also groups around a christological center. The person of Christ is, as Bavinck says, the organic center of revelation. The incarnation, on this picture, appears to function as a constitutive principle as well: "If Christ ... is the incarnate Word, then the incarnation is the central fact of the entire history of the world."[62] But how do these two—the unified decree and the incarnation—relate as constitutive principles? Is the decree to become incarnate the organic center of the divine counsel itself and therefore the true constitute principle of organism *ad extra*? To further understand the relation between the decree and incarnation, attention now needs to be given to one final matter: the election of Christ.

The Election of Christ

Predestination, at least in terms of the optimal end, culminates in election for Bavinck.[63] As expected, Bavinck's organicism fills outs the depth and breadth of the discussion. Although it remains beyond dispute for Bavinck that human beings—whether fallible or fallen—are viewed as objects of election in Scripture, Bavinck also thinks that the elect are viewed not only atomistically, but also as a unified organism.[64] Most properly, the object of election is Jesus Christ and the church, his mystical body, as opposed to a mere (and nameless) aggregate of individuals.[65] The decree of predestination, therefore, includes Christ as the first object of election, wherein the election of the church logically follows that of Christ.[66] In terms of organic arrangement, Christ's human nature was from eternity—at the designation of the Father—foreordained to union with the divine nature and therefore a mediatorial office.[67] This does not mean that Christ was made the ground of election for Bavinck. Strictly speaking, Christ is the meritorious cause of salvation and instrumental cause of election (i.e., election is realized in and through Christ). Election in Christ entails the impartation of divine benefits to the church through Christ alone because Christ is the organic center and head of the

---

61. Bavinck, *RD* 2:392.
62. Bavinck, *RD* 3:274.
63. Bavinck, *RD* 2:399.
64. Bavinck, *RD* 2:402.
65. Bavinck, *RD* 2:390.
66. Bavinck, *RD* 2:403.
67. Bavinck, *RD* 2:403.

church. In other words, the real object of election is the mystical Christ, the Head and the body united as perfect organism.[68] Precisely because of this organic unity, one can conceive of election as a fixed decree without falling victim to the austere picture of supralapsarianism.[69]

The election of Christ with the church and Christ's existence as the organic center of creation now leads us to consider the incarnation directly. Again, the incarnation of the Son of God is the "climax, crown, and completion" of God's (self)-revelation. "All revelation," says Bavinck, "tends toward and groups itself around the incarnation as the highest, richest, and most perfect act of self-revelation."[70] Given Bavinck's thoroughgoing commitment to the incarnation as the heart of the organism *ad extra*, one might expect Bavinck's organicism to lead him to endorse a species of the incarnation anyway argument, wherein the Son would be moving toward incarnation apart from consideration of the fall into sin per se. Bavinck understands why theologians gravitate to this position, even though he does not hold it himself and finds it outside the bounds of the scriptural witness.[71] The necessity of the incarnation turns on soteriology for Bavinck. The rationale is straightforward: the Fall occurred, so the Fall was decreed by God as it occurred; "there is no room for any reality other than the existing one."[72] By corollary, no Reformed theologian can say the fall into sin occurred outside of God's one, eternal counsel. In God's eternal counsel, therefore, "the incarnation on account of sin also has a place."[73] "Creation and fall, preservation and governance, sin and grace, Adam and Christ—all contribute, each in his or her own way, to the construction" of the perfect organism built to the honor and glorification of the triune God.[74]

In the end, Bavinck appears to be, as Bruce Pass has argued, a "consistently inconsistent" supralapsarian.[75] As Pass further explains, "For all his talk of system, Bavinck is reluctant to tie off all the loose ends. In fact, at the critical juncture, namely, the place the incarnation occupies in the ordering of the decrees. Bavinck refuses to square the circle."[76] Whatever larger critiques one might mount against

---

68. Bavinck, *RD* 2:404.
69. Bavinck, *RD* 2:404.
70. Bavinck, *RD* 3:278.
71. Bavinck considers the motivating deductions as follows: (1) the incarnation cannot be accidental and grounded solely in human sin; (2) sin does not destroy God's ultimate plan; (3) religion before the fall cannot differ in essence to religion after the fall; (4) Christ's person and work cannot be exhausted in salvation; and (5) the church exists for Christ, not vice versa. See Bavinck, *RD* 3:279.
72. Bavinck, *RD* 3:279.
73. Bavinck, *RD* 3:279.
74. Bavinck, *RD* 2:405.
75. Pass argues that Bavinck's organicism, in fact, "presupposes a consistently inconsistent supralapsarianism." Pass, *The Heart of Dogmatics*, 125.
76. Pass, *Heart of Dogmatics*, 125.

Bavinck's use of the organic worldview as a deductive principle to move from Scripture to world history, it is certainly the case that Bavinck fails to make good on the relation between his implied supralapsarian Christology and the divine decrees in his theology. It remains unclear why Bavinck—precisely because of the emphasis on coordination across eternity within the organic motif—can only countenance a soteriological relation between the Fall and the incarnation. Thus, Bavinck's overall critique of the infra- and supralapsarian debate and his attending insights begs for an organically integrated answer to the questions *Cur mundus?* and *Cur Deus homo?* Unfortunately, Bavinck does not provide such an answer.

Karl Barth and Purified Supralapsarianism

It is not a stretch to say that Karl Barth developed his theology as he cut his teeth on historic Reformed thought, whether Calvin or later orthodox divines.[77] Such engagement often led Barth to part ways with this tradition, even as he remained appreciative of the Reformed outlook.[78] On this score, Barth's engagement with the lapsarian controversy is particularly important. As Shao Kai Tseng has recently demonstrated, it was Barth's wrestling with the theological perspectives at work in the lapsarian controversy that shaped Barth's christological doctrine of election as we know it.[79]

The beginning of Barth's formal engagement with the lapsarian controversy can be found in *Göttingen Dogmatics* §18.IV (published lectures from 1924 to 1925),[80] even though Barth had already tentatively proclaimed himself a supralapsarian as early as *Römerbrief* II (published in 1922).[81] Even still, it was not until 1936 when the preliminary fruit of Barth's wrestling with the lapsarian problem revealed itself. Occasioned both by his earlier lapsarian convictions and a lecture by Pierre Maury on predestination, Barth developed his understanding of the relationship between Christology and predestination in a set of lectures published in the series *Theologische Existenz heute* (Issue 47) under the title *Gottes Gnadenwahl*.[82]

77. Cf. John Webster, *Barth's Earlier Theology* (London: T&T Clark, 2005), 1.
78. As Barth put it during his time at Göttingen, Reformed dogmatics "does not have to involve a mere repetition of the Reformed tradition." *Göttingen Dogmatics: Instruction in the Christian Religion*, vol. 1, ed. Hannelotte Reiffen and trans. Geoffrey W. Bromiley (Grand Rapids, MI: Wm. B. Eerdmans, 1991), 456.
79. Shao Kai Tseng, *Karl Barth's Infralapsarian Theology: Origins and Development (1920–1953)* (Downers Grove, IL: IVP Academic, 2016).
80. Barth, *Göttingen Dogmatics*, 466–75.
81. Karl Barth, *Der Römerbrief 1922* (Zweite Fassung), in *Gesamtausgabe* II.47, ed. Cornelis van der Kooi and Katja Tolstaja (Zurich: TVZ, 2010), 237.
82. Karl Barth, *Gottes Gnadenwahl* (München: Chr. Kaiser Verlag, 1936). On the relationship between Barth and Maury, see Simon Hattrell, ed., *Election, Barth, and the French Connection: How Pierre Maury Gave a "Decisive Impetus" to Karl Barth's Doctrine of Election* (Eugene, OR: Pickwick Publications, 2016).

2. Lapsarianism Problematized and Purified

Tseng contends, quite appropriately, that "the central theological question that [Barth] tackles in *Gottes Gnadenwahl* is the lapsarian debate."[83] In this work, Barth expressly demonstrates his preference for the supralapsarian position:

> In the so-called supralapsarian opinion on election, as it was worked out among several of the reformed of the 17th century in the successors of Calvin and Beza, one should not see scholastic sophistry. It was, in truth, not speculation, but stood against the majority of theologians at that time holding an infralapsarian opposite-opinion, which wanted to distinguish the omnipotence, goodness, and wisdom of God in creation from his justice and mercy in reconciliation as first and original. But there is … no higher will in God than his gracious will.[84]

The aforementioned separation of creation and reconciliation proves to be a—if not the—major and abiding concern for Barth. As Barth responded in the printed *Fragebeantwortung* (Q&A), "From the perspective of the infralapsarian doctrine, creation and reconciliation are separated … . In this tearing apart and splitting of creation and reconciliation, I already see dawning the danger of a natural theology."[85] Already at work in *Gottes Gnadenwahl*, therefore, is what would form the bulk of his critique and purification of lapsarianism in *CD* §33: the danger of natural theology, God's gracious election as the "truth of revelation" (*Offenbarungswahrheit*) in its thoroughly christological form,[86] and double predestination as christological *Aufhebung*.[87] "We cannot know our election in Jesus Christ," Barth writes, "without first and above all knowing in Him our

---

83. Tseng, *Karl Barth's Infralapsarian Theology*, 187.

84. Barth, *Gottes Gnadenwahl*, 8: "Man darf in der sogen. supralapsarischen Ansicht von der Erwählung, wie sie von einigen Reformierten des 17. Jahrhunderts in der Nachfolge von Calvin und Beza herausgearbeitet worden ist, keine scholastische Spitzfindigkeit sehen. Spekulation war in Warheit nicht sie, sondern die von der Mehrzahl der damaligen Theologen vertretene infralapsarische Gegenansicht, die die Allmacht, Güte und Weisheit Gottes in der Schöpfung von seiner Gerechtigkeit und Barmherzigkeit in der Versöhnung als ein Erstes und Eigentliches unterscheiden wollte. Es gibt aber … in Gott keinen höheren Willen als seinen Gnadenwillen."

85. Barth, *Gottes Gnadenwahl*, 43: "In der Sicht der infralapsarischen Lehre werden Schöpfung und Versöhnung getrennt … . In dieser Auseinanderreißen und Zerspaltung von Shöpfung und Versöhnung sehe ich bereits die Gefahr einer natürlichen Theologie heraufsteigen."

86. Barth, *Gottes Gnadenwahl*, 13.

87. *Aufhebung*, for Barth, entails the dialectical and Hegelian notion of the negation of a negation, though maintaining the overriding purpose and intelligibility of the older negation in the new affirmation. See G. W. F. Hegel, *Georg Wilhelm Friedrich Hegel: Encyclopedia of the Philosophical Sciences in Basic Outline*, Part 1: The Science of Logic, ed. and trans. Klaus Brinkmann and Daniel O. Dahlstrom (Cambridge: Cambridge University Press, 2010), §§79–82.

reprobation."[88] In Barth's typical prose, Jesus Christ—and he alone—is both the right and left hand of God, the divine Yes and No.[89] As God's elect, Jesus Christ takes human reprobation upon himself, and, in so doing, "our reprobation is sublated" (*unsere Verwerfung aufgehoben*).[90]

As is evident, the heart of the material critique Barth proffers with regard to the lapsarian question in CD §33.1 is somewhat established by the time he starts writing CD II/2 in the winter of 1939/40 (published in 1942). That said, Barth's small print excursus lays bare his pressing theological concerns in great detail and specificity. As such, Barth's lapsarian excursus in CD §33.1 will form the bulk of the material analyzed in assessing Barth's critique, even though other salient portions from the *Church Dogmatics* will be explored in order to further clarify the nature of Barth's supralapsarian purification. Such will be the case with Barth's articulation of *das Nichtige* and its importance for filling out the contours of Barth's lapsarian inquisition.

The Lapsarian Excursus of Church Dogmatics *§33.1*

Barth's excursus in §33.1 follows from his dogmatic assertion that "the divine predestination is the election of Jesus Christ."[91] He further suggests Christ's election carries in itself the double theological pronouncement that Jesus Christ is both the electing God and elected man. For Barth, this leads to a vigorous maintenance of one point: "there is no such thing as a *decretum absolutum*."[92] As Barth would baldly state later in §33.2, "this decree is Jesus Christ, and for this very reason it cannot be a *decretum absolutum*."[93] Such substitution becomes "the decisive point in the amendment of the doctrine of predestination."[94] It is not a surprise then that Barth isolates the lapsarian controversy for an extended excursus. The debate itself concerns all the matters close at hand: the object of predestination, the will of God in eternal election, and the relation of economies of providence (creation) and reconciliation.

The Common Presuppositions After his historical introduction to the lapsarian question, Barth discusses what he finds as the "equally unassailable presuppositions" between infralapsarianism and supralapsarianism.[95] Ironically, each point Barth perceives as an area of agreement in the debate corresponds precisely to a

---

88. Barth, *Gottes Gnadenwahl*, 20: "Wir können unsere Erwählung in Jesus Christus nicht erkennen, ohne zuerst und vor allem wiederum in Ihm unsere Verwerfung zu erkennen."
89. Barth, *Gottes Gnadenwahl*, 19.
90. Barth, *Gottes Gnadenwahl*, 22.
91. Barth, CD II.2, 103.
92. Barth, CD II.2, 115.
93. Barth, CD II.2, 158.
94. Barth, CD II.2, 161.
95. Barth, CD II.2, 133.

2. Lapsarianism Problematized and Purified

critique of the tradition. As we shall see, at the heart of each of these critiques is the relationship between God's freedom and the extent of God's being known in Christ. The latter part of this relationship corresponds to what has been helpfully called Barth's "principal christocentrism" with respect to his theological method and exegesis.[96]

The first presupposition Barth isolates is the discrepancy between the objects of predestination and Jesus Christ as the elected and rejected man. According to Barth, "it is in the election of some [individuals] … that the man Jesus Christ plays a specific and indispensable part as the first of the elect. With the rejection of the others he has nothing whatever to do."[97] That is, when it comes to the objects of predestination—especially the object of reprobation—Jesus Christ remains far too absent. Instead, "a proper solution is found in the individual x or y," whether that be as *creabilis* and *labilis* or *creatus* and *lapsus*.[98] Put in question form, it may be phrased thus: Are the objects of predestination always "*homo x* or *y*," and if so, how does Christ relate to them?

---

96. In terms of Barth's methodology, see Dolf te Velde's detailed discussion in *The Doctrine of God in Reformed Orthodoxy, Karl Barth, and the Utrecht School: A Study in Method and Content* (Boston: Brill, 2013), 259–336; and Tyler R. Wittman, *God and Creation in the Theology of Thomas Aquinas and Karl Barth* (Cambridge: Cambridge University Press, 2019), 129–250. The term "principal Christocentrism" is taken from David Gibson, via Richard Muller, in *Reading the Decree: Exegesis, Election and Christology in Calvin and Barth* (New York: Bloomsbury T&T Clark, 2009). According to Gibson, principal Christocentrism refers to the exegetical method that follows from Barth's understanding of the relationship between Christ and revelation. More to the point, Christology becomes *the* epistemological access point and conceptual control upon all doctrinal loci (e.g., doctrine of God). Wittman makes a similar point in his exposition of God's self-correspondence within Barth's theology. In particular, Barth refuses to allow any criterion other than Jesus Christ to determine how we conceive of the relation between God's internal and external activity. The form and content of the divine decree, therefore, become functionally synonymous because the correspondence possesses no intelligibility apart from Jesus Christ. See especially Wittman, *God and Creation in the Theology of Thomas Aquinas and Karl Barth*, 220–43. Cf. Barth, *CD* II.2, 157. This also forms the basis of Barth's critique of the *pactum salutis*: "[The federal theologians'] doctrine of a purely intertrinitarian pact did not enable them to give an unequivocal or binding answer to the question of the form of the eternal divine decree as the beginning of all things" [*CD* IV.1, 66]. For Barth, therefore, there existed for these theologians a covenant of nature above, beyond, and before Jesus Christ; hence, "their view of the covenant became dualistic" [*CD* IV.1, 66]. I will return to these points again as the discussion unfolds below. For a critique of Barth's christological maximalism and method, which nevertheless remains appreciative of his theological instincts, see Steven Duby, *God in Himself: Scripture, Metaphysics, and the Task of Christian Theology* (Downers Grove, IL: IVP Academic, 2019), 132–87.

97. Barth, *CD* II.2, 133.

98. Barth, *CD* II.2, 133.

Second, Barth wants to ask whether or not God's eternal decree of predestination implies a fixed system in time, which binds both God and mankind. On Barth's interpretation, the Reformed tradition, both in its supralapsarian and infralapsarian articulations, "presuppose and maintain that that system is in any case from all eternity, and that it is indeed fixed and unalterable, so that not merely individuals, but God himself as its eternal author is bound to it in time."[99] The divine decrees understood in this sense strip both God and humans of true freedom. For Barth, a straitjacket is applied to God when God relates to time in this manner. This critique stands as part and parcel of Barth's larger revision of God's eternity and immutability in terms of God's constancy, livingness, and faithfulness in Jesus Christ, which is once again in keeping with his method.[100] As Barth writes later in IV.1,

> [God's] eternal being of and by Himself has not to be understood as a being which is inactive because of its pure deity, but as a being which is supremely active in a positing of itself which is eternally new. His immutability is not a holy immutability and rigidity, a divine death, but the constancy of His faithfulness to himself continually reaffirming itself in freedom.[101]

For Barth, God's freedom and faithfulness are only fully revealed in Jesus Christ. In this vein, the incarnation of Jesus Christ reveals (or just is) the connection of time and eternity,[102] which is always made present in the Holy Spirit.[103] One must note, however, that Barth conceives of God's eternal time and man's time asymmetrically, even if the bridge between them is located christologically. God's eternity comprehends time, but time does not comprehend God's eternity. It is a one-way street for Barth—lest one constrain God's freedom and open the door to a natural theology. To put it succinctly: God's triune eternality enfolds temporality

---

99. Barth, *CD* II.2, 134.

100. On the relation of time and eternity in Barth's theology, see the following: James Cassidy, *God's Time for Us: Barth's Reconciliation of Eternity and Time in Jesus Christ* (Bellingham, WA: Lexham Press, 2016); John Colwell, *Actuality and Provisionality: Eternity and Election in Theology of Karl Barth* (Eugene, OR: Wipf and Stock, [1989] 2011); Daniel Griswold, *Triune Eternality: God's Relation to Time in the Theology of Karl Barth* (Minneapolis, MN: Fortress Press, 2015); and George Hunsinger, "Mysterium Trinitatis: Karl's Barth's Conception of Eternity," in *Disruptive Grace: Studies in the Theology of Karl Barth* (Grand Rapids, MI: Eerdmans, 2000).

101. *CD* IV.1, 561. Barth's understanding of immutability is indebted to the critical reconstruction of the doctrine by Isaak Dorner, even as Barth parses freedom and necessity differently. On Barth's critical reception of Dorner on *Unveränderlichkeit* in the doctrine of God, see Sang Eun Lee, *Karl Barth und Isaak August Dorner: eine Untersuchung zu Barths Rezeption der Theologie Dorners* (Frankfurt: Peter Lang, 2014), 153–98.

102. Cf. Griswold, *Triune Eternality*, 164.

103. Cf. Barth, *CD* IV.2, 344–7.

2. Lapsarianism Problematized and Purified

in Jesus Christ.[104] In terms of the lapsarian question, this christologically actualistic reconceptualization of time and eternity problematizes any system that fixes God in time for Barth. The essence of Barth's second critique is summarized lucidly by Dolf te Velde: "The older theology loses sight, in Barth's view, of the living nature of God's decree."[105]

The third common presupposition Barth mentions flows from the second. According to Barth, both parties in the debate speak of fixed symmetry in the decree of predestination.[106] God is glorified "equally in the eternal blessedness of the elect and the eternal damnation of the reprobate."[107] Election corresponds to the demonstration of mercy, while reprobation corresponds to that of justice. If this critique is turned into a milder question, then it amounts to this: Is God's will to self-glorification—if it remains true that some are elected to eternal blessedness and others are rejected—necessarily symmetrical along the lines of mercy and justice? Obviously, this question cuts with a sharper edge if it is conceded that God's eternal decree, as Barth would posit the tradition as arguing, "implies the setting up of a fixed system which the temporal life and history of individuals can only fulfill and affirm."[108]

Most problematic for Barth is the fourth and final presupposition he finds: "above all—the hidden basis of all other agreement—all parties were agreed in their understanding of the divine good-pleasure which decided between election and rejection and this determined the concrete structure of the system appointed from all eternity for time."[109] Barth considers the appeal to God's good pleasure as an utter *decretum absolutum*—a hidden and unquestionable decree. Barth forcefully asks of the tradition: where is the picture of God in Jesus Christ? Given Barth's methodological approach—Jesus Christ as *principium cognoscendi*—this question seems unavoidable. Barth asks it poignantly in his later discussion of the eternal will of God in the election of Jesus Christ: "Is there a continuity between the christological center and telos of the temporal work of God which was so clearly recognized by the older theologians, and the eternal presupposing of that work in the divine election which was no less clearly recognized by them?"[110] The answer was most certainly no for Barth. The older theologians did not see continuity,

---

104. Cf. Barth, *CD* II.1, 616–17.

105. Dolf te Velde, *The Doctrine of God in Reformed Orthodoxy, Karl Barth, and the Utrecht School*, 412. Cf. *CD* II.2, 181–4.

106. Again, this is not historically accurate because an analogy not symmetry per se is operative in the debate. Nevertheless, Barth's concerns remain theological in the sense that, despite what protestations Reformed divines might have, the lapsarian conclusions yield some sort of symmetry in the end (in Barth's theological mind). Bavinck, as we saw earlier, registered a similar critique.

107. Barth, *CD* II.2, 134.

108. Barth, *CD* II.2, 134.

109. Barth, *CD* II.2, 134.

110. Barth, *CD* II.2, 149.

and, even further, "they had no desire to bring the two doctrines together in this way."[111] Again, the decisive point was always the hidden and absolute decree—the inscrutability of God's good pleasure—for Barth. As Barth concludes:

> Behind both of these views (at a different point, but with the same effect in practice), there stands the absolute God in himself who is neither conditioned nor self-conditioning, and not the picture of the Son of God who is self-conditioned and therefore conditioned in His union with the Son of David; not the picture of God in Jesus Christ.[112]

The Advantages and Deeper Problems of Infralapsarianism After taking stock of the "doubtful presuppositions" of the two lapsarian views, Barth begins to chart out the relative strengths and weaknesses of both, as well as whether one or the other might be amended so as to prove theologically serviceable. For reasons that I will soon explore, Barth prefers the supralapsarian position. Yet before going down that path it is instructive to highlight what Barth appreciates within the infralapsarian position, even though he ultimately (and vehemently) rejects it as a Trojan horse for the "theological Enlightenment."[113] Let me begin with the particular advantages—of which there are only two—that Barth recognizes.

First, Barth argues that infralapsarianism mitigates against the possibility of collapsing theology into anthropology. According to Barth, the rigidity in which the supralapsarian scheme rises above the infralapsarian one actually—although unwittingly—makes human beings "the measure and center of all things."[114] Infralapsarians, in logically subordinating the decree of predestination to the decrees of creation and the Fall, at least "knew of another secret of man apart from the fact that he is either elect or reprobate."[115] The supralapsarian opinion, on the other hand, emphasized how the course of each human being was already plotted and fixed, each existence having only one prospect of fulfilment. According to Barth, supralapsarianism held open the door for a confusion of the divine work with human self-seeking. Practically speaking, however, infralapsarianism also held to the dubious presupposition of a fixed system, even though it theoretically questioned this rigidity by supposing something higher in the decrees of creation and the Fall. In this way, the theoretical safeguard within infralapsarianism was itself a pathogen leading unto an even worse anthropological disease—the naturalistic doctrine of man apart from and above revelation. Given Barth's opprobrium for a fixed system, the infralapsarian advantage doesn't really amount to much; in fact, it seems more like a bandage on a mortal wound.

---

111. Barth, *CD* II.2, 149.
112. Barth, *CD* II.2, 135.
113. Barth, *CD* II.2, 144.
114. Barth, *CD* II.2, 137.
115. Barth, *CD* II.2, 137.

2. Lapsarianism Problematized and Purified 75

The second and final "obvious advantage of infralapsarianism consists naturally in its greater reserve with respect to the reality of the fall and the presence of evil in the world."[116] This, as we saw with Turretin, was a central feature of the infralapsarian polemic against supralapsarianism. Although, as Barth recognizes, the infralapsarians attributed the reality of sin and evil to God's eternal counsel, they did it in such a manner as to remove any lingering doubt that God might be the positive author of sin. The supralapsarians, on the other hand, were much bolder and harsher in their presentation because "[in] their eyes the more pressing danger was that of opening up the slightest chink to dualism."[117] In the infralapsarian scheme, evil "assumes a more enigmatical character, being enfolded in an impenetrable darkness."[118] On this point, Barth thinks the infralapsarian position can bring out the truth—in a clearer, although perhaps not better manner—that the economies of evil and redemption are not coordinate. Barth puts it as follows:

> They can state much more decidedly that in our redemption a moral judgment is executed and a victory won for the almightiness of God. They can also state that God has not foreordained anyone for evil, not even the reprobate … They were better able to avoid the temptation to find an excuse in the fact that the divine purpose includes evil for the sake of election and rejection.[119]

Despite these advantages, the correctness of the infralapsarian position remains strictly relative. It serves only to demonstrate the dangers of the supralapsarian position without proposing a more tenable theological solution itself. In fact, the solution it sets up is far worse in Barth's mind. Within the framework of the common presuppositions mentioned in the previous section, Barth believes infralapsarianism proves to be theologically unworkable because it sets the stage for a "cleavage between natural and revealed theology."[120] The danger Barth mentioned in *Gottes Gnadenwahl* is now emphasized with force. The infralapsarian scheme may well follow the sequence of the biblical picture with regard to the realization of salvation, but it "shrank from the deduction" that the "framework and the basis of all temporal occurrence is the history of the covenant with God and man."[121] By introducing a natural order above the economy of salvation and alongside the *decretum absolutum*, infralapsarianism "defended in the long run something that could not be defended" and as such has no prospect of being amended.[122] For Barth, infralapsarianism only proved to be a failure of nerve,

---

116. Barth, *CD* II.2, 138.
117. Barth, *CD* II.2, 138.
118. Barth, *CD* II.2, 138.
119. Barth, *CD* II.2, 138–9.
120. Barth, *CD* II.2, 136.
121. Barth, *CD* II.2, 136.
122. Barth, *CD* II.2, 144.

a failure of dogmatic thinking, which in the end "carried within it the seed of theological Enlightenment and its own dissolution."[123] In short, infralapsarianism neither desired nor was able to amend the "doubtful presuppositions" based on its attempt to see and understand the decrees of creation, providence, and the Fall in their inward relationships to each other and this apart from the decree of predestination. The system placed an a priori prohibition on bringing together creation and predestination christologically, and, as a result, the will and good pleasure of God became doubly obscure. Supralapsarianism, on the other hand, "with no material alteration to the thesis concerning *homo labilis* can be developed in a christological direction."[124]

Purified Supralapsarianism According the Barth, supralapsarianism does not need a wholesale alteration, but a detachment and purification from the doubtful presuppositions of the older theology. If the older presuppositions are truly necessary and unshakable, then certainly the "Supralapsarian God threatens to take on the appearance of a demon."[125] Thankfully, Barth maintains, they can be removed without setting aside the basic and nonspeculative thought that "the first and chief order which is normative and decisive for all others and for the realization of all others in time" is the order of God's mercy and justice, the order of supernatural predestination that seeks "to understand the causative will of the Creator and the permissive will of the One who overrules even the fall as the will of this God of mercy and justice."[126] The older supralapsarians might have been theistic monists, but at least it was a "biblical and Christian monism which they envisaged."[127]

With this material core in mind, Barth seeks to remove the shackles of the other presuppositions, especially and above all else the "idolatrous concept of a *decretum absolutum*."[128] As he proceeds to unpack the positive contours of this purification in his small print excursus, Barth reveals the hallmarks of his theological program. The first move involves thinking through the eternal reality, determination, comprehension, and will of God not *in abstracto* but *in concreto*.

> God wills man: not the idea of man, not humanity, not human individuals in the mass or in particular ... He wills man, His man, elected man, man predestined as the witness to His glory and the object of his love. In this man, but only in him, He wills humanity and every individual man and what we may describe as the idea of humanity.[129]

---

123. Barth, *CD* II.2, 144.
124. Barth, *CD* II.2, 143.
125. Barth, *CD* II.2, 140.
126. Barth, *CD* II.2, 135.
127. Barth, *CD* II.2, 135.
128. Barth, *CD* II.2, 143.
129. Barth, *CD* II.2, 141.

The man, of course, is Jesus Christ, the *God-man*. God intends that Jesus Christ—and all those in Christ—should testify to God's glory and thus "reveal and confirm and verify positively what He is and wills."[130] The same happens negatively: "A marking off, a separating, a setting aside" is revealed and confirmed and verified in Jesus Christ.[131] As Barth explains more fully,

> It is not a second Yes on God's part, but a No which is of God only to the extent that it corresponds and is opposed to the Yes, a No which forms the necessary boundary of the Yes: so assuredly is God God and not not God; so assuredly does He live in eternal self-differentiation from all that is not God and is not willed by God. In this sense God is and is not: He wills and does not will.[132]

Although it is not God's will that "elected man fall into sin," it is God's will that sin—that which exists as a result of God's not willing—should be "repudiated and rejected and excluded" by Christ.[133] By this Barth means that Jesus Christ, as the elected man, should repudiate what God repudiates and in so doing reveal and proclaim the greater Yes of God. God wills and affirms Christ as the sinful man—"as man laden with sins and afflicted by humanity's curse and misery"—for the sake of the "fullness of His glory, the completeness of His covenant with man, for the sake of the perfection of His love."[134] Christ was predestined to utter this same No and thus corroborate the divine Yes, to confront and be confronted by what God repudiates. Even still, this confrontation and defeat in creaturely time cannot exist in the same self-evident form that it does for God in eternity. In the case of humanity, it must take the form of a historical event. "It must become the content of a history: the history of an obstacle and its removing; the history of a death and a resurrection; the history of a judgment and a pardon; the history of a defeat and a victory."[135] It must become, in other words, the entire history of Jesus Christ.[136] If the human creature is to be a witness to the divine glory, this victory

---

130. Barth, *CD* II.2, 141.
131. Barth, *CD* II.2, 141.
132. Barth, *CD* II.2, 141.
133. Barth, *CD* II.2, 141.
134. Barth, *CD* II.2, 141.
135. Barth, *CD* II.2, 141.
136. When considering Barth's supralapsarian vision as a whole, one feels the force of Berkouwer's critique: "Barth's revised supralapsarianism blocks the way to ascribing *decisive* significance to history." That said, Berkouwer does not take Barth as conceiving history as merely the illustration or playing out of an eternal idea. Berkouwer instead worries whether Barth's consistent attempt to expunge every element of "double bookkeeping" (i.e., the separation of creation and reconciliation) actually blurs the distinction between creation and redemption such that the transition in history from being under God's wrath to being under God's grace is obscured, which in the end "fails to do justice to the harmony of the multicolored witness of Scripture." G. C. Berkouwer, *The Triumph of Grace in the Theology of Karl Barth: An Introduction and Critical Appraisal*, trans. Harry R. Boer (Grand Rapids,

must assume the form of a history. For this reason, God wills the confrontation of humanity "by the power of evil" and "wills Himself as the One who must and will give man the victory."[137] Thus the human creature relies totally and utterly upon divine grace. All of this leads Barth to the supralapsarian conclusion that needs no sigificant alteration: "God wills *homo labilis*, not in order that he may fall, but in order that when he has fallen he may testify to the fulness of God's glory."[138] God wills and elects *homo labilis*, not for the Fall, but for "the demonstration in time, in the creaturely sphere, of His eternal self-differentiation."[139] In this particular instance, self-differentiation does not mean within God's being, but a differentiation between what God positively wills for mankind (i.e., Himself as the covenant partner) and what God doesn't will (i.e., not God).

This then is Barth's supralapsarian purification and vision. Creation and fall do not represent separate spheres existing apart from the predestination of and reconciliation found in Jesus Christ. It is all of a piece; it is one theological package and seeks to articulate the deep teleological aspect of God's Yes for all of creaturely existence. Given Barth's complex, one might say dizzying, reasoning regarding the election of *homo labilis* and the place of the Fall in this supralapsarian narrative, it is now necessary to explore a bit further his theological understanding of sin, covenant, and the Fall. Below we will explore the manner in which Barth rejects aspects of a *felix culpa* while nonetheless holding to, in some sense, the teleological necessity of the Fall vis-à-vis *das Nichtige* and its defeat in Jesus Christ.

Supralapsarianism, Covenant, and das Nichtige

In his discussion of Barth's revision of supralapsarianism, Berkouwer notes how "Barth's preference for the supralapsarian view is nothing else than the reverse side of the ontological impossibility of sin."[140] Matthias Wüthrich makes a similar point in his study of Barth's doctrine of *das Nichtige*: "The resulting supralapsarian preference is not only reflected in the primacy of the doctrine of election in *KD*, but also extends structurally to the justification of the reality of nothingness in §50."[141]

MI: Wm. B. Eerdman, 1956), 256–8. This then leads Berkouwer to consider the possibility and problem of universalism in Barth's theology. Barth, in fact, responds to Berkouwer's critique in *CD* §69.3 [*CD* IV.3.1, 173–80]. On the accusation of *Geschichtslosigkeit,* see also Matthias Dominique Wüthrich, *Gott und das Nichtige: eine Untersuchung zur Rede vom Nichtigen ausgehend von § 50 der Kirchlichen Dogmatik Karl Barths* (Zürich: Theologischer Verlag Zürich, 2006), 273–335.

137. Barth, *CD* II.2, 141.
138. Barth, *CD* II.2, 141–2.
139. Barth, *CD* II.2, 142.
140. Berkouwer, *Triumph of Grace in the Theology of Karl Barth*, 256.
141. Wüthrich, *Gott und das Nichtige*, 50: "Die daraus folgende *supralapsarische Präferenz* spiegelt sich nicht nur in der Vorrangstellung der Erwählungslehre in KD, sondern *reicht strukturell bis in die Begründung der Wirklichkeit des Nichtigen in §50 hinein.*"

2. Lapsarianism Problematized and Purified

Admittedly, Barth argues the same: the "ontic context in which nothingness is real is that of God's activity as grounded in his election, of His activity as the Lord of His creatures, as the King of the covenant between Himself and man which is the goal and purpose of his creation."[142] In order to better situate and understand the reality of *das Nichtige*, it is helpful to first articulate the "goal and purpose of [God's] creation," namely the presupposition of the covenant which undergirds Barth's doctrines of creation, *das Nichtige*, and reconciliation.

For Barth, creation and covenant are correlative terms. Creation is the external basis of the covenant, and covenant is the internal basis of creation.[143] Barth's account remains rigorously teleological in the sense that creation can only be understood in light of Jesus Christ and "that reality which God destines of fellowship with Jesus Christ."[144] In this way, the presupposition of creation is the covenant of grace, which is nothing more than the work of Jesus Christ in history. "What is creaturely exists in order to be serviceable to the glory of God in the work of his Son."[145] Such creaturely serviceability entails (inherently) a double determination. Barth utilizes a string of phrases to describe this: God's Yes and No; God's positive and negative willing; God's *opus proprium* and *opus alienum*; the work of God's right and left hands. At the most basic level, Barth suggests that the positive (and thoroughly christological) willing and affirmation of creation involves the "necessary rejection of everything which by His own nature God cannot be ... which ... God cannot will and create."[146] Creation is "not rejection, but election and acceptance" in Christ.[147] Nevertheless, there is a rejection, a potent non-willing on God's part. Barth clarifies the christological nature of this twofold determination in his discussion of "Creation as Justification":

> God created man to lift him in His own Son into fellowship with Himself. This is the positive meaning of human existence and all existence. But this elevation presupposes a wretchedness of human and all existence which His own Son will share and bear. This is the negative meaning of creation. Since everything is created for Jesus Christ and his death and resurrection, from the very outset everything must stand under this twofold and contradictory determination ... It has subsistence; yet it does not have such subsistence as it can secure and maintain for itself ... This is how He has created it to be.[148]

Tellingly, Barth argues that God's Yes (the christological end of creation) presupposes the embrace of God's No by the human creature, which is that

---

142. Barth, *CD* III.3, 351.
143. Barth, *CD* III.1, 94, 228.
144. Webster, *Karl Barth*, 98.
145. Barth, *CD* III.1, 370.
146. Barth, *CD* III.1, 331.
147. Barth, *CD* III.1, 331.
148. Barth, *CD* III.1, 376.

wretchedness which Jesus Christ will share and bear. Although this might seem to indicate an infralapsarian preference—that is, the human creature as *creatus and lapsus*—Barth's emphasis falls on the incapacity of the human creature to fulfill their end apart from God's preservation and intervention. On the one hand, the language of the covenant as God's *opus proprium* "offers a way of talking about the ordered mutuality of God and humanity in which God elects a people to have their obedient consent to their election."[149] On the other hand, God's *opus alienum* includes the inevitability of the Fall, the human creature as *homo labilis*. God "has appointed [human beings] to stand firm on this frontier," Barth writes, "to say No in covenant with Him to what he has not willed but negated. But He knows man's incapacity to fulfill this destiny."[150] Man, therefore, has to be "defended against the menace of nothingness."[151]

So what, then, is *das Nichtige*? According to Barth, *das Nichtige* is "neither God nor His creature."[152] Barth also resists the Augustinian trope: "It would be foolhardy to rush to the conclusion that it is therefore nothing, i.e., that it does not exist."[153] Although *das Nichtige* does not fall within the genus of God or creature, it is "not simply to be equated with what is *not*."[154] Consistent with Barth's method, this peculiar way of phrasing the reality of *das Nichtige* means it can only be known christologically.[155] Positively construed, *das Nichtige* is that which is overcome in Jesus Christ; negatively, it is the reality of God's No, God's not willing. Ontically, *das Nichtige* exists as a potent force "so long as God is against it."[156] So, again, the ontic context is "God's activity as grounded in His election," which includes a Yes and a No. "Grounded always in election," Barth writes, "the activity of God is invariably one of jealousy, wrath, and judgment. God is also holy, and this means that His being and activity take place in a definite opposition, in a real negation, both defensive and aggressive."[157] In this way, *das Nichtige* exists as the "impossible possibility," though still the powerful and effective work of God's "rejection, opposition, negation, and dismissal."[158] God's non-willing remains effective, even if alien and improper to God's being. God, nevertheless, knows *das Nichtige*. God "knows that which He did not elect or will as the Creator" and "knows how inevitably it imperils His creature."[159] But God also knows that

---

149. Webster, *Karl Barth*, 118–19.
150. Barth, *CD* III.1, 384.
151. Barth, *CD* III.1, 387.
152. Barth, *CD* III.3, 349.
153. Barth, *CD* III.3, 349.
154. Barth, *CD* III.3, 349.
155. As Tseng appropriately comments, "In other words, '*das Nichtige*' is primarily a predestinarian term." Shao Kai Tseng, "Karl Barth on Nothingness: A Christological-Predestinarian Defiance of Theodicy," *Sino-Christian Studies* 20 (2015): 48.
156. Barth, *CD* III.3, 353.
157. Barth, *CD* III.3, 351.
158. Barth, *CD* III.3, 351–2.
159. Barth, *CD* III.3, 358.

das Nichtige has no power over God and thus no perpetuity. By extension, the security God grants creation against *das Nichtige* is the "perpetuity which He wills to grant it in fellowship with Himself, and which cannot be lacking in this fellowship but is given it to all eternity."[160] Concretely, this means that *das Nichtige* is overcome and eliminated in the victory of Jesus Christ, in God's faithfulness to God's *opus proprium* in its eschatological consummation. "Because Jesus is Victor, nothingness is routed and extirpated."[161]

Precisely in this way, reconciliation presupposes the covenant of grace for Barth. Because God had pledged in his will to be the covenant partner of humankind in the Son, Barth conceives of reconciliation as the "maintaining, restoring, and upholding of that fellowship in face of an element which disturbs and disrupts and breaks in."[162] The doctrine of reconciliation, in other words, operates on the same assumption as the doctrine of creation: God wills to be in fellowship with the human creature, to be God with us. As Barth puts it:

> From all eternity He determined that men would be those for whom He is God: His fellow-men. In willing this, in willing Jesus Christ, He wills to be our God and He wills that we should be His people. Ontologically, therefore, the covenant of grace is already included and grounded in Jesus Christ, in the human form and human content which God wills to give His Word from all eternity.[163]

The incarnation and the atonement, therefore, remain conceptually inseparable for Barth such that he can abruptly announce "Jesus Christ is the atonement."[164] In putting it this way, Barth means atonement as the actualization of the will of God—which is first and foremost the destiny of the Son of God—in history as it meets the sin of the creature and the reality of *das Nichtige*.[165] Of course, such an understanding of atonement is descriptive and broad, corresponding more to the language of faithfulness and constancy to the presupposition already laid down in the covenant of grace. Despite such broadness, an essential element within Barth's supralapsarian narrative has been recognized: the defeat of *das Nichtige* as a necessary event in history.

Reflecting at large on Barth's supralapsarian narrative and the reality of *das Nichtige*, Edwin Chr. van Driel has proposed a "creational entropy" thesis.

---

160. Barth, *CD* III.3, 360.

161. Barth, *CD* III.3, 363. One sees clearly here the fruit of Barth's notion of christological *Aufhebung*.

162. Barth, *CD* IV.1, 22.

163. Barth, *CD* IV.1, 45.

164. Barth, *CD* IV.1, 34.

165. Barth, *CD* IV.1, 35. Or, as Barth states closely thereafter, "The work of atonement in Jesus Christ is the fulfillment of the communion of Himself with man and of man with Himself which he willed and created at the very first." *CD* IV.1, 36.

According to van Driel, Barth's articulation of God's election (willing) and rejection (non-willing) establishes various *possibilia* such that the rejected (non-created) *possibilia* have causal force in the form of *das Nichtige*.[166] The causal force tethered to *das Nichtige* is strictly entropic because, as van Driel suggests, "all of what is not God necessarily lapses into evil unless God incorporates it into God's own life."[167] God's life, in contradistinction, cannot be threatened by *das Nichtige* because God's trinitarian life is "self-grounded and self-renewing."[168] *Das Nichtige* is the reality accompanying God's No; human creatures are, by extension, those inevitably drawn to *das Nichtige* apart from incorporation into the divine life through the incarnation, death, and resurrection of Christ. They are inevitably drawn because they, unlike God, are not *a se* and self-grounded. For van Driel, this indicates a necessity of sin in Barth's supralapsarian narrative, as well as a construal of creation, time, and human agency as simply an intermezzo in God's history in Jesus Christ.

Even still, God does not positively will human sin or even positively will a fall into sin. God wills humanity's confrontation with sin in order that they may reject it. But this is exactly what they cannot do as creatures apart from divine intervention. As was discussed above, this directly corresponds to Barth's "purification" of supralapsarianism.

> [God] wills the confrontation of man by the power of evil. He wills man as the one assailed by this power. He wills him as the one who, as man and not God, has not evolved this power of himself but is subjected to it. He wills Himself as the One who must and will come to the help of man in this subjection, who alone in this subjection can and will give to man the victory ... God wills man *homo labilis*, not in order that he may fall, but in order that when he has fallen he may testify to the fulness of God's glory.[169]

According to van Driel, this also suggests an adherence to a form of the *felix culpa* argument, wherein God is greater in and by the very fact that God defeats sin and *das Nichtige*.[170] Such an interpretation, however, is difficult to sustain given Barth's awareness of the *felix culpa* tradition and rejection of part of it explicitly. In his rejection, Barth isolates not the *"felix culpa"* per se, but the *"meruit habere"* as that which goes "too far."[171] The human creature does not deserve or achieve or

---

166. van Driel, *Incarnation Anyway*, 121–4. On unactualized "possibles" in Barth's account, see also Nicholas Wolterstorff, "Barth on Evil," *Faith and Philosophy* 13, no. 4 (1996): 584–608. For a critique of Wolterstorff's interpretation, see Tseng, "Karl Barth on Nothingness," 35–64.
167. van Driel, *Incarnation Anyway*, 122.
168. Barth, *CD* III.3, 80.
169. Barth, *CD* II.2, 141–2.
170. van Driel, *Incarnation Anyway*, 126–30.
171. Barth, *CD* IV.1, 69.

2. Lapsarianism Problematized and Purified

win anything on account of sin. Instead, human sin stands "in opposition to and conflict with the gracious will of God."[172] Precisely in this opposition, the grace of God does not abandon the creature, "but only because it makes good what we have spoiled, and therefore only in that humiliation of us which brings us help and comfort, but which is inescapable in this wealth of help and comfort."[173]

As Barth begins to unpack the scope of his rebuttal of the *felix culpa* tradition, he ventures into the waters of God's wisdom. "The wisdom of God which allows this episode in order to make, not the episode itself, but the overcoming of it an occasion to magnify His grace and to reveal and actualize it—we have to say for the first time—as free grace in it, in accordance with His eternal will and purpose."[174] This should not be confused with "pseudo-wisdom," which tries to make this episode "necessary" in order to "excuse or exculpate the man who is responsible for it."[175] To embrace such "pseudo-wisdom" is tantamount to calling evil good. All theological thinking, according to Barth, must never transgress this boundary, even though it is undeniable that God makes good what human creatures have spoiled.[176]

What, we may now ask, is the import of this for fleshing out the overall dimensions of Barth's critique? Within Barth's supralapsarian narrative, God is certainly not rendered greater for defeating *das Nichtige*. The defeat of *das Nichtige* occurs as part and parcel of the temporal enactment of God's eternal election, an election which also speaks of a rejection.[177] But, as always, the thoughtform must remain christological. For this reason, the atonement, as John Colwell comments, "is not just God's counter to man's sin but the accomplishment of His original will, his eternal covenant in Jesus Christ."[178] In Barth's theological scheme, Christology, predestination, creation, covenant, and reconciliation are thoroughly and eternally integrated.[179] Such integration signals the heart of Barth's preference for supralapsarianism, and why Barth refuses to alter materially the object

---

172. Barth, *CD* IV.1, 69.
173. Barth, *CD* IV.1, 69.
174. Barth, *CD* IV.1, 69.
175. Barth, *CD* IV.1, 69.
176. Barth, *CD* IV.1, 70.

177. This seems to breathe, as Hans van Balthasar noted, "the spirit of Hegel," despite the fact that Barth adamantly rejected any sort of synthetic development that must necessarily run through the contradiction of evil. For a strong denial of this Hegelian spirit in Barth's doctrine of sin, see Wolf Krötke, *Sin and Nothingness in the Theology of Karl Barth*, trans. and ed. Philip G. Ziegler and Christina-Maria Bammel (Princeton: Princeton Theological Seminary, 2005), 30–4. Balthasar is quoted in Krötke, 30.

178. Colwell, *Actuality and Provisionality*, 240.

179. Such integration, however, trades on a strange (and often inconsistent) mixture of dialectic and actualism. On the ambiguity of Barth's actualism, see Brandon Gallaher, *Freedom and Necessity in Modern Trinitarian Theology* (Oxford: Oxford University Press, 2016), 128–41.

of predestination as *homo labilis*. The object cannot be *homo lapsus* precisely because God wills the inevitable confrontation of the human creature with *das Nichtige*, a confrontation which man *in abstracto* is hopeless to overcome.[180] But, theologically, *homo* cannot and does not exist *in abstracto*, but only *in Christo*. This has important ramifications when interpreting Barth's self-claimed "purification" of supralapsarianism. Although Barth has not "materially" altered the object, he has christologically restructured the discussion to such an extent that the original categories are significantly refashioned. *Homo* is not simply *creabilis et labilis in abstracto*, but already *in Christo*. In this way, Barth has also significantly altered the telos of the overall supralapsarian vision. God's end in creation is no longer God's glory in the form of mercy and justice as was considered in the seventeenth-century controversy among supralapsarians like Twisse or Mastricht, but God's glory in the form of justice and mercy as concretely, solely, and relentlessly manifest in Jesus Christ, who is God's will-to-covenant. To be God's covenant partner, by extension, is to corroborate God's Yes and No, to affirm what God affirms and reject what God rejects. Or, in other words, to affirm that God's covenant will in Jesus Christ is the only true ontological reality for every human creature; to affirm what one already is universally in Christ. There is no such thing as *homo in abstracto* but only *in Christo*. One can once again see the integrative force of Barth's supralapsarian narrative, this time with anthropology.

Theological Summary

It is now time to take stock, and, in so doing, lay out the central features of the theological critiques of Bavinck and Barth. These critiques provide the launching point for further dogmatic reflection. In particular, the manner in which Bavinck and Barth engaged and critiqued the lapsarian debate sets in sharp relief a set of dogmatic questions and concerns worthy of theological response. My own dogmatic work will seek to work through these questions and concerns through a retrieval of the theology of Jonathan Edwards. Before proceeding, it is important to recognize that my prior discussions of Barth and Bavinck did not attempt to bring cohesion to the full scope of their theological thinking, nor adjudicate internecine disputes among secondary interpreters. For example, I did not attempt to draw out all of the implications of Barth's christological doctrine of predestination for the doctrine of God or human election/rejection,[181] nor did I attempt to consider any

---

180. Cf. Barth, *CD* III.2, 146.

181. The interpretive landscape in Barth studies with regard to the full implications of Barth's doctrine of election, both in the doctrine of God and human election, is extremely divisive, to say the least. For a helpful overview, see the collection of essays edited by Michael Dempsey: *Trinity and Election in Contemporary Theology* (Grand Rapids, MI: Wm. B. Eerdmans, 2011). For more general introductions to Barth's doctrine of election see, Wolf Krötke, "Erwählungslehre," in *Barth Handbuch*, ed. Michael Beintker (Tübingen: Mohr

development in Barth's theology.[182] Something similar was true for my discussion of Bavinck's theology. Without integrating all of their thinking, I chose to focus instead on the key challenges they presented to the lapsarian debate, as well as the theological questions and insights such challenges unearthed. To those insights I now turn, beginning with Bavinck.

From Bavinck's perspective, the seventeenth-century lapsarian debate fails to satisfy theological thinking for primarily three reasons. First, neither infralapsarianism nor supralapsarianism fully grasp the unity and diversity, the mechanical and teleological at work within God's decrees. Given the presuppositions, neither could grasp the interconnected (i.e., organic) nature of the decrees. This is why, on Bavinck's interpretation, each camp eventually retreated into the opposing position. Second, predestination is not simply about the eternal states of rational creatures, especially if taken to mean the manifestation of God's glory strictly and ultimately in the form of mercy (heaven) and justice (hell). Such a portrait only yields a "step-wise" understanding of foreordination, wherein even the Fall is a positive step toward the predetermined eternal state. This corresponds to the third aspect of Bavinck's critique: Christology. God's glory is positively revealed christologically. All theological thinking must consistently place Jesus Christ at the center of the decretal organism in such a way that it can truly be said "all things in him hold together" (Col. 1:17b). Christ himself is the center and goal of creation and election, not the eternal states of rationale creatures *tout court*. But on this last point, it must be said, Bavinck himself was consistently inconsistent.

Like Bavinck, Karl Barth also took issue with the way in which certain theologians engaging in the lapsarian debate structured the telos of creation around God's glory in the form of mercy and justice, as well as their overall failure to incorporate Christology into the discussion. Unlike Bavinck, however, Barth attempted an idiosyncratic "purification" of supralapsarianism for his own theological project. The supralapsarian position appealed to Barth based on its integration of creation and reconciliation. The problem for Barth is that the older theology failed to integrate the two christologically. Where the older theology spoke (abstractly) of God's good pleasure, Barth went further and viewed the *beneplacitum Dei* exclusively in christological terms. One cannot speak of God's will apart from Jesus Christ. With this christological amendment in place and the older presuppositions removed, the supralapsarian framework proved not only theologically serviceable but necessary, and this precisely because the framework

---

Siebeck, 2016), 221–6; and J. Christine Janowski, "Gnadenwahl," in *Barth Handbuch*, ed. Michael Beintker (Tübingen: Mohr Siebeck, 2016), 321–8.

182. On the question of development, see Matthias Gockel, *Barth and Schleiermacher on the Doctrine of Election: A Systematic-Theological comparison* (Oxford: Oxford University Press, 2006), 104–97; Bruce McCormack, *Karl Barth's Critically Realistic Dialectical Theology: Its Genesis and Development 1909–1936* (Oxford: Clarendon Press, 1995); and, most recently, Shao Kai Tseng, *Trinity and Election: The Christocentric Reorientation of Karl Barth's Speculative Theology, 1936–1942* (New York: T&T Clark, 2023).

prioritizes unity and integration around the christological telos. Obviously, as Barth was aware, this presents a difficulty with regard to sin and evil, a difficulty which Barth attempted to overcome in his theological presentation of *das Nichtige*. In all of this, as Berkouwer notes, there is a remarkable consistency in Barth's thinking: "a christological doctrine of creation, a biblical Christian monism, a corrected supralapsarianism, wrath as the 'form of grace.'"[183] The latter of which—wrath as the form of grace—coincides with Barth's correlation of reprobation and Christology.

Apart from Barth's concern for the integration of creation and reconciliation within the supralapsarian framework, it is tempting to read Barth's self-proclaimed "purification" of predestination as a "thoroughgoing refutation of Reformed orthodoxy."[184] In one sense, this is surely true: the full scope of Barth's christological purification, especially regarding Christ's reprobation, bears little resemblance to earlier Reformed dogmatics. Yet, in another sense, it is not accurate. As shown in Chapter 1, the christological integration of creation and grace was not a foreign concept to someone like Thomas Goodwin; it is, in fact, the centerpiece of Goodwin's supralapsarian system. Of course, the manner in which Barth carried out the integration is quite different. Barth's manner of supralapsarian integration creates as many theological problems as Barth believes it solves. One problem, as Steven Duby has pointed out, is that Barth's approach "implicitly—and against some of Barth's own theological instincts—ends up compromising God's aseity and freedom in the incarnation."[185] In his insistence that there exists no hidden will behind Jesus Christ, Barth comes to the striking conclusion that both created being and *das Nichtige* are rooted in Christ's incarnation and Christ's justification. Such a position is rigorously supralapsarian. As Barth himself confesses, "Created being as such needs salvation."[186] When worked out in Barth's system, this appears to have the odd effect of swallowing up the interval between God, sin, and humanity. Mercy and justice are already bound together with the *Logos ensarkos* in whom is carried all humanity—*homo creabilis et labilis*. This, as should be obvious, is far removed from the supralapsarianism of Thomas Goodwin. Barth's integration, in the end, proves too strong, too pure.

Overall, given Bavinck's and Barth's critiques and insights, a set of interrelated questions may now be positively formulated. These questions lie at the heart of dogmatics and come through with penetrating force in the lapsarian debate.

1. What theological connection exists between God's decreed end in creation and the decreed end of the Son's incarnation?

---

183. Berkouwer, *Triumph of Grace in the Theology of Karl Barth*, 258.

184. Lindsay, *God Has Chosen*, 170.

185. Duby, *God in Himself*, 175. See also Tyler Wittman's similar critique in *God and Creation in the Theology of Thomas Aquinas and Karl Barth*, 253–95.

186. Barth, *CD* IV.1, 8.

2. In what sense does Holy Scripture, specifically in its witness to Jesus Christ, invite a more positive parsing of the divine will (i.e., the *decretum absolutum*) in the acts of creation, incarnation, and predestination?
3. Given the answers to the first two questions, what entailments does this have for the correlation of the predestination of rational creatures and election of Christ?
4. What precise manner of asymmetry exists between particular election and rejection?
5. How does one locate (the decree of) the Fall, and subsequently sin, in this theological picture?

In addition to these questions, a set of preliminary *desiderata* in answering them may also be provided in keeping with the insights unearthed in the criticisms of Bavinck and Barth:

1. With Bavinck and Barth, the end of predestination should not be construed as mercy mixed with justice.
2. With Bavinck and Barth, Jesus Christ should be considered as primary in God's decretal will.

To be sure, a preoccupation of contemporary dogmatics, whether Reformed or otherwise, seems to be with Barth's answers to the aforementioned questions. If it was true in the ancient world that all roads led to Rome, then the cliché of modern, Reformed theology seems to be that the doctrine of predestination and its attendant concerns radiate from Barth. But my goal is not polemical but positive: to dogmatically offer an alternative path forward in the integration of creation, Christology, and predestination through a retrieval of the theology of Jonathan Edwards. In particular, I seek to answer the aforementioned questions that emerged from the criticisms of Bavinck and Barth as I think theologically with Jonathan Edwards. The proof, as they say, is in the pudding. As such, it is now time to turn to the theology of Jonathan Edwards.

Part II

JONATHAN EDWARDS AND LAPSARIANISM

Chapter 3

CREATION, CHRIST, AND THE DECREES

In what respects is Christ God's elect?[1]

—Jonathan Edwards

All communicated glory to the creature must be by the Son of God, who is the brightness or shining forth of his Father's glory. And therefore when the external world comes to receive its greatest brightness and glory, it will doubtless [be] by him, and it will be by him as God-man.[2]

—Jonathan Edwards

All the works and dispensations of G[od] in all parts of the Creation & in all ages of it are such as shew forth the Infinite value G[od] has for & delight he has in his son.[3]

—Jonathan Edwards

The lapsarian question, as witnessed in Reformed theological discussions in the seventeenth and twentieth centuries, reaches deep into the doctrines of God, Christology, and creation. In a certain sense, then, how one approaches the material and formal nature of God's predestination is already partially informed by one's prior theological construal of the integration of creation and grace, and the relation to God therein. This is no less true for Jonathan Edwards. That Edwards articulated something akin to the necessity of creation is a well-trodden

---

1. "Questions on Theological Subjects," *WJEO* 39.
2. "Miscellanies," no. 952, *WJE* 20:221.
3. Sermon 699. Heb. 2:7-8 (March 1743) [L. 1v.], Box 11, Folder 816, Beinecke Rare Book and Manuscript Library, Yale University. The transcription of this sermon was graciously provided to me by Kenneth Minkema, Director of the Jonathan Edwards Center at Yale University.

path in scholarship.⁴ What is not so well known—and, in fact, significantly underdeveloped in the literature—is the relationship between the election and predestination of Jesus Christ and the act of creation.⁵ The election of Jesus Christ—articulated rather unsystematically across Edwards's corpus, especially in his sermons and "Miscellanies" notebook—conditions Edwards's doctrine of creation to such an extent that any discussion of Edwards's doctrine of creation apart from his doctrine of election remains incomplete.

At the heart of the matter lies Edwards's explication of the divine decrees along trinitarian and christological lines, which, in turn, provides the foundation for articulating the telos of creaturely existence. More precisely, creation follows as a consequence of the Father's election of the Son of God, who is the "one grand medium" of God's communication and glorification. All of this, according to Edwards, summarily falls under the umbrella of predestination: "That grand decree of predestination, or that sum of God's decrees, called the purpose which God purposed in Christ Jesus, the appointment of Christ, or the decree respecting his person (in the order wherein we must consider these things), must be considered first."⁶ Predestination, here, does not first and foremost refer to the election or rejection of individual human beings or even an elect covenant people (even though it does refer to these realities by extension), but rather the christological conditioning and ordering of creation as such. The decretal ordering of creation toward Christ, in this sense, follows the election of Jesus Christ. As Edwards puts the matter in a 1744 sermon, "God's design in the creation of all things is to glorify his Son, and through him to glorify himself."⁷

The aforementioned sermonic point provides a helpful gloss on the inherent relation between predestination and creation within Edwards's theology as a whole. More comprehensively stated, God's decree to bring creation into existence *ex nihilo* is internally refracted through the Son of God as God's elected mode of self-communication and self-glorification. According to Edwards, creation not only exists as a theater of the Son's infinite fullness and glory, but it does so in order to communicate the glories of the Son of God, and by extension the Father and Holy Spirit, through an affective union with human beings, who compose the one mystical body or "spouse" of Christ. The goal of this chapter is to unpack the scope of these claims, and to show that these claims remain stable across

---

4. For an overview of this tension (seen most acutely in his dissertation, *End of Creation*), see McClymond and McDermott, *Theology of Jonathan Edwards*, 207–23. This will be discussed in greater detail below.

5. Here underdeveloped does not mean unnoticed. See Schafer, "Jonathan Edwards's Conception of the Church," 52–4; Michael David Bush, "Jesus Christ in the Theology of Jonathan Edwards" (PhD Diss., Princeton Theological Seminary, 2003), 54–82; Sang Hyun Lee, *The Philosophical Theology of Jonathan Edwards*, exp. edn (Princeton: Princeton University Press, 2003), 223–31; and Holmes, *God of Grace and God of Glory*, 126–36.

6. "Miscellanies," no. 1245, *WJE* 23:180.

7. "Approaching the End of God's Grand Design" (December 1744), *WJE* 25:117.

Edwards's lifetime even if systematically underdeveloped. In order to accomplish this, attention will first be given to the relationship between God and the world in recent scholarship on Edwards, followed by a larger situation of Edwards's thought that considers his overarching commitment to election of Jesus Christ as the driving force behind the creation of all things.

The Relationship between God and the World

Whence and whither the world? The manner in which one answers this question, especially as it relates to God's freedom in creation, takes one to the heart of theology. Yet the specific contours and content of God's freedom for creation are not self-evident. It requires discrimination. This question was especially pertinent for Jonathan Edwards and drew forth sustained reflection over the course of his life.[8] His theological reflections ultimately culminated in a final work being prepared for publication before his death: *Dissertation I: Concerning the End for which God Created the World*.[9] Famously—or maybe infamously—Jonathan Edwards wrote in *End of Creation* that "we may suppose *that a disposition in God, as an original property of his nature, to an emanation of his own infinite fullness, was what excited him to create the world; and so that the emanation itself was aimed at by him as a last end of the creation*."[10] According to Edwards, such a disposition in God to see God's internal glory (or fullness) diffused "must be prior to the existence of the creature, even in intention and foresight."[11] What is more, Edwards indicates that God "looks on communication of himself, and the emanation of the infinite glory and good that are in himself to belong to the fullness and completeness of himself, as though he were not in his most complete and glorious state without it."[12]

The "as though" within Edwards's previous statement has generated a flurry of interpretations, ranging from pantheism to normative Reformed orthodoxy, albeit in new idiom, given his burgeoning context.[13] Put simply, the "as though" signals the interplay and tension latent in Edwards's theology between God's "freedom" on the one hand and the "necessity" of creation on the other. This tension can

---

8. Edwards's ruminations on the end of creation begin as early as 1723 ("Miscellanies," no. *gg*) and extend to the end of his life.

9. The manuscript of the *Two Dissertations* was posthumously transcribed by Samuel Hopkins and published in 1765. For more details, see Ramsey, "Editor's Introduction," in *WJE* 8:114, n. 7. Hereafter, *Dissertation 1* will be referred to as *End of Creation*.

10. *WJE* 8:435 (italics original).

11. *WJE* 8:438.

12. *WJE* 8:439.

13. Charles Hodge, *Systematic Theology*, vol. 2 (Grand Rapids, MI: Wm. B. Eerdmans, 1977), 220; Kyle Strobel, *Jonathan Edwards's Theology: A Reinterpretation* (London: Bloomsbury T&T Clark, 2014), 75–104.

be construed, roughly, along two interpretive models: (1) the actuality-increase model; and (2) the creative necessity model.[14]

Let me begin with the actuality-increase model, which finds its most astute articulation in the interpretation of Sang Hyun Lee. According to Lee, Edwards's understanding of the God-world relation follows from his reconception of the divine essence as an eternal disposition to actuality.[15] When considering God's being *ad intra*, Lee maintains that, for Edwards, disposition and actuality perfectly coincide in the beauty of consenting relations among the triune persons, thereby preserving God's self-sufficiency and aseity. "God's motive in creating the world is the further exertion of his *original dispositional essence*, which is already fully exercised within God's internal being."[16] The corresponding effect of creating involves a "self-enlargement of God" *ad extra*, such that "the world is internally related to the triune God in the sense that the world repeats God's internal prior actuality through God's external exercise of his original dispositional essence."[17] God's self-enlargement, Lee contends, is God's infinite and temporal self-repetition, not God's self-realization. In this way, God's aseity is preserved, though significantly redefined as a consequence of Edward's dynamic reconception of the divine being. On Lee's rendering, time and space gain significance for God's own life by literally "adding to" the divine being. According to Lee, "for Edwards, although God does not need temporality for his internal actuality and perfection, God needs or uses the world in space and time to exercise his dispositional essence outside of his own internal being."[18] This should not be construed, Lee argues, as an "increase" to the divine being; "it is rather what God does in and through the world in time and space that affects the divine being by adding to it,"[19] with addition taken in the sense of "constituting the external extension of God's internal fullness."[20] God's fullness of actuality *ad intra* is a fullness "that becomes fuller" *ad extra*.[21]

Overall, Lee's interpretive model seeks to make sense of the sundry and consistent statements across Edwards's corpus, especially in *End of Creation*, that "God's exercising his perfection to produce a proper effect is not distinct from the emanation or communication of his fullness."[22] Or, as Edwards further puts the matter in terms of emanation and remanation,

---

14. Both of these "models" run straight through Edwards's vast oeuvre and are often emphasized with greater or lesser frequency depending on the agenda of the interpreter.

15. See Lee, *Philosophical Theology of Jonathan Edwards*, 170–96.

16. Lee, *Philosophical Theology of Jonathan Edwards*, 199. Emphasis in original.

17. Lee, *Philosophical Theology of Jonathan Edwards*, 203.

18. Sang Hyun Lee, "God's Relation to the World," in *The Princeton Companion to Jonathan Edwards*, ed. Sang Hyun Lee (Princeton: Princeton University Press, 2005), 68.

19. Lee, *Philosophical Theology of Jonathan Edwards*, 68.

20. Lee, *Philosophical Theology of Jonathan Edwards*, 209.

21. Lee, *Philosophical Theology of Jonathan Edwards*, 210.

22. *WJE* 8:527.

in the creature's knowing, esteeming, loving, rejoicing in, and praising God, the glory of God is both exhibited and acknowledged; his fullness is received and returned. Here is both an *emanation* and *remanation*. The refulgence shines upon and into the creature, and is reflected back to the luminary. The beams of glory come from God, and are something of God, and are refunded back again to their original. So that the whole is *of* God, and *in* God, and *to* God; and God is the beginning, middle and end in this affair.[23]

But there is more. Lee also contends that the creation of the world in terms of the actuality-and-increase model can be, in a larger sense, attributed to the Son of God in particular. The Son creates the world because the Son also possesses, as God, the primordial disposition toward actuality; the world, in this way, is created "to become a perfect image of the perfect image of God,"[24] wherein the incarnate Christ—the Son of God visible in time and space—is the "one event or life in which God's exertion of the divine disposition ad extra is accomplished 'without measure'—that is, to a full degree."[25] The rhythms of world history before and after Christ are repetitions of the Son's prior actuality—foreshadowing before and increasing after in the church.

Lee's overall thesis has been strongly challenged by a number of interpreters who have attempted to make sense of Edwards's dispositional language in other ways. One such interpreter is Oliver Crisp, who argues that, given Edwards's ontological framework, "Edwards constructs a version of panentheism that includes a doctrine of continuous creation, and occasionalism, with the creation as the necessary output of the divine nature."[26] According to Crisp, Edwards maintains that "God is necessarily, eternally creative"[27] insofar as God's divine disposition corresponds to divine attributes that cannot remain eternally dormant but require creation in order to be exercised. This, in short, is the heart of the creative necessity model. Lee is incorrect, on Crisp's reading, insofar as disposition need not entail a wholesale restructuring of the divine being; the language of disposition should instead be construed as a perfection of God's essence, a perfection that is morally determinative for God such that God must create a world. Put another way, God necessarily creates some world because God possesses a moral perfection that makes God "necessarily, eternally creative."[28] This does not vitiate divine freedom because freedom, whether divine or human according to Edwards, does not

---

23. *WJE* 8:531 (italics original).
24. Lee, *Philosophical Theology of Jonathan Edwards*, 226.
25. Lee, *Philosophical Theology of Jonathan Edwards*, 227.
26. Oliver Crisp, "Jonathan Edwards on God's Relation to Creation," *Jonathan Edwards Studies* 8, no. 1 (2018): 12.
27. Oliver Crisp and Kyle Strobel, *Jonathan Edwards: An Introduction to His Thought* (Grand Rapids, MI: Eerdmans, 2018), 95.
28. Oliver Crisp, *Jonathan Edwards on God and Creation* (New York: Oxford University Press, 2012), 50.

hinge upon liberty of indifference. God's freedom is commensurate with moral determinism. God can be free and morally constrained by God's nature to create a world in order to express God's glory, or fullness, through a necessary display of all of God's attributes.

The heart of Crisp's interpretative model—at least in terms of the necessary determination of God's freedom for creation—is textually grounded in Edwards's *Freedom of the Will*. There, Edwards argues God's will is morally and necessarily determined by God's "own infinite all-sufficient wisdom in everything"[29] such that the greater the moral determination to that which is most wise, the greater the freedom. In other words, God is morally constrained by God's own nature to act in the wisest manner possible. Moral necessity stands in contradistinction to "natural" necessity, wherein an agent has the (meta)physical ability (or natural power) to act or not act. For Edwards, God is bound by moral necessity with regard to creation, though not natural necessity. That is, God's freedom for creation must be understood along the lines of liberty of spontaneity as opposed to liberty of indifference. On this way of conceiving the matter, God is morally determined by the perfection of God's nature to create a world that communicates the fullness of the divine being unto an external effect in the wisest possible manner.

Overall, Crisp sees Edwards's emphasis on self-glorification and the work of creation as amounting to the same thing: a moral determination of the divine being for self-communication to and through creatures able to comprehend such divine communication intellectually and affectionately. Yet, God's moral determination (creative necessity) compromises neither metaphysical nor psychological aseity on God's part because, according to Crisp, God needs nothing, strictly speaking.[30] Crisp's conclusion is striking: "So, in Edwards's hands, the creation is the mechanism by which God comes to gaze on himself reflected in the image of his creatures, who he then draws to himself in an everlasting process of divinization, whereby creatures are made ever more like the Creator—yet never becoming identical to the Creator."[31]

This brief mapping of two influential interpretive models of the relation between God and the world within Edwards's theology now sets the stage for the reinterpretation that follows. It does so in two ways. First, it takes note of, even if significantly revising, three important emphases in Edwards's theological reasoning as found in these models: (1) creation is structured around God's self-communicative actuality in Jesus Christ (Lee); (2) the triune God is essentially creative (Crisp); and (3) the triune God is perfectly self-sufficient and ontologically independent from creation (Lee and Crisp). What stands in need of revision, however, is the manner in which the predestination of Jesus Christ conditions creation in Edwards's theological reasoning. In what follows I will attempt this revision. It will not be so much a wholesale reinterpretation, but a new accent

---

29. *WJE* 1:380.
30. Crisp, *Jonathan Edwards on God and Creation*, 77–90.
31. Crisp, *Jonathan Edwards on God and Creation*, 86.

and structure for approaching Edwards on the possibility and telos of creation. In particular, the election of Jesus Christ—*ad intra* and *ad extra*—will be shown to provide the necessary architecture for coherently approaching Edwards's on the end of creation as a whole.

The Election of the Son of God ad intra: *The Father's Election of the Son*

In "Miscellanies" no. 769, Edwards argues "Christ is chosen of God [the Father] as to his divine and human nature."[32] As witnessed in this entry, election primarily has a twofold referent for Edwards: (1) God *ad intra*, as to the Son's divinity; and (2) God *ad extra*, as to the God-man, Jesus Christ. The former is a natural election, while the latter pertains to God's "free and sovereign" election (i.e., an election by will). Such language is rather perplexing. What does it mean that the Father chooses the Son as to the Son's divinity? The Father's choosing of the Son qua divine nature has nothing to do with the "essential glory" of the Son or "real happiness which is infinite." The election of the Son of God, in other words, is not Arian, nor is it indicative of an internal subordination in the triune life. Instead, the Son is chosen of God as to "[his] great declarative glory."[33] "His election as it respects his divine nature," Edwards writes, "was for his worthiness, and excellency, and infinite amiableness in the sight of God; and perfect fitness for that which God chose him to his worthiness, was the ground of his election."[34] Tellingly, the election of the Son of God qua divine nature refers back to the worth of the Son of God as such—a worth of natural necessity as the second person of the Trinity, as the Son of the Father. In contrast to the election of the human nature, which was "free" and "sovereign," the election of the Son functions as necessary corollary of the Son's hypostatic self-differentiation from the Father. The *ad intra* choosing of the Son by the Father naturally and necessarily follows from the Son's procession from the Father. Immanently, procession and election function coordinately.

In order to further comprehend this correlation between procession and election, Edwards's theological reasoning on God's trinitarian self-differentiation needs tracing out. In an April 1734 sermon on Heb. 1:3 entitled, "Jesus Christ is the Shining Forth of the Father's Glory," Edwards explains the Father and the Son are not distinguished from each other in their "excellency of nature."[35] Each divine person possesses "numerically the same individual glory."[36] What distinguishes the Son from the Father, according to Edwards, is the mode of

---

32. "Miscellanies," no. 769, *WJE* 18:415.
33. "Miscellanies," no. 769, *WJE* 18:415.
34. "Miscellanies," no. 769, *WJE* 18:415.
35. Jonathan Edwards, "Jesus Christ as the Shining Forth of the Father's Glory," in *The Glory and Honor of God: Previously Unpublished Sermons of Jonathan Edwards*, vol. 2, ed. Michael D. McMullen (Nashville, TN: Broadman and Holman, 2004), 227.
36. "Jesus Christ as the Shining Forth of the Father's Glory," 228.

subsistence: the Son proceeds from the Father. Rather importantly, this indicates for Edwards that the Son, in his mode of subsistence, is the shining forth of the person (not simply essence) of the Father. The Son of God is "in himself by virtue of his personal properties" the shining forth of the Father's glory. "This is not merely an honor conferred upon him by the good pleasure of God," states Edwards, "but 'tis what he himself necessarily is."[37] Furthermore, the happiness of the Father consists in the beholding of divine glory (i.e., the Father's own glory) in the Son: "The infinite happiness of God the Father is in beholding this his own perfect image."[38]

Edwards's reasoning here is consequential for clarifying the manner of the election, or choosing, of the Son of God *ad intra*. Foremost, the Father's election of the Son is one of natural necessity; the glory of the Father necessarily shines forth, or is necessarily declared, in the Son. The Father "chooses" the Son as to his divine nature because the Father lovingly, delightfully, and necessarily beholds the perfections of the divine nature and his own image in the Son. As Edwards specifies in a 1743 sermon on Heb. 2:7-8, "Election as it respects the Person as the Object of God[']s Et[ernal] delight is necessary. [I]t is not as in men Election of meer men."[39] Edwards especially utilizes the language of communication to fill out this notion of the election *ad intra*. The Son is the chosen of God as to "[his] great declarative glory"[40] *ad intra* because the Son is the personal and perfect communication of the Father's glory. Election, in its deepest sense, specifies the entire communicative movement that transpires between the Father and Son in the Holy Spirit.[41] Election *ad intra* refers to the Father's "peculiar" love for the Son.[42]

This is not the whole story, however. Edwards also believes God the Son, as one who possesses the fullness of divinity *in se*, is further inclined to communicate the fullness of the divine life to another. In this way, the doctrine of election not only specifies the Father's election of the Son *ad intra*, but also simultaneously specifies the election of the Son of God *ad extra*. According to Edwards, the further communication of the perfection of God's life to creatures remains entirely dependent on the fuller sense of the election of Jesus Christ.

---

37. "Jesus Christ as the Shining Forth of the Father's Glory," 226.

38. "Jesus Christ as the Shining Forth of the Father's Glory," 230.

39. Sermon 699. Heb. 2:7-8 (Mar. 1743) [L. 2v.].

40. "Miscellanies," no. 769, *WJE* 18:415.

41. Importantly, the act of election *ad intra* remains fully trinitarian. In a fragmentary piece on "The Equality of the Persons of the Trinity" Edwards writes, "The Father has good, and though the Son receives the infinite good, the Holy Spirit, from the Father, the Father enjoys the infinite good through the Son. He is the end of the other two in their acting *ad intra*, and also in his acting *ad extra*, in all they do in redemption and their distinct economical concerns. The end of the Father in electing is the Spirit. He elects to a possession of this benefit." *WJE* 21:146-7. As this fragmentary musing indicates, the Spirit closes the loop, as it were, in election without collapsing it.

42. Sermon 699. Heb. 2:7-8 (March 1743) [L. 2v.].

The Election of the Son of God ad extra: *Election as Creative Communication*

Edwards asks in an early "Miscellanies" entry on the end of creation,

> Why, then, did God incline further to communicate himself, seeing he had done [so] infinitely and completely? Can there be an inclination to communicate goodness more than adequately to the inclination? To say so is to say, that to communicate goodness adequate to the inclination is not yet adequate, inasmuch as he inclines to communicate further, as in the creation of the world. To this I say, that the Son is the adequate communication of the Father's goodness, is an express and complete image of him. But yet the Son has also an inclination to communicate himself, in an image of his person that may partake of his happiness: and this was the end of the creation, even the communication of the happiness of the Son of God; and this was the only motive hereto, even the son's inclination to this (see No. 115). And man, the consciousness or perception of the creation, is the immediate subject of this.[43]

The qualification Edwards alludes to in "Miscellanies" no. 115 involves the communicative movement in the godhead as it follows the trinitarian processions. According to Edwards, the Father cannot be the object of the Son's communicative goodness in the same manner that the Son is the object of the Father's communicative goodness because of the order of subsisting relations. These early remarks indicate a consistent reflex in Edwards's theology: God's triune relationality grounds the positive contours of God's internal and external works. When it comes to God's decree for creation, the hypostatic self-differentiation of the Father and the Son, as well as the necessary delight of each other therein, stand as the reason for God's creative movement *ad extra*.[44]

In order to fully understand the scope of this claim within Edwards's theology, it is pertinent to turn again to Edwards's mature argument in the *End of Creation*

---

43. "Miscellanies," no. 104, *WJE* 13:272.

44. It seems to be a hallmark of much of modern theology to attempt to think carefully and positively through the act of creation as a trinitarian act such that one can differentiate the specific contributions of individual persons in the act itself. Conceptually, this means saying more than the typical restriction of inner-trinitarian relations as relations of origin. This, of course, should not mean that one says something in contradiction to that. In contemporary theology, Wolfhart Pannenberg and Christoph Schwöbel provide two penetrating examples of positively tracing out the meaningfulness of God's hypostatic self-distinction in the act of creation. See Christoph Schwöbel, "God as Conversation: Reflections on a Theological Ontology of Communicative Relations," in *Theology and Conversation: Towards a Relational Theology*, ed. J. Haers and P. De Mey (Leuven: Leuven University Press, 2003), 62–6; and Wolfhart Pannenberg, *Systematic Theology*, vol. 2, trans. Geoffrey Bromiley (Grand Rapids, MI: Wm. B. Eerdmans Publishing, 1994), 20–35.

regarding the relationship between God's disposition to self-communication *ad extra* and God's aseity. As Edwards writes in the *End of Creation*,

> For though these communications of God, these exercises, operations, effects and expressions of his glorious perfections, which God rejoices in, are in time; yet his joy in them is without beginning or change. They were always equally present in the divine mind. He beheld them with equal clearness, certainty and fullness in every respect, as he doth now. They were always equally present, as with him there is no variableness or succession. He ever beheld and enjoyed them perfectly in his own independent and immutable power and will. And his view of, and joy in them is eternally, absolutely perfect, unchangeable and independent. It can't be added to or diminished by the power or will of any creature; nor is in the least dependent on anything mutable or contingent.[45]

All of the divine perfections, as well as their operations, effects, and so on, are contained within the divine mind. But Edwards takes the matter further by appropriating all of the "divine ideas" to the Son in particular. According to Edwards, the hypostasis of the Son contains all of God's ideas regarding God's perfections.[46] More precisely, the Son is the idea (or wisdom or understanding) of God in subsistence.[47] The Father, therefore, perfectly beholds in the Son—as the perfect, independent, and necessary communication of the divine essence, as well as the necessary and express image of his person—all of the divine perfections in affective delight (i.e., in the Holy Spirit). God's "exercises, operations, effects and expressions of his glorious perfections" present themselves in the divine mind "without beginning or end" as they are "declared," or manifest, in the Son.

But what, one may now ask, is the import of all of this for understanding of Edwards's position on God's relation to the world, especially as it pertains to the "necessity" of creation and God's disposition to self-communication as a perfection of divinity? As witnessed in Sang Lee's interpretation, God's "excitement" to create the world is in some sense bound up with the "communicative inclination" (or disposition) inherent in the elect Son of God. For Edwards, this means that God's inclination toward creation is entirely conditioned by the Son's hypostatic

---

45. *WJE* 8:448.

46. For a treatment of Edwards's metaphysical commitment to idealism and its ramifications for Christology and creation, see S. Mark Hamilton, *A Treatise on Jonathan Edwards: Continuous Creation and Christology* (JESociety Press, 2017); and Seng-Kong Tan, "Jonathan Edwards's Dynamic Idealism and Cosmic Christology," in *Idealism and Christian Theology*, ed. Joshua Harris and S. Mark Hamilton (New York: Bloomsbury Academic, 2016), 177–96.

47. Cf. *WJE* 21:121. As Edwards writes in "Miscellanies" no. 94: "Tis also said that God's knowledge of himself includes the knowledge of all things; and that he knows, and from eternity knew, all things by the looking on himself and by the idea of himself, because he is virtually all things." *WJE* 15:257.

distinction from the Father. The movement must not, however, be construed as binitarian; it remains thoroughly trinitarian because the Holy Spirit "actuates" the Son's "communicative inclination."[48] Seng-Kong Tan's comments are perceptive here.

> Insofar as God is Trinity only in the coming forth of the Spirit—"the end of all procession," virtual ideas of creation exist in God's love toward his Son. The creation of the world is decreed in the conjunct processions of Son and Spirit … The future creation of the universe, as with all things decreed by God, is "virtually done in the sight of the Father" by the Son in the Spirit. It is an act of election by the triune God.[49]

Such an articulation of creation is fairly novel from the perspective of older Reformed dogmatics, and one needs to be precise here in order to understand the novelty of Edwards's theological position. Such might be accomplished by juxtaposing Edwards against the scholastic tradition. In Thomas Aquinas and most Reformed orthodox theologians following after him, God's will *ad extra* first terminates upon all things known by God as possible participations or imitations of the divine essence, which then terminates on actual created things by the ordering of divine wisdom and power, moving creatures from potentiality (nonexistence) to actuality (existence). In this classical sense, there exists no new motion in God with regard to creation; no new will enters God, only a new external work proceeds from God's eternal and efficacious will. This is in keeping with a classical understanding of God as perfect actuality (*actus purus*) with no passive potency.[50] But this classical position is nuanced for Edwards. The divine

---

48. Edwards expounds upon this role of the Spirit in "Miscellanies" no. 108: "Now we have shown [No. 104], that the Son of God created the world for his very end, to communicate himself in an image of his own excellency … . He who by his immediate influence gives being every moment and by his Spirit actuates the world, because he inclines to communicate himself and his excellencies, doth doubtless communicate his excellency to bodies, as far as there is any consent or analogy. And though beauty of face and sweet airs in man are not always the effect of the corresponding excellencies of mind, yet the beauties of nature are really emanations, or shadows, of the excellencies of the Son of God." *WJE* 13:279.

49. Tan, "Jonathan Edwards's Dynamic Idealism and Cosmic Christology," 179–80. Tan references *WJE* 19:192, even though that reference, in context, implicitly refers to the covenant of redemption.

50. For a summary explanation of these matters in relation to modern theology, see Steven Duby, "Election, Actuality, and Divine Freedom: Thomas Aquinas, Bruce McCormack, and Reformed Orthodoxy in Dialogue," *Modern Theology* 32, no. 3 (July 2016): 325–40; and Steven Duby, "Divine Immutability, Divine Action and the God–World Relation," *International Journal of Systematic Theology* 19, no. 2 (April 2017): 144–62. Walter Schultz takes Edwards's metaphysics of modality as a species of medieval exemplarism, which he calls "complete representation exemplarism." In particular, Schultz argues that

will first terminates on all things known by God as possible participations in the Son of God, who is God's wisdom subsisting via an extension of the doctrine of appropriations, which then terminates on actual created things as ordered by the Son and actuated by Spirit.[51] Conceptually, this means the Son's mediation in creation is not simply that of a structural principle of rationality (e.g., divine ideas united in and mediated abstractly through the Logos), but the ground, possibility, and origin of all creaturely existence as those creaturely realities participate in and reflect the image of the Son.[52] Moreover, the Son—in his self-distinction from the Father—manifests an inherent determination to communicate his self-possessed divine glory to another. Edwards articulates the matter like this in his *Discourse on the Trinity*:

> The love of God as it flows forth *ad extra* is wholly determined and directed by divine wisdom, so that those only are the objects of it that divine wisdom chooses. So that the creation of the world is to gratify divine love as that is exercised by divine wisdom. But Christ is divine wisdom, so that the world is

---

the modal statuses of all effects *ad extra* are rooted in God's ability *ad extra*, abilities of which God has direct and eternal awareness. Such direct representational awareness of God's ability *ad extra* "constitutes all real possibilities." *Jonathan Edwards' Concerning the End for Which God Created the World: Exposition, Analysis, and Philosophical Implications* (Göttingen: Vandenhoeck & Ruprecht, 2020), 159–69.

51. In a certain respect, this sounds similar to Thomas Aquinas' trinitarian doctrine of the Word, especially as "begotten Wisdom." See Thomas Aquinas, *Summa Theologiae* I, q. 34, a. 1, ad. 2. As Dominic Legge explains in his exposition of Aquinas' Christology, "it is *impossible* that God would make *anything* except through his Word, because the Father always acts in the world through the Word, the eternal conception of his wisdom." *The Trinitarian Christology of St. Thomas Aquinas* (Oxford: Oxford University Press, 2017), 70 (emphasis in original). All created things are made through the Word, Aquinas argues, because the Word "contains the ideas [*rationes*] of everything created by God." Thomas Aquinas, *Summa Contra Gentiles* IV, c. 42, as quoted in Legge, 68. Legge further explains: "the second person of the Trinity is the exemplar of all creatures insofar as he proceeds by way of intellect as the divine Word" (71). To be sure, the overarching trinitarian structure of the creaturely *exitus* from God and *reditus* to God is strikingly similar in the theologies of Aquinas and Edwards. But, as I am tracing it here, Edwards goes much further in his integration of creation and Christology than Aquinas.

52. Again, Tan: "While all ideas are comprehended in the divine Logos, the creation of the universe is not a temporal communication of the divine Idea or divine Love. The universe is not a *self*-communication of God, but is a created image of the Son's own person. Only as the Son gives his Spirit to redeemed creatures does this constitute a divine self-communication *ad extra*—the end of creation." "Jonathan Edwards's Dynamic Idealism and Cosmic Christology," 180. This recognition of the Son's fullness concretely communicated, as opposed to an abstract structural principle in creation, is significant for interpreting Edwards's understanding of the occasion of the Fall (see Chapter 5).

made to gratify divine love as exercised by Christ, or to gratify the love that is in Christ's heart, or to provide a spouse for Christ—those creatures which wisdom chooses for the object of divine love as Christ's elect spouse, and especially those elect creatures that wisdom chiefly pitches upon and makes the end of the rest.[53]

Summarily stated, God's decree to create and to communicate God's fullness to a created other coincides with the absolutely necessary existence of the Son of God *ad intra*, as well as the absolutely necessary communal and communicative relationship between the Father and the Son as bound and ordered by the Spirit. The divine will and divine love, therefore, terminate on possible participations in the hypostasis of the Son precisely because the Son, as God's declarative glory *ad intra*, mediates the declarative communication of divine goodness and love *ad extra*. In this sense, God's hypostatic self-differentiation provides the interpretive key for understanding Edwards's claim that God's communication of the divine perfections *ad extra* is a "necessary consequence of his delighting in the glory of his own nature."[54] God delights in the glory of his own nature, not abstractly, but concretely in God's hypostatic self-distinction. This means God's will for creation cannot be construed in a morally deterministic fashion *tout court*, but in keeping with the strictest trinitarian logic.[55] Creation arises as an outworking of the Son's election *ad intra*, an outworking of the glory of God's own nature as declared in the Son.

Edwards's overall trinitarian logic may now be articulated as follows. The possibility of the decree for creation arises from the Father's immanent and perfect delight in the Son's divine nature and perfections, as well as the reciprocal delight of the Son toward the Father.[56] The order of relations remains foundational: the processions of the divine persons reveal—in fact, simply *are*—the possibility and causal basis for creation.[57] Because the Father is the fount of deity, the Father has relational priority according to mode of being.[58]

---

53. *WJE* 21:142.
54. *WJE* 8:447.
55. For an argument that Edwards paints a picture of God's moral perfection as necessarily determinative of a best possible world, see William Rowe, *Can God Be Free?* (Oxford: Clarendon Press, 2004), 54–73. As mentioned previously, Oliver Crisp holds a similar, though somewhat more complex, position. See *Jonathan Edwards on God and Creation*, 146.
56. In using the language of "arises" I am not speaking temporally but structurally (*in signo rationis*). For Edwards, God's creative decree has its *foundation* in the trinitarian processions and does so precisely in the manner specified above.
57. Tan states the principle as follows: "The reality of this universe is virtually comprehended in the generation of the Son." "Jonathan Edwards's Dynamic Idealism and Cosmic Christology," 178. Cf. Thomas Aquinas, *Scriptum super libros Sententiarum* I, d. 14, q.1, a. 1; *Summa Theologiae* I, q. 45, a. 6, resp.
58. So Edwards in "Miscellanies" no. 1062 says: "Tis fit that the order of the acting of the persons of the Trinity should be agreeable to the order of their subsisting: that as the

Within this relational order, the Father's communicative movement terminates perfectly on the Son as the Father beholds the perfections of the divine essence and the image of his person in the Son, and as the Father is present to the Son in loving delight. Here, the spiration of the Holy Spirit is just the loving delight that the Father and the Son have in each other, which constitutes the one divine life of mutual indwelling. The communication of the divine fullness is given and returned perfectly, not as a willed decision in God or as a coming-to-be of God, but necessarily as the one divine triune life.[59] God's communicative perfection is already fully actualized apart from the created order, and therefore not contingent in any ontologically real sense. "[God's] being and existence can't be conceived of but as prior to any of God's acts or designs: they must be presupposed as the ground of them," so Edwards argues in *End of Creation*. "[God] can't create the world to the end that he may have existence; or may have such attributes and perfections, and such an essence."[60] Miklos Vetö's overall commentary on Edwards is salient: "The world, far from being the necessary term of a 'communicative need' of God, can only be understood from the adequate resolution of this 'need' from inside divinity itself, in 'the felicity of the communion of the persons of the Trinity.'"[61]

Because divine aseity and divine unity are not in question for Edwards, his theological reasoning allows him to idiosyncratically parse God's creative act in terms of the Son's loving and communicative perfection as it exists *ab ipso*:

> God the Son, having the infinite goodness of the divine nature in him, desired to have a proper object to whom he might communicate his goodness: to have this object in the nearest, strictest union with himself, and therefore desires (to speak of him after the manner of men) a spouse to be brought and presented to himself in such a near relation and strict union as might give him the greatest advantage to communicate his goodness to her.[62]

Father is first in the order of subsisting, so he should be first in the order of acting; that as the other two persons are from the Father in their subsistence, and as to their subsistence naturally originated from him and dependent on him, so that, in all that they act, they should originate from him, act from him and in a dependence on him; that as the Father, with respect to the subsistences, is the fountain of the Deity, wholly and entirely so, so he should be the fountain in all the acts of the Deity. This is fit and decent in itself." *WJE* 20:431.

59. Cf. Edwards, "Jesus Christ as the Shining Forth of the Father's Glory," 226–9.

60. *WJE* 8:469.

61. Miklos Vetö, *La pensée de Jonathan Edwards: avec une concordance des différentes editions de ses Œuvres, nouvelle édition remaniée* (Paris: L'Harmattan, 2007), 99: "Le monde, bien loin d'être le terme nécessaire d'un 'besoin de communication' de Dieu, ne se comprend qu'à partir de la résolution adéquate de ce 'besoin' à l'intérieur de la divinité elle-même, dans 'la félicité de la communion des personnes de la Trinité' [*WJE* 16:415]."

62. "Approaching the End of God's Grand Design" (December 1744), *WJE* 25:117.

In beholding himself in the Son, the Father necessarily communicates the divine fullness to the Son such that the Father necessarily chooses the Son to declare the divine fullness, or glory. To commandeer a biblical idiom, the Father has given all things to the Son in election, even the Son's freedom to communicate the fullness of the triune life to another.[63]

This is what has been glossed previously as the election of the Son *ad intra*. But, as shown above, Edwards takes the matter further. Because the love between the Father and the Son is already reciprocated perfectly in the Spirit, the Son's reflexive act on the divine perfections does not yield another communicative work *ad intra*.[64] "For the Father is not a communication of the Son," so Edwards argues, "and therefore not an object of the Son's goodness."[65] Robert Jenson helpfully catches the implications of God's communicative movement *ad intra* for God's work *ad extra*: "The Son thinks the fellowship in and by which he responds to the Father's self-communication, and *so* there is a world."[66] The movement is external, bestowing being and bringing creatures to life therein. As Edwards writes in "Miscellanies" no. 704 with respect to God's creative decree, "the decree of God's communicating his goodness to such a subject don't so much as presuppose the being of the subject, because it gives being."[67] The election of the Son of God gives being to creation because, as we saw, the Son is the positive, theological content of God's declarative glory and goodness. Vetö isolates the metaphysical implication: "Christ, Son and Word of God, is the paradigm of all duplications and all manifestations, as well as the conceptual spring of a metaphysics which manages to think newness without subjecting it to becoming."[68]

---

63. For an interpretation of Edwards on "fullness" and "communication" that places the emphasis directly and more narrowly—I think too narrowly at times—on the person of the Spirit, see James R. Salladin, *Jonathan Edwards and Deification: Reconciling Theosis and the Reformed Tradition* (Downers Grove, IL: IVP Academic, 2022), 19–64. Salladin's project focuses upon "fullness" as the category that enables Edwards to endorse a form of graced "participation" in the divine life without blurring Creator-creature categories.

64. Logically, if such a movement were essential and internal, then it could be possible to continue *ad infinitum*. That is, every reflexive act on the divine essence by a divine person could yield another subsistence. This is a criticism raised by Oliver Crisp in assessing Edwards's a priori trinitarian argument (*Jonathan Edwards on God and Creation*, 122–4). It seems to me, however, that this criticism is slightly wide of the mark when one considers Edwards's overarching trinitarian claims, especially his emphasis on the relational order of the trinitarian processions. The reflexive act *ad intra*, in other words, is exhausted in the Son.

65. "Miscellanies," no. 115, *WJE* 13:282.

66. Robert Jenson, *America's Theologian: A Recommendation of Jonathan Edwards* (Oxford: Oxford University Press, 1988), 47.

67. "Miscellanies," no. 704, *WJE* 18:321.

68. Vetö, *La pensée de Jonathan Edwards*, 478: "Le Christ, Fils et Verbe de Dieu, est le paradigm de tous les dédoublements et de toutes les manifestations, il est également le ressort conceptuel d'une métaphysique qui parvient á penser la nouveauté sans la

Up until now, the impression might have been implicitly given—by utilizing the categories of *ad intra* and *ad extra*—that Edwards separates the internal and external election of the Son of God in some way or another. Yet this is not so. Edwards consistently refers to the one election of Jesus Christ in a twofold sense: "Christ is chosen of God as to his divine *and* human nature."[69] To be clear, Edwards neither concludes nor implies that there is triune self-realization with or in God. God exists *a se* and remains complete *in se*. Nevertheless, Edwards's overall reasoning clearly indicates that the election of the Son as to his divine nature includes (in some sense) the election of the Son to a creaturely nature. Jesus Christ's election is one theological package. The former is an absolute, or natural, necessity *ad intra*; the latter may be classified as a fitting necessity *ad extra*. Edwards speaks in precisely this manner in a 1743 sermon on the topic.

> The Heart of G[od] has been from Et[ernity] determined & Engaged to Give Great Testimonies & manifesta[tions] of this his Love to his son[.] Tis *fit* that it should be Testified & declared. [N]ot that [Christ] needed anything. [A]s it was not because G[od] needed any thing that it was his will to Glorify hims[elf]. [B]ut it was a *condecent* thing ... & it was the will of G[od] to shew forth his own Glory & that in a Great degree so it was his Et[ernal] will greatly to shew forth his Love to his son ... this was Gods Et[ernal] design & purpose & seems to be called by *way of Eminency his decree*.[70]

For Edwards, the election of the Son *ad extra* is a "fit" and "condecent thing." Modally, fittingness (*convenientia*) falls somewhere between absolute necessity and hypothetical necessity (i.e., necessity of the supposition) for Edwards; as such, its modality is also stronger than mere possibility.[71] Unlike discussions of

soumettre au devenir." According to Vetö, Edwards's theological program contains an overall revision of metaphysics: "Le jaillissement-dédoublement qui est l'avènement de Fils, son engendrement trinitaire, est le ressort métaphysique de l'être-acte en tant que désir et croissance" ["The outpouring-duplication which is the advent of the Son, his trinitarian generation, is the metaphysical spring of being-act as desire and growth"] (477).

69. "Miscellanies," no. 769, *WJE* 18:415 (emphasis mine).

70. Sermon 699. Heb. 2:7-8 (March 1743) [LL. 3v.-4r.] (emphasis mine).

71. On the modality of fittingness, see Corey Barnes, "Necessary, Fitting, or Possible: The Shape of Scholastic Christology," *Nova et Vetera*, Eng. edn 10, no. 3 (2012): 657–88; and Gilbert Narcisse, O.P., *Les raisons de Dieu: Argument de convenance et esthétique théologique selon saint Thomas d'Aquin et Hans Urs von Balthasar* (Fribourg: Éditions Universitaires, 1997). Narcisse defines fittingness (*convenance*)—via Thomas Aquinas—as "un possible réalisé" ["a realized possible"] (109). More technically, "*la convenance est l'unité du possible probable et du réalisé nécessaire,* dans la stricte mesure où cette unité est pensée d'une manière strictement *théologique*" ["fittingness is the unity of the probable possible and the necessary realized, to the extent that this unity is thought of in a strictly theological manner"] (137). Narcisse will later demarcate this sort of necessity as a theological necessity because "la nécessité qui en résulte est qualifieé par le type particulier de science que

contingency and necessity that follow from theological judgments about divine power—*potentia ordinata* and *potentia absoluta*[72]—and divine volition, fittingness is instead negotiated along the lines of divine wisdom.[73] This is certainly true for Edwards: God acts as "being limited and directed in nothing but his own wisdom, tied to no other rules and laws but the direction of his own infinite understanding."[74] Fittingness, in this sense, eliminates what have been traditionally called "compossible worlds" for Edwards, though it does not eliminate the contingency of this world as such in some sort of modal collapse. Recall, only the election of the Son *ad intra* is absolutely necessary. Creation remains, in Edwards's terminology, "arbitrary": "Creation is an arbitrary production. They are the effects of the mere good will and pleasure of God. God when he creates anything he doesn't create it by necessity of nature, but voluntarily. But the Son of God proceeds from the Father naturally and necessarily."[75] By arbitrary, Edwards does not mean capricious. God's arbitrary operation means, as Crisp recognized, something akin to a movement of the will that is free from external compulsion (i.e., liberty of spontaneity); God is an "arbitrary" being in the sense that God's will is wholly determined by God's wisdom. As we saw above, divine wisdom is parsed along trinitarian lines for Edwards. The Son, rather uniquely, is divine wisdom subsisting. It appears that "arbitrary" and "fitting" (condecent) function synonymously and christologically

---

constitue la *sacra doctrina*" ["the necessity which results is qualified by the particular type of science which constitutes *sacra doctrine*"] (533). That is, fittingness acquires a theological necessity based on the analogy of faith as the intellect operates—even if speculatively—within the domain of theological science (i.e., divine revelation). See also the helpful article by Fellipe do Vale: "On Thomas Aquinas's Rejection of an 'Incarnation Anyway,'" *TheoLogica: An International Journal for Philosophy of Religion and Philosophical Theology* 3, no. 1 (2019): 144–64. Do Vale summarizes well Thomas's position on fittingness: "So, by definition, *x* is fitting if (a) it proceeds from or belongs to *y* by reason of *y*'s nature and/or (b) is the means to achieving some end that brings together the most goods and avoids the greatest evils" (150). Do Vale also argues, rather persuasively, that fittingness functions for Thomas as a "modal concept *springing forth from his persuasions about the nature of the canon and theological interpretation*" (157, italics original).

72. For a helpful discussion of God's absolute and ordained power vis-à-vis possibility and necessity, see William J. Courtenay, *Capacity and Volition: A History of the Distinction of Absolute and Ordained Power* (Bergamo: Lubrina, 1990); Hester Goodenough Gelber, *It Could Have Been Otherwise: Contingency and Necessity in Dominican Theology at Oxford, 1300–1350* (Leiden: Brill, 2004), especially 309–49; and Muller, *Divine Will and Human Choice*.

73. So Narcisse: "La problématique de la convenance est bien un essai de scruter le *pourquoi* de la Sagesse divine." ["The problematic of fittingness is rightly an attempt to scrutinize the *why* of divine Wisdom."] *Les raisons de Dieu*, 523. Cf. Narcisse, *Les raisons de Dieu*, 101–13.

74. "Miscellanies," no. 1263, *WJE* 23:202–3.

75. Edwards, "Jesus Christ as the Shining Forth of the Father's Glory," 228.

for Edwards.[76] Fittingness becomes a way of specifying the wise correspondence between the election of Christ *ad intra* and *ad extra*; thus, the election of Jesus Christ—in its twofold sense—provides the internal basis for creation within Edwards's decretal theology. The election of Christ fittingly entails a creative act and qualifies the nature of God's freedom for creation: the election of Jesus Christ is creative communication.[77]

The Election of Christ and Supralapsarian Christology

What has been more or less muted so far in this account of the relation between creation and the election of Jesus Christ is Edwards's repeated emphasis that election pertains to Jesus Christ as the God-*man*. Edwards articulates the matter like this in a 1744 sermon on the subject:

> *Inq.* What is this one great design that God has in view in all his works and dispensations?
>
> *Ans.* 'Tis to present to his Son a spouse in perfect glory from amongst sinful, miserable mankind, blessing all that comply with his will in this matter and destroying all his enemies that oppose it, and so to communicate and glorify himself through Jesus Christ, God-man. This I take to be the great design of the work of creation [and the] work of providence. God has appointed but one head of the whole creation, and that one head is Jesus Christ, God-man.[78]

It is not enough, according to Edwards, to confess that the external and creative movement entailed by the election of the Son of God pertains merely to the general communication of divine wisdom as refracted through the Son, say in a similar vein to the function of Logos in early Christian thought as a rationally ordering principle within creation. The fuller logic of Edwards's treatment of the election of Jesus Christ and creation is, much like in Thomas Goodwin's theology, a species of supralapsarian Christology, wherein the divine motive for the incarnation is not primarily redemption.[79] The emphasis falls on Jesus Christ as mediator in

---

76. One might also call this sort of necessity in Edwards's theology a "communicative necessity" based on its overall theological function. Other interpreters have also noticed this fitting or communicative necessity in Edwards's understanding of God's glory and triune fullness, though they do not parse it in christological terms as I have done here. See especially Krister Sairsingh, "Jonathan Edwards and the Idea of Divine Glory: The Trinitarian Foundation of Edwards' Theology and Its Ecclesial Import" (PhD Diss., Harvard University, 1986), 183.

77. Cf. Scholl, "Excellency of Minds," 199–200.

78. "Approaching the End of God's Grand Design" (December 1744), *WJE* 25:116.

79. On Edwards's supralapsarian Christology, see also S. Mark Hamilton, "Jonathan Edwards on the Election of Christ," *Neue Zeitschrift für Systematische Theologie und Religionsphilosophie* 58, no. 4 (2016): 525–48. For systematic and historical perspectives on

protological and eschatological terms,[80] as opposed to strictly soteriological.[81] In Edwards's reasoning, the election of the Son of God as the communicative medium *ad extra* includes the elective elevation of human nature to a personal union with God: human creatures are "elected in [Christ's] election."[82] The culmination of Edwards's theological reasoning is found in a late "Miscellanies" entry, no. 1245.[83] In that notebook entry, Edwards succinctly weaves together the prominent theological themes we have been exploring thus far (the election of Jesus Christ *ad extra*) and those that have remained in the background (union, incarnation, and individual election). As such, it is beneficial to take an extended excursus in order to examine his thoughts in "Miscellanies" no. 1245.

"Miscellanies" no. 1245

Edwards begins "Miscellanies" no. 1245 by setting forth what it does not mean to be chosen in Christ. First, in a typical anti-Arminian move, Edwards follows Thomas Goodwin explicitly in noting that it "cannot be a being chosen because it is foreseen we shall believe in Christ."[84] Second, being chosen in Christ does not entail a foresight of Christ's "satisfactions and merits as our surety."[85] "Christ purchased our salvation," Edwards writes, "but not our election."[86] Christ's redemptive work is not, in other words, the impulsive cause of individual election.

---

supralapsarian Christology, see van Driel, *Incarnation Anyway*; Crisp, "Incarnation without the Fall," 215–33; and Hunter, *If Adam Had Not Sinned*.

80. Robert Jenson makes a somewhat similar point: "Christ is conceived … as universal mediator, as between God and all creatures, so also within the triune life and within the world of creatures, and in both connections as mediator both of what is separated by evil and of what is separated merely by nature." *America's Theologian*, 104.

81. Francis Turretin, for example, is unequivocal in his soteriological assessment: "no other end of the advent of Christ and of his incarnation is ever proposed (whether in the Old or in the New Testament) than that he might save his people from sin." *Inst*.13.3.4. English Translation: *Institutes of Elenctic Theology*, trans. George Musgrave Giger and ed. James T. Dennison, Jr., vol. 2 (Phillipsburg, NJ: P&R Publishing, 1992), 300.

82. "Miscellanies," no. 769, *WJE* 18:418. One should not launch into any Barthian comparisons too quickly, even if some are warranted. Barth's overall thought works in a direction at odds with Edwards's theological vision. Even still, as Robert Jenson suggests, "Edwards' doctrine of election anticipates at most key points the justly praised 'Christological' doctrine of election in Karl Barth." *America's Theologian*, 106.

83. Robert Jenson observes that "Miscellanies" no. 1245 amounts to a "full draft systematic analysis" of the election of Christ. *America's Theologian*, 105.

84. "Miscellanies," no. 1245, *WJE* 23:177. In this entry, Edwards references Thomas Goodwin's sermon on Eph. 1:4-5, which is "Sermon V" in *Works* 1:65–82.

85. "Miscellanies," no. 1245, *WJE* 23:177.

86. "Miscellanies," no. 1245, *WJE* 23:177.

Edwards then proceeds to unpack how the text of Ephesians indicates that we are chosen so that we might *be holy*, not that we might *be in Christ*. For Edwards, like Thomas Goodwin before him, such a thought underscores the reality that "our being looked upon in him is some way the ground of our being chosen from eternity to be holy and happy."[87] Edwards's reasoning here marks a shift from his previous thought as articulated in "Miscellanies" no. 769. Earlier Edwards had argued that Christ is the "head of all elect creatures, and both angels and men are chosen in him in some sense, i.e. chosen to *be in him*."[88] Edwards's shift involving the verb "to be" is subtle, but he is now seeking to affirm that individual election unto holiness is predicated upon the fact that, "in some sense," human creatures are already virtually "in Christ." Even still, this does not mean that individual saints were elected with Christ simultaneously. God's election of Jesus Christ is "first in the affair" and "some way or other the ground of our being chosen."[89]

After setting forth the negative boundary markers, Edwards proceeds to unpack the matter positively. His explication focuses on four key points: (1) "All things that God ever decreed," writes Edwards, "he decreed for the sake of his beloved"[90] (i.e., the Son); (2) the sum of God's purposes in creating the world was to "procure a spouse, or a mystical body, for his Son";[91] (3) the object of God's determination to communicate himself in the fullness of his grace and love is not multiple but one, namely, the mystical body of Christ; and (4) God chose the "race of mankind" in particular to communicate his love and goodness in Christ.

First, in God's works *ad extra*, God purposes all things *for* Christ and purposes to accomplish all things *in* Christ. "Therefore probably it is that," Edwards notes with reference to Eph. 3:11, "the sum of God's decrees is called the purpose which he purposed in Christ."[92] What is important to note here is that Edwards considers God's work *ad extra* from a general point of view. He does not mention, in any explicit manner, particular events or persons. Edwards is simply stating that the determination of all of God's communicative works *ad extra*—as was specified with greater detail in the above discussion of the election of the Son *ad extra*—will be purposed in the Son. Once again, according to this line of reasoning, God's summative decree *ad extra* does not have any other ultimate end in mind other than the Son. The Son is "the end of all of God's works *ad extra*," and all was decreed to "be brought to pass by the Son."[93] As Edwards argues in his 1743 sermon from Hebrews with regard to the Father's love for the Son, "All the wo[rks] & d[ispensations] of G[od] with Regard to all Parts of the C[reation] & in all ages

---

87. "Miscellanies," no. 1245, *WJE* 23:177.
88. "Miscellanies," no. 769, *WJE* 18:418.
89. "Miscellanies," no. 1245, *WJE* 23:178.
90. "Miscellanies," no. 1245, *WJE* 23:178.
91. "Miscellanies," no. 1245, *WJE* 23:178.
92. "Miscellanies," no. 1245, *WJE* 23:178.
93. "Miscellanies," no. 1245, *WJE* 23:178.

of it[,] they are for this Purpose & theref are [] ~~sovereignly~~ so performed ~~to~~ as to answer this End."⁹⁴

After establishing the preeminence of Christ in God's purposes *ad extra* from a general perspective, Edwards moves to examine the issue more precisely. Here he finds that—more narrowly defined—God's end was to procure a spouse for the eternal Son. The "purpose of the whole series of events" in creation was to provide a "mystical body" for the Son to lavish his love upon.⁹⁵ Once again, Edwards foregrounds the Son's communicative goodness within his discussion of God's eternal purpose in creating the world. The same point is made in *End of Creation*, wherein Edwards notes that the church is called the fullness of Christ, "as though he were not in a complete state without her."⁹⁶ Within this larger determination to provide a "mystical spouse" for the Son, the election of individual created beings is referred to as election "in Christ," or the "purpose which God purposed in Christ Jesus."⁹⁷ What Edwards has in view primarily involves the strict union decreed between Christ and his "chosen" body.

So, Edwards's third emphasis: "though many individual persons were chosen, yet they were chosen to receive God's infinite good and Christ's peculiar love in union, as one body, one spouse, all united in one head."⁹⁸ The communication of the Son's "fullness" occurs not otherwise than through union with the Son. "They are chosen singly," Edwards writes, "but in their very first election there is respect to their union in the body of Christ."⁹⁹ The decreed order is highly significant: Edwards identifies union with and conformity to Jesus Christ as conceptually prior to individual election. In making this point, Edwards is providing the requisite context for considering the order of the divine decrees, particularly post-Fall. This is seen most explicitly when he continues his discussion by referring to the "individual circumstances of the individual chosen members."¹⁰⁰ Only after consideration of the "very first election in Christ" is one able to consider the "circumstances" of the individual chosen members. The circumstances include their being "sinful and miserable, etc.," as well as "the appointment of the particular way how they should

---

94. Sermon 699. Heb. 2:7-8 (March 1743) [L. 4r.].
95. "Miscellanies," no. 1245, *WJE* 23:178.
96. *WJE* 8:439-40. The theme of God creating the world to provide a spouse for his Son is a consistent theological point for Edwards. Indeed, it spans from his early musings in the "Miscellanies" (cf. "Miscellanies," no. 271) to his late thoughts in the *End of Creation*. For example, Edwards writes in his "Notes on Scripture" concerning Eph. 1:22-23: "This seems to be the good that Christ sought in the creation of the world, who is the beginning of the creation of God, when all things were created by him and for him, viz. that he might obtain a spouse that he might give himself to and give himself for, on whom he might pour forth his love, and in whom his soul might eternally be delighted." *WJE* 15:187.
97. "Miscellanies," no. 1245, *WJE* 23:179.
98. "Miscellanies," no. 1245, *WJE* 23:179.
99. "Miscellanies," no. 1245, *WJE* 23:179.
100. "Miscellanies," no. 1245, *WJE* 23:179.

come to conformity and participation with the head, how way should be made for it by Christ's satisfaction, righteousness, etc."[101] The "very first election" pertains to conformity to the head in the larger, more general sense, namely union with the Son vis-à-vis participation as a creature made to affectively and intellectually know God's goodness in Christ; the "individual circumstances" of the individual chosen members pertain to their creaturely condition post-Fall.

This brings us to Edwards's final point in "Miscellanies" no. 1245: God's choice of the "race of mankind" to communicate his peculiar love and goodness in Christ. God chose human beings to "be that species of creatures out of which he would take a number to constitute one created, dear child and one body of his Son."[102] It is telling that this is the first mention of human beings in Edwards's account of what it means to be "chosen in Christ." Only after laying the architectonic of election as christological communication does Edwards focus on humankind. Here, Edwards argues God decrees that one from the seed of mankind "should have the most transcendent union with the eternal *Logos*."[103] In this respect, Jesus Christ is more especially called the "elect of God."[104] Although the Son of God is loved by necessity of his divine nature, the person of Jesus Christ—the God-*man*—is the "first elect" and loved with respect to this sovereign election. Once again, the operative category for Edwards is union. In the language of predestination, the Son was predestined to hypostatically unite with a particular human nature, the yet-to-be-created human nature of Jesus Christ. The Son of God was, in this sense, *incarnandus*.[105]

Edwards concludes his discussion in "Miscellanies" no. 1245 by stating in the "grand decree of predestination, or that sum of God's decrees," we must consider "the appointment of Christ, or the decree respecting his person" as first in the order of the decrees.[106] Jesus Christ was appointed as the "author and foundation" with respect to the rest of the decrees, wherein God leaves everything for him to accomplish and bring into effect. Edwards then proceeds to make some

---

101. "Miscellanies," no. 1245, *WJE* 23:179.
102. "Miscellanies," no. 1245, *WJE* 23:179–80. Cf. *WJE* 18:418.
103. "Miscellanies," no. 1245, *WJE* 23:180.
104. "Miscellanies," no. 1245, *WJE* 23:180.
105. Important to remember here is the *anhypostasis-enhypostasis* distinction, which teaches that the human nature of Jesus Christ has no self-standing existence apart from its union with the Logos. As articulated in the *Leiden Synopsis*: "So that flesh has no subsistence apart from the Son of God, but it exists and subsists in him, and by him it is borne and supported." Henk van den Belt, ed., *Synopsis Purioris Theologiae: Latin and English Translation*, vol. 2, trans. Riemer A. Faber (Leiden: Brill, 2016), 79. The distinction remains important because Edwards does not adhere theologically to any version of the eternal God-manhood of Jesus Christ, and he still preserves the distinction between the Son's aseity and economic activity. It is proper to speak of the Son as *incarnandus*, though not eternally incarnated.
106. "Miscellanies," no. 1245, *WJE* 23:179.

discriminating remarks about individual election and rejection. In particular, God's decree to communicate the divine fullness in Christ and unite all the elect as his body is not the "reason of distinction in election, or why one was elected and not another, which was of God's sovereign pleasure."[107] Christ is the first elect, with election of individual persons logically following after this in the decree. Conformity to the head and intimate communion with God through Christ is the purpose of election, though not the impulsive cause of the election of individual creatures.

The End of the Incarnation

Based on the overview of Edwards's ideas just provided, a driving theological motive within Edwards's reasoning on the incarnation becomes clear: elective union and communion. That said, a careful distinction between the election of the Son *ad extra* and the Son's incarnation needs to be made and maintained. It is a distinction somewhat underspecified in Edwards's twofold understanding of the election of Jesus Christ. Foremost, the election of the Son of God *ad extra* entails an elective union with a creaturely nature for the purpose of communicating the glory of the divine perfections as beheld in the Son (see above). Creative communication through elective union, however, does not imply that this union would occur—by absolute necessity—with a human nature. Recall, for Edwards, the election of Jesus Christ as to his union with human nature was not based upon "works or worthiness" of human nature as such, but strictly a sovereign determination. Although the election of Jesus Christ *ad extra* gives being to creaturely reality in general and demands communicative union, this does not mean that it demands hypostatic union with a human nature. According to Edwards, the hypostatic union with a human nature remains a hypothetical necessity. Counterfactually considered, the Son could have assumed, for instance, an angelic nature, although the Son did not determine to do so. As Edwards argues in "Miscellanies" no. 769,

> His election as he was man was a manifestation of God's sovereignty and grace. God had determined to exalt one of the creatures so high that he should be one person with God, and should have communion with God, and glory in all respects answerable, and so should be the head of all other elect creatures, that they might be united to God and glorified in him. And his sovereignty appears in the election of the man Jesus various [*sic*] ways. It appears in choosing the species of creatures of which he should be, viz. the race of mankind, and not the angels, the superior species.[108]

Elect angels, nonetheless, benefit from Christ's election as the God-man.

---

107. "Miscellanies," no. 1245, *WJE* 23:179.
108. "Miscellanies," no. 769, *WJE* 18:416.

> All creatures have this benefit by Christ's incarnation, that God thereby is as it were come down to them from his infinite height above them, and is become a fellow creature, and all elect creatures hereby have opportunity for a more free and intimate converse with God, and full enjoyment of him than otherwise could be; and though Christ is not the Mediator of the angels in the same sense that he is of men, yet he is a middle person between God and them, through whom is all their intercourse with God and derivations from him.[109]

Edwards's further speculative musings on the fall and confirmation of angelic creatures prove instructive for understanding the inner workings of his supralapsarian Christology.[110] As Edwards speculates early on in "Miscellanies" no. 320,

> It seems to me probable that the temptation of the angels that occasioned their rebellion was that when God was about to create man, or had first created him, God declared his decree to the angels that one of that human nature should be his Son, his best beloved, his greatest favorite, and should be united to his eternal Son, and that he should be their head and king; that they should be given to him and should worship him and be his servants, attendants and ministers. And God, having thus declared his great love to the race of mankind, gave the angels the charge of them as ministering spirits to men.
>   Satan, or Lucifer, or Beelzebub, being the archangel, one of the highest of the angels, could not bear it, thought it below him and a great debasing of him; so he conceived rebellion against the Almighty and drew away a vast company of the heavenly hosts with him. But he was cast down from the highest pitch of glory to the lowest hell for it, and himself was made an occasion of bringing that to pass which his spirit so rose against. Yea, his spite and malice was made an occasion of it, and that same act of his by which he thought he had entirely overthrown the design; and that same person in human nature, which they could not bear should rule over them in glory and should be their king and head to communicate happiness to them, by this means proves their king in spite of them and becomes their judge; and though they would not be his willing subjects, they shall be his unwilling captives; he shall [be] their sovereign to make them miserable and pour out his wrath upon them. And mankind, whom they so envied and scorned, are by occasion of them advanced to higher glory and honor and greater happiness, and more nearly united to God; and though they disdained to be ministering spirits to them, yet now they shall be judged by them as assessors with Jesus Christ.[111]

---

109. "Miscellanies," no. 744, *WJE* 18:389.
110. For a discussion of the confirmation of angels within the framework of the covenant of works, see Chapter 4. For a larger discussion of Edwards's angelology, see also McClymond and McDermott, *Theology of Jonathan Edwards*, 273–94; and Amy Plantinga Pauw, "Where Theologians Fear to Tread," *Modern Theology* 16, no. 1 (January 2000): 39–59.
111. "Miscellanies," no. 320, *WJE* 13:401–2.

Tellingly, this early notebook entry reveals two consistent theological motifs for Edwards: (1) God's declared determination to love of human beings in and as the God-man proved to be the occasion for Satan's fall, such that Satan (and the fallen angels) refused to be ministering spirits to the race of mankind;[112] and (2) human beings, because of God's free determination, were elevated through their union with Christ as the highest of all created beings. The union of the Son of God with human nature, therefore, is the great stumbling block for angelic creatures. When viewed from the perspective of history, seeing Christ in flesh "was the greatest trial of the [unfallen] angels' obedience that ever was."[113] Moreover, unfallen angels were only "confirmed" in righteousness after the work of redemption, that is, after the humiliation and exaltation of the God-man, Jesus Christ. This, for Edwards, corresponds to the end for which angels were created, namely to "to be ministering spirits to Christ, in the great work of his exalting and glorifying beloved mankind."[114] "But the angels had not any great opportunity to do this business," Edwards writes, "till this work of Christ's glorifying mankind had been carried on considerably in the world."[115] The ascension—which entails permanent exaltation of the Son's assumed human nature—becomes the "confirming" moment for unfallen angels; for Satan and his fallen lot, the ascension further manifests their unwillingness to answer the end for which they were created.[116]

112. Cf. "Miscellanies," no. 702, *WJE* 18:306: "This well accounts for that exceeding enmity that Satan manifests against Christ and the race of mankind, in that it was for their sakes that he was cast down from heaven to hell. That was the sin for which he was condemned and cast down, viz. that when God revealed the great love he had to this race, and his design of exceeding honor and happiness to them and to one in their nature, especially that should be his Son, and that the angels should minister to this race, and should be subject to this elect one of the race, and worship him and serve him as their Lord, they envied them this honor, and could not bear to yield it to them, and for this was cast into eternal [misery]." See also Edwards's extended citation of Thomas Goodwin on the occasion of the fall of Satan, wherein Goodwin indicates it was the hypostatic union in particular that led to Satan's primordial apostasy (*WJE* 23:213–14).

113. "Miscellanies," no. 515, *WJE* 18:59.

114. "Miscellanies," no. 939, *WJE* 20:198.

115. "Miscellanies," no. 939, *WJE* 20:198.

116. It should be noted, however, that this is not the entire story. Edwards indicates that angels were created to be more than ministering spirits to elect human beings (generally speaking). They were created to be subservient to Christ in the work of redemption (cf. *WJE* 20:196). This raises a theological question: Is redemption prioritized over creation? If so, how can this be? In Christian theology, this type of exaltation of the human creature as a result of the fall can be classified as a *felix culpa* (happy fault). McClymond and McDermott acknowledge Edwards's adherence to some sort of *felix culpa* and do so precisely in their exposition of his angelology. See McClymond and McDermott, *Theology of Jonathan Edwards*, 282. Similarly, in discussing the ultimate condemnation of Satan in Edwards's theology, Pauw makes the following observation: "In [Satan's] eternal hatred of God and fellow creatures, undertones of tragedy and divine vulnerability keep intruding into

Overall, Edwards indicates both angelic and human creatures benefit from Christ's communicative and mediatorial office, even though the relation between human creatures and God is superior. For "confirmed" angelic creatures, they receive greater manifestations of the God's perfections by witnessing the external mission of Son of God, "especially in the death and suffering of Christ."[117] These angels also rely upon the God-man, Jesus Christ, for the increase of their holiness and reward of eternal life.[118] "So that it can truly be said of the angels," Edwards argues, "that they have eternal life by sovereign grace through Christ in a way of self-emptiness, self-diffidence and humble dependence on him."[119]

For human beings, the benefit is far superior, even if both angels and human beings eternally receive "heavenly" life. Simply put, the eternal reward for humans is superior because it involves beatitude through union with Christ; humans are "elected in Christ's election." Herein the teleological thrust of Edwards's notion of election and corresponding supralapsarian Christology appears as a norming factor: "Christ was made flesh, and dwelt among us in a nature infinitely below his original nature, for this end, that we might have as it were the full possession and enjoyment of him."[120] By full possession and enjoyment of Christ, Edwards means beatific fellowship with the Son in an analogous manner to the fellowship between the triune persons. Such a reward angels merely observe.

> Again it shows how much God designed to communicate himself to men, that he so communicated himself to the first and chief of elect men, the elder brother and the head and representative of the rest, even so that this man should be the same person with one of the persons of the Trinity. It seems by this to have been God's design to admit man as it were to the inmost fellowship with the deity ... The saints' enjoyment of Christ shall be like the Son's intimate enjoyment of the Father.[121]

Overall, Edwards's theological reasoning might be heuristically mapped onto that theological maxim common among Reformed divines in discussions of divine predestination: that which is last in execution, ought to be first in intention. The last executed act is the beatific vision in its thoroughly christological form; the first in intention is the election of Jesus Christ.[122]

Edwards' eschatological victory song." "Where Theologians Fear to Tread," 50–1. That such a tension runs straight through Edwards's theology at precisely this point will be the focus of the following chapters.

117. "Miscellanies," no. 937, *WJE* 20:197.
118. Cf. "Miscellanies," no. 940, *WJE* 20:199.
119. "Miscellanies," no. 937, *WJE* 20:196.
120. "Miscellanies," no. 741, *WJE* 18:367.
121. "Miscellanies," no. 741, *WJE* 18:367. Cf. Jenson, *America's Theologian*, 180–2.
122. See chapter five for an explication of Edwards's understanding of the beatific vision in its christological register.

Summary

According to Edwards, the election of Jesus Christ determines not only the *why* of creation (it is the most fitting necessity), but also the *end* of creation (communication of the fullness of the triune relations and perfections as beheld in the Son of God) and the *principal means* for attaining the end therein (personal union of human beings with the Son). The election of Jesus Christ, therefore, serves as the internal basis for creation,[123] with protology and eschatology converging in Jesus Christ. Edwards refers to this as that "grand decree of predestination," or the "sum of God's decrees."[124] Put in sharper terms, creation arises *ex nihilo* as a fitting consequence of the election of Jesus Christ *ad intra* and *ad extra* in order to communicate the fullness of God's triune life and perfections to creatures, which occurs in and through Jesus Christ, the one "grand medium" of communication.

> The creature is no further happy with this happiness which God makes his ultimate end than he becomes one with God ... the union will become more and more strict and perfect; nearer and more like to that between God the Father and the Son; who are so united, that their interest is perfectly one.[125]

And, as was shown above, union derives its fullest sense from the hypostatic union for Edwards. The hypostatic union takes communicative priority over all other forms of union. This facilitates a unique conclusion: Edwards not only believes creation to be a fitting (condecent) necessity but believes this creation to be the best possible one. This is true for Edwards, not in a Leibnizian sense, but simply because the best possible world is a creation internally structured around Jesus Christ. When God creates, it is necessarily bound to the election of the Son of God, therein making it the best because created history, whatever its possibilities, is purposed to Jesus Christ.

In terms of the significance of these findings for the order of the divine decrees in the theology of Jonathan Edwards, a preliminary schematization may be offered at this point.

1. The election of Jesus Christ *ad extra*, which entails
   1a. The decree of the glorification of divine perfections (excellency) *ad extra* in and through the Son.

---

123. Edwards's theological reasoning certainly bears some material similarity to Karl Barth's understanding of creation as the formal presupposition of the covenant, and covenant as the material presupposition of creation. Or, in other words, creation provides the external basis of the covenant, and covenant provides the internal basis for creation. See Barth, *CD* III.1, §41.3.

124. "Miscellanies," no. 1245, *WJE* 23:180.

125. *WJE* 8:533.

1b. The decree to communicate the glory of the divine perfections *ad extra* to a particular object of the Son's love, namely a "spouse" in strict union with the Son.
1c. The decree to create this world.

2. The decree of the incarnation, which entails
2a. The hypostatic union of the Son with a human nature.
2b. The elevation of human creatures as the chosen "spouse" of the Son.

By way of anticipation of the arguments given in Chapters 4 and 5, the relationship between Edwards's understanding of election in Christ and redemption deserves a note. In "Miscellanies" no. 744, Edwards observes that God's works *ad extra*, from the beginning of the universe to the end, "appears to be but one." "'Tis all one design carried on," Edwards writes, "one affair managed in all God's dispensations, towards all intelligent beings, viz. the glorifying and communicating himself in and through his Son Jesus Christ as God-man and by the work of redemption of fallen man."[126] According to Edwards, Christ's person and Christ's redemptive work are logically distinct aspects of God's one design, but never really disassociated in the mind of God with reference to God's work *ad extra*. Even still—and like Thomas Goodwin to whom Edwards appealed—Edwards believes the person of Christ remains preeminent over the redemptive work insofar as the work does not make the person glorious; rather, the work discloses or reveals the prior glory and perfection of the Son of God. Furthermore, the priority of God's decree to communicate the fullness of the divine life in the Son of God determines why the incarnation of the Son of God—quite apart from his work as redeemer—benefits all intelligent creatures, both angels and mankind: "God thereby is as it were come down to them from his infinite height above them, and is become a fellow creature, and all elect creatures hereby have opportunity for a more free and intimate converse with God, and full enjoyment of him than otherwise could be."[127]

Yet a related issue emerges with regard to this last point, namely the correspondence between the end of the incarnation and the decrees of the Fall and redemption. As Edwards argues in his 1733 sermon series, "Wisdom Displayed in Salvation," "Man is hereby brought to a greater and nearer union with God ... The fall is the occasion of Christ becoming our head, and the church his body."[128] Or again: "Man's misery is made an occasion of increasing both [the union to a proper object and relish of the object] by the work of redemption."[129] On this point, we see again Edwards's theological similarity

---

126. "Miscellanies," no. 744, *WJE* 18:388.

127. *WJE* 18:388.

128. "Wisdom Displayed in Salvation," in *Works of President Edwards*, vol. IV (New York: Leavitt & Allen, 1857), 154.

129. "Wisdom Displayed in Salvation," 156.

to Thomas Goodwin in Edwards's refusal to endorse a counterfactual form of supralapsarian Christology. So Edwards specifically argues in "Miscellanies" entry from the early 1730s:

> Hence we may learn something how vastly greater glory and happiness the elect are brought to by Christ than that which was lost by the fall, or even than that which man would [have] attained to if he had not fallen. For then, man would never have had such an advantage for an intimate union and converse with the Father or Son, Christ remaining at an infinite distance from man in the divine nature, and man remaining at an infinite distance from the Father, without being brought nigh by an union to a divine person.[130]

The incarnation clearly remains temporally contingent upon the Fall in this entry, even as the logical motive for the incarnation appears to rise above it (*supra lapsum*) within Edwards's larger reasoning on the election of Christ.

All of this, then, raises an important theological question: how does Edwards relate his grand theological statements regarding the election of Jesus Christ and its attendant ramifications for the end of the incarnation to the decree of the Fall and redemption? This is especially pertinent because Edwards appears to prioritize redemption over creation in many places. This, for instance, is a serious critique raised by Stephen Holmes: "Edwards must be described as uncompromisingly supralapsarian after all. Regardless of the place of the decree of reprobation, God's first thought emphatically is that he will redeem, not that he will create."[131] Such a sentiment appears in the penultimate sermon of Edwards's famous series "The History of the Work of Redemption."

> This Work of Redemption is so much the greatest of all the works of God, that all other works are to be looked upon either as part of it, or appendages to it, or are some way reducible to it. And so all the decrees of God do some way or other belong to that eternal covenant of redemption that was between the Father and the Son before the foundation of the world; every decree of God is some way or other reducible to that covenant.[132]

So, which is it? Is the predestination of Christ the sum of God's decrees? Or is it the covenant and work of redemption? There seems to be a tension at work in Edwards's theology between the christologically conditioned end of creation and the christologically conditioned work of redemption. It is a tension, I argue, that manifests itself in Edwards's covenant theology (Chapter 4) and in his understanding of individual election and rejection (Chapter 5). To this I now turn.

---

130. "Miscellanies," no. 571, *WJE* 18:510–11. Cf. "Miscellanies," no. 510, *WJE* 18:54–5.
131. Holmes, *God of Grace and God of Glory*, 131.
132. *WJE* 9:513.

Chapter 4

COVENANT, CHRIST, AND THE DECREES

And all the eternal counsels and decrees of God, so far as God has been pleased to inform us concerning them, seem all subservient to that grand purpose of God, the redemption of the elect, and are all in some sort, appurtenances of the eternal covenant of redemption.[1]

—Jonathan Edwards

This seems to be the good that Christ sought in the creation of the world, who is the beginning of the creation of God, when all things were created by him and for him, viz. that he might obtain a spouse that he might give himself to and give himself for, on whom he might pour forth his love, and in whom his soul might eternally be delighted.[2]

—Jonathan Edwards

'Tis all one design carried on, one affair managed in all God's dispensations, towards all intelligent beings, viz. the glorifying and communicating himself in and through his Son Jesus Christ as God-man and by the work of redemption of fallen man.[3]

—Jonathan Edwards

In the new preface to his republished *Jonathan Edwards and the Covenant of Grace*, Carl Bogue notes how, despite the voluminous amount of scholarship on the theology of Jonathan Edwards since 1975, there still appears "no such work" addressing the scope and impact of Edwards's covenantal thought.[4] That fact remains

---

1. "Terms of Prayer" (May 1738), *WJE* 19:775–6.
2. "235. Ephesians 1:22-23," *WJE* 15:187.
3. "Miscellanies," no. 744, *WJE* 18:388.
4. There are notable exceptions. See especially Carl Bogue, *Jonathan Edwards and the Covenant of Grace*, The Jonathan Edwards Classic Studies Series (Eugene, OR: Wipf & Stock, 2008); John Gerstner, "The Covenants," in *The Rational Biblical Theology of Jonathan Edwards*, vol. 2 (Powhatan, VA: Berea Publications, 1992), 79–141; Michael McClymond

true, especially regarding the manner in which his covenantal views interpenetrate his other theological commitments. This chapter begins to address just such an overlap, although it is not (nor do I claim for it to be) an exhaustive presentation of Edwards's covenant theology. Within this chapter, I intend to explore the manner in which Edwards's tri-covenantal structure—the covenant of works, the covenant of redemption, and the covenant of grace—relates, theologically, to the warp and woof of Edwards's commitment to the christologically conditioned end of creation and the divine decrees (see Chapter 3). One may recall from the end of the previous chapter that Edwards indicates "the decrees of God do some way or other belong to that eternal covenant of redemption that was between the Father and the Son before the foundation of the world; every decree of God is some way or other reducible to that covenant."[5] Given Edwards's statement that "every decree" has its beginning and mooring—in some way or another—in the covenant of redemption, it is necessary to investigate how such a foundation relates to Edwards's theological commitment to Jesus Christ as the sum of God's decrees. The covenantal structure of Edwards's thought, therefore, needs to be analyzed in order to fully account for Edwards's decretal theology and lapsarianism.

Before proceeding, however, it is best to briefly explain the form of covenantal thought within the broad landscape of Reformed orthodoxy of which Edwards was an inheritor, in particular the covenant of works, covenant of grace, and covenant of redemption.[6] Let's begin with the covenant of works. Although the origin of the covenant of works (*foedus operum*) in Reformed theology has been a difficult issue to trace, the concept was without doubt firmly fixed in the Reformed mind by the seventeenth century.[7] The *Westminster Confession*, for example, forthrightly

---

and Gerald McDermott, "Edwards's Calvinism and Theology of the Covenants," in *The Theology of Jonathan Edwards* (New York: Oxford University Press, 2012), 321–38; Cornelis van der Knijff and Willem van Vlastuin, "The Development in Jonathan Edwards' Covenant View," *Jonathan Edwards Studies* 3, no.2 (2013): 269–81; Reita Yazawa, "Covenant of Redemption in the Theology of Jonathan Edwards: The Nexus Between the Immanent and Economic Trinity" (PhD Diss., Calvin Theological Seminary, 2013); Paul James Hoehner, "The Covenantal Theology of Jonathan Edwards" (PhD Diss., University of Virginia, 2018); and Gilson Ryu, *The Federal Theology of Jonathan Edwards: An Exegetical Perspective* (St. Bellingham, WA: Lexham Academic, 2021).

5. "Sermon Twenty-Nine" (August 1739), *WJE* 9:513.

6. For a larger, though still general, overview, see Michael S. Horton, "Covenant," in *The Oxford Handbook of Reformed Theology*, ed. Michael Allen and Scott Swain (Oxford: Oxford University Press, 2020), 433–45.

7. See Richard Muller, "The Covenant of Works and the Stability of the Divine Law in Seventeenth-Century Reformed Orthodoxy: A Study in the Theology of Herman Witsius and Wilhelmus à Brakel," in *After Calvin: Studies in the Development of a Theological Tradition* (New York: Oxford University Press, 2003), 175–89; and J. V. Fesko, *The Covenant of Works: The Origins, Development, and Reception of the Doctrine* (Oxford: Oxford University Press, 2020).

states, "The first covenant made with man was a covenant of works, wherein life was promised to Adam; and in him to his posterity, upon condition of perfect and personal obedience."[8] As Westminster's confessional statement betrays, the theological details of the covenant of works attempt to describe the nature of the relationship between God and human creatures before the Fall. Despite the rather straightforward tenor of this statement, the larger conversation surrounding the covenant of works—that is, its relation to the covenant of grace, redemptive history, the Mosaic law, the nature of Adam's reward, and so on—is complex.[9]

Upon the violation of the covenant of works by Adam and Eve, many Reformed orthodox theologians spoke of the enactment of the covenant of grace. Again, the *Westminster Confession* provides a programmatic summary: "Man, by his fall, having made himself uncapable of life by that Covenant, the Lord was pleased to make a Second, commonly called the covenant of grace; wherein he freely offereth unto sinners life and salvation by Jesus Christ; requiring of them faith in him, that they may be saved, and promising to give unto all those that are ordained unto eternal life his Holy Spirit, to make them willing, and able to believe."[10] Immediately put into effect after the Fall, the covenant of grace stands as "perpetually and immutably one in matter and substance," even though it is administered differently under the Old and New Testaments.[11] The difference between the covenant of works and the covenant of grace is often expressed as the difference between law and gospel: "In the covenant of works, righteousness was commanded. In the covenant of grace, it was furnished by Christ. In the former, man was obligated to be justified by works, and in the latter by faith. In the former, law is preached, and in the latter, gospel."[12] An important divergence between the covenants, therefore, is the setting forth of a Mediator and Testator, which was often articulated along the lines of an eternal pact: the covenant of redemption.

The covenant of redemption (*pactum salutis*) stands as a unique development and contribution from Reformed theology to the wider theological landscape.[13] During the era of high orthodoxy (c. 1640–1725), the doctrine of the *pactum*

---

8. *Westminster Confession* 7.2.

9. See, for example, Mark Jones, "The 'Old' Covenant," in *Drawn into Controversie: Reformed Theological Diversity and Debates within Seventeenth-Century British Puritanism*, ed. Michael A. G. Haykin and Mark Jones (Göttingen: Vandenhoeck & Ruprecht, 2011), 183–203; and Sebastian Rehnman, "Is the Narrative of Redemptive History Trichotomous or Dichotomous? A Problem for Federal Theology," *Nederlands archief voor kergeschiedenis* 80 (2000): 296–308.

10. *Westminster Confession* 7.3.

11. Johann Heidegger, *The Concise Marrow of Theology*, trans. Casey Carmichael (Grand Rapids, MI: Reformation Heritage Books, 2019), 11.20 (p. 80).

12. Heidegger, *Concise Marrow of Theology*, 11.21 (p. 81).

13. On the covenant of redemption, see Richard Muller, "Toward the *Pactum Salutis*: Locating the Origins of a Concept," *Mid-America Journal of Theology* 18 (2007):11–65; J. V. Fesko, *The Covenant of Redemption: Origins, Development, and Reception* (Göttingen: Vandenhoeck & Ruprecht, 2016); Woo, *Promise of the Trinity*; and Scott Swain,

salutis occupied a fixed theological locus. Since then, it has had its defenders (less so) and its detractors (more so) among Reformed dogmaticians.[14] At its heart, as B. Hoon Woo notes, the covenant of redemption "provides a pretemporal, inviolable foundation of the covenant of grace in Reformed federal theology."[15] Despite divergences among Reformed theologians over the particularities of the covenant—for example, is it a third covenant or not?—all agreed that the *pactum* speaks of "Christ as the surety (*sponsor*) of the covenant of grace for the elect."[16] It does so by specifying the eternal transaction between the persons of the Trinity as it touches upon the economic application of redemption (in its entirety). R. Scott Clark summarizes the overarching theology:

> In its most developed form, the *pactum salutis* or counsel of peace (*consilium pacis*) held that the Father and the Son entered into an agreement as part of which the Son agreed to become the guarantor (or *sponsor*) or surety of the redemption of the elect, requiring him to provide the perfect, substitutionary obedience and death owed by the elect, and the Father agreed to give a people to the Son and to accept his vicarious obedience.[17]

The covenant of redemption, for many (not all) Reformed thinkers, provides the eternal mooring for the manifestation of one, unified covenant of grace in history.

With this brief overview in hand, we can now turn to examine the relation between the election of Christ *ad extra* and Edwards's covenantal thought. First, I will unpack Edwards's understanding of the covenant of works, especially his position on the question of Adamic and angelic rewards. Edwards's position is similar to that of Thomas Goodwin, which evinces a stark difference between the first Adam and the second Adam, creation and grace. I then proceed to chart out the distinctions between the covenant of redemption and the covenant of grace in Edwards's theology. For Edwards, the covenant of grace most properly refers the direct relationship between Christ and the church, which Edwards identifies as the marriage covenant; in contradistinction, the covenant of redemption refers to the eternal pact between the Father and the Son, and only then by gracious extension to believers as Christ's mystical body. Contrary to many interpreters—and, in some sense, the baldness of some of Edwards's statements about the covenant of redemption—I will demonstrate that the covenant of grace is not subservient

---

"The Covenant of Redemption," in *Christian Dogmatics: Reformed Theology for the Church*, ed. Michael Allen and Scott Swain (Grand Rapids, MI: Baker Academic, 2016), 107–25.

14. For a representative defender, see Michael Horton, *The Christian Faith: A Systematic Theology for Pilgrims on the Way* (Grand Rapids, MI: Zondervan, 2011), 45; for a representative detractor, see Karl Barth, *CD* IV.1, 63–8.

15. Woo, *Promise of the Trinity*, 14.

16. R. Scott Clark, "Christ and Covenant: Federal Theology in Orthodoxy," in *A Companion to Reformed Orthodoxy*, ed. Herman J. Selderhuis (Boston: Brill, 2013), 428.

17. Clark, "Christ and Covenant," 407.

to the covenant of redemption in Edwards's theology. Instead, the covenant of grace, taken primarily as the marriage covenant between Christ and the church, functions as an extension of the election of Jesus Christ *ad extra* and itself logically precedes the covenant of redemption in the decrees. The implications of Edwards's covenantal thought will then be applied to further refine the order of the decrees as schematized at the end of the previous chapter.

The Covenant of Works

The covenant of works was, according to Edwards, the covenant made with Adam "stating the condition of eternal life."[18] As Edwards writes in an early sermon on the nature of justification in the covenant of works, "The goodness of God appeared in the first Covenant which proposed justification by works. It was an act of God's goodness and condescension towards man to enter into any Covenant at all with him. And that he would become engaged to give eternal life to him upon his perfect obedience."[19] He continues: "In the first covenant respect was had to the goodness or loveliness of works in fixing them as the condition of life."[20] For Edwards, the covenant of works was entirely conditioned upon Adam's consent and obedience. The order is irreversible: consent first, then obedience. "Adam's consent before he fell must be supposed, for his dissent would have been sin, which, to suppose before he sinned, is a contradiction."[21] In consenting to the covenant, Adam consented to do the "work of the covenant." Consent, properly speaking, is not a "work" for Edwards. "In the first covenant, after man had consented," Edwards writes, "he was yet to do that work which was the condition of the covenant; and therefore that is a covenant of works."[22] In this way, Adam's consent to the covenant of works stands in continuity with the manner in which believers exercise faith (consent) in the covenant of grace. Consent, neither in the covenant of works nor in the covenant of grace, should be conceived of as a work. "The consent of mankind is no more express to the covenant of grace under the gospel than Adam's consent before the fall."[23]

---

18. "Miscellanies," no. 30, *WJE* 13:217.
19. Sermon 153. Rom. 4:16 (1729) [L. 2r.], *WJEO* 45 (type modified).
20. Sermon 153. Rom. 4:16 (1729) [L. 5v.], *WJEO* 45.
21. "Miscellanies," no. 1215, *WJE* 23:147.
22. "Miscellanies," no. 299, *WJE* 13:386.
23. "Miscellanies," no. 1215, *WJE* 23:147. The same point is made by Edwards in an early "Miscellanies" entry: "In the second covenant, there is nothing to do but only to consent: there is no work to be done afterwards; the work is done by Christ. This therefore is not a covenant of works; for although faith be a good work, yet in such a case 'tis no more properly called a work than Adam's consenting to the first covenant was part of the work of that covenant." "Miscellanies," no. 299, *WJE* 13:386.

By consenting to the work of the covenant, Adam also accepted the promises contingent upon obedience and curses contingent upon disobedience. If Adam obeyed, then God promised blessing and immortal life; if Adam disobeyed, God promised death. The former corresponds to justification: "If Adam had finished his course of perfect obedience, he would have been justified; and certainly his justification would have implied something more than what is merely negative; he would have been approved of, as having fulfilled the righteousness of the law, and accordingly would have been adjudged to the reward of it."[24] The latter corresponds to both temporal and eternal death, the full threatening of which Edwards summarizes in his commentary on Gen. 2:17: "This expression denotes not only the certainty of death, but the extremity ... and so it properly extends to the second death, the death of the soul, for damnation is nothing but extreme death."[25] Rather importantly, Adam's consent also corresponds to his acceptance of his role as covenant head of the whole human race:

> And therefore [like the blessings for obedience], when Adam is threatened with a being deprived of all these on his disobedience, Adam must understand it in like manner as a calamity to come on the whole race; and consequently the implicit promise of life, or the confirmation and increase of the blessing, respects also the whole race. Hence the covenant must be made with Adam, not only for himself, but all his posterity.[26]

The threatening of death was total and eternal, both for Adam and his posterity.

Adam's consent, as mentioned already, had to be followed by Adam's obedience. The manner of this obedience had to be perfect because the qualification for justification is measured against God's holiness. The qualification arises "from the holiness of God ... from his delight in the beauty of holiness and his abhorrence of the deformity of sin."[27] Adam's righteousness required perfect, active, and sustained conformity to God's "nature and will," which are "absolutely necessary to God's acceptance of a man to eternal life."[28] Such an "absolute" necessity corresponds to all of God's covenant dealings with creatures. According to Edwards, God so ordered the "covenant of grace that it should agree with a mere covenant of works [in] that respect."[29] The qualifications for justification remain identical across the

---

24. "Justification by Faith Alone" (1738), *WJE* 19:150. On the specific nature of Adam's reward, see the next section.

25. "77. Genesis 2:17," *WJE* 15:72. Cf. *WJE* 24:134; "Miscellanies," no. 785, *WJE* 18: 467–72; *WJE* 3:258–9.

26. "398. Genesis 1:27–30," *WJE* 15:396. Cf. "Miscellanies," no. 844, *WJE* 20:145; See also Edwards's argument in *Original Sin* (*WJE* 3:245–61).

27. "'Controversies' Notebook: Justification," *WJE* 21:365.

28. "'Controversies' Notebook: Justification," *WJE* 21:354–5.

29. "'Controversies' Notebook: Justification," *WJE* 21:365. As will be evidenced shortly, the covenant of grace should be taken here as synonymous with the covenant of redemption in its historical execution.

various covenants (and for all time). As Carl Bogue correctly notes, "whatever the circumstance, the 'principle' and 'habit' of total obedience must remain constant."[30] On this point, Edwards registers how total obedience applied to more than the single command annexed to the forbidden fruit. The positive precept of the law was not the "main rule" given to Adam, but presupposed "the great rule of righteousness written in his heart."[31] The particularized law stood as an isolated test case for the entire moral law.

> It presupposes the sum of the law of nature to have been already established and known by Adam, viz. that man owed God a supreme and perfect respect, and to be regarded above all other things, and that he ought to be entirely subject to him, and to improve his faculties and God's good creatures, that were given him, only in a way agreeable to the will and designs of the Creator of all; and that if he refused, he deserved to be destroyed by his Creator.[32]

Of course, Adam disobeyed and abrogated (in a limited sense) the covenant of works. As a result, all human beings stand condemned in Adam, are taken into sin (i.e., Adam's sin is imputed), and "share in the abrogation of the covenant of works."[33] Once abrogated, the covenant of works can no longer serve as the "proper means to bring the fallen creature to the service of God" as it did "with man in the state of innocency."[34] Such abrogation, according to Edwards, only applies to justification by human obedience and works, not to the covenant itself. By breaking the covenant of works, Adam and his posterity forfeited the promises of the covenant of works and stand under the universal dominion of sin with all of its consequences. Nevertheless, "it would be a complete misrepresentation of Edwards," Carl Bogue rightly argues, "if one concluded … that the covenant of works ceased to be in effect after Adam's sin."[35] As Edwards writes early on in "Miscellanies" no. 35, "There have never been two covenants [the covenant of works and the covenant of grace], in strictness of speech, but only two ways constituted of performing of this covenant: the first constituting Adam the representative and federal head, and the second constituting Christ the federal head; the one a dead way, the other a living way and an everlasting one."[36] Although I shall unpack this

---

30. Bogue, *Jonathan Edwards and the Covenant of Grace*, 151.
31. "Miscellanies," no. 884, *WJE* 20:143.
32. "Miscellanies," no. 884, *WJE* 20:142.
33. Bogue, *Jonathan Edwards and the Covenant of Grace*, 152. On the consequences of Adam's disobedience and the imputation of Adam's sin, see Edwards's argument in *Original Sin* (*WJE* 3:380–412).
34. "244. Romans 6:14," *WJE* 15:198.
35. Bogue, *Jonathan Edwards and the Covenant of Grace*, 156.
36. "Miscellanies," no. 35, *WJE* 13:219. Or, as Edwards argues in "Miscellanies" no. 30: "But if we speak of the covenant God has made with man stating the condition of eternal life, God never made but one with man to wit, the covenant of works; which never yet was abrogated, but is a covenant stands in full force to all eternity without the

reality further in the discussions of the covenants of grace and redemption that follow, it is sufficient at this point to make clear that, in strictness of speech, the covenant of works is never truly abrogated; it stands as unfilled by Adam, wherein Adam (and all human creatures in Adam) becomes incapable of fulfilling it after the Fall. To be more precise, Adam possesses no moral desire to fulfill the covenant of works because of his forfeiture of the supernatural image of God at the Fall.[37]

Because the covenant of works remains in effect, two important results follow. First, God makes good on the covenant stipulations of punishment ensuant upon Adam's disobedience.[38] For Edwards, there are only two possibilities: either one stands under the judgment of the covenant of works or one does not. The latter reality, as will be explained further shortly, only takes shape around God's gracious initiative in Jesus Christ in the covenant of redemption. The second result of the continuity of the covenant of works is its function as a necessary condition for receiving eternal life, even though no natural person is able to fulfill it. Again, from the divine perspective, God never abrogates a covenant once made. As such, the "condition" of righteousness must be fulfilled by God's covenant partner. This is why, for Edwards, the covenant of grace pertains to the "righteousness of the law" already revealed in the covenant of works.[39] Notwithstanding this continuity, a key difference emerges: in the covenant of grace, the "righteousness of the law" is fulfilled for us instead of by us. In other words, "what Christ did, was to fulfill the covenant of works."[40] "The same law is a law of subjection to those that are under the covenant of works," Edwards states in "Miscellanies" no. 1030, "that is the law of liberty to those that are under the covenant of grace. Christ in this respect, as well as others, did not come to destroy the law but to fulfill, as he says in *Matthew 5:17*."[41] Reconciliation and eternal life depend on the fulfillment of the covenant of works by Jesus Christ.

But this is not the only difference ensuant upon Adam's covenant failure. According to Edwards, the covenant of grace offers a greater reward than the covenant of works. Thus, an important question emerges: what kind of life was promised to Adam had he fulfilled the covenant of works?

---

failing of one tittle. The covenant of grace is not another covenant made with man upon the abrogation of this, but a covenant made with Christ to fulfill it. And for this end came Christ into the world, to fulfill the law, or covenant of works, for all that receive him." *WJE* 13:217. Although Edwards specifies that the "covenant of grace" fulfills the covenant of works, this is not entirely accurate from the perspective of Edwards's overall thought in which he clarifies how the covenant of redemption, technically, fulfills the covenant of works. See my argument in the sections below.

37. See *WJE* 3:380–8.
38. Cf. "Miscellanies," no. 717, *WJE* 18:348.
39. "Miscellanies," no. 1030, *WJE* 20:368. Once again, covenant of grace needs to be understood in this context as the historical manifestation of the covenant of redemption.
40. "Justification by Faith" (1738), *WJE* 19:219.
41. "Miscellanies," no. 1030, *WJE* 20:368.

4. *Covenant, Christ, and the Decrees* 129

Adam's Reward and the Covenant of Works

Within Reformed theology, the issue of Adam's reward was not a hotly debated topic, even though diverse opinions existed.[42] On the one hand, Reformed divines such as Francis Turretin and Thomas Boston took eternal life to mean heavenly life;[43] on the other hand, theologians such as Thomas Goodwin disagreed, taking eternal life to mean a continuation of earthly life, although without sin.[44] The theological point is not arcane. How one answers this question betrays, in a deep sense, how one construes the relationship between nature and grace, creation and beatitude. This is no less true for Jonathan Edwards.

Edwards, like Goodwin, emphatically denied heaven would have been Adam's reward had he not sinned. "Heaven is not the promise of the FIRST COVENANT WITH ADAM," writes Edwards in a "Miscellanies" entry from late 1739, "but is only the promise of the covenant of grace, and the inheritance which is alone by the purchase of Christ."[45] According to Edwards, the reward of heavenly life is not to be conflated with eternal (earthly) life, even though, "doubtless if [Adam] had stood, he would have been advanced to a much greater happiness."[46] Edwards's argument

---

42. Herzer, "Adam's Rewards: Heaven or Earth?" 162–82.

43. See Turretin, *Inst.* 8.6.3; and Thomas Boston, *The Whole Works of the Late Thomas Boston of Ettrick*, ed. Rev. Samuel McMillan (Aberdeen: George and Robert King, St. Nicholas Street, 1850), 8:17.

44. See Goodwin, *Works* 7:49.

45. "Miscellanies," no. 809, *WJE* 18:512. This "Miscellanies" entry can be dated between August 1739 and January 1740 (See Chamberlain, "Editors Introduction," *WJE* 18:42–8). Edwards's theological thoughts in this entry appear to be a minor development from his position in the summer of 1731. That summer, Edwards preached a sermon entitled "East of Eden" based on Gen. 3:24, wherein he argued: "Man in the state wherein he was created was in a very happy condition in paradise, as we have already shown. But doubtless, if he had stood, he would have been advanced to a much greater happiness. 'Tis most reasonable to suppose that the blessedness he enjoyed even while in a state of trial shouldn't be so great as after he had done his work and come to receive his reward. He now enjoyed life, but if he had stood he would have been called to the tree of life to eat of that, and his life should not only have been ascertained to him forever, but he would have advanced to a higher degree of life. Eternal life was then, as it is now, the great promise of God. It was the promise of the covenant of works as well as the covenant of grace. And as eternal life don't now, so it did not then, only denote a continuance of man's life forever so that he should never die, but it denotes a most glorious and blessed life." *WJE* 17:337. The development, or so it seems to me, does not involve a wholesale change but a theological clarification of the nature of the "glorious and blessed life" that Adam would have enjoyed had he been confirmed in righteousness and granted to eat from the tree of life. In "East of Eden," Edwards vaguely construes such life as an immortal and "higher degree" of life in a similar though not exact manner to unfallen and confirmed angels (*WJE* 17:337–8). Edwards clarifies the issue by 1739 as he contrasts a higher degree of life with heavenly life.

46. "East of Eden" (1731), *WJE* 17:337.

in "Miscellanies" no. 809 reveals what lies at the heart of the difference: the promise of grace pertains to a higher order than the reward annexed to the covenant of works. In particular, the reward of heaven is fellowship with the Father as made possible by and in Jesus Christ, who enables human creatures to "partake of the very happiness of God himself."[47] It is worthwhile to consider Edwards's argument carefully.

Foremost, Edwards maintains that the promise of an "unseen world" was never annexed to the covenant of works. The performance of perfect obedience by Adam and the covenant promises guaranteed therein never entailed the expectation of heaven. Nothing else was implied in the covenant God made with Adam except that "man's life should be perpetuated and the happy circumstance of it on eating the fruit of the tree of life."[48] This yields an important implication: Adam's performance in the original state could never merit heavenly life. The natural order cannot, even in perfect obedience, merit heaven apart from God's gracious condescension in Jesus Christ.[49]

Exegetically, Edwards argues for the impropriety of heaven as a reward for Adam based on Paul's words in 1 Cor. 15:44-49, wherein a distinction is made between the natural and spiritual body, the image of the earthly and the image of the heavenly.[50] The earthly represents Adam and his position as humanity's representative; the spiritual represents Christ and his position as federal head. So Edwards reasons:

> If he had never fallen, we should have been conformed to him in these respects. We should have dwelt in natural earthy bodies, though in the most perfect state of such bodies, and without sin. So we should, by a parity of reason, have been conformed to him in the place of his habitation. The first Adam was earthy and of the earth in respect to the place of the habitation of his person, in the world he was of and belonged to, as well as in the habitation of his soul, or the body that [he] dwelt in; and in both we should have been conformed to him.[51]

---

47. "Miscellanies," no. 809, *WJE* 18:515.

48. "Miscellanies," no. 809, *WJE* 18:512.

49. In fact, Edwards also indicates in an early sermon that God is under no obligation to give a reward for any act of obedience. "Adams Obedience if he had Perfectly Obeyed the Law, and Performed the Condition of the Covenant of works would no Otherwise have deserved Eternal life than by vertue of Gods Covenant. If he had strictly Required Obedience to not only to the moral Law but many Positive and the Abstaining from the forbidden fruit but many other Positive precepts without any Promise of or hopes of Reward the pa it would have been most Reasonable that he should Obey and God Could no way be Accused of Injustice if he had bestowed no Reward[.]" Sermon 54. Luke 17:19 (1727) [L. 2r.], *WJEO* 42. Cf. "Glorious Grace" (Summer 1722), *WJE* 10:391–2.

50. Coincidentally, Thomas Goodwin's theological reasoning on Adam's earthly reward depends upon the same exegesis of 1 Cor. 15. See Goodwin, *Works* 7:44–74.

51. "Miscellanies," no. 809, *WJE* 18:513.

The inverse applies to those found in Christ. "They shall have spiritual heavenly bodies, and shall dwell in heaven."[52] Central to Edwards's distinction between the earthly realm and the heavenly realm is the dissolution of the world as occasioned by the Fall. On this point, Edwards concedes a form of the *felix culpa*: "One reason why heaven is bestowed is because this world is ruined by the fall, and is to be destroyed; therefore, Christ will come and take away his elect to another world, a better world than this is, or ever was."[53] The Fall becomes, on Edwards's line of reasoning, the occasion for a greater happiness of the saints.[54] As a corollary to this point, Edwards mentions how the occasion of the Fall and the advancement of human beings into heaven showcases Satan's defeat. "[Satan] is cast down from his high seat of glory in heaven," Edwards writes, "and men, that he envied and destroyed, are taken in his room; and what he does against [them] to destroy them is made an occasion of bringing it about."[55] Satan's destructive schemes prove, in the wisdom of God, to be an occasion for human advancement as opposed to eternal ruination. McClymond and McDermott note the irony well: "For Edwards, the devil undoes himself."[56] In an argument reminiscent of Anselm's in *Cur Deus Homo*, Edwards also speculates how human creatures "fill up the place in heaven that he was cast out from."[57] Overall, humanity's ascension into heaven follows as a result—and only as a result—of the descension and ascension of the Son of God. One of mankind had to belong to heaven already in order for the rest of mankind to inherit such a habitation. The hypostatic union, according to Edwards, enables human creatures to share in God's happiness in a manner impossible for the natural state of humanity.[58] "None ever ascended to heaven but mystical Christ, and there is no way of any others' ascending to heaven but by being members of him."[59] Jesus Christ, as the God-man, descended from the heavenly world in order to gain for human beings "the place of the residence of God's glory."[60] This, as Edwards repeatedly notes, is the "peculiar promise" of the covenant of grace.[61] But there is more. Another peculiarity follows from the occasion of the Fall and the Son's descension and ascension. Not only do saints receive the reward of heavenly

---

52. "Miscellanies," no. 809, *WJE* 18:513.

53. "Miscellanies," no. 809, *WJE* 18:514.

54. See Chapter 5 for a larger discussion of the decree of the Fall, especially the idea of "greater happiness."

55. "Miscellanies," no. 809, *WJE* 18:515.

56. Michael McClymond and Gerald McDermott, "The Angels in the Plan of Salvation," in *The Theology of Jonathan Edwards* (New York: Oxford University Press, 2012), 283.

57. "Miscellanies," no. 809, *WJE* 18:515. Cf. "Miscellanies," no. 616, *WJE* 18:147; Cf. Anselm, *Cur Deus Homo*, 1.16–18.

58. The term state is employed here to draw a distinction between ontology and operation/orientation.

59. "Miscellanies," no. 809, *WJE* 18:514.

60. "Miscellanies," no. 809, *WJE* 18:515.

61. "Miscellanies," no. 809, *WJE* 18:514–16.

life and greater happiness, but unfallen angelic creatures likewise receive the reward of "eternal life" at the hand of Christ. Edwards's arguments for the angelic reward, in fact, further reveal the priority Edwards places on the christological end of creation.

The Angelic Covenant and Reward

In a string of "Miscellanies" spanning nos 935–947, Edwards spent considerable mental energy contemplating the fall, purpose, and reward of angels. According to Edwards, God brought angels into existence to serve the Son of God, particularly in their ministrations to those human creatures beloved by the Son.[62] Given that angels are intelligent and voluntary beings, Edwards believes God transacts with them by way of covenant. One must not suppose "that God would make them, and not make known to 'em what they were made for, when he entered into covenant with them, and established the conditions of their eternal happiness."[63] The covenant God made with the angels was another covenant of works, which bears similarity to its Adamic counterpart: "The faithfulness of the angels in that special service must be the condition of their reward or wages; and if this was the great condition of their reward, then we may infer that it was their violating this law, and refusing and failing of this condition, that was that by which they fell."[64]

The condition, of course, was violated. Satan and a host of other angelic creatures refused to comply, violated the covenant, and fell from heaven. For those angels who did not follow in the way of Satan (i.e., the elect angels), a period of probation immediately began. In a similar manner to before the angelic fall, the obedience of the unfallen angels would lead either to confirmation (and reward) or banishment. Yet, unlike before, confirmation for the elect angels will yield an increase in holiness and happiness. "The fall of the angels laid a foundation for the greater holiness of the elect angels," Edwards speculates, "as it increased their knowledge of God and themselves, gave 'em the knowledge of good and evil, and was a means of their being emptied of themselves and brought low in humility."[65] Once again, the *felix culpa* looms large. Rebellion proves to be an occasion for increase. According to Edwards, the fall of Satan—and eventually human creatures—allowed for greater manifestations of God's perfections in Jesus Christ. The operative terms for revealing God's perfections are "empty" and "humility," which further highlight the total reliance of the creature upon the Creator for Edwards.

---

62. "Miscellanies," no. 939, *WJE* 20:198. So as to not unnecessarily repeat details from Chapter 3, I will concentrate here on elements related to the end for which angels were created and the manner of God's dealings with them. See Chapter 3 for an earlier discussion of angels.
63. "Miscellanies," no. 939, *WJE* 20:198.
64. "Miscellanies," no. 939, *WJE* 20:198.
65. "Miscellanies," no. 940, *WJE* 20:199.

The ultimate test of angelic abasement rests in their willingness to serve Christ in the work of redemption. "So that it can truly be said of the angels," Edwards muses, "that they have eternal life by sovereign grace through Christ in a way of self-emptiness, self-diffidence and humble dependence on him."[66] As Pauw notes, "For the angels, eschatological bliss and security in heaven required a humility willing to give up the superior status and dignity of heaven."[67] By giving up their superior status—a giving up Satan was not willing to do—elect angels mirror the Son's giving up. After "humbly" attending to Christ in his humiliation, the angels were confirmed and exalted by Christ in his exaltation. After the ascension, Christ himself confirmed the angels in their covenant obedience, thereby granting them rest until the full reception of their reward at the consummation of all things.[68]

Edwards's overall christological concentration is key to understanding the creation and end of the existence of angels.[69] In the language of the preceding chapter, angels derive the entirety of their existence from the splendor of Jesus Christ as the God-man, either in rejecting him (fallen angels) or accepting him (elect angels). For the latter, "Jesus Christ, God-[man], is he through whom and in whom they enjoy the blessedness of the reward of eternal [life], both as the head of influence through whom they have the Spirit, and also as in Christ, God-man, they behold God's glory and have the manifestations of his love."[70] The Holy Spirit, rather strikingly for Edwards, is given to confirmed angels, albeit in a different manner than to elect human creatures. The angels are not united to the Son by the Spirit; nevertheless, they "actually continually and eternally derive" the Spirit from Christ as their "head of life and divine influence."[71] Edwards appeals to typology and the tree of life to illumine his point. The tree of life in Eden is a type of Christ, who is the tree of life in paradise from which all inhabitants of heaven receive the fruit unto eternal life. Just as the tree of life in Eden would not have yielded its fruit until Adam was confirmed in obedience, the fruit of heaven was not ripe for consumption until the incarnation, sufferings, death, resurrection, and exaltation of the Son of God.[72] Edwards writes,

> But what is the fruit that grows on this heavenly tree, the second person of the Trinity, but the fruit of the Virgin Mary's womb, and that fruit of the earth spoken

---

66. "Miscellanies," no. 937, *WJE* 20:196.
67. Pauw, "Where Theologians Fear to Tread" : 45.
68. "Miscellanies," no. 947, *WJE* 20:203–4. As Edwards writes in "Miscellanies" no. 937, "They did not enjoy perfect rest till he ascended and confirmed them, so that the angels as well as men have rest in Christ, God-man." *WJE* 20:197.
69. Pauw is correct to assert, in a comparison to Bonhoeffer, that "For Edwards, angelic existence was not a heavenly sinecure but a 'participation in the being of Jesus.'" "Where Theologians Fear to Tread," 46.
70. "Miscellanies," no. 937, *WJE* 20:197.
71. "Miscellanies," no. 937, *WJE* 20:196.
72. "397. Genesis 2:9 and 3:22–24," *WJE* 15:394.

of, *Isaiah 4:2*, that son born, that child given, etc … . When this holy child had gone through all his labors and sufferings, and had fulfilled all righteousness, and was perfected … then he was seen of angels, and received up into glory, and then the fruit was gathered. Christ, as full ripe fruit, was gathered into the garner of God, into heaven, the country of angels, and so became angels' food. Then the angels fed upon the full ripe fruit of the tree of life, and received of the Father the reward of everlasting life … . Thus the fruit of this tree of life did not become the food of life to either men or angels till it was ripe.[73]

This certainly raises a question about the function of typology for Edwards before the Fall. Types function in history to lay a conceptual foundation for understanding the full significance of later events in God's ordained plan for that same history. According to Edwards, both "men and angels" receive heavenly and eternal life from the Son of God and do so only after his incarnation and redemptive work. Apart from Christ, no heavenly reward will or can be received. If this is true, what heavenly significance does the tree of life hold for Adam, especially if Adam was never promised heavenly life? The "ripe" fruit of Christ promised at the end of (redemptive) history, or so it seems for Edwards, is already typologically present in Eden.[74] Yet, Edwards is clear that the "ripe fruit" that would have been given to Adam was not heavenly. So, again, how can the christological fruit of redemption be typologically available to Adam in a covenant never intended to yield such fruit? The answer to this quandary lies, in part, in Edwards's understanding of the covenant of redemption. To this I now turn.

The Covenant of Redemption

Jonathan Edwards, like Reformed theologians before him, vigorously endorsed the covenant of redemption.[75] Unlike so many of those theologians, however, Edwards did not view the covenant of grace as a historical outworking of the covenant of

---

73. "397. Genesis 2:9 and 3:22-24," *WJE* 15:394.

74. Interestingly, Thomas Aquinas specifies that Adam was given knowledge of Christ in Eden (though not redemption). "Nothing prevents an effect from being revealed to one to whom the cause is not revealed. Hence, the mystery of the Incarnation could be revealed to the first man without his being fore-conscious of his fall. For not everyone who knows the effect knows the cause." *Summa Theologiae* III, q.1, a.3, ad 5.

75. For other overviews of Edwards on the covenant of redemption, see Yazawa, "Covenant of Redemption in the Theology of Jonathan Edwards"; Amy Plantinga Pauw, *The Supreme Harmony of All: The Trinitarian Theology of Jonathan Edwards* (Grand Rapids, MI: Wm. B. Eerdmans Publishing Co., 2002), 91–118; Fesko, *Covenant of Redemption*, 122–39; Bogue, *Jonathan Edwards and the Covenant of Grace*, 95–124; and Hoehner, "Covenantal Theology of Jonathan Edwards," 97–164.

redemption *tout court*.[76] Edwards made (and maintained) an important distinction between the covenant of grace and the covenant of redemption. Strictly speaking, Edwards took the covenant of grace as the marriage covenant between Christ and the church (i.e., his spouse), whereas the covenant of redemption refers to the eternal covenant between the Father and the Son. In terms of this latter covenant, Edwards baldly asserts that "all the eternal counsels and decrees of God, so far as God has been pleased to inform us concerning them, seem all subservient to that grand purpose of God, the redemption of the elect, and are all in some sort, appurtenances of the eternal covenant of redemption."[77] This raises several important questions. First, if all of the decrees are appurtenances of the covenant of redemption (literally arising from and subordinated to), then does Edwards eternally and absolutely prioritize redemption over creation? Second, if this is true, what exact relation does the "summative" decree pertaining to the Son's "spouse" bear to the covenant of redemption? Is it, in fact, subordinate?

In order to answer these questions, it is prudent to begin with "Miscellanies" no. 1062, wherein Edwards comes closest to a systematic presentation of the covenant of redemption. After establishing the ontological equality of the persons of the trinity, Edwards proceeds to unpack the fitness that exists between the immanent and economic works of God. In short, Edwards adheres to the theological maxim that trinitarian missions follow processions.[78] This leads to a necessary point when broaching the covenant of redemption: "This order [or] economy of the persons of the Trinity with respect to their actions *ad extra* is to be conceived of as prior to the covenant of redemption, as we must conceive of God's determination to glorify and communicate himself as prior to the method that his wisdom pitches upon as tending best to effect this."[79] It remains non-negotiable for Edwards that God's inclination toward glorification as communication stands prior to the ordination of the (wise) method of execution. Edwards continues: "Therefore this particular invention of wisdom, of God's glorifying and communicating himself by the redemption of a certain number of fallen inhabitants of this globe of earth, is a thing diverse from God's natural inclination to glorify and communicate himself in general, and superadded to it or subservient to it."[80]

Several matters are worthy of note. First, Edwards explicitly refers to the covenant of redemption as a "superaddition" to God's "inclination" to communication. As argued extensively in the previous chapter, God's glorifying and communicative

---

76. This is contrary to the refrain of, as far I am aware, every interpreter, even Robert Jenson: "The foundation of all history is the 'covenant of redemption,' the pure inner-triune concert which allows reality other than God." *America's Theologian*, 136. Given Jenson's overall argument about God's decrees and the election of Jesus Christ, it is peculiar that he made the same move.
77. "The Terms of Prayer" (May 1738), *WJE* 19:775–6.
78. Cf. "Miscellanies," no. 1062, *WJE* 20:431.
79. "Miscellanies," no. 1062, *WJE* 20 20:430.
80. "Miscellanies," no. 1062, *WJE* 20:432.

movement takes trinitarian form around the election of Jesus Christ *ad intra* and *ad extra*. By reason of parity—and this is key—the covenant of redemption should be taken as superaddition to Christ's election. Second, Edwards quickly moves from God's eternal and communicative "inclination" to the redemption of fallen creatures, skipping over creation itself. This could be taken in one of two directions: either (1) Edwards takes creation and fall as necessary means following God's communication and glorification in the wise form of redemption; or (2) Edwards's reasoning assumes a fixed order, wherein the covenant of redemption conceptually follows (in the decree) upon the supposition of the Fall within the created order and its given (and ultimate) end. Edwards's argument favors the latter:

> There is something else new besides a new, particular determination of a work to be done for God's glorifying and communicating himself: there is a particular covenant entered into about that very affair, settling something new concerning the part that some, at least, of the persons are to act in that affair.[81]

The first "new" determination is redemption; the second "new" component is the covenant of redemption. What is not "new," however, is the eternal order of the trinitarian processions and God's ultimate end of glorification through communication in Christ to an object of the Son's love.

On Edwards's reasoning, God could have also redeemed apart from the covenant of redemption. God's determination to redeem is a determination "not implied in the economy of the Trinity, as indeed the determination of no particular work is implied in the establishment."[82] In general, God is under no natural necessity to redeem; more particularly, if God determined to redeem, God is still under no natural necessity to redeem in a specific manner.[83] For Edwards, the only natural necessity is, again, that the order of the missions follows the order of the processions: "The establishment of the economy is a determination that, in whatever work is done, the persons shall act in such a subordination; but the determining what works shall be done is not implied in that establishment."[84] By subordination, Edwards means order of processions, that is, the Son is eternally begotten of the Father and not the reverse. God's works *ad extra* are not divided; neither are they confused.

With the qualification that the covenant of redemption is neither an internal nor external necessity for God, Edwards is free to speak of the wise determination

---

81. "Miscellanies," no. 1062, *WJE* 20:432–3.
82. "Miscellanies," no. 1062, *WJE* 20:438.
83. The coherence of Edwards's claim here will be further analyzed in the final chapter, at least insofar as Edwards's theological reasoning leads him into a position wherein God's determination to create in Christ (i.e., election *ad extra*) entails a commitment to redeem in Christ.
84. "Miscellanies," no. 1062, *WJE* 20:438.

4. Covenant, Christ, and the Decrees

and perfect consent among the triune persons to redeem.[85] The precise outworking of this divine determination to redeem is a "new" and "superadded" covenant between the Father and the Son. The transaction, as it were, occurred solely between the Father and the Son because the Son alone subjects himself to humiliation and assumes the additional role of soteriological mediator. To construe this as functionally binitarian—as "alarmingly reminiscent of classical social contract theory"—would be to miss the subtlety of Edwards's position.[86] The Holy Spirit, according to Edwards, is present as a consenting partner but not a covenanting partner because no reward was promised to the Spirit upon fulfillment of the covenant. "The covenant of redemption was the covenant in which God the Father made over an eternal reward to Christ mystical, and therefore was made only to Christ, the head of that body."[87] For Edwards, the Holy Spirit is the eternal reward and the foundation of the real union between Christ and his mystical body.[88] The concern of the Spirit in the covenant of redemption is not as a party covenanting, but as the "moving cause of the whole transaction" and as the "great good covenanted for."[89] The Holy Spirit is the "end of the covenant."[90] Edwards, in fact, elsewhere contends that the Holy Spirit is "represented as that wherein the communicative fullness of Christ consists."[91] Having received the Spirit without measure, Jesus Christ communicates the Spirit to believers without measure, and thereby communicates himself. The qualification of "without measure" becomes a key difference for human creatures before and after the Fall.[92]

In summary, Edwards does not really deviate in material substance from the Reformed tradition when unpacking the overall structure of the covenant of redemption: the Son entered into a free, covenant arrangement with the Father wherein the Son, out of love for sinners, subjected himself to obedience—obedience

---

85. Cf. "Miscellanies," no. 1062, *WJE* 20:442.

86. Pauw, *The Supreme Harmony of All*, 115.

87. "Miscellanies," no. 1062, *WJE* 20:442.

88. See Robert W. Caldwell III, *Communion in the Spirit: The Holy Spirit as the Bond of Union in the Theology of Jonathan Edwards* (Colorado Springs, CO: Paternoster, 2006), 60–7.

89. "Miscellanies," no. 1062, *WJE* 20:443.

90. "Miscellanies," no. 1062, *WJE* 20:443.

91. Sermon 819. Gal. 3:13-14 (April 1746), ed. Tom Koontz. Unpublished and edited MS provided to me by Kenneth Minkema, Director of the Jonathan Edwards Center at Yale University. Edwards's previously unpublished sermons on Galatians have since been published as follows: Kenneth P. Minkema, Adriaan C. Neele, and Allen M. Stanton, eds., *Sermons by Jonathan Edwards on the Epistle to the Galatians* (Eugene, OR: Cascade Books, 2019).

92. As Edwards articulates the matter in *Religious Affections*, "The inheritance that Christ has purchased for the elect, is the Spirit of God; not in any extraordinary gifts, but in his vital indwelling in the heart, exerting and communicating himself there, in his own proper, holy or divine nature: and this is the sum total of the inheritance that Christ purchased for the elect." *WJE* 2:236. See also Caldwell, *Communion in the Spirit*, 71–3.

even unto death—in order to merit eternal life for those same (elect) sinners.[93] Nevertheless, what remains to be addressed are the finer details of how the covenant of redemption relates to Edwards's larger covenantal theology, as well as the order of the decrees. It is in these finer details where Edwards's uniqueness within the Reformed tradition becomes apparent.

Relation to the Covenant of Works

Fundamentally, Edwards takes the covenant of redemption as the fulfillment by Christ of the covenant of works made with Adam. As mentioned previously, God never abrogates the covenant of works on the divine side. The Son, in the covenant of redemption, becomes the guarantor of its fulfillment. Like the covenant of works, God the Father makes the covenant of redemption with one party serving as federal head. The difference, however, pertains to the covenanting party. In the covenant of redemption, the covenant partner is the eternal Son of God, who actively fulfills all righteousness in the state of his humiliation.[94] After the Fall, God the Father never transacts with sinners directly, but only as they are found in mystical union with the covenant head, Jesus Christ. As Edwards writes in "Miscellanies" no. 1091:

> God the Father makes no covenant and enters into no treaty with fallen men distinctly, by themselves. He will transact with them, in such a friendly way, no other way than by and in Christ Jesus, as members and as it were parts of him. The friendliness and favor shall not be to them in their own name, but it shall all be to Christ, and all acts of friendship and favor shall be to him, and all promises made to him, and the fulfillment of promises also shall be to him, and to believers only as being in him, and under the covert of his name, and as being beheld and reckoned as parts of him.[95]

---

93. Edwards concisely summarizes his view in a sermon on Heb. 13:8 (April 1738): "The Covenant of Redemption or that Eternal Covenant that ~~is betw~~ there was between the F & the Son which X ~~was~~ undertook to stand as mediatour for fallen men & was appointed thereto of the Father in that Covenant all ~~things were agreed & [-] between X & his Father~~ & concerning Xs execution of his mediatorial office were agreed between X & his F & established by them & this Cov. & Et. agreemt is the highest [-] Rule that X acts by in his office." Sermon 470. I Cor. 13:1-10(b), 470. Heb. 13:8 (438) [L. 6v.], *WJEO* 53.

94. Christ's sinlessness (or perfect holiness) is, therefore, necessary for salvation: "That it should have been possible that Christ should sin, and so fail in the work of our redemption, does not consist with the eternal purpose and decree of God, revealed in the Scriptures, that he would provide salvation for fallen man in and by Jesus Christ, and that salvation should be offered to sinners through the preaching of the gospel." *WJE* 1:286.

95. "Miscellanies," no. 1091, *WJE* 20:477.

God the Father will only transact with sinners in Christ because Christ, functioning as the mediator between God and man in the covenant of redemption, fulfills the righteousness of the law required in the covenant of works. This is why Edwards is adamant that the only "condition" annexed to the covenant of redemption is Christ's perfect righteousness: "So Christ's righteousness is the alone proper condition of eternal life to the second Adam and his spiritual seed, according to the tenor of the new covenant made with him."[96]

For Edwards, the covenant of redemption functions, in part, as the christological reduplication of the covenant of works; or, more properly, the christological perfection of the covenant of works. Jesus Christ assumes the role of covenant head as the second Adam. The promises made to the Son of God in the covenant of redemption are, in this sense, applied eternally to the whole mystical body of Christ as they were "virtually" contained in the representative head. Edwards writes,

> And therefore the promises are in effect not only made to Christ, but his members. For they were made to the whole mystical Christ, and though the whole of Christ mystical was not yet in being, only the head of the body as yet is in being, and the members only existing in God's decree. And as in process of time the members, one after another, come into being, and then the same promises that were virtually made to 'em before are expressly revealed to 'em, and directed to 'em. Yet this does not make the promises, as revealed and directly made to the members, a different covenant from the promises that were before made to the head, that existed before 'em and stood for 'em.[97]

The promises Edwards has in mind pertain to Christ's reward for his obedience—active and passive—in the affair of redemption. As Edwards notes elsewhere, "In the promise of the Father's covenant with the Son are included eternal life, perseverance, justification; and not only so, but regeneration or conversion; the giving faith, and all things necessary in order to faith, [such] as the means of grace, God's Word and ordinances: for all these things are included in the success of what [Christ] has done and suffered and are parts of his reward."[98] In God's eternal covenant of redemption, these promises find purchase foremost in Christ as head and then, by extension, to the spouse "virtually" hidden in the Son as members not yet in being but "only existing in God's decree." Those hidden in the Son in the decree as his "spouse" have been, according to Edwards, given to the Son by the Father. But this raises a question central to this study: are those hidden in and given to the Son (i.e., the "object" of the Son's love) already considered in the decree as logically created and fallen or not? In the idiom of the lapsarian debate, are they *creatus et lapsus* or *creabilis et labilis*? Or, perhaps in more rarefied air,

---

96. "Miscellanies," no. 1091, *WJE* 20:478.
97. "Miscellanies," no. 1091, *WJE* 20:475.
98. "Miscellanies," no. 617, *WJE* 18:149.

homo creandus and *lapsurus*?⁹⁹ For, as Edwards notes, "God the Father did in that covenant of redemption, give such and such persons by name to Jesus Christ from his eternal love to them."¹⁰⁰ Yet, on the other hand, Edwards appears to claim in "Miscellanies" no. 1245 that the Father gave the Son his elect "spouse" by name prior to the covenant of redemption. It is best to quote Edwards at length:

> The election of all Christ's elect people is for the sake of Christ in two respects: first, it was for the sake of Christ that God determined there should be a created body for the special communications of his goodness. It was that his Son might have a spouse provided. But this is not a reason of the distinction in election, or why one was elected and not another, which was of God's sovereign pleasure. Secondly, it was [for] the sake of Christ that God set his love on the elect and determined to make 'em holy and happy. Because he had chosen 'em to be members of Christ's body, and gave 'em to Christ to that end, and so, looking upon them as now his, he loved them for his sake. It must needs be so, the nature of things shows. For as after the Father had given the particular persons to Christ, Christ himself thenceforward looked upon them and loved them as his own, and had their names written on his heart, so it must be that God the Father, after he had given them to Christ, must love 'em as his Son's on account of their belonging to him. And this is a quite different thing from his justifying them and accepting them as the objects of complacence and favor for the sake of Christ's righteousness. The former is loving them for Christ's infinite, divine, eternal dignity and glory. The latter is accepting them on the account of the righteousness Christ performed as their mediator in their stead, the price he paid after he was incarnate to purchase favor and rewards for them.¹⁰¹

This leads us to inquire further about Edwards's construal of the "spouse" in the decree. On this point hangs Edwards's idiosyncratic distinction between the covenant of grace as the marriage covenant and the covenant of grace as the covenant of redemption. The former pertains to a communication of Christ's "infinite, divine, eternal dignity and glory," while the latter pertains to Christ's mediatorial humiliation for the sake of redemption.

Relation to the Covenant of Grace

Commenting on Edwards's understanding of relationship between the covenants of grace and redemption, Carl Bogue notes that they are "inseparably united," even if the covenant of grace is primarily identified as the "manifestation of the eternal covenant of redemption."¹⁰² Paul Hoehner expresses a similar conclusion: "For

---

99. On this latter distinction, see the discussion of Petrus van Mastricht in Chapter 1.
100. "The Everlasting Love of God" (March 1736), *WJE* 19:480.
101. "Miscellanies," no. 1245, *WJE* 23:181.
102. Bogue, *Jonathan Edwards and the Covenant of Grace*, 115.

Edwards, the eternal Covenant of Redemption includes and is the foundation for the Covenant of Grace, which in one sense is merely the temporal progressive revelation and outworking of the Covenant of Redemption in history."[103] For most interpreters, then, the covenant of redemption provides the eternal footing for the covenant of grace in Edwards's theology. Bogue puts the matter bluntly: "Had there been no covenant of redemption, there would be no covenant of grace."[104]

That such a common, even if ultimately misleading, interpretation prevails when analyzing Edwards's statements about the covenant of grace is easy to understand. For example, in an April 1738 sermon on Heb. 13:8, Edwards preaches that "the Cov. of Grace ~~his~~ is not essentially diff. from the Cov. of Redemption it is ~~only that Cov. of Redem~~ but an expression of it tis only that Cov of Redemption partly Revealed to mankind for their encouragement faith & comforts."[105] Or, as Edwards writes in "Miscellanies" no. 1091, "There are promises of God the Father made to believers, and not only made to Christ for them, before the world was. And yet it will not follow there is a distinct Covenant of Grace between God the Father and believers, besides the eternal Covenant of Redemption that God made with is Son."[106]

Despite this fact, Edwards also conceptually distinguishes between the covenants of grace and redemption by appealing to the concept of marriage:

> There is doubtless a difference between the covenant that God makes with Christ and his people, considered as one, and the covenant of Christ and his people between themselves. The covenant that a father makes between a son and his wife, under one or considered as one, must be looked upon different from the marriage covenant or the covenant of the son and his wife between themselves.[107]

Edwards maintains this same point in "Miscellanies" no. 1091: "But the covenant between Christ himself and his church, by virtue of which she is united to him, is interested [in] him, and becomes his spouse and his mystical body, is an entirely distinct thing."[108] The central distinction between the covenants of grace and redemption, according to Edwards, rests on the parties contracting together in the covenant. In the covenant of redemption, it occurs between the Father and the Son (which includes all of the elect contained virtually in the Son). In the covenant of grace, the contracting parties are Christ and the church, which, according to Edwards, admits of no mediator. Edwards summarizes this well in "Miscellanies" no. 825:

---

103. Hoehner, "The Covenantal Theology of Jonathan Edwards," 191.
104. Bogue, *Jonathan Edwards and the Covenant of Grace*, 111.
105. Sermon 470. I Cor. 13:1-10(b), 470. Heb. 13:8 (438) [L. 7v.], *WJEO* 53.
106. "Miscellanies," no. 1091, *WJE* 20:475.
107. "Miscellanies," no. 667, *WJE* 18:148.
108. "Miscellanies," no. 1091, *WJE* 20:477.

> There is another covenant that is the marriage covenant between Christ and the soul, the covenant of union, or whereby the soul becomes united to Christ. This covenant before marriage is only an offer or invitation. "Behold, I stand at the door, and knock: if any man hear my voice, and open the door, I will come in to him, and will sup with him, and he with me" [Revelation 3:20]. In marriage, or in the soul's conversion, it becomes a proper covenant. This is what is called the covenant of grace, in distinction from the covenant of redemption.[109]

For Edwards, then, the covenant of grace primarily denotes the "marriage covenant" or "covenant of union" between Christ and his "spouse" directly.

We can now recognize the twofold sense in which Edwards employs the covenant of grace. In one sense, the covenant of grace refers to the salvific and mediatorial work of Christ as it historically enacts the eternal covenant of redemption. That is, the covenant of grace becomes a helpful way for Edwards to refer to temporal unfolding of God's eternal covenant to save sinners. This is how, as we saw earlier in the discussion of the covenant of works, Edwards is able to refer to the covenant of grace as a fulfillment of the covenant of works: "God never made but one with man to wit, the covenant of works … The covenant of grace is not another covenant made with man upon the abrogation of this, but a covenant made with Christ to fulfill it."[110] Recall, however, that strictly speaking only the covenant of redemption fulfills the covenant of works because the condition of both covenants is perfect righteousness. God the Father only transacts with believers by federal extension of the covenant with Christ, the only truly righteous one.[111] "The covenant that God the Father makes with believers," Edwards maintains, "is indeed the very same with the covenant of redemption made with Christ before the foundation of the

---

109. "Miscellanies," no. 825, *WJE* 18:537.

110. "Miscellanies," no. 30, *WJE* 13:217. Although this is an early "Miscellanies" entry, it should be taken as representative of Edwards's overall thought. On my reading, Edwards's covenantal scheme undergoes refinement over time, but never undergoes a wholesale change.

111. It is worthy of mentioning here that, from Edwards's perspective, justification is an immanent and eternal act in God, an act which leans heavily into Edwards's understanding of union with Christ. For Edwards, humans are justified in Christ, though not with Christ. This leads to a bold conclusion: just as there is only one person who fulfills the covenant of works, there is only one truly justified man: Jesus Christ. This should not be taken to mean that human beings are eternally justified themselves. Although this might be true virtually (in the decree and in the covenant of redemption), their actual justification occurs in time under the condition of faith, the condition of closing (uniting) with the Righteous One by the Holy Spirit. Once again, Edwards's similarity to Thomas Goodwin is striking. See Jones, *Why Heaven Kissed Earth*, 230–8; and Robert McKelvey, "Eternal Justification," in *Drawn into Controversie: Reformed Theological Diversity and Debates within Seventeenth-Century British Puritanism*, ed. Michael A. G. Haykin and Mark Jones (Göttingen: Vandenhoeck & Ruprecht, 2011), 223–62.

world, or at least is entirely included in it."[112] The proper referent for covenant between the Father and Son is the covenant of redemption; however, if one refers to the covenant between the Father and Son as extended to the "spouse" in history as it fulfills the covenant of works, it is not improperly called the covenant of grace. The covenant of redemption as revealed in history benefits fallen creatures, and, just so, demarcates the history of grace.

In another sense, however, the covenant of grace refers to the more direct interaction between Christ and the church, and it should not be taken to mean the covenant of redemption/covenant of works. This other sense is what Edwards refers to as the "marriage covenant" or "covenant of union." While the first sense of the covenant of grace qua covenant of redemption admits of no proper conditions for believers because Christ alone fulfills all the conditions of righteousness, the second sense of the covenant of grace qua marriage covenant admits of one condition: the consent of faith, or a closing with Christ. As Edwards writes, "But in the covenant between Christ and his members or spouse, she is by herself a party in the covenant, and that in this party by which alone, according to the tenor of the covenant, she is interested in the benefit of union and propriety in Christ (which is the benefit directly conveyed in this covenant) is her believing in Christ, or her soul's active union with him."[113] No mediator is needed, argues Edwards, "between Christ and sinners to bring about a marriage union between Christ and their souls."[114] On this point, Edwards understands the term mediator most basically as "one who interposes as another person between parties at variance or difference, to reconcile them or unite them."[115] Because the covenant of grace qua marriage covenant unfolds directly between Christ and believer as a single entity, no mediator is technically required. "That which Christ conveys and confirms to believers, is his own proper possession. That eternal inheritance which he gives, is properly his own. It is his own independently and absolutely, so that 'tis his to dispose of."[116] In other words, the grace and love which Christ bestows upon his "spouse" flows from his own communicative inclination.

Seen from the whole of Edwards's theology, it becomes clear that Edwards prefers to use mediator as a soteriological concept annexed to the covenant of redemption. The Father transacts with believers indirectly through the mediatorial

---

112. "Miscellanies," no. 1091, *WJE* 20:477–8.

113. "Miscellanies," no. 1091, *WJE* 20:478–9.

114. "Miscellanies," no. 1091, *WJE* 20:478.

115. "Jesus Christ is the Great Mediator and Head of Union in Whom All Elect Creatures in Heaven and Earth Are United to God and One Another," in *The Blessing of God: Previously Unpublished Sermons of Jonathan Edwards*, ed. Michael D. McMullen (Nashville, TN: Broadman & Holman, 2003), 314.

116. Sermon 534. Heb. 9:15-16 (January 4, 1740), ed. R. Craig Woods. Unpublished and edited MS provided to me by Kenneth Minkema, Director of the Jonathan Edwards Center at Yale University. The transcription (edited) is published as follows: P534, *WJEO* 55.

office of the Son. Nevertheless, it is not theologically improper to apply the term mediator in non-soteriological ways for Edwards, namely Christ as the protological and eschatological mediator. Given the arguments from the previous chapter, the human nature of Christ assumed in the hypostatic union becomes the mediatorial "medium" for communication of the Son's fullness and enabler of the beatific vision. Thus, "communicative medium" and "mediator" can function synonymously in Edwards's theology when discussing the election of Jesus Christ *ad extra* without reference to the covenant of redemption. Within the framework of the covenant of redemption, though, Christ serves as soteriological mediator between the Father and sinners.

With the distinction between the marriage covenant and the covenant of redemption now in place, we must ask: which covenant has conceptual priority? Does the covenant of grace qua marriage covenant remain, to use Bogue's logic, "eternal in a [logically] derivative rather than an absolute sense"?[117] At first glance, two factors appear to corroborate such an interpretation. First, there is Edwards's failure to refer to the "marriage covenant" as eternal. Edwards reserves the adjective eternal specifically for the covenant of redemption, which seems to validate the derivative nature of the covenant of grace taken as the "marriage covenant." Apart from this consideration, the greater corroboration seems to be Edwards's constant refrain that "all decrees may one way or other be referred to the covenant of redemption."[118] Take, as another example, Edwards's running comments on Eph. 3:9 in the *Blank Bible*:

> This is here mentioned from respect to the reason why God "created all things by Jesus," viz. because the creation of all things was with an aim and subordination to that great work of Christ as mediator, viz. the work of redemption. It was not only God's design in all the works of providence from the beginning of the world, as in the foregoing words, but also in the creation of the world itself. And therefore God "created all things by Jesus Christ." Christ was to be the great means of God's glory, and that by which chiefly he was to be so was the work of redemption, which he was to work out, and to which all other works, and even the creation of the world itself, were subordinate, which the following verse confirms. It was meet therefore that, seeing the principal work was to be wrought by Christ, that other works subordinate thereto should be so likewise. And therefore both the beginning of the world and the end of the world are by Christ, for both are subordinate to the great purposes of the work of redemption. He is therefore both the creator and the judge of the world. He is, as he says in the Revelation, the Alpha and the Omega [Rev. 1:8].[119]

---

117. Bogue, *Jonathan Edwards and the Covenant of Grace*, 134.
118. "Approaching the End of God's Grand Design" (December 1744), *WJE* 25:119.
119. *WJE* 24:1100–1.

Or, even more starkly, there are Edwards's musings in "Miscellanies" no. 833: "Indeed, all the works of God that were before the fall of men were parts of the work of preparation for the work of redemption."[120]

Such conceptual priority, if true, poses potential difficulties within Edwards's thought as we have been tracing it. Framed as question, the difficulty would be thus: Is God's conceptual priority of thought redemption in Christ or creation in Christ? The question, it should be stated, does not pertain to the de facto realities of history. These realities unfold in keeping with God's sole determination to save fallen creatures in the work of redemption. Human creatures know no other history than redemptive history. Nevertheless, if Edwards maintains a conceptual priority of redemption in the decree over everything else, then not only is he supralapsarian, but he is rigorously so. This, I take, is the heart of Stephen Holmes's critique: "Edwards must be described as uncompromisingly supralapsarian after all. Regardless of the place of the decree of reprobation, God's first thought emphatically is that he will redeem, not that he will create."[121] That is, the question of the place of reprobation (or the object)—which I will address directly in the next chapter—becomes somewhat irrelevant if redemption has conceptual priority over everything else in the decree.

Yet, as Oliver Crisp notes, Holmes seems to equivocate on the covenant of redemption and the work of redemption, such that Holmes misconstrues redemption itself as the ultimate end of creation in Edwards's theology.[122] Holmes, as a result, "misunderstands the logical sequence of the decrees" because God's self-glorification actually comes first in the decree.[123] Despite the interpretive correction, Crisp still registers a critique along similar lines. Edwards upholds, according to Crisp, a logical priority of God's self-glorification primarily through redemption, which, in God's decree, awkwardly construes election as a derivative means to redemption. This is, so Crisp argues, problematic. How can God logically redeem apart from a sinful object (i.e., an object in need of redemption), whether that object is conceived of as possible or actual? When fleshed out, "election is dependent upon the way in which God construes the covenant of redemption."[124] On Crisp's interpretation, Edwards's argument is

---

120. "Miscellanies," no. 833, *WJE* 20:43.
121. Holmes, *God of Grace and God of Glory*, 131.
122. Crisp, *Jonathan Edwards and the Metaphysics of Sin*, 17. A point of order: Crisp uses the language of "chief" end to specify what I refer to as "ultimate" end in this sentence. We mean the same thing: the "original ultimate end" that stands above all other ends in creation, as expressed by Edwards in his "Explanation of Terms" in *End of Creation* (*WJE* 8:413).
123. Crisp, *Jonathan Edwards and the Metaphysics of Sin*, 22. To be fair, Holmes actually argues that Edwards takes God's desire to glorify and communicate himself as basic (see Holmes, *God of Grace and Glory*, 134), even though the manner in which Holmes works this out does not invalidate Crisp's overall critique.
124. Crisp, *Jonathan Edwards and the Metaphysics of Sin*, 20.

ultimately (and fatally) flawed because, in the end, Edwards maintains God as decreeing redemption both apart from sin (supralapsarian), as well as with sin as a necessary requirement (infralapsarian).[125] Edwards wants to have his cake and eat it too, or so it seems.

But, similar to Crisp's qualm with Holmes, I take issue with Crisp's interpretation of the conceptual order of the decrees. Edwards does not stipulate that God decrees his self-glorification through redemption first and foremost. Rather, God decrees his self-glorification as the election of Jesus Christ *ad extra*, which, in the logical order, does not yet specify redemption or an object in need of redemption. The work of redemption—which follows as a consequence of the covenant of redemption—is a *superadded means* to God's ultimate end in Christ. Edwards's assertion that "all the eternal counsels and decrees of God ... are all in some sort, appurtenances of the eternal covenant of redemption" must be read through his larger theological commitment to God's elected mode of self-glorification (i.e., God's ultimate end). As was argued in the previous chapter, Edwards construes God's self-glorification *ad extra* as christological communication. God's ultimate end *ad extra* is to communicate the perfections of the Son. "All the works and dispensations of G[od] in all parts of the Creation & in all ages of it are such as shew forth the Infinite value G[od] has for & delight he has in his son."[126] The *primary* means to actualize such communication is elective, hypostatic union of the Son with a human nature. Redemption, therefore, is logically subservient as a means to the end of election, not vice versa. The sum of God's purposes in creation and "the whole series of events" was to "procure a spouse" for the Son.[127] God's first thought is election in the Son, not redemption. This entails an important corollary: the marriage covenant cannot exist as an appurtenance of the eternal covenant of redemption either. Conceptually, the covenant of redemption is eternally derivative from the virtual union already presupposed between the Son and his spouse. In the covenant of redemption, the "spouse" is already put in the decree, as it were.

If the covenant of grace qua marriage covenant should not be conceptually collapsed (in the decree) into the covenant of redemption but stands as prior, what does this mean for logical quality of the "spouse" in the decree (i.e., *lapsus* or *labilis*)? To fully attend to this question, the contours of the "marriage covenant" need to be further traced out, especially in relation to its eternality or lack thereof. After doing so, I will synthesize (in broad strokes) Edwards's unsystematic covenantal schema as it pertains to the election of Jesus Christ *ad extra* and its

---

125. Crisp, *Jonathan Edwards and the Metaphysics of Sin*, 22.

126. Sermon 699. Heb. 2:7-8 (March 1743) [Col. 2].

127. "Miscellanies," no. 1245, *WJE* 23:178. So, Paul Ramsey's conclusion, in his editorial commentary on the *End of Creation*, is mistaken: "The work of redemption was in the counsels of God before time was, and that was the original and independent end for which God created the world." *WJE* 8:532, n. 1.

import for further refinement of the intended end, order, and objects of God's decrees in Edwards's thought.

The Marriage Covenant and the Election of Jesus Christ

In Part I of the *End of Creation*—a part ostensibly devoted to the use of pure reason apart from biblical exegesis—Edwards argues for the intimate connection between Christ and the church: "Thus the church of Christ (toward whom and in whom are the emanations of his glory and communications of his fullness) is called the fullness of Christ: as though he were not in his complete state without her."[128] Again, the procurement of a "spouse" for the Son of God stands as the "sum of [God's] purposes with respect to the creatures."[129] The shorthand way of expressing this communicative purpose is the election of Jesus Christ *ad extra*, with the election of Jesus Christ *ad extra* framing Edwards's thoughts on the covenant of grace as the marriage covenant. In this sense, the enactment of the marriage covenant in history finds its eternal mooring not in the covenant of redemption *tout court*, but in the election of Jesus Christ and "the designs of Christ's love to the children of men" directly.[130] For this reason, the focus of the marriage covenant is Christ himself, "full possession and enjoyment of him."[131] Through possession of Christ, the spouse's "enjoyment of Christ shall be like the Son's intimate enjoyment of the Father."[132] This is God's primary design.

But what, we may ask, of Edwards's lack of reference to the marriage covenant as eternal? The lack of reference can be explained by attending to the precise manner in which Edwards employs the notion of a covenant. Strictly speaking, a covenant cannot exist where a covenant partner does not exist in actuality to submit to the terms of the covenant. In the covenant of redemption, the covenant partner is the Son of God in the Son's eternal and actual existence as the Son of the Father; in the covenant of works, it is Adam in his historical and actual existence; and, in the marriage covenant, the covenant partner is the human being in their *historical* existence. For Edwards, the marriage covenant is not properly called a "covenant till it is consented to."[133] Edwards means here the consent of faith, wherein the soul closes with Christ.[134] Before the historical existence of creatures in their actual being, the "marriage covenant" only exists virtually as annexed to the election of Jesus Christ. The spouse of Christ (i.e., the elect) exists virtually in the decree, although they have yet to come into being temporally. It makes no

---

128. *WJE* 8:439–40.
129. "Miscellanies," no. 1245, *WJE* 23:178.
130. *WJE* 24:1101.
131. "Miscellanies," no. 741, *WJE* 18:367.
132. "Miscellanies," no. 741, *WJE* 18:367.
133. "Miscellanies," no. 617, *WJE* 18:150.
134. Cf. "Miscellanies," no. 1091, *WJE* 20:479.

sense, technically speaking, to refer to the "marriage covenant" as eternal, just as it makes no sense to refer to the covenant of works as eternal. The foundation of each may exist in the decree, but the creature can only consent to such covenants as actual beings in time. Nevertheless, the material promises that are given in the marriage covenant are eternal. In other words, the eternal substance is the election of Jesus Christ *ad extra*, while the historical form is the "marriage covenant." For Edwards, the focal point is communicative communion through union with the Son of God.

> And indeed we may say that the sum of all that Christ promises in his covenant with his people, is that he will give himself to them. In marriage the persons covenanting, giving themselves to each other, do give what they have to each; the union which they mutually consent to infers [and] confers communion.[135]

By acknowledging the marriage covenant's eternal mooring in the election of Jesus Christ, the difficulty involving Edwards's lack of qualification of the marriage covenant as eternal fades away. It simply isn't eternal, only the election of Jesus Christ and the attendant promises to his spouse are.

So where does this leave us? What does a synthesis of Edwards's commitment to the election of Jesus Christ and his covenantal thought look like? What may we say about the order and, rather significantly, the objects in the decree?

A Covenantal Synthesis

At the headwater of Edwards's covenantal theology lies the election of Jesus Christ *ad extra*. As argued in the previous chapter, all that God decrees is decreed for the sake of the Son of God. Materially, God's external decree mirrors the election of Jesus Christ *ad intra* such that the operative term for election is communication. The material center of elective communication is always the Son of God. Formally, Edwards believes the decree for communicating the Son's fullness *ad extra* takes shape around the procurement of a "spouse" (or mystical body) as that spouse is united to the Son by the Holy Spirit. God's "special aim" was to unite individual and intelligent creatures together as one entity in order to render perceptive the Son's "unspeakable and transcendent goodness and grace."[136] In unpacking the strictures of this special aim for God, Edwards narrows on the hypostatic union as the manner of the Son's enabling the broader communicative union with creatures in time. By extension, the election of Jesus Christ *ad extra* enfolds (virtually) those human creatures not yet created whom the Holy Spirit will mystically unite in a union of hearts to the God-man. This union of hearts (or the union of the soul with Christ) in creaturely time assumes the form of

---

135. "Miscellanies," no. 617, *WJE* 18:149.
136. "Miscellanies," no. 1245, *WJE* 23:179.

a covenant—the "marriage covenant" or "covenant of union." The continuity of which rests in the material promise: the sum of the promises given in the "marriage covenant" is the splendor of Jesus Christ himself. In this very limited sense, all other covenants subordinate themselves to the "marriage covenant." Building upon the summary from the end of the previous chapter on the order of the decrees, we may now include the logical "object" in our schematization. The objects specified here are, of course, not Edwards's own terminology, but rather terminology borrowed from the historical lapsarian discussion in Chapter 1 in order to bring analytic clarity to Edwards's reasoning. The order and objects are as follows:

1. The election of Jesus Christ *ad extra*, which entails
   1a. The decree of the glorification of divine perfections (excellency) *ad extra* in and through the Son.
   1b. The decree to create this world.
   1c. The decree to communicate the glory of the divine perfections *ad extra* to a particular object of the Son's love, namely a "spouse" in strict union with the Son. The object is, at this point, *creabilis*.

2. The decree of the incarnation, which entails
   2a. The hypostatic union of the Son with a human nature. The particular human nature of Christ is, in this moment, *creandus*; the Son is, by extension, *incarnandus*.
   2b. The elevation of human creatures as the chosen "spouse" of the Son. This spouse also exists as *creandus* in the decree.

With such an understanding in place, we can proceed to locate the covenant of redemption. The covenant of redemption, as Edwards argues, needs to be distinguished from God's natural inclination to glorify and communicate himself. Again, God's "natural" movement to glorification and communication is entirely conditioned by the election of Jesus Christ. As we saw, the language Edwards employs to speak of the distinction between God's natural communication and the covenant of redemption is superaddition. For Edwards, superaddition distinguishes a decreed end from the means of execution. The covenant between the Father and the Son (in the Spirit) is a contrivance and intervention of wisdom for executing the decree of redemption. As is evident in "Miscellanies" no. 1062, the intervention of wisdom supposes objects in need of redemption: "But we must conceive of the determination that a redemption shall be allowed for fallen men as preceding the covenant or agreement of the persons of the Trinity relating to the particular manner and means of it."[137] For Edwards, the decree for redemption necessarily precedes the covenant of redemption, with the covenant

---

137. "Miscellanies," no. 1062, *WJE* 20:433.

of redemption thereafter establishing the most fitting means for executing the decree. So, logically, "all of the decrees" cannot "belong to" the covenant of redemption. What Edwards intends is that the means for executing God's decrees are further specified by the covenant of redemption. The covenant of redemption logically follows both God's decreed end for creation and the decree of redemption. As such, distinctions need to be made and maintained between (1) the decree of redemption; (2) the covenant of redemption; and (3) the historical work of redemption.

The preceding discussion has an important implication: the superadded covenant put in place for executing the decree of redemption cannot unmoor itself from God's prior (christological) end in creation in such a manner as to foster another ultimate end. God's end in creation is but one, and therefore independent of all conditions. In the covenant of redemption, therefore, the Son's transaction with the Father (in the Spirit) explains the appended end-to-which of the election of Jesus Christ *ad extra* (i.e., redemption), and does so without altering the end-for-the-sake-of-which (i.e., the splendor of the person of Jesus Christ, God-man).[138] Seen from this perspective, redemption—which includes the decree of redemption and the covenant of redemption—might be thought of utilizing Edwards's own terms from the *End of Creation*, as a hypothetical or consequential end. Such an end, although agreeable in itself to an agent, "arises on the supposition or condition of such and such circumstances or on the happening of a particular case."[139] What such a supposition or condition fully means for Edwards from within the framework of God's decree will have to wait for the next chapter; it is sufficient for now to recognize it as the Fall.

Given the condition of fallen creatures (i.e., the condition of sin), the marriage covenant cannot be enacted in creaturely time apart from consideration of the covenant of redemption. In the de facto realities of history, union with Christ and redemption intertwine each other, so much so that the promises and conditions of each covenant appear harmonious. "Hence it appears that many of the things promised in both these covenants are the same," writes Edwards, "but in some things different. So that those things that are promises in one of these covenants, are conditions in another. Thus regeneration and closing with Christ, is one of the promises of the covenant of the Father with Christ, but is the condition in the covenant of Christ with his people."[140]

To reiterate: the marriage covenant and the covenant of redemption are, from the perspective of creaturely history, inseparably bound. God offers no

---

138. The terminology introduced here is not Edwards's own, but a helpful tool for clarifying what Edwards intends. I will bring the full meaning of these distinctions to bear on Edwards's theology as I construct a corrective picture of his lapsarianism in the final chapter.

139. *WJE* 8:410. For further deployment of these distinctions, see Chapter 5.

140. "Miscellanies," no. 617, *WJE* 18:149.

covenant of marriage apart from the work—incarnation, life, death, resurrection, and ascension—of the Redeemer. In other words, the history surrounding and culminating in Jesus Christ is the only history available to creatures: God's history with and for creatures in Jesus Christ as demarcated by the eternal covenant of redemption. Thus, Edwards's conclusion on the unified design of history: "'Tis all one design carried on, one affair managed in all God's dispensations, towards all intelligent beings, viz. the glorifying and communicating himself in and through his Son Jesus Christ as God-man and by the work of redemption of fallen man."[141] The conjunction employed by Edwards is significant. Conceptually, Edwards thinks the "principal means by which God glorifies his Son in the world that is created is by providing him a spouse, to be presented [to] him in perfect union, in perfect purity, beauty and glory."[142] But Edwards also argues that, within this principal means, the "spouse" would not only be mankind per se, but mankind as fallen.

> The way in which the eternal Son of God is glorified in the creation is by communicating himself to the creatures, not by receiving anything from the creatures ... And because it was a spouse to communicate his goodness to that he desired, therefore that she might be one fit not to give but receive good, one was pitched upon that was remarkably empty and poor in herself, not of the highest order of creatures, but mankind—and not man in his first and best estate, but in a fallen, miserable, helpless state: a state wherein his emptiness and need of goodness did more remarkably appear. And because it was his design to communicate his goodness, therefore that he might do it the more fully, those were chosen that were unworthy; because the more unworthy the more is free goodness exercised, and so Christ's end the more answered in his seeking a spouse to communicate of his goodness to. Hence, not the angels but the miserable race, [the] ruined, sinful race of mankind, was pitched upon. And because the design was that Christ should communicate goodness, therefore such an one was chosen that needed that Christ should suffer, and it was the will of Christ to suffer because suffering is the greatest expression of goodness and manifestation of kindness. The great design was that Christ in this way should procure or obtain this his spouse, bring her to come to him, present her to himself and make her perfectly beautiful, perfectly and unspeakably happy.[143]

Incorporating Edwards's aforementioned reasoning here into our schematization on the order and objects of the decrees, a modified picture emerges:

---

141. "Miscellanies," no. 744, *WJE* 18:388.
142. *WJE* 24:117.
143. *WJE* 24:117–18.

1. The election of Jesus Christ *ad extra*, which entails
   1a. The decree of the glorification of divine perfections *ad extra* in and through the Son.
   1b. The decree to create this world.
   1c. The decree to communicate the glory of the divine perfections *ad extra* to a particular object of the Son's love, namely a "spouse" in strict union with the Son. The object is, at this point, *creabilis et labilis*.

2. The decree of the incarnation, which entails
   2a. The hypostatic union of the Son with a human nature. The particular human nature of Christ, in this moment, is *creandus*; the Son is, by extension, *incarnandus*.
   2b. The elevation of human creatures as the chosen "spouse" of the Son. This spouse now exists as *creandus et lapsurus* in the decree.

3. The decree of the Fall.
4. The decree to redeem, which entails
   4a. The decree for the fit means as specified by the covenant of redemption. At this juncture, the objects are *creatus et lapsus*.

Left for consideration is the place of the covenant of works. Recall, God did not promise, according to Edwards, a heavenly reward to Adam if he fulfilled all righteousness. Heaven rests solely on the "peculiar promise" of the marriage covenant and, by extension, the covenant of redemption. It might seem, then, that the positive value of the covenant of works corresponds to its ability to reveal creaturely insufficiency and dependence upon Jesus Christ and, by extension, to magnify the fuller reality of God's perfections—holiness, grace, justice, and so on—in redemption, heaven, and even hell. Edwards seems to suggest such within his speculations on angels in "Miscellanies" no. 937:

> As the perfections of God are manifested to all creatures, both men and angels, by the fruits of those perfections, or God's works—the wisdom of God appears by his wise works, and his power by his powerful works, his holiness and justice by his holy and just acts, and his grace and love by the acts and works of grace and love—so the glorious angels have the greatest manifestations of the glory of God by what they see in the work of men's redemption, and especially in the death and sufferings of Christ.[144]

Given this and other similar statements, Robert Jenson concludes, "Within Edwards's thought as a whole, this covenant [of works] was made to be broken."[145]

---

144. "Miscellanies," no. 937, *WJE* 20:197.
145. Jenson, *America's Theologian*, 136.

If taken apart from Edwards's strong christological commitments, Jenson's conclusion seems to be on target. However, such a conclusion equivocates on a crucial point: an anthropological "made to be broken" is conflated with the christological made to be fulfilled. This does not alleviate the theological difficulties, but it does seem more faithful to Edwards's thought. In Edwards's reasoning, the manner in which the covenant of works relates to the covenant of redemption involves an intensified christological disclosure of God's perfections as beheld in the Son. For Edwards, Christ's obedience especially reveals the contours of God's perfections and invites creatures into a greater apprehension of their "excellencies" as manifest concretely in the God-man.[146] This need not be taken to mean, as Jenson suggests, that the covenant of works was made to be broken, even if it would be broken by human creatures. It leads to a different conclusion: the covenant of works was preparatory for the fuller revelation of the Son of God in the flesh. In the idiom of typology, the Adamic covenant of works—like the tree of life—serves as a type (or shadow) of Christ's obedience, which is part and parcel of a greater symphonic movement leading to Christ being the creature's (both angelic and human) all in all—"all its strength, all its beauty, all its life, its fruits, its honor and its blessedness."[147] The covenant of works never possessed an integrity apart from Christ. It was not made for Adam to break but for Jesus Christ to fulfill. Seen in light of its Adamic abrogation though, the covenant of redemption specifies not only Christ's life of righteousness (active obedience) but his "superadded" work in absorbing the consequences—death, punishment, and estrangement—following disobedience (passive obedience). The Son humbles himself in an obedience, even an obedience unto death.

Taking the covenant of works into account, a fuller decretal picture can be presented as follows:

1. The election of Jesus Christ *ad extra*, which entails
   1a. The decree of the glorification of divine perfections *ad extra* in and through the Son.
   1b. The decree to create this world.
   1c. The decree to communicate the glory of the divine perfections *ad extra* to a particular object of the Son's love, namely a "spouse" in strict union with the Son. The object is, at this point, *creabilis et labilis*.

2. The decree of the incarnation, which entails
   2a. The hypostatic union of the Son with a human nature. The particular human nature of Christ, in this moment, is *creandus*; the Son is, by extension, *incarnandus*.

---

146. This is poignantly seen in Edwards's famous sermon, "The Excellency of Christ" (*WJE* 19:560–94).

147. "Miscellanies," no. 936, *WJE* 20:193. Cf. "Miscellanies," no. 702, *WJE* 18:309 (see *Corol.* 11).

 2b. The elevation of human creatures as the chosen "spouse" of the Son. This spouse now exists as *creandus et lapsurus* in the decree.

3. The decree of the covenant of works with the object existing as *creatus et lapsurus*.
4. The decree of the Fall
5. The decree to redeem, which entails
 5a. The decree for the fit means as specified by the covenant of redemption. At this juncture, the objects are *creatus et lapsus*.

The Remainder

If the aforementioned interpretation is correct, then we have been led to a place that intensifies and clarifies a difficulty at work in Edwards's theology. Given Edwards's commitment to the election of Jesus Christ *ad extra*, the intensification and clarification centers on his adherence to a form of the *felix culpa*. That Adam broke the covenant of works was not happenstance. Foreknowledge, of the Arminian sort, is not a solution either. For Edwards, the Fall proves to be an occasion for a greater apprehension of Christ's glory precisely in the work of redemption, so much so that there appears to be an overall positivity to the Fall within his theology. By positivity, I mean the positive use of evil by God, such that the Fall might not truly be a fall but a necessary means to some sort of creaturely elevation. By focusing on the relationship between the election of Jesus Christ and the covenants in this way, an acute pressure point concerning the decree of the Fall has now been located. The pressure point centers on Edwards's twin commitment: the christological end of creation (decreed apart from a sinful object) and the christological end of redemption (decreed upon the supposition of a sinful object). The former depends upon the incarnation, while the latter depends upon the incarnate Redeemer. Yet the ultimate end remains stable: communicative union with Jesus Christ. So, we are driven to ask: whence the *felix culpa*?

 This question sets the stage for the remaining interpretive work. In particular, how does Edwards account for the reality (and decree) of sin in his construal of the election of Jesus Christ *ad extra*? What does this mean, in turn, for the integrity of the individual objects, not only of election (the spouse), but also the individual objects of rejection? And, when it is all before us, what decretal portrait are we left with?

Chapter 5

PARTICULAR PREDESTINATION, CHRIST, AND THE DECREES

Such is his wisdom in his decrees, and all acts and operations, that if it were not for wise connection that is regarded, many things would not be decreed. One part of the wise system of events would not have been decreed, unless the other had been decreed, etc.[1]

—Jonathan Edwards

This scripture [Rom. 9:21] will hardly justify our expressing ourselves so that God gives reprobates a being to that end, that he might glorify himself in their destruction.[2]

—Jonathan Edwards

Up to this point, an interpretation of Edwards's theology has been set forth wherein Christology—specifically the election of Jesus Christ *ad intra* and *ad extra*—functions as a heuristic principle for bringing together a nexus of theological emphases across Edwards's corpus, especially creation and covenant. In this chapter, we will investigate how this principle comes to bear on Edwards's construal of the order and objects of individual predestination. What does it mean for Edwards that all of the decrees—including the decrees of individual election and rejection—maintain cohesion around and are summed up in the one integrative end: the communication of divine glory in Jesus Christ? In this integrative and christological sense, we will see why Edwards's overall decretal theology is supralapsarian in structure, even as his understanding of the objects of particular election and rejection remain *creatus et lapsus*—an ostensibly infralapsarian take.

But Edwards's lapsarian vision is not without internal difficulties. As recognized at the end of the previous chapter, a tension exists between the christological end of creation (decreed apart from a sinful object) and the christological end

---

1. "Part V on Predestination," in *"Controversies" Notebook*, WJEO 27.
2. *WJE* 24:1023.

of redemption (decreed upon the supposition of a sinful object). In this chapter, we will see how this tension manifests itself in another area: the expression of vindictive justice. The expression of divine glory in the form of justice factored heavily into the infra- and supralapsarian debate in the seventeenth century (see Chapter 1). Although Edwards does not side with the strict supralapsarians in their construal of divine justice as an ultimate end in God's program of self-glorification, he still thinks of vindictive justice as necessary in some sense. The manner in which he carves out space for the expression of (vindictive) justice leads one into the heart of his argument for the *felix culpa*. According to Edwards, God decrees the Fall as an occasion for a deeper perception of the infinite riches and fullness of the Son of God. This includes the expression of vindicative justice. In order to adjudicate all of these matters, we will first explore the formal order of the decrees as they harmonize around the election of Christ *ad extra*. Then we will examine Edwards's most sustained discussion of the infralapsarian and supralapsarian debate as found in "Miscellanies" nos 700 and 704, and this with an eye to the decrees of particular election, rejection, and damnation. Finally, we will turn to Edwards's theological depictions of the Fall and hell, and their significance within the communicative matrix of God's self-glorification in Jesus Christ.

The Order of the Decrees

Ingredient to the lapsarian debate, as witnessed in the discussion of Chapter 1, is the order of the decrees. Recall Bavinck's formal characterization: infralapsarians prefer the historical order, while supralapsarians prefer the teleological order. Even though the picture is more complicated than this, the overall point remains valid: the order of the decrees, however construed and with whatever degree of complexity, helps situate a thinker and their theology vis-à-vis the lapsarian question. Like much of Edwards's theological endeavors already explored, and in large part due to the unsystematic nature of Edwards's thought on this subject, his full understanding of the order of the decrees—especially when considering particular election and reprobation—needs to be gleaned from across his private notebooks and published works in order to paint a coherent picture. The overall picture that emerges does not fit easily into either a historical or teleological order but bears some similarity to the organic order of Herman Bavinck; or in Edwards's own idiom, it is a harmonious order maintaining cohesion around Jesus Christ.

The Harmony of the Decrees

Early on in his "Miscellanies," Edwards tries to adjudicate between God's absolute and conditional decrees. Instead of arguing for a hard bifurcation between the two, Edwards inserts the language of harmony and excellency in order to reorient the discussion: "God decrees all things harmoniously and in excellent order; one decree harmonizes with another, and there is such a relation between all the

5. Predestination, Christ, and the Decrees

decrees as makes the most excellent order."[3] Edwards provides an example in order to make his point clear. Does God decree rain in a drought because God decrees the earnest prayers of his people? Or does God decree the prayers of his people because he decrees rain? The answer, for Edwards, is both. Despite the infelicity associated with the use of the word "because"—an impropriety of which Edwards is all too aware[4]—Edwards resolves that the relation between the two decrees needs to be taken in such a way as to not make one decree the strict condition of the other. There exists a harmony between both the decree of the blessing of rain and the decree of the prayers of the people, which is a concrete expression of the harmony that exists among all of God's decrees.

Harmony—like its counterparts of proportionality and excellency—is a metaphysical term of art for Edwards. As such, it requires further specification in order to grasp the import of its significance for Edwards in his conceptualization of the divine decrees. Edwards's early metaphysical understanding of harmony can be found in "Miscellanies" no. 64, an entry dating from 1723. In this entry, Edwards compares the harmony and proportion found in God's natural (i.e., lawlike) operations in the world to God's spiritual operations. The key difference hinges on the extendedness of proportionality: spiritual operations "being the highest kind of operations of all are done in the most general proportion, not tied to any particular proportion, to this or that created being; but the proportion is with the whole series of acts and designs from eternity to eternity."[5]

Edwards elaborates upon this understanding of proportion and harmony in his private notebook, "The Mind." For Edwards, "proportion is complex beauty."[6] With reference to natural objects and laws, complex beauty consists in relations, specifically their correspondence, symmetry, and regularity, all of which Edwards resolves into "equalities."[7] Complex beauty stands in juxtaposition to simple beauty because complexity admits of irregularity for the sake of greater proportionality. That is, several objects or laws may appear irregular with regard to their simple beauty (i.e., proportionally among themselves), though they appear proportioned and beautiful when seen from the whole. In this sense, "particular disproportions sometimes greatly add to the general beauty, and must necessarily be, in order to a more universal proportion—so much equality, so much beauty—though it may be noted that the quantity of equality is not to be measured only by the number, but the intense-ness, according to the quantity of being."[8] What is more, beauty corresponds to "consent" and "dissent" within the relation, which is representative

---

3. "Miscellanies," no. 29, *WJE* 13:216.

4. "I acknowledge, to say God decrees a thing 'because,' is an improper way of speaking, but not more improper than all our other ways of speaking about God." "Miscellanies," no. 29, *WJE* 13:216.

5. "Miscellanies," no. 64, *WJE* 13:235.

6. *WJE* 6:333.

7. *WJE* 6:335.

8. *WJE* 6:335.

of metaphysical "intense-ness." The more intense and extensive the consent, the greater the beauty and, by extension, excellency. "Excellency," writes Edwards, "may be distributed into greatness and beauty," with the latter taken as "being's consent to being."[9] Of course, on the level of entities incapable of sensible consent (i.e., nonrational objects), natural objects and laws operate according to God's fixed operations and express either simple or complex beauty from whatever vantage they are viewed by perceiving creatures. John Bombaro summarizes well Edwards's metaphysics in relation to excellency and beauty:

> 'Excellency' or being consists, therefore, in *relations*. Beauty is proportion; proportion is excellence; and excellency is relational plurality or existence itself. Thus, to be is to be in relation. Excellency emerges, then, as the aesthetic expression of relations of consent—the principle components of ontological structures.[10]

The matter proceeds differently—at least in terms of complexity—for spiritual harmonies because the "proportions are vastly oftener doubled, and respect more beings, and require a vastly larger view to comprehend them."[11] Technically speaking, spiritual harmonies differ because they take into account spiritual beings, creatures capable of "consent" and "dissent" as ontologically distinct entities (minds) from God. Furthermore, spiritual harmonies transcend the natural operations of God and find their true ground in God's arbitrary operations. Edwards's thoughts in "Miscellanies" no. 1263 prove instructive here, wherein he specifies that arbitrary does not mean capricious but ordered according to divine wisdom.

> Thus, let us proceed which way we will in the series of things in the creation, still the higher we ascend, and the nearer we come to God in the gradation or succession of created things, the nearer it comes to that: that there is no other law than only the law of the infinite wisdom of the omniscient first cause and supreme disposer of all things who, in one, simple, unchangeable, perpetual view, comprehends all existence in its utmost compass and extent and infinite series.[12]

Commenting on such an understanding of harmony and causality, Paul Ramsey interprets Edwards's position as favoring a "constant correlation of events" in keeping with his idealism.[13] That is, things "are" because they are perceived

---

9. *WJE* 6:382.

10. John Bombaro, *Jonathan Edwards's Vision of Reality: The Relationship of God to the World, Redemption History, and the Reprobate* (Eugene, OR: Pickwick, 2012), 62.

11. *WJE* 6:336.

12. "Miscellanies," no. 1263, *WJE* 23:211.

13. Paul Ramsey, "Editor's Introduction," in *WJE* 1:36. Ramsey situates Edwards rather close to Hume in rejecting efficient causality. But this, it seems to me, is mistaken. Edwards

immediately and in their entirety by God. As Edwards specifies in the *Freedom of the Will* concerning divine foreknowledge, God "sees" a connection between a subject (possible event) and predicate (future existing) such that the connection is "firm and indissoluble."[14] "But if future existence be firmly and indissolubly connected with that event," maintains Edwards, "then the future existence of that event is necessary."[15] On this point, Edwards employs the scholastic notion of futurity: "That if there must be some reason of the futurition of the thing, or why the thing is future, this can be no other than God's decree; or, the truth of the proposition, 'Such a thing will be,' has been determined by God."[16] Edwards believes—as we saw in Mastricht—that the certain futurity of an event occurs antecedently to certain knowledge, both of which occur logically posterior to God's decree. This is a straightforward anti-Arminian position: God foreknows the future certainty of an event because God decrees the event (and all other events). The larger and thornier question, however, pertains to the manner in which Edwards conceives the harmony of God's decrees within the divine mind. Or, in other words, what does the harmony of such an infinitely decreed series "look like" to God?

Harmony and Christ

Within Edwards's species of idealism, "Things as to God exist from all eternity alike. That is, the idea is always the same, and after the same mode. The existence of things, therefore, that are not actually in created minds, consists only in power, or in the determination of God that such and such ideas shall be raised in created minds upon such conditions."[17] Such conditions arise according to the specification of divine wisdom: "Such is [God's] wisdom in his decrees, and all acts and operations, that if it were not for wise connection that is regarded, many things would not be decreed. One part of the wise system of events would not have been decreed, unless the other had been decreed, etc."[18] Divine volition, at least for Edwards, remains entirely determined by divine understanding and wisdom.[19]

---

clearly upholds the reality of secondary causes (see, e.g., "Miscellanies," nos 1003 and 1263). The real question, which Mark Hamilton rightly pinpoints, involves the manner in which Edwards squares secondary causality with occasional causality [cf. Hamilton, *A Treatise on Jonathan Edwards*, 48–9]. My purpose in this study is not to explore Edwards's metaphysics of causality, but simply to register that Edwards's understanding of the "harmony" of the decrees entails the use of secondary causes within the matrix of perception.

14. *WJE* 1:265.
15. *WJE* 1:265.
16. "Part V on Predestination," in *"Controversies" Notebook*, *WJEO* 27.
17. *WJE* 6:355.
18. "Part V on Predestination," in *"Controversies" Notebook*, *WJEO* 27.
19. *WJE* 1:376.

When worked out, Edwards holds that God's will is necessarily directed to what is most wise given the moral perfection of God's nature.[20]

As argued in Chapter 3, God's morally perfect knowledge of created realities is contained virtually in the subsistence of the Son of God.[21] Virtually, the possibilities for created realities coinhere in the Son, who is the idea of the Father's divine essence in distinct subsistence.[22] Given this fact, it follows that the vast harmony of the decrees finds its grounding virtually in the Son of God. As Seng-Kong Tan comments, "God [the Father] beholds all created ideas *ad extra* as one in reality corresponding to the virtual, perfect, series of ideas in Christ."[23] Christ himself—as God-man—exists as the center of the union of virtual and created ideas; all decreed events are eternally connected to and present with the Son. The utmost compass of existence and the infinite series of events maintain a harmonious-teleological cohesion in Jesus Christ.[24] In terms of the order of intention in the decrees, Edwards prioritizes christological communication. The decrees unfold around the excellency—that is, the greatness and beauty—of their intended center: the Father's love for the Son. The Son's excellency, in turn, must be realized and communicated in the passing of creaturely time. Human minds are meant to perceive (in an ever-increasing manner) the harmonious connection between the Son and every decreed operational—spiritual or natural—reality, which, in the end, showcases the glory of the Son.

> The Son of God created the world for his very end, to communicate himself in an image of his own excellency. He communicates himself properly only to spirits; and they only are capable of being proper images of his excellency, for they only are properly beings, as we have shown. Yet he communicates a sort of a shadow or glimpse of his excellencies to bodies, which, as we have shown, are but the shadows of being, and not real beings. He who by his immediate influence gives being every moment and by his Spirit actuates the world, because he inclines to communicate himself and his excellencies, doth doubtless communicate his excellency to bodies, as far as there is any consent or analogy.

---

20. *WJE* 1:380. Edwards's emphasis on the moral perfection of God's nature resonates with Katherine Sonderegger's attempt to ethicize omnipotence and relocate discussions of the divine will as the bridge term between God's inner life and economic activity. See Katherine Sonderegger, *Systematic Theology*, vol. 1, *The Doctrine of God* (Minneapolis, MN: Fortress Press, 2015), 151–326, as well as Matthew Wilcoxen's appropriation of Sonderegger against the theological construal of Karl Barth in Wilcoxen, *Divine Humility: God's Morally Perfect Being* (Waco, TX: Baylor University Press, 2019), 145–87. For a discussion of divine power, possibility, and actuality in early modern Reformed thought, see Muller, *Divine Will and Human Choice*, 258–82.

21. Cf. "Miscellanies," no. 94, *WJE* 13:259–60.

22. Cf. *WJE* 21:142.

23. Tan, "Jonathan Edwards's Dynamic Idealism and Cosmic Christology," 184.

24. Cf. Bavinck, *Christian Worldview*, 125.

And though beauty of face and sweet airs in man are not always the effect of the corresponding excellencies of mind, yet the beauties of nature are really emanations, or shadows, of the excellencies of the Son of God.[25]

The decreed connection holds true, according to Edwards, even in relation to futurition of sin: "Sin is an evil, yet the futurition of sin, or that sin should be future, is not an evil thing. Evil is an evil thing, and yet it may be a good thing that evil should be in the world."[26] As will be explained further below, this should not be taken in a generally aesthetic sense, but in a strictly christological sense. The disharmony that is evil—even though not decreed for its own sake—exposes the depth of the decretal center.[27]

This harmonious-teleological determination of the decrees—what I have shorthanded throughout as the election of Jesus Christ *ad extra*—proves essential to the interpretation of Edwards's overall lapsarian vision. That is, the election of Jesus Christ *ad extra* proves determinative for how Edwards construes the decrees of particular election and reprobation, both the order and objects therein. The most systematic presentations Edwards provides on this subject occur in "Miscellanies" nos 700 and 704.

"Miscellanies" nos 700 and 704

In these "Miscellanies" entries, Edwards wants to specify what constitutes logical priority and posteriority in the decree of individual predestination, especially as it concerns conditionality. The latter of which, in his estimation, has "occasioned difficulty in controversies concerning the decrees."[28] Of particular importance is the sinfulness of the human creature vis-à-vis the decree of damnation. As Edwards makes clear in these entries, a proper consideration of order follows upon a technical understanding of an ultimate

---

25. "Miscellanies," no. 108, *WJE* 13:279.

26. "Part V on Predestination," in *"Controversies" Notebook*, *WJE0* 27. Edwards refers elsewhere to this as "fitting": "God may permit sin, though the being of sin will certainly ensue on that permission: and so, by permission, he may dispose and order the event. If there were any such thing as chance, or mere contingence, and the very notion of it did not carry a gross absurdity (as might easily be shown that it does), it would have been very unfit, that God should have left it to mere chance, whether man should fall or no. For chance, if there should be any such thing, is undesigning and blind. And certainly 'tis more fit that an event of so great importance, and that is attended with such an infinite train of great consequences, should be disposed and ordered by infinite wisdom, than that it should be left to blind chance." "The Justice of God in the Damnation of Sinners" (May 1735), *WJE* 19:346.

27. Cf. Jenson, *America's Theologian*, 107–10.

28. "Miscellanies," no. 704, *WJE* 18:321.

end. Because distinct notions of end prove so important within the context of "Miscellanies" nos 700 and 704, it is necessary to first have the explanation of Edwards's various uses of end ready in hand. This is best accomplished by attending to Edwards's introduction in *End of Creation*. After carefully parsing these terms, we can then see how they coordinate with his discussion of the order of the decree of predestination.

Original and Hypothetical Ends

In his introduction to *End of Creation*, Edwards carefully explains the way he will be using the term "ultimate end" within the dissertation. In particular, Edwards draws a distinction between an "ultimate end," which is desirable for its own sake, and a "subordinate end," which is sought only for the sake of something else. A subordinate end, when seen from a larger perspective, functions in an equivalent manner to means. In the context of *End of Creation*, Edwards speaks of God's ultimate end in creation in the highest possible sense, namely as the one, original ultimate end. Such an original, ultimate end must be considered prior in the mind of God to everything else (i.e., an end independent of all conditions and valued for its own sake).

Edwards then goes on to make a more nuanced distinction between (1) an original end independent of all conditions (just discussed), and (2) a hypothetical or consequential end.[29] A hypothetical or consequential end is agreeable to an agent for its own sake, although it does not exist antecedently to all conditions. According to Edwards, a hypothetical end arises upon the supposition or condition of a particular case or happening.[30] Rather importantly, a hypothetical end is not strictly synonymous with a subordinate end because a hypothetical end may be valued for its own sake and not for the sake of another and greater end. Thus, Edwards indicates the possibility of two sorts of ultimate ends with reference to God's will: independent and original, and dependent and hypothetical.[31] For ease of reference, I will shorthand the former as "ultimate$_1$," and the latter as "ultimate$_2$," in the argument throughout the remainder of this chapter.

Interestingly enough, the examples Edwards provides of the difference between an ultimate$_1$ and ultimate$_2$ end pertain to the exercise of divine attributes. The first attribute mentioned is God's justice. Although justice itself is agreeable to God's nature as such, there is no necessity in God that induced God to create intelligent beings and then "order the occasion of doing either justly or unjustly."[32] Edwards clarifies as follows: "The justice of God's nature makes a just regulation agreeable, and the contrary disagreeable, as there is occasion, the

---

29. *WJE* 8:411.

30. *WJE* 8:411.

31. For a more elaborate analysis, see Schultz, *Jonathan Edwards' Concerning the End*, 62–75.

32. *WJE* 8:412.

subject being supposed and the occasion given: but we must suppose something else that should incline him to create the subjects or order the occasion."[33] The next attribute Edwards isolates is faithfulness. Faithfulness to fulfill promises could not, according to Edwards, be God's ultimate$_1$ end in giving creatures being, even if the exercise of faithfulness toward creatures upon the supposition of God's promise to them is itself amiable to God for its own sake.[34] The isolation of attributes in these examples is significant, especially since the glorification of justice appears as a point of contention in the lapsarian debate in general, as well as Edwards's discussion of it within "Miscellanies" no. 704 in particular. I shall return to this point in the subsequent discussion of reprobation. For now, one salient feature concerns Edwards's willingness to concede hypothetical, albeit still ultimate, ends. Such ends touch upon God's determination to act in accord with God's nature upon the supposition of certain occurrences, although they are not determinative for God's decretal will as such. In other words, hypothetical ends are not determinative for God in the same sense as God's ultimate$_1$ end. Edwards argues as follows:

> It may be further observed that the original ultimate end or ends of the creation of the world is alone that which induces God to give the occasion for consequential ends by the first creation of the world, and the original disposal of it. And the more original the end is, the more extensive and universal it is. That which God had primarily in view in creating, and the original ordination of the world, must be constantly kept in view, and have a governing influence in all God's works, or with respect to everything that he does towards his creatures.[35]

The implication is that there could exist multiple hypothetical ends that are not subordinate to each other, even if they remain subordinate to the original, ultimate$_1$ end in creation. The various intended hypothetical ends exist coordinately, though again not in such a way as to produce the subordination of ends and means between themselves.[36] What is more, though different hypothetical ends remain logically independent of each other qua intended end, this does not mean they cannot condition each other in the order of execution (see the next section). Precisely in this way—as we saw in Bavinck's organicism—"the whole picture is marked by immensely varied omnilateral interaction."[37]

---

33. *WJE* 8:412.
34. *WJE* 8:412.
35. *WJE* 8:413.
36. Although William Twisse articulates the ultimate end differently from Edwards, he too refuses to admit of subordination in God's intention in precisely this way. Thus, Twisse allows for a coordination of differing means and ends that are not subordinate to each other. Cf. Twisse, *A Treatise of Mr. Cottons*, 4–5.
37. Bavinck, *RD* 2:392.

Priority and Posteriority in "Miscellanies" nos 700 and 704

With these distinctions in hand, we are now able to generate a proper interpretation of Edwards's ordering of the decree of individual predestination. Beginning with "Miscellanies" no. 700—which is roughly a paragraph in length—Edwards qualifies the nature of antecedence at work in individual election and reprobation. Edwards's point is straightforward. In the decree of individual election, God decrees the "creature's eternal happiness antecedent to any foresight of good works, in a sense wherein he does not, in reprobation, decree the creature's eternal misery antecedent to any foresight of sin."[38] According to Edwards, the notion of election coincides with God's ultimate$_1$ end in decreeing, namely "that God will communicate his happiness and glorify his grace (for these two seem to be coordinate)."[39] Reprobation, however, functions differently because "the being of sin is supposed in the first things in order in the decree of reprobation."[40] But Edwards is quick to clarify that this should not be construed in an Arminian sense, "so that the creature's determination in this decree is properly to be looked upon as antecedent to God's determination, and [that] on which his determination is consequent and dependent."[41] So Edwards has established two preliminary principles in this "Miscellanies" entry: (1) antecedence is not based on Arminian foreknowledge; and (2) a strong asymmetry exists between election and reprobation. Even with these principles in place, it remains unclear as to the place of sin in the decree. Edwards appears to argue the decree of reprobation both depends upon and does not depend upon the creatures' being in sin. What does Edwards mean?

Edwards clarifies his understanding of antecedence in "Miscellanies" no. 704, an entry roughly seven times the length of no. 700. Edwards begins by technically specifying what constitutes priority in the decrees. First, there is the end decreed prior to (and apart from) the means necessary to achieving that end. These sorts of ends, drawing upon the distinctions from *End of Creation*, take the form of ultimate ends. "That which stands in the place of the ultimate end in the decree," explains Edwards, is "the shining forth of God's glory, and the communication of his goodness."[42] Apart from the priority of ends in the aforementioned respect, Edwards designates, secondly, how priority in the decrees considers the "capableness or aptness of the means to obtain the end, before he fixes on the means."[43] So, before God fixes on the means, two things must be considered: (1) the end; and (2) the "capacity and fitness" of means to an appointed end.

---

38. "Miscellanies," no. 700, *WJE* 18:283.
39. "Miscellanies," no. 700, *WJE* 18:283.
40. "Miscellanies," no. 700, *WJE* 18:283.
41. "Miscellanies," no. 700, *WJE* 18:283.
42. "Miscellanies," no. 704, *WJE* 18:316. As shown in Chapter 3, God's ultimate end as glory and communication takes shape around the election of Jesus Christ.
43. "Miscellanies," no. 704, *WJE* 18:315.

This leads Edwards to consider the sinfulness of the reprobate within the logical order of the decrees. The sinfulness of the reprobate, according to Edwards's line of reasoning, is prior to the decree of damnation because "sinfulness is the foundation of the possibility of obtaining" the end of glorifying God's justice by means of punishing the wicked.[44] God decrees damnation based upon (1) the sinfulness of the reprobate (fit means); and (2) the decree to glorify God's justice in punishing sinfulness (the end). The decree of damnation, therefore, occurs logically "posterior to the consideration of the sin of men."[45] Both the glory of divine justice and the sinfulness of the creature "may properly be said to be before the decree of damning the reprobate" and, as a result, "the ground of the decree of damnation."[46] Evident throughout Edwards's discussion is the distinction between the decree of reprobation and the decree of damnation, which is typical in (supra)lapsarian schemes. Edwards is careful to note the decree of damnation (i.e., punishment) always supposes a sinful object, whereas he remains more circumspect regarding the decree of reprobation itself.

On the distinction between damnation and reprobation, Edwards latches on to the place and purpose of vindictive justice in the decree. Vindictive justice (i.e., punishing justice) should not be confused with the glory of God's justice *tout court* because it does not stand in the place of an ultimate$_1$ end. God's glorifying God's justice in punishing sin is a "certain way and means for the glorifying of an attribute."[47] The failure to make such a distinction "has led to great misrepresentations and undue and unhappy expressions about the decree of reprobation."[48] Edwards has in his mind the stronger form of supralapsarianism such that "the glorifying of God's vindictive justice on such particular persons has been considered as altogether prior in the decree to their sinfulness; yea, [to] their very beings."[49] This is a great mistake according to Edwards because vindictive justice exists as a means to glorifying God's justice upon the supposition of a sinful object, wherein sinfulness must be conceived of as logically prior to possibility of the means for obtaining the end of glorifying justice.[50] As Edwards argues further in "Miscellanies" no. 704, "God's decree of the eternal damnation of the reprobate, is not to be conceived of as prior to the fall, yea, and to the very being of the person."[51] Edwards clearly locates the decree of damnation as posterior to the fall and being of the person. But what of the decree of reprobation itself? Edwards's answer is nuanced. Certain elements in the decree of reprobation are placed prior to the Fall and others are not. "But nothing in the decree of reprobation is to be

---

44. "Miscellanies," no. 704, *WJE* 18:315.
45. "Miscellanies," no. 704, *WJE* 18:316.
46. "Miscellanies," no. 704, *WJE* 18:315.
47. "Miscellanies," no. 704, *WJE* 18:316.
48. "Miscellanies," no. 704, *WJE* 18:316.
49. "Miscellanies," no. 704, *WJE* 18:316.
50. Cf. Vetö, *La pensée de Jonathan Edwards*, 237.
51. "Miscellanies," no. 704, *WJE* 18:317.

looked upon as antecedent in one of those respects to man's being and fall, but only that general decree that God will glorify his justice, or rather his holiness and greatness, which supposes neither their being nor sinfulness."[52] Nevertheless, "whatsoever there is in this decree of evil to particular subjects, is to be considered as consequent on the decree of their creation, and permission of their fall."[53] For Edwards, the general decree to glorify "justice" as annexed to the decree of reprobation is the only portion of the decree antecedent to the creation and fall of particular objects. Framing it this way, however, raises a question about the glorification of divine justice because, as mentioned in the previous section, the glorification of divine justice itself stands as a hypothetical end upon the (logical) supposition of an object and occasion. What does Edwards mean here?

Because the divine perfection of justice factors heavily into Edwards's reasoning, it is necessary to spend a brief moment unpacking some of its structures for God *in se*. Divine justice, in Edwards's metaphysics, corresponds to the idea of divine excellency. As discussed above, divine excellency may be distributed into greatness and beauty; according to Edwards in "Miscellanies" no. 704, justice functions as a metonym for greatness and holiness. By parity of reason, excellency may be distributed into justice and beauty. Justice, in this line of metaphysical reasoning, corresponds to the degree of agreeableness or disagreeableness to God's being. For God *in se*, justice corresponds to God's infinite agreeableness or regard for God's own being. Edwards brings these concepts together cogently in "Miscellanies" no. 1077:

> GOD'S HOLINESS is his having a due, meet and proper regard to everything, and therefore consists mainly and summarily in his infinite regard or love to himself, he being infinitely the greatest and most excellent Being. And therefore a meet and proper regard to himself is infinitely greater than to all other beings; and as he is as it were the sum of all being, and all other positive existence is but a communication from him, hence it will follow that a proper regard to himself is the sum of his regard. TRINITY.[54]

Edwards's final emphasis on God's triunity directs us to how divine excellency is demarcated theologically for him. God's infinite consent to God's own being—that is, God's excellency—just is the *relations* between the Father, Son, and Spirit.[55] Undergirding the entire metaphysical language of consent is God's triune love. When we put this entire picture together, justice functions as a description of the mode and manner of God's triune love *ad intra*. "There is God's holiness," Edwards

---

52. "Miscellanies," no. 704, *WJE* 18:317.
53. "Miscellanies," no. 704, *WJE* 18:317.
54. "Miscellanies," no. 1077, *WJE* 20:460.
55. Cf. *WJE* 6:364; *WJE* 21:131. Along these lines, Edwards appropriates the divine perfection of holiness to the Holy Spirit in particular, who is the bond of mutual love between the Father and the Son.

tells us, "but it is the same ... with his love to himself. There is God's justice, which is not really distinct from his holiness."[56] In this sense, justice does not appear to be, strictly speaking, a discrete "perfection" at all. Divine justice aesthetically describes God's being *ad intra*, in particular the infinite extent of the harmonious, loving, and self-giving aspects of God's triune life. The repercussions for understanding the decree to glorify God's justice *ad extra* pertain to the way in which God relates to and orders the world, in particular what Michael McClymond has called the principle of proportionate regard.[57] God necessarily orders the world in such a way that it analogically mirrors God's triune life of love. Human creatures, in this sense, were made to proportionately love God after the manner of God's love *in se*. Thus, "Injustice is not to exert ourselves towards any being as it deserves, or to do the contrary to what it deserves in doing good or evil, or in acts of consent and dissent."[58]

Although the fuller correlation between divine justice and the decree concerning the permission of sin will be explored in the sections that follow, we can at least see at this point how the glorification of justice fits into the order of the decree of reprobation. Foremost, the decree to glorify divine justice does not function as a control such that it inclines God in the decrees of creation, election, and reprobation. Divine justice, in fact, cannot function this way because it is more a description of the mode and manner of God's triune being. Because justice pertains to the *extent* and *agreeableness* of the loving relations among the triune persons, the decree to glorify God's justice *ad extra* needs to be seen (in the most general sense) as hypothetically coordinate with God's communicative and ultimate$_1$ end. This is significant for interpreting Edwards's claim that the "general decree that God will glorify his justice, or rather his holiness and greatness" supposes neither the being nor sinfulness of the creature. Whereas the execution of justice supposes an object and occasion, whether sinful or not, the decree to glorify divine justice remains descriptive of God's overall communicative movement to creatures.

This, then, leads us back to Edwards's interpretation of the order of individual predestination within "Miscellanies" no. 704. Again, "God's decree to glorify his love and communicate his goodness, and to glorify his greatness and holiness" stands logically prior to creation and the Fall and, in fact, gives being to creation. As argued in Chapter 3, this is simply the election of Jesus Christ *ad extra*,

---

56. *WJE* 21:131.

57. On this principle, see Michael McClymond, "Creation in Jonathan Edwards" (PhD Diss., University of Chicago, 1992), 183–94; and Michael McClymond, *Encounters with God: An Approach to the Theology of Jonathan Edwards* (Oxford: Oxford University Press, 1998), 53–4. For Edwards, another feature of this principle is that all sin is against God. And, as will be mentioned in the discussion of hell, Edwards employs the principle of proportionate regard to argue for the infinite nature of punishment in hell. See, for example, Edwards remarks in the sermon, "The Justice of God in the Damnation of Sinners" (May 1735), *WJE* 19:342–3.

58. *WJE* 6:364.

wherein the election of Jesus Christ gives being to creation because Jesus Christ is the positive, theological content of God's communicative goodness and love. Along these lines, Edwards can distinguish between election prior and posterior to the Fall. Prior to the being and fall of the creature, election corresponds to the integration of creation and Christology; posterior to the Fall, election corresponds to the integration of creation, Christology, and soteriology. This is precisely why Edwards argues that "all that is in the decree of election, all that respects the good to the subjects ben't posterior to the being and fall of man; yet both the decrees of election and rejection or reprobation, as so styled, must be considered as consequent on the decrees concerning the creation and fall."[59] The ultimate end of election, so Edwards reasons, resonates across the Fall in keeping with the divine communicative and christological end.

In terms of reprobation, however, the case is different. Prior to the Fall, only the general decree within reprobation to glorify God's justice (i.e., consent to God's triune love) is taken into account. But since justice at this logical juncture in the decree does not involve punishing justice, it is difficult to understand what this actually entails theologically. When read against Edwards's claims regarding God's justice *in se*, it appears that the end of reprobation, when taken in its general sense, is nothing other than a further description of the ultimate$_1$ end of creation: God creates the world as a communicative theater to display the glory of the Father's love for the Son, with justice functioning as a descriptor for the necessary agreeableness of creaturely consent to and necessary disagreeableness of dissent from the Son. Although the general claims about justice are coherent, Edwards's attempt to speak of divine justice (in general) as a part of reprobation prior to the Fall is, one must admit, confused and confusing. It would have been better for Edwards to speak of the entirety of the decree of reprobation as posterior to the Fall, something he in fact does at the end of the "Miscellanies" entry: "The first decree of evil or suffering implies that in it, for there is no evil decreed for any other end but the glory of God's justice; and therefore, the decree of the permission of sin is prior to all other things in the decree of reprobation."[60] The Fall—that is, the permission of sin—is decreed for the glory of justice *apart from* any logical consideration of reprobation and punishing justice. Importantly, this means God does not decree the Fall for the purpose glorifying justice in the damnation of a class of human creatures known as the reprobate. As Edwards insists in his exegesis of Rom. 9:21, "this scripture will hardly justify our expressing ourselves so that God gives reprobates a being

---

59. "Miscellanies," no. 704, *WJE* 18:317–18. Once again, though now stated differently from that in Chapter 4, this offers a subtle, though significant, correction to Crisp's interpretation that Edwards is supralapsarian on election and infralapsarian on rejection. For Edwards, election has a broader theological range than reprobation such that election has both supralapsarian and infralapsarian elements. This point is clearly recognized, for example, by Joe Ben Irby in "Changing Concepts of the Doctrine of Predestination in American Reformed Theology," 87–90.

60. "Miscellanies," no. 704, *WJE* 18:321.

to that end, that he might glorify himself in their destruction."⁶¹ Failure to register this point might lead one to interpret Edwards as seeing the decrees of election and reprobation as equally basic to God's self-glorification.⁶² Both election and reprobation lead to God's glorification, but they do not do so in equally basic (i.e., symmetrical) ways. An asymmetry exists between election and reprobation that turns on protology and teleology. The end of election remains stable across the Fall, whereas reprobation finds no such resonance strictly speaking. Election and creation are correlative; creation and reprobation are not.

Based on Edwards's understanding of election as containing broader (apart from the supposition of sin) and narrower (upon the supposition of sin) elements, Edwards can argue that the glorification of God's mercy to elect individuals cannot be the ultimate₁ end of individual predestination. Analogously to vindictive justice vis-à-vis divine justice, both redemptive grace and mercy serve as "certain ways or means for the [sic] glorifying the exceeding abundance and overflowing fullness of God's goodness and love."⁶³ And like the decree of particular reprobation, the decree of glorifying God's grace and mercy "presupposes" the object to be miserable and sinful.⁶⁴ Posterior to the creation of the human being and their fall, the decrees of individual election and rejection both "have respect to the distinction or discrimination that is afterwards made amongst men in pursuance of these decrees."⁶⁵ Whatever is "prior" to the actual act of particular election and rejection must also be considered "in some respect prior to the decree concerning the distinction."⁶⁶ This is true because all that comes before is already put in the decree. Hence, the particular election (and rejection) of human beings in history presupposes their existence and fallen condition. In this way, Edwards believes "the decrees of God must be conceived of in the same order, and as antecedent to

---

61. *WJE* 24:1023.

62. Michael Allen, in his reflection on "Miscellanies," no. 704, argues that both "election and reprobation serve the greater and simple goal of God's self-glorification and are equally complex (requiring two grounds: one of purpose, the other of necessity)." Allen, "Jonathan Edwards and the Lapsarian Debate," 309. In making this point, Allen misquotes Edwards as saying "the decree of *reprobation* may properly be said, in different respects, to be because of both these [the sinner qua sinner and the divine intent to magnify God-self through just punishment of sin]' (308); in the primary text, Edwards says "The decree of *damnation* may properly be said, in different respects, to be because of both these." "Miscellanies," no. 704, *WJE* 18:315. The decrees of damnation and reprobation are not synonymous, and Allen builds an argument upon the premise that they are—for Edwards at least.

63. "Miscellanies," no. 704, *WJE* 18:317.

64. "Miscellanies." no. 704, *WJE* 18:317. Edwards creates, according to Vetö's interpretation, a subtle parallelism between election and reprobation, without subjecting the divine will to "narrow exigences" (exigences étroites) of a "symmetry" between mercy and justice. *La pensée de Jonathan Edwards*, 238.

65. "Miscellanies," no. 704, *WJE* 18:318.

66. "Miscellanies," no. 704, *WJE* 18:318.

and consequent on one another, in the same manner as God's acts in execution of those decrees."[67]

Although the correspondence between the logical order of intention and "acts of execution" appears to entail only an efficiently causal order, Edwards attempts to clarify his complex understanding of priority within God's unified decree by providing a rather perplexing illustration of a straight line of infinite length that runs parallel to itself. Although the full illustration remains obscure to me, the overall point seems to be this: in the order of the decrees, as it concerns priority and posteriority, there exists a harmonious coordination between hypothetical ends and means such that no new motion enters God's one will. I emphasize hypothetical (ultimate$_2$) ends because the entire illustration only applies to decrees logically posterior to the decreed ultimate$_1$ end of all things. Edwards writes,

> In one respect, the end that is afterwards to be accomplished is the ground of God's acting; in another respect, something that is already accomplished is the ground of his acting, as 'tis the ground of the fitness or capableness of that act to obtain that end. There is nothing but the ultimate end of all things, viz. God's glory and the communication of his goodness, that is prior to God's first act in creating the world in one respect, and mere possibility in another. But with respect to after acts, other ends are prior in one respect, and other preceding acts are prior in another, just as I have shown it to be with respect to God's decrees.[68]

The difference between ultimate$_1$ and ultimate$_2$ ends becomes the key to understanding the order of the decrees in Edwards's lapsarian picture. There is only one ultimate$_1$ end in God's decree: the election of Jesus Christ *ad extra*, which specifies the content of God's glory and communication of divine goodness. For this very reason, for example, Edwards can draw a distinction between the decree of the end of election (ultimate$_1$) and the decree of bestowing salvation on an elect soul (ultimate$_2$). The former remains "unconditioned" as to other decrees, while the decree to bestow salvation on the elect remains "conditioned" upon other decrees—that is, the decree of the permission of sin, the decree of giving faith, and so on. Hence, God's "decreeing and giving the happiness of the elect is not so founded on faith" because it presupposes no decree prior to Christ which is able to condition it.[69] Although Edwards does not argue for it explicitly in "Miscellanies" no. 704, his coordination of "end" and "fit means" applies here as well. The ultimate

---

67. "Miscellanies," no. 704, *WJE* 18:318.
68. "Miscellanies," no. 704, *WJE* 18:319.
69. Technically speaking, this is not true. As seen in the previous chapter, one "condition" is consent to the marital union with Christ. For Edwards, consent is a "fit means" that follows from the end so rendered.

end entails an ultimate fit means: Jesus Christ and beatific union with him. Once one descends lower than this in the decrees, there exists a harmonious and immensely complex interconnectedness and conditionality.[70] These lower decrees "may in some sort be conditions of decrees," Edwards argues, "so as that it may be said that God would not have decreed some things had he not decreed others."[71] This is certainly the case with the decree of damnation: "For with respect to eternal punishment, it may be said that God would not, yea, could not, have decreed or executed it had he not decreed and permitted sin."[72]

All of this leads Edwards to endorse a *modified* supralapsarian order in the divine decrees. Taking into account insights from the previous chapters, Edwards's lapsarian picture may now be schematized as follows:

1. The election of Jesus Christ *ad extra*, which entails
    1a. The decree of the glorification of divine perfections *ad extra* in and through the Son.
    1b. The decree to create this world.
    1c. The decree to communicate the glory of the divine perfections *ad extra* to a particular object of the Son's love, namely a "spouse" in strict union with the Son. The object is, at this point, *creabilis et labilis*.

2. The decree of the incarnation, which entails
    2a. The hypostatic union of the Son with a human nature. The particular human nature of Christ, in this moment, is *creandus*; the Son is, by extension, *incarnandus*.
    2b. The elevation of human creatures as the chosen "spouse" of the Son. This spouse now exists as *creandus et lapsurus* in the decree.

3. The decree of the covenant of works with the object existing as *creatus et lapsurus*.
4. The decree of the Fall.
5. The decree to redeem, which entails

---

70. As Edwards argues: "But if we descend lower than the highest end, if we come down to other events decreed that ben't mere ends but means to obtain that end, then we must necessarily bring in more things as in some respect prior, in the same manner as mere possibility is in this highest decree; because that more things must necessarily be supposed, or considered as put in the decree, in order to those things decreed reaching the end for which they are decreed. More things must be supposed in order to a possibility of these things taking place as subordinate to their end; and therefore, they stand in the same place, in these lower decrees, as absolute possibility does in the decree of the highest end." "Miscellanies," no. 704, *WJE* 18:316.
71. "Miscellanies," no. 704, *WJE* 18:321.
72. "Miscellanies," no. 704, *WJE* 18:320.

5a. The decree for the fit means as specified by the covenant of redemption. At this juncture, the objects are *creatus et lapsus*.

6. The decree of particular election and rejection with the object as *creatus et lapsus*. This also entails
   6a. The decree of the fit means of election (i.e., sin and grace/mercy as understood from the perspective of the covenant of redemption).
   6b. The decree of the fit means of reprobation (i.e., sin).

7. The decree of damnation. The object is *creatus et reprobus*.

As seen in Chapter 1, whether one is slotted as an infralapsarian or supralapsarian cannot rest solely on the definition of the object of predestination. Even supralapsarians like Mastricht and Maccovius had infralapsarian nuances in their theology. As a result, the designation supralapsarian and infralapsarian—both historically and theologically—is best adjudicated according to the integrative function of "ends" in the architectonic. Although the "objects" of particular election and rejection are clearly *creatus et lapsus* for Edwards,[73] the overall integration around the election of Jesus Christ *ad extra* pre- and post-Fall yields a modified supralapsarian picture. Just so—and in a similar manner to Mastricht and Goodwin—Edwards draws a distinction between the decree of election in general (prior to the consideration of the Fall) and the decrees of particular election and rejection/damnation (posterior to the Fall and sinfulness of the object). "Hence God's decree of the eternal damnation of the reprobate," argues Edwards, "is not to be conceived of as prior to the fall, yea, and to the very being of the person; as the decree of the eternal glory of the elect is."[74] Furthermore, the decrees to glorify God's mercy and justice assume a certain form post-Fall, a form which cannot be conceived as prior to the being and permission of the fall of the object. The obvious ramification being the ultimate end of the decree of individual predestination is not God's self-glorification in the form of mercy and justice. Edwards has certainly parted ways from the supralapsarian picture of Mastricht (and most supralapsarians historically) in this way, though his theological picture still resonates with Thomas Goodwin's modification.[75] With

---

73. Take, as another example, Edwards's unambiguous remarks on Rom. 9:21: "But that mass, in which both the chosen and rejected lie undistinguished, and from whence their distinction first begins by the hands of God the potter, is the corrupt mass of fallen mankind." *WJE* 24:1023.

74. "Miscellanies," no. 704, *WJE* 18:317.

75. I take this as a clear departure from Edwards's earlier reasoning in "Miscellanies" no. 292, wherein he argues that "man's fall was intended that God might glorify himself this way, by [manifesting] his mercy and his just wrath, for that is properly the end of God's determining the fall." *WJE* 13:384. Edwards's opinion in "Miscellanies" no. 292 appears to be, for the most part, abandoned by the time of "Miscellanies" no. 704.

these caveats in mind, Edwards's lapsarianism is best characterized under the umbrella of supralapsarianism because of the integrative function of the ultimate$_1$ end across the Fall, even as the objects of particular election and rejection in the decree are considered *infra lapsum*. Unlike the infralapsarian picture of Francis Turretin, for example, Edwards refuses to divide the orders of creation and grace around the chasm of the Fall. The Fall, in Edwards's scheme, is itself integrated into the ultimate$_1$ end. The question remaining is how.

The Decree Concerning the Permission of Sin, Felix Culpa, *and Redemption*

Edwards's supralapsarianism modification places the spotlight on the decree of the Fall and by extension the *felix culpa*. The overall theological portrait that has emerged so far presses us to inquire further about the correspondence of the election of Christ *ad extra* across the Fall, especially the relation between creation in Christ, redemption, and the being and terminus of the elect and reprobate in their particularity. In other words, what is the relationship between the decree of the Fall and the election of Christ *ad extra*?

The Image of God and the Holy Spirit

Inherent to Edwards's understanding of the Fall, which will further shed light on God's permission of the Fall, is the distinction between the natural and spiritual image of God. As Edwards explains in *Original Sin*, God first made humankind with two principles: natural and supernatural. The former corresponds to the natural image of God and consists in the capacity of the human being for God. Human dispositions come to be rightly and fully actualized only under divine influence. For this reason, Edwards insists upon superior or supernatural principles as those which "immediately depend upon man's union and communion with God, or divine communications and influence of God's Spirit."[76] Existing above mere human nature, supernatural principles were meant to govern and guide the natural principles. As Edwards maintains, "These divine principles thus reigning, were the dignity, life, happiness, and glory of man's nature."[77] Important to recognize, however, is the distinction between the glory of human nature (i.e., its created end) and the ontological structures as such. Without superior principles, a human being still remains a human being. Because these superior principles are not ontologically internal to human nature, no ontological change occurs upon their removal (or forfeiture).

The Fall, therefore, hinges upon the overriding of the superior principles by the natural principles. In other words, Edwards construes the Fall as an independent exercise of natural principles. The fact that the natural faculties override the superior

---

76. *WJE* 3:382.
77. *WJE* 3:382.

principles follows as a result of God's withholding confirming grace.[78] Once Adam sinned, the partially present superior principles (i.e., the external influences of the Holy Spirit) were completely removed, leaving the human being completely under the reign of natural principles. The servants in the house then became the masters. God does not implant or infuse wicked principles in this theological picture; they follow inevitably in the creature apart from the motion of the Holy Spirit. Without grace, the human creature drifts toward sin. Created nature, in this sense, is unable to exercise its capacities rightly without grace. Human creatures, in the words of Kathryn Tanner, are "miserable and fundamentally incapacitated without it."[79] In terms of the lapsarian question as I have been pursuing it, the important matter is not so much the (causal) mechanism of withholding grace and the subsequent fall and total corruption, but the divine intent in doing so.[80] Why did God permit the fall into sin and sin as such? Why refrain from issuing confirming grace in the moment of Adam's temptation? This leads us directly to Edwards's notion of the *felix culpa*.

Permission of Sin and the Felix Culpa

In order to grasp Edwards's reasoning on the *felix culpa*, the nature of sin and moral evil needs to be further explored.[81] Without question, sin has an aesthetic orientation within Edwards's theology. Recall Edwards's notion of excellency as distributed into greatness and beauty, wherein that latter trades on the language of consent and dissent, and the former corresponds to the "intense-ness" of the relation. Also recall Edwards's understanding of proportionality: complex beauty may admit of irregularity for the sake of the greater proportionality. Without covering every detail, it follows that dissent is one such irregularity among spiritual

---

78. Cf. "Miscellanies," no. 290, *WJE* 13:382.

79. Kathryn Tanner, *Christ the Key* (Cambridge: Cambridge University Press, 2010), 132. One such way of understanding the Fall and original sin is explored by Daniel Houck in his recent volume *Aquinas, Original Sin, and the Challenge of Evolution* (Cambridge: Cambridge University Press, 2020). Houck proposes a new Thomist view of original sin, which consists of two core claims: "Original sin is the lack of sanctifying grace in the human being, and the human being with original sin retains human nature." *Aquinas, Original Sin, and the Challenge of Evolution*, 202. This view, at least on my reading, is congruent with one dominant thread within Edwards's theological reasoning. Coincidentally, this is also the exact position of Thomas Goodwin, who conceives of the Fall as rooted in the mutability of the human creature apart from the supernatural operations of God's grace. See Goodwin, *Works* 7:3–34.

80. For a discussion of the former, see Crisp, *Metaphysics of Sin*, 25–53; cf. Kearney, "Jonathan Edwards's Account of Adam's First Sin," *Scottish Bulletin of Theology* 15, no. 2 (Autumn 1997): 127–41.

81. I limit the discussion to moral evil because natural evil brings in a host of other issues not directly germane to the discussion.

beings. Metaphysically then, sin is dissent from Being and, as such, an irregularity within the matrix of Being and beings. Consent, on the other hand, finds it mooring in the perfection of love. "All primary and original beauty or excellence that is among minds is love."[82] God's infinite beauty—as the primary and original Being existing *a se*—is "his infinite mutual love of himself."[83] God's beauty is peculiar—to use Edwards's language—because it is self-grounded and self-sufficient. It is also important to recall from earlier that such language corresponds directly to that of divine justice *ad intra*. Undergirding the entire metaphysical language of consent is the extent and agreeableness of God's love among the divine persons, with the implication that God's attributes are positively ethicized according to God's triune mode of in-being. Sin and therefore deformity, both in Edwards's metaphysics and theology, is want of God's love in its triune movement.

With this understanding in hand, it is now possible to see how Edwards's *felix culpa* hinges upon "perception" of divine excellency. As Edwards muses in his private notebook on the "History of Redemption,"

> END IN PERMITTING THE FALL OF AN MEN & ANGELS. God aimed at 3 Things in this. 1 A Greater more full and prop manifestation of his own Glariou[s] Excellency & Perfection. 2 The more excellent Holiness of the Creature in its being holy in a greater degree & excercising [*sic*] Holiness in a more amiable & Excellent manner. 3. The more exquisite Happiness & sweet Joy of the Creature.[84]

Given the argument of prior chapters, such "excellency" cannot be understood abstractly, but only as refracted through and logically coordinate with the election of Jesus Christ *ad extra*. Ingredient to the Son's election *ad extra* is the communication of the fullness of the triune relations and perfections as beheld in the Son of God. This truly is the ultimate$_1$ end of creation.[85] Unlike the traditional *felix culpa*—which functions as a shorthand for the theological position that human creatures receive greater benefits (chiefly Christ's person and redemption) as a result of the Fall[86]—Edwards's notion of the *felix culpa* functions in such a manner as to allow for a fuller "perception" of the excellency

---

82. *WJE* 6:362.
83. *WJE* 6:363.
84. "History of Redemption Book II," in *"History of Redemption" Notebooks*, WJEO 31.
85. To reiterate a prior point: "For God glorifies himself in communicating himself, and he communicates himself in glorifying himself. Jesus Christ, and that as God-man, is the grand medium by which God attains his end, both in communicating himself to the creatures and [in] glorifying himself by the creation." Edwards, "Approaching the End of God's Grand Design" (December 1744), *WJE* 25:117.
86. John Hick takes this sort of outcome to be a clear presupposition of the *felix culpa*, an insight he believes "to be one of the cornerstones of Christian theodicy." John Hick, *Evil and the God of Love* (New York: Harper & Row, 1966), 182. He finds this in Barth as well.

of divine love which exists between the Father, Son, and Spirit. This benefit does not correspond to addition (nothing is merited!) but to depth.[87] In this way, the Fall functions to expose the depth of the reality that already is. God's intention in the Fall, therefore, is twofold for Edwards: (1) to reveal the depth of the love existing between the Father and the Son as it corresponds to the ultimate$_1$ end of creation;[88] and (2) to reveal the fact that to be a human creature is to be entirely sustained in and by this love. The "happiness" and "joy" is greater by spiritual perception.[89] In Edwards's metaphysical idealism, greater perception (if ordered properly) yields greater consent. The contrary is also true: if disordered, it yields greater dissent.

One may now see the import of Edwards's understanding of the Fall. Apart from the stability of God's gracious motion via the Holy Spirit, human creatures will inevitably sin, drifting toward self-sufficiency and self-love (i.e., dissent). God knows this. And, as we have seen, Edwards's species of supralapsarian Christology already prioritizes incorporation (not ontological) into the divine life on the front end. That is, the Son's hypostatic union with a human nature enables adoption into the divine life so as to share in the divine love that exists between the Father and the Son. But, according to Edwards's manner of reasoning, being adopted into the divine life is not enough. Because human creatures cannot, nor will they ever, perceive identically in the way God perceives, the Fall allows for a closer perception to that of God's perception than would otherwise be possible apart from it. The telos—the end-for-the-sake-of-which—of the incarnation itself has not changed, namely communication of the Son's fullness through beatitude; the Fall, from this perspective, does not determine the fact of the incarnation. Even still, God permits the Fall in order to reveal the depth of that same end. In other words, human creatures cannot correctly perceive their natural state and the depth of their true end apart from the Fall. "God's design was first to show the creature's emptiness in itself and then to fill it with himself in an eternal, unalterable fullness and glory."[90] Edwards is not arguing that the Fall makes creatures empty. The Fall, rather, reveals the emptiness of the creature apart from God's grace and love. The Fall reveals to creatures that they are indeed creatures. According to Edwards, the creature needs to be brought to see "their own emptiness" in order to then "be brought to an entire dependence on the sovereign grace and all-sufficiency of God,

---

87. As stated at the end of Chapter 3, I am aware that Edwards's thoughts in the 1733 sermon series "Wisdom Displayed in Salvation," as well as elsewhere, appear to contradict this portrayal of the Fall. For example: "Man's misery is made an occasion of increasing both [the union to a proper object and relish of the object] by the work of redemption." In *The Works of President Edwards*, vol. IV, reprint of the Worcester edition (New York: Leavitt & Allen, 1857), 156. I will address this dissonance directly in the final chapter.

88. In Edwards's theology, the depth and perfection of this love has a name *ad intra*: the Holy Spirit.

89. See Edwards's discussion of spiritual perception (sense) in *WJE* 2:271–2.

90. "Miscellanies," no. 936, *WJE* 20:192.

to be communicated to them by his Son as their head."[91] Again, in this theological and metaphysical picture, greater perception yields greater consent or dissent.

At this juncture, it is important to ask how Edwards's reasoning here squares with his aesthetic reasoning elsewhere that the sense of God's perfections would be imperfect and faint without the knowledge of sin and evil. As Edwards argues in "Miscellanies" no. 348 (an entry labeled "Decrees"),

> And as it [is] necessary that there should be evil, because the glory of God could not but be imperfect and incomplete without it, so it is necessary in order to the happiness of the creature, in order to the completeness of that communication of God for which he made the world; because the creature's happiness consists in the knowledge of God and the sense of his love, and if the knowledge of him be imperfect, the happiness must be proportionably imperfect. And the happiness would also be imperfect upon another account; for as we have said, the sense of good is comparatively dull and flat without the knowledge of evil.[92]

Edwards reaches this conclusion based upon the relation between God's essential glory and its expression *ad extra*. "It is highly proper that the effulgent glory of God should answer his real excellency."[93] The permission of sin allows for, at least in this early "Miscellanies" entry, the proper communication and perception of all of God's perfections, which includes justice in the form of punishment. Overall, this entry appears to place Edwards, as John Hick dubbed it, within the framework of an Augustinian-style aesthetic theodicy.[94] Sin and evil—from the divine perspective—appear to yield something greater, for example, the glorification of all of God's perfections. While this sort of aesthetic conclusion certainly seems warranted in this particular "Miscellanies" entry, there is also a piece of the puzzle missing. Recall, based on Edwards's larger reasoning on divine justice, nothing about divine justice per se demands that God order the world toward the expression of justice in the mode of vindictive punishment. God, in other words, does not create in order to display God's glory in punishing.

This is where the relation between God's essential glory and effulgent glory as worked out in "Miscellanies" no. 348 needs to be read in conversation with Edwards's claims regarding the election of Jesus Christ *ad extra*, as well as the

---

91. "Miscellanies," no. 936, *WJE* 20:192. Edwards says something similar in his sermon "God Glorified in Man's Dependence" (1731): "And we are not only indeed more dependent on the grace of God, but our dependence is much more conspicuous, because our own insufficiency and helplessness in ourselves is much more apparent, in our fallen and undone state, than it was before we were either sinful or miserable." *WJE* 17:204; Cf. "Miscellanies," no. 1127, *WJE* 20:498.

92. "Miscellanies," no. 348, *WJE* 13:420–1.

93. "Miscellanies," no. 348, *WJE* 13:419.

94. Hick, *Evil and the God of Love*, 76–95.

permission of the Fall as subservient to that ultimate$_1$ end. Without doing such, it would be easy to interpret Edwards as endorsing wholesale the following theological picture: (1) God decrees his self-glorification through the necessary exercise and expression of all of the divine attributes; (2) justice is such an attribute; (3) divine justice includes punishing justice; and so (4) God decrees the permission of the Fall and subsequent sin in order to display punishing justice, which, in turn, allows creatures to appreciate the fullness of justice as such. While this is clearly the plain teaching of "Miscellanies" no. 348, Edwards also takes this aesthetical insight in a christological direction. With the christological aspect in place, one is able to integrate Edwards's thoughts on the end of creation, the Fall, and the end of redemption.

Felix Culpa *and the Work of Redemption*

According to Edwards, God aims at the fullest manifestation of God's excellencies and perfections in the created order only insofar as they are communicated christologically. As witnessed in the prior chapters, Edwards ties this closely to the work of redemption, so much so that it is possible to have the impression that Edwards prioritizes the work of redemption over creation. But this is, as I have argued, a misjudgment. The decree of redemption remains subordinate to the decree concerning the election of Christ *ad extra*: "All the works and dispensations of G[od] in all parts of the Creation & in all ages of it are such as shew forth the Infinite value G[od] has for & delight he has in his son."[95] Given Edwards's understanding of the Fall, the work of redemption follows upon the supposition of sin so as to amplify the christological telos of creation as to perception. Precisely in this way, Edwards can say—not infelicitously—that the work of redemption is, "as it were, the sum of God's works of providence" and that "God intended the world for his Son's use in the affair of redemption."[96]

This interpretation becomes particularly acute for correctly assessing Edwards's understanding of the communication and glorification of the divine perfections within the temporal mission of the Son vis-à-vis the crucifixion. For Edwards, the work of redemption allows one to perceive the depth of love that exists between the Father and Son, the same love in which humans were created to share through adoptive union, which is the "peculiar benefit of the covenant of grace."[97] "It was the will of G[od] to shew forth his own Glory," Edwards writes, "& that in a Great degree so it was his Et[ernal] will greatly to shew forth his Love to his son … this was Gods Et[ernal] design & purpose & seems to be called by way of Eminency his decree."[98]

---

95. Sermon 699. Heb. 2:7-8 (March 1743) [L. 1v.].
96. "Sermon Thirty," *WJE* 9:518.
97. "Miscellanies," no. 1093, *WJE* 20:482.
98. Sermon 699. Heb. 2:7-8 (March 1743) [LL. 3v.- 4r.].

For this reason, Edwards insists that divine justice "is more gloriously manifested in the sufferings of Christ for the elect than in the damnation of the wicked."[99] In Edwards's theological and metaphysical reasoning, justice is most properly about the order of divine love. Christ, in his passion, preeminently manifests "an infinite regard for the honor of God's justice."[100] As further witnessed in his sermon, "Excellency of Christ," the passion uniquely reveals a particular conjunction of excellencies in Christ, "viz. his infinite regard to God's justice, and such love to those that have exposed themselves to it, as induced him thus to yield himself a sacrifice to it."[101] Of particular importance is Christ's love. For Edwards, justice is more gloriously manifested in Christ's passion because self-giving love is the excellency of God's triune life.[102] That is, love of this sort positively mirrors divine justice *ad intra*. Rather uniquely in Christ's passion, then, God's self-giving manifests itself in God's ability to reveal the disagreeableness of sin to God's being (i.e., vindictive justice), as well as the plentitude and perfection of divine love (i.e., divine justice per se) which is set in relief by it.

Returning to the *felix culpa*, God orders the Fall not only to reveal human insufficiency apart from God's love (i.e., that they are in fact creatures), but also to reveal (in coordination) the depth of the sufficiency and perfection of God's love as it exists between the Father and the Son in the Spirit. "Here is a great occasion," Edwards argues with regard to the Fall, "for the manifestation of the fullness of God's heart. In the creatures' unworthiness and misery is [an] extraordinary occasion for opening the treasury of infinite riches and fullness of the divine nature."[103] In particular, Christ's willing submission to the vindicatory aspect of justice expresses the depths of God's self-giving love, as well as reveals the complete dependence of the creature upon God. So conceived, the "greatest manifestation of evil" and "dreadful nature of sin" truly appear in the crucifixion.[104] At the cross, the full magnitude and reality of human dissent (i.e., sin) is revealed in that human beings actually reject and crucify the Lord of glory.[105] The cross also reveals the extent of God's dissent from sin, chiefly in the fact that only the incarnate Son can—as the

---

99. *WJE* 24:1024.
100. "Excellency of Christ" (August 1736), *WJE* 19:577.
101. "Excellency of Christ" (August 1736), *WJE* 19:578.
102. This need not be taken to mean—as Brandon Gallaher does following Balthasar—that there exists a sort of *Ur-kenosis* in the divine life, a hypostatic modality of readiness of the Son to obedience and self-surrender. Christ might well be conceived of as the divine *Uridee* of involving a non-divine world in the trinitarian life of love, though not in the sense of a "pre-sacrifice." See Gallaher, *Freedom and Necessity*, 203–50. Also, *pace* Barth, the obedience of the Son in his sacrificial death should not be projected into the eternal being of God with the result that divine humility is rendered voluntaristically as a form of eternal divine obedience. On this point, see Wilcoxen, *Divine Humility*, 109–44.
103. "Approaching the End of God's Grand Design" (December 1744), *WJE* 25:119.
104. "Miscellanies," no. 941, *WJE* 20:199.
105. "Miscellanies," no. 1005, *WJE* 20:330.

only truly righteous one—restore dissenting creatures by substituting himself "in their stead."[106] It is important to recognize, however, that God's dissent from sin did not render the Son himself odious to God: "Christ suffered the wrath of God for men's sins in such a way as he was capable of, being an infinitely holy person who knew that God was not angry with him personally, knew that God did not hate him, but infinitely loved him." Christ "became" sin, according to Edwards, in that he had in his soul "a great and clear sight of the infinite wrath of God against the sins of men, and the punishment they had deserved," and this in such way that "our sins were his tormenters."[107]

Most importantly, the work of redemption reveals the glorious depths of the love that exists between the Father and Son. This same love is that which the Son temporally enacts, and therefore reveals, in his passion:

> Christ never did anything whereby his love to the Father was so eminently manifested, as in his laying down his life, under such inexpressible sufferings, in obedience to his command, and for the vindication of the honor of his authority and majesty; nor did ever any mere creature give such a testimony of love to God as that was: and yet this was the greatest expression of all, of his love to sinful men, that were enemies to God.[108]

The passion, in this sense, is not antithetical to God's love. It is the temporal unfolding of its beauty. Precisely in beholding and experiencing the benefits of the work of redemption, human creatures are given a deeper perception of God's life *ad intra*.[109] This is similarly true for angels: "The glorious angels have the greatest manifestations of the glory of God by what they see in the work of men's redemption, and especially in the death and sufferings of Christ."[110] The angels, however, are never incorporated into the divine life through adoptive union, even as Christ remains the "head" of their election in an extrinsic sense. The angels see God's love, though they never—to use one of Edwards's favorite analogies—taste it.

Particular Election and Reprobation

Without question, Edwards endorsed the sovereign election and rejection of individual persons in the same vein as the *Westminster Confession*.[111] As Edwards

---

106. "Miscellanies," no. 1005, *WJE* 20:332.
107. "Miscellanies," no. 1005, *WJE* 20:329–30.
108. *WJE* 19:577.
109. This focus on perception, or "sense," comes through clearly in "Miscellanies" no. 1127, wherein Edwards discusses the fittingness of a state of probation before confirmation in beatitude. See *WJE* 20:499. Cf. Miklos Vetö, *La pensée de Jonathan Edwards*, 292–3.
110. "Miscellanies," no. 937, *WJE* 20:197.
111. Cf. *WCF* 4.5–7.

specifies in a sermon on Rom. 11:7, "is only in the distinctions that sovereign Grace makes among them some are Elected and others are Left ... those that G[od] of his sovereign Good Pleasure has been pleased to ... set his Love upon from Et[ernity] & ordain [them] to Et[ernal] Life others he has Left to perish."[112] The manner in which Edwards articulated God's reason in this distinction post-Fall between the elect and reprobate is both clear and straightforward: God's sovereign good pleasure.[113] In this very limited sense, Edwards's discussion is both traditional—in keeping with the particularism of Reformed orthodoxy in contrast to the Remonstrant position—and confessionally standard. This does not mean it is not possible to further analyze Edwards's position on particular predestination in terms of causality, knowledge, and freedom, both divine and human, either with reference to the Reformed tradition or in terms of his metaphysics.[114] It certainly is, and Edwards has much to say about those matters. But Edwards's views on causality and contingency are not the primary concern here. While the relation between the divine decree, divine causality, and human choice is an important theological topic, it has only an indirect bearing on the question at hand. The direct concern is the correspondence between the election of Jesus Christ *ad extra* as the harmonious center of the decrees and the particular objects of election and rejection, especially the end of their existence. Is it true—in Thomas Schafer's memorable turn of phrase—that reprobate persons serve only as "ontological ciphers" within Edwards's theological program?[115] Or, as Amy Plantinga Pauw has argued, does Edwards's dynamic understanding of God's beautiful being and works—all summarized under the category of union—falter eschatologically? This leads her to a startling conclusion about the non-elect within Edwards's vision: "Instead of a cosmic redemption, there is a cosmic holocaust: the earth created by God is annihilated in a paroxysm of apocalyptic violence, and the vast majority of God's creatures are eternally bereft of the communications of God's goodness and love that were God's end in creation."[116] In order to address these questions, this final section turns to consider the terminus of individual election

---

112. Sermon 552. Rom. 11:7(b) (May 1740) [L. 1v.], *WJEO* 55.

113. Cf. "Miscellanies," no. 1245, *WJE* 23:180.

114. This, for example, is the approach of Philip Fisk. According to Fisk, Edwards's insistence on causal (moral) necessity—universal determining providence—obliterates the classic Reformed distinction on freedom as freedom *ad utremlibet*, and, as a result, an ontology of true contingency. See Philip John Fisk, *Jonathan Edwards's Turn from the Classic-Reformed Tradition of Freedom of the Will* (Göttingen: Vandenhoeck & Ruprecht, 2016), especially chapter 6 and the conclusion. Another issue that often arises in these discussions is Edwards's adherence to a species of occasional causation. See, for example, Oliver Crisp, "How 'Occasional' was Edwards's Occasionalism," in *Jonathan Edwards: Philosophical Theologian*, ed. Paul Helm and Oliver D. Crisp (Burlington, VT: Ashgate, 2003), 61–77.

115. Schafer, "Jonathan Edwards's Conception of the Church," 54.

116. Pauw, *The Supreme Harmony of All*, 132.

Christ, the Holy Spirit, and the Elect

Although the predominant focus thus has been on the integration of creation and Christology, the election of Jesus Christ *ad extra* is a thoroughly trinitarian movement for Edwards. To say otherwise would be to misconstrue the relationship that exists between the divine processions, the divine missions, and the christological telos of creation. For God's life *ad intra*, the Holy Spirit is, properly speaking, the end of Father's election of the Son: "And the Holy Ghost is the last that proceeds from both the other two, yet the Holy Ghost has this peculiar dignity: that he is as it were the end of the other two, the good that they enjoy, the end of all procession."[117] The Holy Spirit abides as the "infinite and eternal mutual holy energy between the Father and Son."[118] For this reason, the peculiar glory of the Holy Spirit *ad intra* is to be the "messenger of both the other persons" in their internal actions, so much so that Edwards argues that the Spirit—in one respect—"wholly influences the Father and Son in all they do."[119] The innertrinitarian (and necessary) election of the Son *ad intra* may be further described, in Kyle Strobel's helpful analysis, using the rubric of religious affection in pure act, or God's personal-beatific delight.[120] The communicative and affective joy that the Father and Son have in each other is the Holy Spirit, who is the pure act of love proceeding from the Father and the Son. To speak of the Father's love for and glorification of the Son as a communicative end is to speak of the Holy Spirit, who is that "delight that the Father and Son have in each other."[121]

In terms of the election of Jesus Christ *ad extra*, Edwards's pneumatology crucially comes to bear in two distinct areas. The first involves Edwards's Spirit-Christology. The incarnation of the Son of God, according to Edwards, entails "giving communion of the divine personality to the human nature."[122] This means the incarnation is a trinitarian act wherein the Father sends the Son into the world and "incarnates" him by an act of sanctification. In other words, the hypostatic union results from the creation and (continual) communication of the Spirit to the human nature of Jesus Christ at the behest of the Father. In this trinitarian movement, the Spirit is given without measure to the human nature of Christ so as to bond it with the eternal Logos.[123] Without getting into all of the intricacies of Edwards on the manner of the hypostatic union, this pneumatological rounding

---

117. *WJE* 21:146.
118. *WJE* 8:373.
119. *WJE* 21:147.
120. See Strobel, *Jonathan Edwards's Theology*, 225–8.
121. *WJE* 21:189.
122. "Miscellanies," no. 709, *WJE* 18:334.
123. Cf. *WJE* 24:767; "Miscellanies," no. 487, *WJE* 13:529. For a further analysis of Edwards's Spirit mediated Logos Christology, see Seng-Kong Tan, *Fullness Received and*

out underscores something central about the election of Jesus Christ *ad extra*. As Rowan Williams aptly put it, Christ is seen as the heart and logic of creation because "Christ appears as the *perfect creaturely*."[124] In Christ one sees "an entire human identity as an unbroken embodiment of divine [triune] life; not 'resembling' but enacting it."[125] One sees in Christ the perfect enactment of divine election, which is trinitarian through and through: the temporal enactment of the infinite and complete giving of life between the Father, Son Incarnate, and Spirit. In this way, Jesus Christ qua human nature has the Holy Spirit precisely as the divine Logos does; he "has the Spirit of the only begotten of the Father."[126]

Secondarily, one recognizes in the mission of the Holy Spirit—based on Edwards's emphasis on adoptive incorporation into God's triune life—the mission to effectuate such incorporation by uniting elect human creatures to Christ. Recall, the Holy Spirit is "the end of [the Father and Son] in their acting *ad intra*, and also in [God's] acting *ad extra*, in all they do in redemption and their distinct economical offices."[127] Edwards states the matter more directly: "The end of the Father in electing is the Spirit. He elects to a possession of this benefit."[128] Edwards refers to the Holy Spirit as the end of election because the Holy Spirit—as the hypostatic enabler of divine love *ad intra*—enables affective union with the Son *ad extra*.[129] No vital union is possible without the Spirit's illuminating, regenerating, and infusing action.[130] For Edwards, "'Tis through the vital communications and indwelling of the Spirit, that the saints have all their light, life, holiness, beauty and joy in heaven: and 'tis through the vital communications and indwelling of the same Spirit, that the saints have all light, life, holiness, beauty and comfort on earth; but only communicated in less measure."[131]

In the work of particular election, the saints are, through the new foundation of the Spirit laid in their soul, united to Christ and drawn into the life of love that exists between the Father and the Son.[132] Particular election entails participation in the Son's election as effectuated by the Spirit, though always in a creaturely and

---

Returned: Trinity and Participation in Jonathan Edwards (Minneapolis, MN: Fortress Press, 2014), 108–85.

124. Rowan Williams, *Christ the Heart of Creation* (London: Bloomsbury Continuum, 2018), 226.

125. Williams, *Christ the Heart of Creation*, 239.

126. "Miscellanies," no. 487, *WJE* 13:529.

127. *WJE* 21:146.

128. *WJE* 21:146–7.

129. As Edwards writes in his "Treatise on Grace": "There is a union with Christ, by the indwelling of the love of Christ, two ways: first, as 'tis from Christ, and is the very Spirit and life and fullness of Christ; and second, as it acts to Christ: for the very nature of it is love and union of heart to him." *WJE* 21:195.

130. See, for example, Strobel, *Jonathan Edwards's Theology*, 177–207.

131. *WJE* 2:236–7. Cf. *WJE* 21:195.

132. Cf. *WJE* 2:206.

mediated form. Jesus Christ receives the Spirit without measure and perfectly, therein having an immediate vision of the Father in his human nature.[133] The elect saints, in contradistinction, receive the Spirit permanently but not in the identical manner as Christ. In this sense, the saints' union with Christ remains categorically distinct from the union of the divine and human natures in Christ.[134] To be united to Christ by the Spirit means to be drawn in and ordered to the type of life that Christ possesses.[135] The Spirit further enables a spiritual and heightened perception of the excellency of Christ, and, in so doing, enables the saint to mediately partake of Christ's immediate "child-like relation to the Father."[136] For Edwards, this is beatitude.[137]

The Beatific Vision

For elect human creatures, communicative and adoptive union culminates in the blessed vision of God. Among Protestant theologians, Edwards stands out for his consistent correlation of the beatific vision with Jesus Christ.[138] For Edwards, the beatific vision is not an immediate and intellectual vision of God's essence, but "consists mostly in beholding the glory of God in the face of Jesus Christ, either in his work or in his person as appearing in the glorified human nature."[139] This should come as no surprise given Edwards's understanding of the election of Jesus Christ *ad extra*. It is the clear and consistent trajectory of his thought. Jesus Christ—as God incarnate—is the one and only grand medium of God's

---

133. Cf. *WJE* 18:428.

134. Cf. Caldwell III, *Communion in the Spirit*, 192–3.

135. Note, however, no claims are made here about the "experience" of union. For one intriguing account of such an experience with an eye to the atonement, see Jordan Wessling, *Divine Love: A Systematic Account of God's Love for Humanity* (Oxford: Oxford University Press, 2020), 219–46.

136. "True Saints, When Absent from the Body, Are Present with the Lord" (October 1747), *WJE* 25:234.

137. In his study of Edwards on "participation," W. Ross Hastings lays a desideratum for participation, namely the "appropriate integration of incarnational Christology and pneumatology." Hastings, *Jonathan Edwards and the Life of God: Toward an Evangelical Theology of Participation* (Minneapolis, MN: Fortress Press, 2015), 163. Overall, Hastings sees Edwards as failing in this integration because Edwards's "highly pneumatic version of *theosis*—which needs Christ only in a secondary and forensic manner and involves asymptotic progression in heaven—smacks of Plotinian influence" (319). Given the arguments I have presented throughout, it is hard to see how such a conclusion is even close to sustainable.

138. For fuller treatments of the beatific vision in Edwards's theology, see Hans Boersma, *Seeing God: The Beatific Vision in the Christian Tradition* (Grand Rapids, MI: Wm. B. Eerdmans, 2018), 354–84; and Kyle Strobel, *Jonathan Edwards's Theology*, 125–76.

139. "Miscellanies," no. 1137, *WJE* 20:515.

communicative knowledge.¹⁴⁰ In Christ, elect believers come to partake intimately of the Father-Son relationship. It is not, however, that the believer comes to see the essence of God (the Father) directly and statically; instead, the believer gets caught up in the dynamic of love between the Father and the Son through their union with Christ:

> They being in [Christ] shall Partake of the ~~Immense~~ Love of G[od] the F[ather] to [Christ] and as the son ... Knows the F[ather] so they shall Partake with him in his sight of G[od] as being as it were Parts of him as he is in the Bosom of The F[ather] so are they in the Bosom of the F[ather]. as he has Immense Joy in the Love of the F[ather] so have they Everyone of them in their measure the ~~same~~ Joy in the same Love of the F[ather].¹⁴¹

As articulated in the previous section, Edwards argues that the proper means for being drawn into this divine life is the Holy Spirit. Again, this is not surprising, for the believer partakes of the divine life after the same manner as God exists *ad intra*. Being caught up in the dynamic of love entails a permanent sending forth of the Holy Spirit into the soul of the saint.¹⁴² In beatitude, "the soul shall live perfectly in and upon Christ, being perfectly filled with his Spirit, and animated by his vital influence."¹⁴³ The election of individual believers, therefore, involves being engrafted into the Son's election *ad extra* via the Holy Spirit, which in turn enables a partaking—not ontological—in beatitude of the Son's election *ad intra*. In heaven the saint will enjoy a vision of the Father with and in Christ, not simply by Christ. Believers are "heirs with [Christ] of his happiness in the enjoyment of his Father."¹⁴⁴ Kyle Strobel articulates well the dynamic at work: "Our call is not simply to gaze on the beauty of Christ, to see Christ as beautiful, but to be caught

---

140. According to Edwards, Jesus Christ is the only creature that has an immediate vision of the divine essence. All elect creatures mediately see God [the Father] through Christ. "Jesus Christ is admitted to know God immediately; but the knowledge of all other creatures in heaven and earth is by means, or by manifestations or signs held forth. And Jesus Christ, who alone sees immediately, [is] the grand medium of the knowledge of all others; they know no otherwise than by the exhibitions held forth in and by him, as the Scripture is express." "Miscellanies," no. 777, *WJE* 18:428.

141. Sermon 373. Rom. 2:10(2) (December 17, 1735) [LL. 44v.-45r.], *WJE* 50. It must be noted, once again, how Edwards seemingly indicates that the beatifical vision only follows as a result of the Fall. Immediately following the aforementioned quotation, Edwards says this: "Herein they shall Enjoy G. in a more Exalt & Excellent manner than ... men would have done if he had never Fallen. for doubtless that happiness that [Christ] hims[elf] Partakes of in his Fathers Bosom is transcenden[t]ly sweet & Excellent—. & how happy therf[ore] are they that are admitted to partake of that stream ... of delight with him" (L. 45r.).

142. Cf. Sermon 373. Rom. 2:10(2) (December 17, 1735) [LL. 44v.-45r.], *WJE0* 50.

143. "True Saints," *WJE* 25:231–2.

144. "True Saints," *WJE* 25:234.

up into this beauty itself—that our whole being would consent to his, and that we would partake of his filial relationship with the Father."[145]

Perhaps the most novel aspect of Edwards's thoughts on the beatific vision involves its progressive nature.[146] In a very real sense, the beatific vision begins on earth and increases both in intensity and clarity in heaven. Although the earthly vision is comparatively dim, it is nevertheless the "imperfect beginning of a blessed-making sight of God."[147] Because the vision of God is always mediated christologically, Edwards conceives of the journey toward beatitude as a christological journey wherein faith (consent) and bodily sight become increasingly intertwined.[148] For Edwards, the journey is pedagogical.[149] On this point, we return once again to Edwards's unique reasoning on the *felix culpa*. As a result of the Fall, the saints' perception of and participation in the history of the work of redemption enables them to perceive the depth of God's love; this, in turn, increases the affection that saints have for the beauty of the triune God in beatitude: "but how Greatly then will Heaven be the more Prized by the saints when they Consid[er] … it as the Fruit of the Love of … a Person so Glo[rious] & Excellent. & … one that is so Exceedingly … Beloved by them. & that tis the Fruit of so Great Love Even … Love that … appear[e]d in shedding his own Precious Blood to purchase this Blessedn[ess] for them."[150] In the work of redemption, so Edwards reasons, the glory of the divine perfections—especially divine love— appears "much more brightly."[151] It appears much more brightly not only for the sake of the divine perfections themselves, but for the sake of the one who bears the perfections. The saints are meant to see the Son's glory and in seeing the Son see the Father. Heaven is the world of their love shared with the saints. The saints "shall know that God and Christ will be forever, and that their love will be continued and be fully manifested forever, and that all their beloved fellow

---

145. Kyle Strobel, "Theology in the Gaze of the Father: Retrieving Jonathan Edwards's Trinitarian Aesthetics," in *Advancing Trinitarian Theology: Explorations in Constructive Dogmatics*, ed. Oliver Crisp and Fred Sanders (Grand Rapids, MI: Zondervan, 2014), 160–1.

146. See Paul Ramsey's fine essay, "Appendix III: Heaven Is a Progressive State," in *WJE* 8:706–38. Most of the themes I have been tracing are found in Ramsey's essay, especially Ramsey's claim that the foundation for understanding Edwards's argument in *End of Creation* is Christology (p. 730).

147. "Pure in Heart Blessed" (c. 1730), *WJE* 17:76. Cf. Boersma, *Seeing God*, 377.

148. One is reminded of the structure of Augustine's *De trinitate* as christological quest. For an interpretation of just this point, see Khaled Anatolios, *Retrieving Nicaea: The Meaning and Development of Trinitarian Doctrine* (Grand Rapids, MI: Baker Academic, 2011), 241–80.

149. A similar emphasis on pedagogy is appropriated by Boersma in his dogmatic proposal on the beatific vision. See Boersma, *Seeing God*, 387–429.

150. Sermon 373. Rom. 2:10(2) (December 17, 1735) [L. 46v.], *WJEO* 50. Cf. Pauw, *Supreme Harmony*, 138.

151. "Miscellanies," no. 777, *WJE* 18:430.

saints shall live forever in glory with the same love [i.e., the Holy Spirit] in their hearts."[152]

This emphasis on what we might rightly call Edwards's pedagogy of perception undergirds his argument against the counterfactual claim that God could have created the elect in a heavenly and sinless state and ordered them toward adoptive and beatific union. As Edwards reasons in "Miscellanies" nos 1127 and 1129, God wisely orders the Fall and a state of probation for the elect in order that their interest in and perception of Christ and the riches of God's love, grace, and goodness might increase. The backdrop of sin and misery enables a greater sensibility of "the beauty of holiness" and the "greatness of the benefit of salvation," and so "serves to humble the soul and fit it for exaltation."[153] As Edwards writes in "Miscellanies" no. 1127,

> God's graces and the riches of his love would have been less displayed, as God's creatures would have been less holy and less happy, and so would have reaped less of the fruits of his love; and as they would have for less to have given 'em a sense of their dependence upon and indebtedness to God's rich and free goodness; as they would have been less sensible of the value of the benefits they have by God's goodness, as was before observed, and less to humble them and make them sensible of their own meanness and insufficiency who are the subjects of these benefits; and also as they would [not] have seen that it was owing to God's mere good pleasure that such a difference is made in their state from a state of misery which others, their fellow creatures, are in and they were liable to.[154]

Despite this emphasis on humility, Edwards also indicates in this same "Miscellanies" entry that the Fall—and by extension a state of probation—enables a display of God's moral perfections and government, in particular (vindictive) justice. "Without a state of probation, no such attribute as God's justice would even have been exercised or beheld."[155] While this certainly resonates with Edwards's statements in "Miscellanies" no. 348 about the display of all of God's perfections, it also perpetuates a tension within Edwards's overall theology with regard to divine justice. This tension becomes more acute when considering reprobation because it seems to entail, in Oliver Crisp's words, some sort of quota of elect and reprobate.[156] Do the elect who are united to Christ need to perceive sin, misery, and wrath—not just in Christ's cross, but both in themselves and in others (i.e., the reprobate)—in order to value and incline the heart to the "beauty of God's holiness?"[157] Edwards answers in the affirmative. Based on precisely this sort of

---

152. *WJE* 8:383.
153. "Miscellanies," no. 1129, *WJE* 20:506.
154. "Miscellanies," no. 1127, *WJE* 20:499.
155. "Miscellanies," no. 1127, *WJE* 20:497.
156. Crisp, *Jonathan Edwards on God and Creation*, 184.
157. "Miscellanies," no. 1127, *WJE* 20:498; cf. "Miscellanies," no. 1129, *WJE* 20:506.

reasoning, Edwards's christological and progressive *visio Dei* contains a rather unpleasant element: the vision across the chasm—the vision of hell from heaven (and vice versa).[158] Edwards believes, in some sense, that an increasing perception of God's vindictive justice should "be kept up in the minds of creatures … in order to their right and just apprehensions of his greatness and gloriousness, and that perfect and becoming and answerable joy and happiness, in the spiritual sight and knowledge of him." This perception, in fact, is "needful in order to the proper respect of the creature to God, and the more complete happiness in a sense of his love."[159] When worked out eschatologically, the damnation of the wicked in hell actively serves the happiness of the saints in beatitude. Edwards explains as follows:

> The saints and angels in heaven before whom the wicked will be punished, will doubtless have a very great sight of the infinite greatness and awful majesty of God, against whom sin is committed, and so of the glorious excellency of that Savior and his dying love, that is rejected by sinners … [T]his punishment is designed to raise their idea of God's power and majesty, to impress it with exceeding strength and liveliness upon their minds, and so to raise their sense of the riches and excellency of his love to them.[160]

As odious as this sounds, it need not be taken to mean that the saints in heaven "find their own happiness increased by the torments of others."[161] True, saints will be sensible of the misery of the damned, but it "will not [be] because they delight in seeing the misery of others. Considered absolutely, the damned's suffering divine vengeance will be no occasion of joy to the saints merely as it is other's misery or because that it is pleasant to them to behold other's misery merely for its own sake."[162] The saints delight in the "sense" of God's justice, not "torment" per se. As Edwards maintains, "'Tis true that God delights in justice for its own sake, as well as in goodness; but it will by no means follow from thence, that he delights in the creatures' misery for its own sake as well as [in their] happiness."[163] So it is with

---

158. According to Edwards, it appears as if "the mis[ery] of the wicke[d] would in some Respect be in the view of the saints in Glor[y] … as the damneds seeing the Happin. of the saints in H will aggravate their mis. so the saints in H seeing the mis. of the d. in Hell will Give them a Greater sense of their own Happ." Sermon 373. Rom. 2:10(2) (December 17, 1735) [L. 47r.-47v.], *WJEO* 50. Cf. Vetö, *La pensée de Jonathan Edwards*, 492–5.
159. "Miscellanies," no. 407, *WJE* 13:469.
160. "Miscellanies," no. 866, *WJE* 20:107.
161. Pauw, *Supreme Harmony*, 177.
162. Sermon 277. Rev. 18:20 (March 1733), [LL. 5v.-6r.], *WJEO* 48. Published as "The End of the Wicked Contemplated by the Righteous" (March 1733), in *Works of President Edwards*, vol. IV, 290.
163. "Miscellanies," no. 461, *WJE* 13:502.

God, so it is with the saints. The more the saints "see of the justice of God," Edwards reasons, "the more will they prize and rejoice in his love."[164]

All of this, as Stephen Holmes has argued, appears to turn on a specific teleology of hell in the sense that the display and perception of vindictive justice stands as a necessary end in God's project of self-glorification.[165] But, as already recognized, this creates a tension in Edwards's theology. Edwards appears committed to two contrary accounts of justice and reprobation: (1) an account of God's self-glorification that requires—as an absolute necessity—the display of vindictive justice in a class of creatures known as reprobate; and (2) an account of God's self-glorification that hypothetically includes vindictive justice on the supposition of sin. But it is hard to see how position (1) can stand alongside Edwards's claim that God does not create and order a world toward the display of divine justice in the form of vindictive justice. As we have seen, justice cannot and does not have such a telic sway over God's decrees. Within Edwards's larger theological and metaphysical reasoning, divine justice is God's infinite and perfect agreeableness or regard for God's own being as worked out in a trinitarian manner. Yet, despite this fact, Edwards repeats—fairly frequently—that hell exists for the display of God's glory, which, in this instance, assumes the form of vindictive justice. What should one make of this ostensibly irreconcilable tension? To answer such a question, we turn to the relation between reprobation, hell, and the election of Christ *ad extra*.

Hell and the Reprobate

Hell, according to Edwards, is a "world of hatred," which God prepared "on purpose for the expression of God's wrath." God has no other use for hell but to "satisfy his hatred of sin and sinners."[166] In this way, as Edwards baldly comments in his sermon on Ezek. 15:2-4, the wicked are only useful in their destruction. The rationale is straightforward: if the human creature refuses to answer actively the ultimate end for which she was created, then God will act upon her "passively" in her destruction, and, in so doing, glorify the hypothetical end of vindictive justice. "When it is thus wicked men are useful only accidentally & not designedly."[167] Though the rhetoric of this sermon—and others like it—is somewhat chilling, Edwards's distinction between active and passive, accident and design needs to be kept in mind. Edwards clearly believes that God does not create in order to damn. As mentioned previously, when commenting on Rom. 9:17—a locus classicus within Reformed exegesis on the divine purpose in reprobation—Edwards

---

164. "The End of the Wicked Contemplated by the Righteous" (March 1733), in *The Works of President Edwards*, vol. IV, 292.

165. Stephen R. Holmes, "The Justice of Hell and the Display of God's Glory in the Thought of Jonathan Edwards," *Pro Ecclesia* IX, no. 4 (2000): 389–403.

166. *WJE* 8:390.

167. "Wicked Men Useful in Their Destruction Only" (July 1734), in *The Works of President Edwards*, vol. IV, 303.

maintains, "This scripture will hardly justify our expressing ourselves so that God gives reprobates a being to that end, that he might glorify himself in their destruction."[168] Even still, Edwards adheres to a position wherein the reprobate becomes a passive and eternal vessel for the perception of vindictive justice and the disagreeableness of sin, and thus actively serves God's self-glorification in Christ. This is what the elect perceive in heaven and how the damnation of the reprobate contributes to their sense of God's love and, by extension, happiness.

As we have also recognized, hell is infinite in duration for Edwards. God cannot bring an end to divine punishment based, in part, on the principle of proportionate regard. For this reason, Edwards could speak of the perfect execution of divine wrath without pity because divine wrath is not a passion in God, at least in the classical theological sense. Wrath is God's—given one element of his definition of divine justice—proportionate response to the dissent of the human creature. Sermonic descriptions such as fury and fierceness, therefore, "denote the Greatest degree of Anger or wrath" and the "effects" of justice as it proportionately meets a sinful object.[169] Yet Edwards also articulated another rationale for the eternal existence of the reprobate in hell, namely, their function within the matrix of perceiving being. God's wrath must be perpetually and increasingly perceived by both the saints in heaven and the damned in hell in order to, as Edwards puts it, reveal the value of the beauty of God's holiness.

Both of these realities—the principle of proportionate regard and the perception of justice—mitigate against the possibility of annihilationism for Edwards.[170] Instead, the reprobate asymptotically approach nothing in an analogical manner to how the consenting human creature (i.e., the elect) asymptotically approaches the relation of love existing between the Father and the Son.[171] Nothing, in this sense, is not ontological but ontic, gaining definitional traction based on the level of consent and dissent from God: "But agreeableness of perceiving being is pleasure, arid disagreeableness is pain. Disagreement or contrariety to being is evidently an approach to nothing, or a degree of nothing, which is nothing else but disagreement or contrariety of being, and the greatest and only evil."[172] Dissenting human creatures (i.e., the reprobate) approach nothing only in the sense that their being becomes increasingly characterized by lack of love. Metaphysically, Edwards refers to God's dissent from dissenting creatures as the "beauty of vindicative

---

168. *WJE* 24:1023.

169. Sermon 322. Rev. 19:15 (April 1734), [LL. 6r.-6v.], *WJEO* 49.

170. Jonathan Kvanvig places Edwards's account of hell withing the domain of the "strong view"; he also finds Edwards's argument that all sin is against God to be the most complete defense in the literature. Jonathan Kvanvig, *The Problem of Hell* (New York: Oxford University Press, 1993). 33. See also Kvanvig, "Jonathan Edwards on Hell," in *Jonathan Edwards: Philosophical Theologian*, ed. Paul Helm and Oliver D. Crisp (Burlington, VT: Ashgate, 2003), 1–11.

171. Cf. *WJE* 8:533.

172. *WJE* 6:335.

justice"¹⁷³ because dissent from dissenting being is "a manifestation of consent to being in general [i.e., God]."¹⁷⁴ To annihilate a dissenting creature would be for God to dissent from God's being, which is an impossibility. Instead, God sustains their ontological status as a perceiving mind, with the ontic irregularity of their dissent contributing to the overall harmony of beauty. For Edwards, then, created substance (i.e., mind) is "more" or "less" based on the "conformity" or "deformity" to God. For a creature to have "less being," so it actually appears, does not mean that they asymptotically approach annihilation. To the contrary, it means that they have "greater dissent" in direct proportion to their perception of reality. Ontologically, the whatness of a created mind does not "increase" or "decrease." Ontically, however, the quality and operation of that mind can be "conformed" or "deformed." To be deformed is to be nothing.

The terrain covered thus far certainly addresses the objectivity of God's wrath and hell, but what of its subjectivity? How does Edwards conceptualize the reprobate's conscious experience of infinite punishment in hell? The experience, as Edwards explains, is best described as hate: "Everything in hell is hateful."¹⁷⁵ The wicked hate God, hate Christ, hate angels, hate saints, and hate one another. "All of the principles which are contrary to love," argues Edwards, "will rage and reign without any restraining grace to them within bounds." And their "hatred and envy will be a torment to themselves."¹⁷⁶ For Edwards, the enactment of wrath in hell occurs by means of the unrestrained wills of the reprobate. Human creatures continually and increasingly dissent from God and from others in hell—the profound antithesis of union with Christ. From this perspective, the human creature in hell eternally wills to possess their self apart from God and does so in full consciousness of God. The sinning, in other words, is the punishment, and it is worked out phenomenologically at the immanent level of the disordered will.¹⁷⁷ Theologically speaking, God's wrath is not experienced—for all of Edwards's vivid, sermonic imagery—in a similar manner to how a human victim experiences torture—either physically or psychologically—at the hands of perpetrator.¹⁷⁸

173. *WJE* 6:365.
174. *WJE* 6:363.
175. *WJE* 8:390.
176. *WJE* 8:391.
177. Cf. "Miscellanies," no. 557, *WJE* 18:101; see also, Miklos Vetö, *La pensée de Jonathan Edwards*, 257–9.
178. A textbook (literally!) example of such imagery is Edwards's infamous Enfield sermon, "Sinners in the Hands of an Angry God." Edwards employs a variety of images—a "wide and bottomless pit," a fiery oven, "great waters damned for the present," a sword, a bow with an arrow "ready on the string" to be made "drunk with your blood," and so on—in order to depict the reality and intensity of God's wrath. *WJE* 22:404–18. To be fair, Edwards doesn't shy away from discussions of physical pain in hell, noting that even the "faculties of the bodies" of the damned will be enlarged in order to be sensible "inlets of more … misery." "Miscellanies," no. 921, *WJE* 20:167. Edwards also muses in an early sermon that those in hell will seek annihilation as an "escape" from the intensity of

Instead, God's wrath is experienced as God's dissenting presence, a presence which increases the knowledge that the damned have of their self as creatures of God, even if they never consent to God in Christ. Edwards's depiction strikingly mirrors Søren Kierkegaard's account of sin and despair. Sin, for Kierkegaard, is fundamentally a position (not an act per se) before God, wherein the human creature, in their sin, wills to be a "self" apart from God. But this is an ontological impossibility because there is no such thing as a self apart from God. "Sin is: before God in despair to will to be oneself."[179]

God, in terms of perception, "enlarges [the reprobates'] capableness of receiving misery or being made miserable, but he don't make 'em strong to bear misery."[180] Though Edwards remains somewhat unclear as to what exactly this means, it appears to entail something like the following: the Holy Spirit—in a manner similar to common grace among the unregenerate—enlarges the reprobates' perception of God's excellency, which in turn increases their misery. This misery is primarily internal, though also experienced externally as individuals in hell "blow the fire of each other's torment."[181] As the reprobates' perception of God's being increases eternally, so does their dissent from God and each other. The "vicious will continues to sink into itself."[182]

When taken all together, Edwards's theology of hell is as follows. The human creature in hell seeks annihilation, characterized not as "nonbeing," but as the furthest dissent from God in the exercise of the disordered/autonomous will. God, in fact, increases for the inhabitant of hell a perception of God's excellency, which in turn revivifies the creature's sin and hatred. This cycle occurs *ad infinitum*. The only thing—or so it seems—that keeps God from allowing the creature's literal annihilation is the principle of proportionate regard taken in conjunction with the necessity of the perception of divine (vindictive) justice within the matrix of perceiving being. The damned exist as perceiving and perceptible objects of dissent.

---

suffering that is experienced, though they will never be granted such a reprieve (Sermon 264. Rev. 6:15–16, [L. 7v.], *WJEO* 47). In any case, the physiological pain of hell should be conceived as opposite the physiological bliss of heaven, wherein the bodily vision of Christ yields spiritual vision which, in turn, produces religious affection—both body and soul.

179. Søren Kierkegaard, *Sickness unto Death: A Christian Psychological Exposition for Upbuilding and Awakening*, ed. and trans. Howard V. Hong and Edna H. Hong (Princeton: Princeton University Press, 1980), 81.

180. "Miscellanies," no. 656, *WJE* 18:197.

181. *WJE* 8:391.

182. Vetö, *La pensée de Jonathan Edwards*, 257: "mais la volonté vicieuse continue à s'enfoncer en elle-même."

Christ and the Reprobate

All of this, then, leads us to finally inquire about the strict relation between the being of the reprobate and the election of Jesus Christ *ad extra*. If all human creatures were made for communicative and beatific union in the Son of God, how is it possible that some human creatures fail to meet their christological end? Are reprobates ordained simply as ontological ciphers, means by which to advance the happiness of the elect in heaven as the elect perceive the increasing deformity of the reprobate in hell?

Given Edwards's commitment to the theological principle that God does not give the reprobate a being (in Christ) in order to glorify God's self actively in their damnation, it hardly seems justifiable to conclude that the reprobate person exists purposefully as an ontological cipher. What is more, Edwards's theologoumenon of the *felix culpa* implies that all human creatures—both elect and reprobate—are permitted to sin in order that the depth of Christ's perfections, especially love, might be revealed within the theater of created and redemptive history. For this very reason, Edwards believes Christ is the medium of God's communication both in heaven and in hell. The saints in heaven consent to Christ's person and partake of his election *ad intra*. The damned in hell dissent from Christ's person and suffer judgment at his hand. Judgment, however, entails the immediate sense of God's glorious presence. And, as Edwards preaches in a sermon on 2 Thess. 1:7-9, the execution of God's wrath upon the wicked shall come forth directly from Christ's presence.[183] Although Edwards remains circumspect about the exact manner of Christ's presence in hell, one may infer from his overall thought that a vision of Christ's glorified humanity enables the "sense of God's wrath" to be made immediately present to the soul in hell.[184] "But the wicked will see Christ by that external light with which he shall shine, though it will be no pleasing, but an infinitely terrible light unto them so that their bodies and organs of sense will be fitted to be acted upon by a quite different medium from what they are [now]."[185] The eternal flame that burns in hell, in Edwards's theological mind, also burns in heaven. Christ's resplendent countenance to one person is "the light of his love," and to another it is, in the same sense, "the flame of his wrath."[186]

Overall, the "sense of God's wrath" need only be taken—in the strict sense—as God's dissenting presence from dissenting being, meaning, by parity of reason, Christ's dissent from dissenting being. This is fitting because, in dissenting from Christ, the reprobate creature corroborates—precisely as the level of their dissent—the christological end of their being. Although unbelievers never value the positive excellency of Christ nor "desire after the enjoyment of Christ,"[187] they partake

---

183. Sermon 392. 2 Thess. 1:7-9 (May 1736), [LL. 6v.-7v.], *WJEO* 51.
184. Cf. "Miscellanies," no. 926, *WJE* 20:169–70.
185. "Miscellanies," no. 926, *WJE* 20:170.
186. "Miscellanies," no. 926, *WJE* 20:170.
187. Cf. "Unbelievers Contemn the Glory and Excellency of Christ" (May 1736), in *The Works of President Edwards*, vol. IV, 364.

remotely of his excellency in their dissent. In Edwards's metaphysical register, the irregularity of dissent to Christ (and, as a result, God's Being) contributes to the beauty of the whole at the level of vindictive justice, a justice always refracted through the person of Christ. Holmes, then, is incorrect to assert that the being of the reprobate is "less" or "differently" human, or Christless.[188] Ontologically, they are human all the way down, though their being is both deformed and deforming. The reprobate never escapes Christ; they continually, sensibly, and increasingly hate him.

Even still, the question remains as to the correspondence between the creation of every human being and the actual end of the reprobate in hell. On this point, Edwards could have availed himself of the sort of theological reasoning found in Thomas Goodwin, wherein only a select number of human creatures were destined for the "super" created end of beatitude before the Fall.[189] All human creatures are certainly created in Christ's election for Goodwin, though not every human creature is destined for Christ in a supernatural and unitive manner. To be sure, this is an odd sort of theological picture. Apart from consideration of the Fall, God elects a set number of humans for super-creation grace, while leaving the remaining in a natural (albeit sinless) state. After the Fall, those non-elect creatures are considered reprobate as their natural state becomes a sinful state apart from God's grace. While Goodwin's lapsarianism alleviates certain difficulties, it magnifies other. In particular, it maximizes the *beneplacitum* of God's will and power. Goodwin's theological picture is certainly consistent with Edwards's species of supralapsarianism, especially when considering his take on the covenant of works, Adam's reward, and the state of human creatures apart from superior and supernatural principles. Whether Edwards was aware of Goodwin's precise position or not is difficult to say. What one can say, however, is that Edwards does not take this route. He roots the distinction made between the elect and reprobate—a distinction made in their *fallen* state—in God's pure good pleasure, and that in accordance with God's antecedent and consequent will.[190] This fact notwithstanding, Edwards's theology—like Goodwin's—leaves him in a position wherein all human creatures possess their beings as a result of Christ's election, though not all receive adoptive union. For Edwards, this does not dehumanize the

---

188. For Holmes, Edwards's notion of reprobation renders the reprobate "less human (or at least 'differently human') than the elect." Holmes, *God of Grace and God of Glory*, 165. Holmes's critique has some force because he too notices—similarly though not identically to the interpretation offered in this study—that creation is enacted christologically and pneumatologically for Edwards. Yet, according to Holmes, this leaves the reprobate with a particularly Christless and Spiritless existence within Edwards's theological picture.

189. See my discussion of Goodwin in Chapter 1.

190. Cf. Vetö, *La pensée de Jonathan Edwards*, 213–15, 238–9.

reprobate because the reprobate still participates in the communicative matrix of being—perceiving and being perceived by Christ.[191]

Conclusion

It is now time to take stock. We may begin by reproducing the schematization of Edwards's lapsarianism. The picture is as follows:

1. The election of Jesus Christ *ad extra*, which entails
   1a. The decree of the glorification of divine perfections *ad extra* in and through the Son.
   1b. The decree to create this world.
   1c. The decree to communicate the glory of the divine perfections *ad extra* to a particular object of the Son's love, namely a "spouse" in strict union with the Son. The object is, at this point, *creabilis et labilis*.

2. The decree of the incarnation, which entails
   2a. The hypostatic union of the Son with a human nature. The particular human nature of Christ, in this moment, is *creandus*; the Son is, by extension, *incarnandus*.
   2b. The elevation of human creatures as the chosen "spouse" of the Son. This spouse now exists as *creandus et lapsurus* in the decree.

3. The decree of the covenant of works with the object existing as *creatus et lapsurus*.
4. The decree of the Fall.
5. The decree to redeem, which entails
   5a. The decree for the fit means as specified by the covenant of redemption. At this juncture, the objects are *creatus et lapsus*.

6. The decree of particular election and rejection with the objects as *creatus et lapsus*. This also entails
   6a. The decree of the fit means of election (i.e., sin and grace/mercy as understood from the perspective of the covenant of redemption).
   6b. The decree of the fit means of reprobation (i.e., sin).

7. The decree of damnation. The objects are *creatus et reprobus*.

---

191. Although Edwards does not argue for it explicitly, it could be the case that the saints in heaven perceive those in hell because, as those creatures united to Christ (i.e., his body), they share Christ's vision of the world.

This overall schematization of Edwards's on the logical instants of the decree, so I have argued, best characterizes him as a modified supralapsarian based on the integrative function of christological communication in his theology, even though the objects of particular election and reprobation are most certainly *creatus et lapsus*. In a similar manner to both Mastricht and Goodwin, Edwards's lapsarianism broadens the category of election such that Edwards is supralapsarian when considering the ultimate$_1$ end of election and infralapsarian when considering certain means of execution. Taken more precisely, Edwards's lapsarianism—just like that of Thomas Goodwin—prioritizes christological communication above all else, which then informs his further theological commitments regarding the covenant of works, the nature of the Fall and supernatural principles, and the centrality of the hypostatic union.

When considering reprobation more broadly, Edwards argues that only God's general decree to glorify his "holiness and greatness" stands prior to the permission of sin because that supposes neither the "being nor sinfulness" of a creaturely object.[192] But this is, strictly speaking, nothing more than a decree to glorify the fullness of God's love *ad intra*. In this very limited sense, Edwards may be styled supralapsarian when considering his own idiosyncratic presentation of the general contours of reprobation. Edwards's general supralapsarian framework has the further implication that particular reprobation and damnation of human creatures cannot unmoor itself from its prior christological reference point. In the end, damnation remains subservient to the manifestation and communication of the excellency of Christ.

When seen from the whole, Edwards articulates a lapsarian vision wherein all of God's decrees maintain a harmonious-teleological determination around Jesus Christ. Said another way, all of God's decrees are subordinate to the election of Jesus Christ *ad extra* and coordinate with each other. Creation in general and human creatures in particular exist to perceive the communicative harmony of the entire cosmos in Christ and, as a result, recommunicate—bask in and consent to—his excellency. For the elect human creature, perception yields consent to Christ; for the reprobate, it yields dissent. Theologically, this corresponds to Edwards's notion of spiritual and natural knowledge. The elect possess—via the permanent indwelling of the Holy Spirit—a spiritual knowledge wherein they perceive the world's structures more and more in line with its christological center, that is, God's arbitrary (wise) operations.[193] This movement is endlessly progressive and joyous. The reprobate, on the other hand, perceive the world naturally, secondarily, and remotely. This perception eternally enflames self-love and hatred. Miklos Vetö's conclusion on the "organic" relation of God's revelation to Christ, therefore, is well justified:

---

192. "Miscellanies," no. 704, *WJE* 18:317.
193. Cf. "Miscellanies," no. 1263, *WJE* 23:211–12.

The justified one who consents to Jesus Christ as his Savior also adheres to all the "articles" of the Christian faith. These items are not isolated lights. They are all taught by and focus on the Son. But whoever relates to the Son by theoretical faith alone will not be able to recognize the mutual harmony between these articles, their organic dependence on the principle of our salvation.[194]

Admittedly, Edwards's unwavering theocentrism will prove unsavory for many: God wisely ordains the Fall so that human creatures can better perceive the fullness of God's triune love as beheld in the Jesus Christ.[195] Or, to speak crudely, to reveal to human creatures how God's love *ad intra* works, and, in so doing, incorporate some of them into that love through union with the Son. However, one aspect of Edwards's theology seems grossly problematic here: the insistence on the eternal and perpetual perception of vindicative justice in the form of eternal punishment. On the face of it, Edwards's christological vision does not appear to be related to vindictive justice at all, especially not the necessary expression of it in the created order. Yet because human creatures are not divine persons, and cannot (ontologically) become divine persons, God's wise method for revealing the width and breadth and height of God's triune love includes setting it against the backdrop of creaturely dissent. As a result of the Fall, human creatures learn, in fact, that they are creatures: not self-sustained, not self-sufficient, not self-governed. The futility and inevitability of the creature's self-making project is fundamentally exposed in Jesus Christ, the one in whom and by whom and for whom all things were created. Human creatures need to see (perceive) and believe (consent) that they are sustained only by the Son's love, apart from which they are deformed and deforming. "The light of God's beauty, and that alone, truly shows the soul its own deformity, and effectually inclines it to exalt God, and abase itself."[196] The

---

194. Vetö, *La pensée de Jonathan Edwards*, 482: "Le justifié qui consent à Jesus-Christ comme son sauveur, adhère aussi à tous les «articles» de la foi chrétienne. Ces articles ne sont pas des lumières isolées. Ils sont tous enseignés par et portent sur le Fils. Or celui qui se rapporte au Fils par seule foi théorique ne saura reconnaître l'harmonie mutuelle entre ces articles, leur dépendance organique du principe de notre salut."

195. Overall, Edwards's theological position is strikingly similar to the Roman Catholic dogmatician Matthias Scheeben. Speculating on the relationship between the Fall and the incarnation, Scheeben writes, "If the race had originally, prior to its sin, received its supernatural goods from the God-man, then the truth would not have been so manifest that He, and He alone, is and can be the source of these goods." *Mysteries of Christianity*, 400. Scheeben—also in a manner resonating with Edwards—endorses a species of supralapsarian Christology rooted in the trinitarian processions (see *Mysteries*, 357–430). Scheeben frames the matter like this: "The answer to the question *Cur Deus homo*? is then also an answer to the question *Cur mundus*? Or *Ad quid mundus*? What direction is given to the world by the Incarnation? This question, although ordinarily too little noted in theological science, is as much place as the first question" (429).

196. "True Grace, Distinguished from the Experience of Devils" (December 1746), *WJE* 25:637.

true light of divine beauty is Christ incarnate, crucified, and risen. Just so, the necessary manifestation of vindictive justice, in Edwards's larger reasoning, is not primarily ordered toward the reprobate in hell but Christ at Calvary. Vindictive justice reveals the propriety of the creature's dependence on the Son's love and the worthiness of the Son as such. Though this does not resolve the difficulty latent in any form of the doctrine of reprobation (i.e., that God actually reprobates), it certainly challenges any claim that Edwards himself bifurcates perdition and God's self-giving in Jesus Christ.[197]

Such an interpretation of reprobation and justice within Edwards's theology slightly modifies, though it does not deny outright, an interpretation that closely intertwines the necessary revelation of God's glory in the form of vindictive justice, reprobation, and the permission of sin. This, for example, is one aspect of Oliver Crisp's interpretation. Recall, according to Crisp, Edwards is committed to the principle that "*necessarily, any created theater of divine glory must be one in which all aspects of that glory are manifested*"; in turn, so Crisp argues, Edwards also seems to be committed to the idea that there must be a quota of elect and reprobate in order to properly manifest the fullness of divine glory because vindictive justice is one such aspect of that glory.[198] Of course, this was not a new insight. John Newton Thomas argues—in the context of a discussion of supra- and infralapsarianism in Edwards's theology—that "the revealing of these attributes [i.e., holiness and justice] through the decree of reprobation is thus in part the end for which sin exists, and therefore the decree of reprobation is prior to the decree of permitting sin."[199] But, as we saw earlier, Edwards explicitly denies that vindictive justice is a divine attribute. It is, instead, a means for glorifying an attribute upon the supposition of sin. Even still, what Crisp and others latch on to is a significant tension I too recognize in Edwards's theological reasoning. The problem centers on Edwards's insistence that creaturely perception of vindictive justice in the divine plan is in some sense necessary. I call this a tension because Edwards's larger christological commitments indicate that even though divine justice in the form of punishment *may* deepen the perception of love, such a display of justice is not absolutely necessary. These are two very different claims, and, on my reading, the tension stands as unresolved within Edwards's theological reasoning. I will return to address this matter in the final chapter.

When seen from the whole, Edwards's theological vision resonates with both Herman Bavinck and Karl Barth. Obviously, there are numerous divergences and, at times, significant ones; but in the supralapsarian elements of Barth's Christology, in Barth's explanation of the *felix culpa*, and in Bavinck's organic and christological structuring of the decrees, there exist strong parallels. Not without reason did Barth confess that his Christian thesis "bears a close resemblance to that of the well-known writings" of Leibniz.[200] The divergence, Barth contends, is

---

197. Cf. Holmes, *God of Grace and God of Glory*, 211–53.
198. Crisp, *Jonathan Edwards on God and Creation*, 178–84.
199. Thomas, "Determinism in the Theological System of Jonathan Edwards," 128.
200. Barth, *CD* III.1, 388.

christological. Leibniz could not and did not represent the *maxio ratio* of the best possible world as the divinity and humanity of Jesus Christ. Like Barth, Edwards believed this created order to be the best possible one, not in a Leibnizian sense, but simply because the best possible world is a creation internally structured around Jesus Christ. Barth's comments about the Fall, then, could just have easily been written by Edwards: "The wisdom of God which allows [the fall] in order to make, not the episode itself, but the overcoming of it an occasion to magnify His grace and to reveal and actualize it—we have to say for the first time—as free grace in it, in accordance with His eternal will and purpose"; but never "necessary" in order to "excuse or exculpate the man who is responsible for it."[201] Edwards, as we saw, in fact did say it: "here is a great occasion for the manifestation of the fullness of God's heart. In the creatures' unworthiness and misery is [an] extraordinary occasion for opening the treasury of infinite riches and fullness of the divine nature."[202]

A final matter is worthy of note. Like Thomas Goodwin, Edwards's lapsarian vision also makes the grace of Christ central to human life. In so doing, Edwards's theology foregrounds the relationship between nature (creation) and grace. This, of course, remains a key divergence between Protestant and Roman Catholic theology, especially in relation to the question of the *donum superadditum*. On my interpretation, Edwards's theological reasoning bears strong similarities to the nature-grace relationship proposed by Kathryn Tanner. According to Tanner,

> The very created character of our existence, the fact, that is, that we are not divine, forms the major impediment to our receiving what God intends to give us in creating us, and constitutes therefore the major impetus behind God's grace. No created version of God's own goodness can ever adequately approach that goodness. If God wants to give it to humans, they have to be elevated beyond what they are themselves as creatures. In short, humans have to be given God in addition to being given themselves. Christ is the highest possible form in which the good of God's own life can be given to us: in him God and the human are one. Therefore, the grace of God in Christ becomes the highest way of addressing the impediment to God's design posed by creation, irrespective of the problem of sin.[203]

Although the language of impediment is, I think, severely misleading, the overall point remains germane: "Christ is the key … to the sort of grace human nature was made to enjoy."[204] The nature-grace relationship—as we saw in Turretin, Goodwin,

201. Barth, *CD* IV.1, 69.
202. "Approaching the End of God's Grand Design" (December 1744), *WJE* 25:119.
203. Tanner, *Christ the Key*, 60.
204. Tanner, *Christ the Key*, 140. Although there are significant differences in the theological pictures painted by Edwards and Tanner, both agree that the incarnation is for entrance into trinitarian relations (cf. Tanner, *Christ the Key*, 144). For a critique of Tanner's supralapsarian vision, see Edwin Chr. van Driel, "Sharing in Nature or Encountering a

and Barth in particular—lies at the heart of the lapsarian question. The whole debate, in fact, turns on it. Does—à la Turretin—a chasm exist between the order of nature and the order of grace? Or—à la Goodwin—are they integrated? Edwards sides with the latter. Christ is truly the sum of God's decrees and integrative center of creation and grace, and this resides *supra lapsum*.

Person: A Tale of Two Different Supralapsarian Strategies," *Scottish Journal of Theology* 75, no. 3 (2022): 193–206.

Part III

SUPRALAPSARIANISM RECONSIDERED

Chapter 6

A MODEST THEOLOGICAL SKETCH

It is confessed that there is a degree of obscurity in these definitions: but perhaps an obscurity which is unavoidable, through the imperfection of language, and words being less fitted to express things of so sublime a nature.[1]

—Jonathan Edwards

Theological Summary

It is now time to summarize the preceding chapters and chart out the contours of Edwards's lapsarian vision so as to reconsider supralapsarianism today. Too often the designation supralapsarian or infralapsarian reduces to the object of predestination. As witnessed in Chapter 1, such a reduction misleads theologically. At the heart of the infra- and supralapsarian debate lies the theological relation between nature and grace, creation and redemption. Are these separate spheres with separate ends or not? How one answers this question predetermines, in a large sense, how one construes the order and objects of predestination. A strict infralapsarian like Francis Turretin believes a chasm separates the two spheres, while a strict supralapsarian like William Twisse brings them together under one intended end. Even still, modifications and mediations abound in the debate. One such modification involves the scope of the genus of predestination. For a majority of the Reformed orthodox, of which Mastricht may be representative, the genus of predestination concerns the eternal states of rational creatures. Yet, for someone like Thomas Goodwin, predestination also includes the election of Jesus Christ precisely because the defining feature of the theological discussion is God's ultimate end in creation. How could one fail to discuss Jesus Christ? As seen in Chapter 2, both Bavinck and Barth—in their own way—recognize this fact and formulate their critiques accordingly. Bavinck's critique places Jesus Christ at the center of the decretal organism; Barth's critique and so-called purification of

[1] *WJE* 8:527.

supralapsarianism makes Jesus Christ both the subject and object of election and reprobation. Despite the vast differences between them, Bavinck and Barth both resist the conclusion that the end of predestination is the display of mercy and justice, whether construed symmetrically or asymmetrically. Such a formulation proves too austere and reductionistic. Where is the picture of God in Christ?

At this juncture enters the theology of Jonathan Edwards. Edwards's lapsarian vision takes shape around the election of Jesus Christ *ad intra* and *ad extra*. In this way, all of God's decrees harmoniously coalesce around one integrative end: the splendor of the God-man. "In that grand decree of predestination, or that sum of God's decrees ... the decree respecting [Christ's] person ... must be considered first."[2] Predestination does not simply apply to the eternal states of rationale creatures but also to God's creative purpose in Jesus Christ as such, and this in such a manner that the decree concerning Christ in predestination logically precedes all else. Within the plentitude of God's triune life *in se*, Edwards employs the nomenclature of election to specify the communicative movement of love that exists as an absolute and natural necessity between the Father and the Son. The glory of all that the Father is perfectly and necessarily shines forth in the Son of God; the Son is the beauty of God the Father's declarative glory. This has an important theological consequence for Edwards. As God's communicative perfection, the Son too inclines to communicate the divine fullness to another outside of the divine life. This is not a bifurcation of wills between the Father and Son, but a different instant of the one will, although this time as refracted through the hypostasis of the Son.[3] Edwards refers to this turn outward as the election of Jesus Christ *ad extra*.

The election of Jesus Christ *ad extra*, so Edwards reasons, fittingly necessitates the creation of the world which exists for the express purpose of communicating the perfections of the divine life as they exist in the exchange of love between the Father and Son, and then, by extension, enfolding human creatures within divine love. "The Heart of G[od] has been from Et[ernity] determined & Engaged to Give Great Testimonies & manifesta[tions] of this his Love to his son[.]"[4] What is more, the Son's incarnation and the creation of this world are coordinate in

---

2. "Miscellanies," no. 1245, *WJE* 23:180.

3. This theological point made here could be elaborated upon in keeping with the Son's aseity, positively construed. That is, the hypostatic differentiation between the Father and the Son is such that Son qua subsistence is from the Father qua subsistence (the same should be said for the modality of the Spirit); however, the Son qua divine is not from the Father qua divine. The Son is God of himself, though never Son of himself. In this precise sense, the Son himself possesses the communicative disposition of divinity, yet in a manner specific to his particular hypostatic existence. Such specificity is revealed to us in—though never exhausted by—the economy. For an elaboration of a trinitarian grammar in keeping with the Son's aseity, see Brannon Ellis, *Calvin, Classical Trinitarianism, & the Aseity of the Son* (Oxford: Oxford University Press, 2012).

4. Sermon 699. Heb. 2:7-8 (March 1743) [LL. 3v.].

the election of Jesus Christ *ad extra*. This insight lies at the heart of Edwards's supralapsarianism. So conceived, the greatest communication to and communion with creatures demands the greatest union. The hypostatic union is just this sort of union. Within Edwards's overall theological reasoning, the incarnation exists for a greater end than redemption. The incarnation enables adoption into the divine life so that human creatures may share in the Father's love for the Son and the Son's love for the Father. The Holy Spirit effectuates this adoptive union—Edwards would say union of hearts—between the believer and Christ (and the Father) because the Holy Spirit is the perfect, reciprocal availability of love between the Father and Son. Apart from the Spirit's uniting work, the Son's election remains un-shareable with human creatures. Yet, as Khaled Anatolios notes in a different context, one's relation to the Spirit is "always mediated by Christ's humanity, which is itself related to the Father through the Spirit."[5] For Edwards, then, "the end of the Father in electing is the Spirit."[6] The Spirit makes available the Father-Son relation precisely as the Spirit of the Son bonds human creatures to the Son and ushers them into the presence of the Father. Such an understanding of the Spirit as the end of election does not, however, undermine the fact that the Son of God, both *ad intra* and *ad extra*, exists as the grand declarative and communicative medium of the divine life. It fails to undermine the Son's declarative primacy because—to borrow another argument from Anatolios with which Edwards would agree—the Spirit's hypostatic particularity is always "outward facing" as the availability of love, the "subsistent readiness whereby the sonship of the Word is eternally disposed in favor of an infinite number of others who would 'lay a claim' upon that word and that sonship."[7]

Another theological consequence of Edwards's christological framing of election involves a reconfiguration of the covenantal schema. The covenant of redemption, in particular, flows out of the covenant of union as a "superaddition" to its christological and therefore adoptive end. The covenant of redemption stipulates the means of redemption, wherein the incarnate Son dies in the stead of ruined sinners by means of his passive obedience. The covenant of redemption also reduplicates the covenant of works as that which was given for Christ to enact as the perfectly elect creature by means of his active obedience. For Edwards, redemption fittingly exposes the depth of the divine life that God possesses *a se* and gifts to creatures. The covenant of redemption—and by extension the economy of redemption—specifies that the Son of God, of himself, freely gives himself for human creatures at the behest of the Father. Insofar as human creatures are created in and ordered to the incarnate Son, their redemption is found as a necessary extension of his incarnate work. Admittedly, Edwards readily endorses a theological vision wherein God decrees to permit the Fall as an occasion for the

---

5. Khaled Anatolios, "Divine *Disponibilité*: The Hypostatic Ethos of the Holy Spirit," *Pro Ecclesia* XII, no. 3 (Summer 2003): 290.

6. *WJE* 21:146.

7. Anatolios, "Divine *Disponibilité*," 301.

magnification of the christological end of creation in the work of redemption. For Edwards, the Fall is decreed to expose the insufficiency of the human creature apart from their gracious incorporation in the divine life of love. Edwards embraces the theological position that God decrees the Fall to allow for an increased creaturely perception of the love that exists between the Father and Son, a love that creates, sustains, and orders creaturely life:

> And thus the whole old creation, both heaven and earth, as to all its natural glory and creature fullness, was to be pulled down, and thus way was to be made for the creation of the new heavens and new earth, or setting forth the whole elect universe in its consummate and everlasting immutable glory, in the fullness of God, in a great, most conspicuous, immediate and universal dependence on his power and sovereign grace, and also on the glorious and infinitely excellent nature and essence of God, as the infinite fountain of glory and love, the beholding and enjoying of which, and union with which, being the elect creature's all in all—all its strength, all its beauty, all its life, its fruit, its honor and its blessedness.[8]

For this very reason, the decree of the Fall and the decree of redemption—in the most general sense—remain coordinate to each other and subordinate to the election of Christ *ad extra*. Christ's cross, then, becomes the great occasion for the manifestation of the fullness of the Son's heart for creation.

Individual election and rejection, unlike Christ's election, follow upon the supposition of the decree of the Fall. In this sense, Edwards holds that God decrees to save some from sin (i.e., the elect) and allows others to remain in sin (i.e., the reprobate) according to the good pleasure of God's will. The elect are those human creatures who, by God's grace, consent to Christ and are adopted into the divine life, wherein they increasingly partake of the love that exists between the Father and the Son in beatitude unto eternity. The reprobate, on the other hand, are those human creatures who dissent from Christ and eternally suffer from the deprivations and desires of their autonomous wills in hell. Despite the infralapsarian take on individual election and rejection, Edwards's overall vision bends in the supralapsarian direction. Election, as a theological category, resonates across the Fall in accordance with the predestination of Christ. Said another way, election has regard to Christ as the end of creation first and foremost, and not simply as an end within the domain of soteriology. Because election has this range within Edwards's theology, his lapsarianism resists facile classification. The predestination of Christ enfolds the decree of the Fall because every decreed event maintains a harmonious connection to the election of Christ *ad extra*. In this precise sense, Edwards's theological vision modifies supralapsarianism. Jesus Christ truly is the sum of God's decrees. All decrees find their harmonious interconnection in his predestination.

---

8. "Miscellanies," no. 936, *WJE* 20:192–3.

Overall, the divine decree arises out of the profound mystery of God's hypostatic self-differentiation, the fullness that is God's triune life *in se*. Positively construed, the divine decree specifies the connection between God's plentiful life apart from creation and God's determination to be with us in Christ. These two, as Edwards is so often at pains to show, are never disjunctive: the absolute/natural necessity of the internal processions entails a fitting necessity of the economic missions.[9] Yet this does not mean, as Robert Jenson would have us believe, that "[the triune God's] predestinating is simply that he lives one way instead of another; and what he predestines is *Christ*."[10] Certainly, this tells us more about Jenson than Edwards. Even still, Jenson's point—stripped of his actualism—has some merit. Even though God's history is not simply the history of Jesus Christ, God does not decree a history apart from us. This is what the incarnation reveals to us. God decrees a history with us because of and through Jesus Christ. For this reason, there are only two categories: those consenting to their being in Jesus Christ and those who do not. What cannot be denied, however, is that all have being in Christ. For Edwards, the history of Jesus Christ is not God's history, but our elected history.

The Problems in Edwards's Account

Edwards's supralapsarian vision is not without difficulties. Throughout my interpretation of his theology, two have risen to the fore. The first corresponds to the reality of the incarnation. For Edwards, the incarnation of the Son of God pertains to both the end of creation and the end of redemption from sin. There exists "one affair managed in all God's dispensations, towards all intelligent beings, viz. the glorifying and communicating himself in and through his Son Jesus Christ as God-man and by the work of redemption of fallen man."[11] Therefore, it is incorrect say that Edwards's supralapsarianism involves an "incarnation anyway" argument, if by "anyway" one means apart from consideration of redemptive realities. Although this may seem counterintuitive, Edwards's harmonious-teleological approach to supralapsarianism frames the incarnation in such a way that one need not appeal to the counterfactual question: would the Son have become incarnate apart from the Fall?[12] Edwards's theological reasoning assumes the end of the incarnation resides *supra lapsum*. Yet, Edwards never fully specifies how his reasoning on the incarnation logically enfolds both the christological end of creation apart from the Fall and the christological end of redemption on the

---

9. See my earlier discussion of "fitting necessity" in Chapter 3.
10. Jenson, *America's Theologian*, 106.
11. "Miscellanies," no. 744, *WJE* 18:388.
12. If Edwards were to frame the question scholastically, it would be similar to that of Bonaventure: what is the primary *ratio* for the incarnation? On this way of framing the question and its differentiation from the counterfactual form, see Hunter, *If Adam Had Not Sinned*, especially chapter six.

supposition of the Fall. But, as I demonstrate below, there are resources in the Thomistic tradition that can address this matter without sacrificing the central tenets of Edwards's supralapsarianism.

The second and more serious difficulty involves Edwards's claim that vindictive justice needs to be perpetually and eternally perceived in God's program of glorification in Christ. It is not obvious why this needs to be the case given Edwards's supralapsarian commitments. In Edwards's species of supralapsarianism, God does not glorify God's self primarily through the manifestation of power, mercy, and justice. In other words, justice is not an end as such, with creation and fall as means to accomplish the end of glorifying the divine perfection of justice in the form of vindictive punishment. Like Thomas Goodwin, Edwards holds that the one, unitive end in creation is the manifestation of and consent to the excellency of Jesus Christ. To render this primary theological vision more coherent, it stands in needs of correction at precisely the point of the display of vindictive justice.

The Motive for the Incarnation

Regarding the motive of the incarnation in Edwards's theology, it is necessary to address a potential objection to the overall interpretive picture I have painted. The objection focuses on those places in Edwards's corpus that suggest the end of incarnation follows in the decree only upon the supposition of the Fall. That is, only as a result of and subsequent to the Fall, God decrees human beings gain the gift of the incarnation and union with Christ. Recall Edwards's argument from his 1733 sermon series: "Man is hereby brought to a greater and nearer *union* with God ... The fall is the occasion of Christ becoming our head, and the church his body."[13] Or again, "Man's misery is made an occasion of increasing both [the union to a proper object and relish of the object] by the work of redemption."[14] With regard to this objection, two matters are relevant. First, some of Edwards's theological insights regarding God's wisdom in the use of the occasion of the Fall have less to do with the incarnation than with the crucifixion, in particular the "sensible" dependence upon God's love and holiness.[15] Edwards never abandons this insight about the cross. It becomes ingredient to my overall interpretation of the *felix culpa* offered in Chapter 5 of this volume.

Second, as noted above, there remains an internal tension within Edwards's theology on the integration of the christological end of creation and christological end of redemption that needs to be addressed. To reiterate, the election of Jesus Christ *ad extra* entails that the decreed end of the incarnation is not logically contingent upon sin because the end of creation (at least for elect creatures) is

---

13. "Wisdom Displayed in Salvation," in *The Works of President Edwards*, vol. IV (New York: Leavitt & Allen, 1857), 154.
14. "Wisdom Displayed in Salvation," 156.
15. Cf. "Wisdom Displayed in Salvation," 154–5.

beatific union with the Son. Yet Edwards also maintains the incarnation, as Bavinck put it, "on account of sin also has a place."[16] But how can these twin realities hold? To bring coherence to this unresolved tension within Edwards's theology, it is helpful to borrow insights from the Discalced Carmelites of Salamanca, a Thomistic school of thought in seventeenth-century Spain.

On the heels of centuries of debate between the Scotists and the Thomists on the motive of the incarnation, the Salmanticenses developed a nuanced position wherein they distinguished (conceptually) between the end *for-the-sake-of-which* (*finis cuius gratia*) and the end *to-which* (*finis cui*) within the genus of final causality and logical order of intention in the decree.[17] In this theological picture, God does not decree the incarnation out of two distinct motives (ends). There exists a single intended end viewed from two logical aspects within the genus of final cause. To better understand what is being described here, it is helpful to first understand the two stages of the single decree. God's unified decree entails two structural stages *in-quo*, wherein God knows all possible states of affairs in God's simple intelligence (stage 1) and, out those possible affairs, wills an actual created order with its attendant combinations and dependencies (stage 2).[18] In the first stage *in-quo*, God knows the possibilities of the incarnation, original sin, redemption, and so on, as well as their mutual interdependence within different genera of cause (i.e., final, material, formal, efficient, etc.); in the second stage *in-quo*, God decrees them into existence. All of this, then, undergirds the argument that there is one intended end with respect to the incarnation, although it can be considered under different aspects within the domain of causality, even within the genus of final causality itself. This leads to the following conclusion: (1) God decrees the glory of Jesus Christ himself—in the genus of final cause—as the end *for-the-sake-of-which* of the incarnation; (2) God decrees the permission of sin—in the genus of material cause—as the matter *concerning which* of the incarnation; and (3) God decrees the human race as to be redeemed—in the genus of final cause—as the end *to-which* of the incarnation. Among the species of final causality itself, *finis cuius gratia* is of greater account than *finis cui*; thus, "Christ … is the first willed and decreed among all things."[19] Yet, as the Salmanticenses contend, this does not prohibit Christ having been willed with a "dependence" on other things across different genera of causality in accordance with the decree. The incarnation is conceptually prior in one aspect and posterior in another. Yet the end itself is stable. How does this scholastic discussion aid in bringing coherence to Edwards's supralapsarianism?

---

16. Bavinck, *RD* 3:279.

17. The Salmanticenses, *On the Motive of the Incarnation*, 5–125, especially 83–5.

18. The Salmanticenses, *On the Motive of the Incarnation*, 19–20.

19. The Salmanticenses, *On the Motive of the Incarnation*, 83. Something similar is at work in Edwards's own distinctions between ends—ultimate, subordinate, chief, and so on. The difference being that the Thomistic discussion distinguishes between aspects of *one* end and not between different ends.

Let us be clear about the end *for-the-sake-of-which* within Edwards's theology: communicative union with the God-man. Creation exists to be the theater of perception and, therefore, consent to the fullness of the Son of God as the eternally begotten and beloved of the Father. In fact, the election of Christ *ad intra* fittingly necessitates his election *ad extra*. All things *ad extra* hold together in Christ because he exists necessarily as the decretal end (the end for-the-sake-of-which) and harmonious center. Yet, as Edwards also argues, God decrees the permission of the Fall as an occasion for the greater manifestation of the Son's excellency. The Fall, in this sense, magnifies the decretal end in keeping with the execution of God's wisdom in decreeing. In so doing, the Fall becomes a matter concerning which of the incarnate Son, and this for no other reason than every single decreed event maintains a harmonious connection to the Son. This does not mean that the Fall functions as a stepwise action in the decree, especially with regard to reprobation. Edwards, like Bavinck, recognizes that the Fall opens up—to speak crudely—many harmoniously related possibilities, one of which is perdition and the execution of vindictive justice. Another such possibility—as least in Edwards's reasoning—is redemption in general and the covenant of redemption in particular, which exists as a "superaddition" to God's communicative end in Christ. Again, the covenant of redemption specifies the *manner* of redemption (i.e., the Son's perfect righteousness and atoning death), and this in such a way as to magnify the depth of love that exists between the Father and the Son. More strikingly—from the perspective of Reformed theology at least—this also pertains to the covenant of works. God institutes the covenant of works, like the covenant of redemption, as an end *to-which* of the incarnation. It was made for Christ—not Adam—to fulfill, even though it possesses a genuine integrity for Adam. Edwards's harmonious approach to the decrees allows for this.

By way of reminder, the entire decretal and conceptual ordering first occurs within the divine mind. This order, of course, then becomes manifest in the de facto realities of history as decreed by God (i.e., the order of execution). Even still, there exists an inscrutable mutual interdependence among decreed events—an immense omni-lateral interaction—which, from the human perspective, appears as priority and posteriority, cause and effect. But things are not so with God.[20] For this very reason, it is perfectly intelligible to maintain one end under two aspects: (1) the end for the sake of which of the incarnation is Christ and beatific union with him (apart from the conceptual consideration of sin) and (2) the end to which of the incarnation is redemption (obviously upon the conceptual supposition of sin). To inquire about God's intended end in creation and the incarnation is not to inquire about counterfactuals per se, but to patiently attend to the contours of God's revelation in Christ. As Bavinck noted, "There is no room for any reality other than the existing one."[21] The Fall occurred and so it too must be integrated into the

---

20. For Edwards, part of spiritual knowledge involves an increasing recognition of the "beauty" of God's decrees in Christ within this harmonious tapestry as they are present to the divine mind.

21. Bavinck, *RD* 3:279.

end of the incarnation of the Son of God. Overall, this Thomistic correction, or so it seems to me, better represents the motive for the incarnation as articulated within Edwards's supralapsarianism.

Vindictive Justice

Another matter needing to be addressed within Edwards's lapsarian vision involves the eternal expression and perception of vindicative justice as part and parcel of God's self-glorification. Edwards grounds his reasoning in two realities: (1) the principle of proportionate regard; and (2) the beauty of vindictive justice within the matrix of perceiving being. In terms of the former, Edwards argues that human creatures are made to proportionately love God after the manner of God's love *in se*. Failure to love God in proportion to God's revelation of God's self—that is, to dissent from God's loving being—is, by definition, an act of injustice. God responds to creaturely dissent, so Edwards reasons, with a proportionate level of dissent. On the level of metaphysics, vindictive justice works itself out as God's eternal dissent from dissenting being, with hell being the place of such dissent.

But Edwards also takes this principle in another direction. Edwards appears to argue that, as Oliver Crisp puts it, "necessarily, any created theater of divine glory must be one in which all aspects of that glory are manifested."[22] Glory manifests itself in this way so as to be regarded as glorious. Vindictive justice is taken as one such aspect (perfection) of glory, and, just so, must be sufficiently expressed and perceived in the created order. God, so it seems, would impugn God's own glory without the eternal display of vindictive justice. Taken further, Edwards thinks the elect human creature would be less happy without the display of vindictive justice because the sense of God's love and perfection would be less for them. Again, we see an aspect of the principle of proportionate regard. If knowledge of God is imperfect, then the creatures' happiness is proportionately imperfect. In this theological picture, the eternal deformity that is sin, evil, and hell appears to maintain a positive contribution to the excellency of the whole. Like subtle dissonance in a Bach composition, the discordant note anticipates and eventually yields a harmonic resolution. The irregularity contributes to the beauty of the regularity.

Given Edwards's larger theological reasoning on the election Jesus Christ *ad extra*, however, it is not clear why the expression of vindictive justice needs to be adopted in this exact form. Edwards's species of supralapsarianism, in fact, prohibits the prioritization of vindictive justice as an ultimate end of creation. Vindictive justice stands as a hypothetical end upon the supposition of sin. Granted, however, Edwards endorsed a theological vision wherein God decrees the permission of sin in order to turn it into an occasion for the deeper perception of Christ. But this is not inherently problematic. Any theological system that endorses creation *ex nihilo*, monotheism, and refuses to consider the Fall as beyond God's sovereign control must navigate between the Scylla of chance and Charybdis of fatalism.

---

22. Crisp, *Jonathan Edwards on God and Creation*, 184.

Edwards grabbed the horns of the dilemma and accepted the burdens that follow as a result. Robert Jenson was quite right in his interpretation of Edwards on this point: "Either there is no God or there is one who can decree evil in order to turn it into good beyond our fathoming."[23] For Edwards, God decrees the Fall to reveal the depth of God's perfect love for and in Christ as set-in relief against the backdrop of creaturely dissent. But, as I have traced it, this christological vision does not comport well with Edwards's strong claims elsewhere that God necessarily orders a world toward the eternal expression of vindictive justice. Is there a way to resolve this tension?

It seems to me that Edwards's twin concerns for the principle of proportionate regard and the beauty of divine justice could be modified—without forfeiting his key insights—in order to depict dissent's damage as the worst form of ontological loss: literal annihilation.[24] Technically speaking, the perceptive knowledge of annihilation (an irregularity of sorts)—along with the perceptive knowledge of Christ's passion—could eternally resonate with consenting and perceiving being, and so still contribute to the harmony of whole. From the perspective of the reprobate, however, there exists the possibility for the eventual consummation of the project of dissent at the level of the disordered will, "which is that of extricating themselves from intimacy with the LORD."[25] Such a theological proposal has the strong advantage of recognizing that the pain and punishment human creatures suffer as a result of sin are always experienced as relational loss and damage, even and especially in hell. Sin is the punishment; annihilation is its end. Of course, Edwards believed eternal punishment in hell to be thoroughly biblical and expressly forbade the possibility of annihilation.[26] Nonetheless, this theological—and no less speculative—option makes good on Edwards's claim that God does not order a world toward the expression of vindictive justice, even though the enactment

---

23. Jenson, *America's Theologian*, 110. So Edwards says: "'Tis acknowledged that sin is, in itself considered, infinitely contrary to God's nature; but it does not follow but that it may be the pleasure of God to permit it, or that it should be agreeable to his will that it should be permitted that it might be notwithstanding, for the sake of the good that he will bring out of it ... But as God permits it, it is not contrary to God's will: for God, in permitting it, has respect to the great good that he will make it an occasion of. If God respects sin, or considers it as man respects it in committing of it, it would be exceeding contrary to his will. But considering it as God decrees to permit it, 'tis not contrary to God's will." "Part V on Predestination," in *"Controversies" Notebook, WJEO* 27.

24. The possibility of self-caused and permanent annihilation is speculatively and persuasively argued for by Paul Griffiths. He argues that sin reduces sinners—some, not all— to what they seek, namely nothing. Paul Griffiths, *Decreation* (Waco: Baylor University Press, 2014), 202. See also Jonathan Kvanvig's somewhat similar "issuant account" in Kvanvig, *Problem of Hell*, 135–6.

25. Griffiths, *Decreation*, 202.

26. Cf. "The Eternity of Hell Torments" (April 1739), in *The Works of President Edwards*, vol. IV, 266–79.

of such justice might be viewed, upon the supposition of sin, as a hypothetical end agreeable to God in itself. The principle of proportionate regard could also be maintained. Rational creatures exist to love the Son after the manner of the Father's eternal love for the Son. The cross reveals the infinite depth of this love; the resurrection reveals its immutable perfection and life. Punitively speaking, dissent from Christ need only entail Christ's proportionated dissent from the creatures' dissent. Because the highest possible form and manifestation (infinite!) of Christ's dissent occurs in his own death and resurrection, the eternal existence of dissenting creatures hardly seems necessary within the matrix of perceiving being. The pain of hell could be taken as the pain of the absence of Christ's love (consent), a pain rendered more acute by Christ's willingness to enter into creaturely dissent and absence. Although the radiance of Christ's countenance via the Spirit illumines hell, it never enlivens it. His presence remains a real absence, opening up the possibility of fulfilling dissent's true desire: nothingness.

The Promise of Edwards's Account

Edwards's supralapsarianism goes a long way toward answering the critical and dogmatic questions intimated in the critiques of Karl Barth and Herman Bavinck (see Chapter 2). Foremost, Edwards roots election in the depths of God's triune life of love, albeit in a manner quite different from Barth's doctrine of God. Unlike Barth, election is not codeterminative of God's triune-being; rather, the plentitude of God's life as Father, Son, and Spirit determines the contours of election for Edwards. Election as a concept specifies—without rendering the mystery transparent—the absolutely necessary communicative movement between the triune persons. The hypostatic particularity of the Son of God is that of the necessarily elect one, the one in whom the perfection of the Father is communicated, declared, and therefore loved without remainder. To see the Son is to see the Father, not in terms of the interchangeability of hypostatic identities but in their indissoluble relation to each other. God lives and only lives as the Triune One. Election, in this sense, demarcates the positive elements of divine aseity, along with its attendant ramifications for speaking of the divine economy. God's decretal will emerges from God's aseity not as God's absolute power (*potentia absoluta*) but as the power of triune love.[27] Although the good pleasure of God's will remains ultimately inscrutable, it is not for that reason only known by way of negation (though that is true). The revelation of God in Christ informs us of another way, directing our gaze to God's triune existence as given to us in the economic missions and therefore inviting us to ponder the splendor of the divine processions. Within the mysterious beauty of the divine processions—in the Edwardsian sense—lies the positive content of God's decrees.

---

27. Cf. Sairsingh, "Jonathan Edwards and the Idea of Divine Glory," 196–7.

In this latter respect, Edwards's trinitarian gloss on election fills out Thomas's oblique comment that the "eternal processions of the persons are the complete cause and reason of the production of creatures, meaning also that the generation of the Son is the complete reason of the production of creation according to which it is said the Father created all things in the Son."[28] The absolute necessity of the election of the Son *ad intra* fittingly necessitates the Son's election *ad extra*.[29] That is, Christ's election *ad extra* becomes fittingly generative of the totality of created existence and necessarily orders it toward the elect Son of God. The Son's elective telos contains two aspects: (1) to declare the Father's love for the Son, and, in so doing, the perfections of the divine life; and (2) to adopt creatures into this divine life through union with the elect Son of God. Like God's life *ad intra*, the divine economy takes shape around declaration (perception) and loving communication (consent). The incarnation, in this sort of theological account, is coordinate with creation within the election of the Son *ad extra*.[30] One does not have priority over the other. On this point, one may well wonder about the danger of pantheism (or, perhaps, panentheism) and the dissolution of the properly mixed relation between God and creation. John Williamson Nevin summarizes a sharp critique of non-hamartiological motives of the incarnation (i.e., any species of supralapsarian Christology) along these lines: "Every such imagination of course, whether it be open or latent only and disguised, reduces the existence of the creature to a mere unsubstantial show, and ends necessarily in the yawning gulf of pantheism."[31] Such a critique presumes that any form of supralapsarian Christology must always and only be built upon an ontological—as opposed to ethical—framework *tout court*. But this is a misjudgment. Edwards's supralapsarianism rests on the integration of protology and eschatology in Jesus Christ such that the incarnation itself is an act of communicative love. The incarnation is not an abstract ontological principle of sublation; the Son is *Emmanuel*, God-with-us. For this very reason, Edwards's emphasis, quite correctly, inherently prioritizes adoptive love over soteriology, although in the wake of the Fall adoption only comes through redemption.

---

28. Thomas Aquinas, *Scriptum super libros Sententiarum* I, d. 14, q.1, a. 1, sol.: "Et quia processiones personarum aeternae, sunt causa et ratio totius productionis creaturarum, ideo oportet quod sicut generatio Filii est ratio totius productionis creaturae secundum quod dicitur Pater in Filio omnia fecisse."

29. See my discussion of fittingness in Chapter 3.

30. Overall, this theological vector within Edwards's thought is stronger than that of similar articulations with the Reformed tradition. Representatively, see John Owen, *Christologia*, in *The Works of John Owen*, vol. 1, ed. William H. Goold (Edinburgh: Banner of Truth, 1965), 146: "And the love of God the Father unto the person of Christ as incarnate, being the first adequate object of divine love wherein there is anything 'ad extra,' is the fountain and cause of all gracious love towards us and in us."

31. John Williamson Nevin, "*Cur Deus Homo?*" in *The Incarnate Word: Selected Writings on Christology*, ed. William B. Evans (Eugene, OR: Wipf & Stock, 2014), 131–2.

Another promise of Edwards's supralapsarianism lies in its ability to incorporate the decree of the Fall. The incorporation of the Fall in the divine counsel signals the truth inherent in both rigorous (William Twisse) and Barthian supralapsarian schemes. Sin and evil never escape God's intent;[32] redemption too cannot be an afterthought or emergency plan.[33] Such integration needs to be maintained because a danger emerges at just this point within many supralapsarian Christologies in that some seem to evacuate sin's horror and the centrality of Christ's historical death and triumph within the gospel story.[34] The Apostle Paul decided to know nothing except Christ and him crucified (1 Cor. 2:2). Supralapsarian Christologies must take into account the significance of the history of redemption lest "the ethical force of sin is wholly swallowed up in theosophico-metaphysical dreams."[35] The incarnation on account of sin has a place too! "This saying is trustworthy and deserving of full acceptance, that Christ Jesus came into the world to save sinners" (1 Tim. 1:16).

The opposite danger must also be resisted. I have in mind here certain emphases within the apocalyptic turn in theology which so heavily prioritize eschatological redemption that one might well conclude that the world was created in order to be destroyed and transformed in Christ's defeat of inimical powers at the cross. This, of course, is not the intent, though it is an implication. The cross gains priority so as to vouchsafe God's "eschatological gift of love that redeems women and men from the world of unlove by an irresistible divine self-giving, thereby conscripting

---

32. Cf. Owen, *Christologia*, 61–2: "Divine wisdom was no way surprised with this disaster ... this is necessary from the infinite wisdom, prescience, and immutability of God ... that [God] is put unto no new counsels, by any events in the works of creation."

33. Cf. Jenson, *Systematic Theology, Vol. 1*, 72. One, of course, can take this too far, as did Schleiermacher in his supralapsarian (and rigorous) subsumption of all things under divine causality. See van Driel, *Incarnation Anyway*, 9–32.

34. This question, for example, looms large over Edwin van Driel's supralapsarian proposal and his resistance to any species of *felix culpa* argumentation. See van Driel, *Incarnation Anyway*, 25–62. Van Driel responds to this material question as raised by apocalyptic theology in a later essay, "'To Know Nothing Except Jesus Christ, and Him Crucified': Supralapsarian Theology and a Theology of the Cross," in *The Wisdom and Foolishness of God: First Corinthians 1–2 in Theological Exploration*, ed. Christophe Chalamet and Hans-Christoph Askani (Minneapolis, MN: Fortress Press, 2015). His response reveals the tendency to minimize the death of Christ in the eschaton: "Because our relationship to Christ is not based on sin, we will also not have to permanently remember either our sin or Christ's sacrifice. Because the cross is not central to our relationship with God, it can at some point be forgotten" (379). Although this is van Driel's supralapsarian conclusion, I take it that such a strong conclusion is not inherent to all articulations of supralapsarian Christology. One can (and should, I think) enfold redemption within eschatological remembrance. Scripture tells us of at least one eschatological anthem: "Worthy is the Lamb who was *slain*" (Rev. 5:12).

35. Nevin, "*Cur Deus Homo?*" 25.

them into his service as creaturely agents of his love and its purposes."[36] Divine power is always the in-breaking of God's gracious, self-giving love in Christ which overthrows the forces of sin, death, and the devil as it ushers in the kingdom of heaven. So conceived, Christ's cross—not Christ himself—becomes the Archimedean point of revelation. This *is* God, God *for us*; the eschaton is cross-shaped. I take the point about the importance of the cross, even though such apocalyptic fervor has the possibility of distorting the dogmatic material with a hypertrophy of soteriology. Edwards's supralapsarianism alleviates this possible distortion by reframing the relationship between protology, soteriology, and eschatology. Such reframing entails that redemption is not God's first and greatest thought; rather it is God's consistent thought. God is *for us* because God is first *with us* in Christ; God is *with us* because we were created *for and in Christ*. "For Christ" and "with us" are coordinate in the decree as to the ultimate end.

Finally, Edwards's supralapsarian logic ultimately—even if inconsistently—wards off framing God's glorification in individual predestination exclusively as the display of mercy in the elect and justice in the reprobate. Although God might well be glorified in these ways, neither mercy nor justice stand as God's ultimate end in creation. In and by itself, neither individual election nor reprobation exists as a final goal; Edwards can truly say with Bavinck, "in the mind of God they never were a final cause."[37] This does not mean, however, that individual election and reprobation do not culminate in a final and total separation. It only means that both election and reprobation are subservient to the election of Christ in the decree. Even reprobation concerns the fundamental grounding of all reality in Christ, and must, in the end, find its truest *ratio* in him. Jesus Christ is the fundamental truth of every creature's being: in him all things hold together.

Desiderata for Supralapsarianism

Before proceeding to the final sections, it will prove helpful to distill Edwards's theological insights into an expanded set of desiderata for constructing a supralapsarian theology today.

1. *The categorical distinction between God and creation should be maintained in all our theological thinking, though not in such a way that divine aseity remains shrouded in apophatic darkness.*
   Such an account of divine aseity will acquire positive content through reflection on the necessary and "ineffable mutual love between the Father and the Son, both in and by that Spirit which proceeds from them

---

36. Philip G. Ziegler, *Militant Grace: The Apocalyptic Turn and the Future of Christian Theology* (Grand Rapids, MI: Baker Academic, 2019), 49.

37. Bavinck, *RD* 2:398.

both."[38] This is revealed in, but not exhausted by, the economy: "God is from himself, and from himself gives himself."[39]

2. *God's decrees should find their ground, not negatively in God's absolute power, but positively in God's internal self-differentiation as Father, Son, and Spirit such that the divine processions prove generative of the decree for creation.*
In the Father's necessary love of his divine essence and perfections as hypostatically present in the self-differentiated Son, the sharing of the divine life of love with another outside of God's life is made possible. On such a view, the relations of origin (to speak in traditional language) and their termination(s) *ad intra* are integral for thinking through the relationship between God's immanent and transient acts.

3. *Creation, though never an absolutely necessary act for God, should be conceived of as a fitting act arising from of the communicative movement of love between the Father and Son in order to "share" the beauty of the divine life as it is manifest in the Son and returned to the Father.*[40]
The Son—as a possessor of the divine essence of himself—necessarily desires to communicate the divine fullness in a similar, though not identical, manner to the Father. This entails the personal giving of the Son of God *with* and *for* a world because the world was created for the Son by way of fitting necessity. It is a world created for the actualization of the infinite possibilities of knowing and loving the Son, in whom creatures also come to know and love the Father. This act gives being to creation. So conceived, the Son is the access point into the divine life for non-divine realities in keeping with his unique hypostatic existence. The Spirit, in his own hypostatic uniqueness, makes the Son available to us.

4. *A christologically structured supralapsarianism should not connote that all is Christology.*
The primary material domain of Christology is the doctrine of God, even though "no element in a system of theology is unrelated to Christology."[41] In this latter sense, Christology and Trinity remain "inseparable and mutually

---

38. Owen, *Christologia*, 145.

39. John Webster, "Life in and of Himself," in *God Without Measure: Working Papers in Christian Theology*, Vol. 1: God and the Works of God (New York: T&T Clark, 2016), 19. Original in italics.

40. On this point, the framework of "mutual, intra-trinitarian glorification" might also be employed, with human existence then characterized as "participation" in trinitarian glorification. Such a framework is ready to hand in Edwards's theology given that glory is explicated along the lines of trinitarian (and christological) communication *ad intra* and *ad extra*. For a contemporary, systematic construction using this sort of doxological framework, as well as the possibility of a rapprochement between East and West in it, see Khaled Anatolios, *Deification through the Cross: An Eastern Theology of Salvation* (Grand Rapids, MI: Wm. B. Eerdmans, 2020), especially 229–85.

41. Webster, "Christology, Theology, Economy," 57.

implicating."[42] Within its deepest structures, therefore, supralapsarianism is christological because it is unwaveringly trinitarian. "For what is revealed in the incarnate life and work of the Son and enjoyed in our eternal fellowship with him is a divine richness that pertains to God's own being, not merely his works *ad extra*."[43] To be oriented to Christ is never to be oriented to Christ alone. To see Christ's glory is to see the glory of him as the Son of the Father and in the Spirit.

5. *The incarnation of the Son and the decree for creation should be viewed as coordinate such that the telos of creation is unified under two aspects: a manifestation of the Son's fullness and adoption into the divine life as made possible by the Son's incarnation.*
    The Son's unique hypostatic enactment of the divine, communicative will entails union based on the principle that the highest communication and communion demands the highest union: God-with-us. In Edwards's language, the Son desires to communicate the divine love to a "spouse" in a covenant of union, and so there is a world.

6. *Theological descriptions of the divine motive in the incarnation should not appeal to counterfactuals.*
    Theological speech regarding the incarnation should take its cue from the following question: what is end of the incarnation? Framing the question in this manner allows one to articulate the end of the incarnation both apart from and upon the supposition of sin. In terms of the former, Christ himself (and, by extension, adoption in him) is the end *for-the-sake-of which*; in terms of the latter, redemption from sin is the end *to-which*.

7. *The spheres of creation (nature) and redemption (grace) should be integrated around the telos of (#5).*
    Both spheres remain intrinsically dependent upon the grace of Jesus Christ, the incarnate One. This dependence has the further entailment that Christ's human life is the only perfect enactment of divine election, even and especially in his death. In Christ one sees "an entire human identity as an unbroken embodiment of divine [triune] life; not 'resembling' but enacting it."[44] Our humanity, *mutatis mutandis*, becomes the embodied enactment of trinitarian life (election) as we are united to Christ by his Spirit. We truly live in and only in his elect life.

8. *Individual election and reprobation should not be viewed atomistically, especially when this means a single naked decision of the divine will concerning the eternal destinies of individual creatures.*
    God does not create for the purpose of damning some in order to express the glory of divine justice. Reprobation too must have an eye to Christ in the organic tapestry of the decrees.

---

42. Webster, "Christology, Theology, Economy," 56.
43. Duby, *God in Himself*, 175.
44. Williams, *Christ the Heart of Creation*, 239. Cf. Tanner, *Christ the Key*, 140–206.

9. *And, finally, the economic outworking of supralapsarianism should follow a covenantal path.*

To speak of the covenant is to speak both of God's faithfulness to himself and a summons to participate in God's faithful activity with and for creatures as it is concretely given. Covenantal communion with God is ever rooted in the God-man: the covenant maker, keeper, and fulfiller. The covenantal paradigm underwrites this relational gift without collapsing transcendence into immanence, the free Lord of the world into the world's organism.[45] "Creation is one long preparation, and therefore the being and existence of the creature one long readiness, for what God will intend and do with it in the history of the covenant."[46]

Thinking Creation, Incarnation, and Fittingness

The mystery of God's decree for creation and the incarnation is a correlate, in Edwards's idiom, of the Son's internal election.

> The Heart of G[od] has been from Et[ernity] determined & Engaged to Give Great Testimonies & manifesta[tions] of this his Love to his son[.] … [B]ut it was a condecent thing … & it was the will of G[od] to shew forth his own Glory & that in a Great degree so it was his Et[ernal] will greatly to shew forth his Love to his son … this was Gods Et[ernal] design & purpose & seems to be called by way of Eminency his decree.[47]

The Father "thinks" creation in the Son as a theater for the display of the Father's love for the Son, and, as such, a display of the fullness and perfection of the divine life as beheld in the Son. The Son, as a unique, subsistent possessor of the divine nature *in se*, too "thinks" creation in loving response to the Father precisely because he exists in the Father and the Father in him. In this triune "thought" the world arises by way of fittingness. So conceived, creation comes into being in order to communicate to another (*aliud*) the triune name in the glorious exchange of divine love: "I made known to them your name, and I will continue to make it known, that the love with which you loved me may be in them, and I in them" (Jn 17:26).

The end of creation is therefore unitive, taking shape necessarily around the Son of God because the Son exists by way of internal election as the necessary declaration of the Father's glory. In this way, the answers to the questions *Cur*

---

45. For a sketch of one sort of covenantal paradigm, see Michael Horton, *Lord and Servant: A Covenant Christology* (Louisville, KY: Westminster John Knox, 2005), 3–21.

46. Barth, *CD* III.1, 231.

47. Edwards, Sermon 699. Heb. 2:7-8 (March 1743) [LL. 3v.-4r.].

mundus? and *Cur Deus homo?* coalesce theologically. As the natural expression of the Father's glory *ad intra*, the Son's natural response to the Father in the Spirit is also externally and fittingly fecund. On this basis, one can conceptualize the sort of theological (fitting) necessity inherent in the divine processions with regard to God's creative love in coordination with the incarnation. "The fact that God has regard to His Son … is the true and genuine basis of creation. To be sure there is no other necessity than that of His own free love. But a genuine necessity is constituted by the fact that from all eternity God willed so to love the world, and did so love the world, that He gave His only begotten Son."[48] One might recall Narcisse's unfolding of the modality of fittingness: "The problematic of fittingness is rightly an attempt to scrutinize the why of divine Wisdom."[49] Incarnation and creation are seen to be fittingly and necessarily entangled as the eye of faith peers into the divine wisdom inherent in the "realized possible" of the history given to human creatures. Just so, and in keeping with the Son's relation *ad intra*, the Son is necessarily the elect One *ad extra*, the one grand medium of God's communication and glorification. "Jesus Christ is admitted to know God immediately … And Jesus Christ, who alone sees immediately, [is] the grand medium of the knowledge of all others; they know no otherwise than by the exhibitions held forth in and by him."[50] Theologically, creation and incarnation remain coordinate in God's decree precisely because union and communication are never torn asunder. Communication of the glory of God's triune love in the incarnate Son is the highest and true end of creation. As a corollary, this means that God loves creatures only in God's self as given unto others in the incarnate Son, though never out of utility or absolute necessity.

From the perspective of the supralapsarian path I have been pursuing, the good pleasure (*beneplacitum*) of God's will in creating is luminously revealed in the incarnate Son (cf. Eph. 1:8). One need not and should not look elsewhere. All things are truly created ἐν αὐτῷ, δι' αὐτοῦ, and εἰς αὐτὸν (Col. 1:15-16). The qualifier ἐν αὐτῷ stands in distinction from Christ's instrumentality—especially *mere* instrumentality—in creation (i.e., "διά" Christ).[51] Theologically, all things (τὰ πάντα) find their ground "in" Christ.[52]

The Son, furthermore, "acts in the mode proper to him, that is, according to the hypostatic character which is his in the immanent processions of the godhead and which 'surfaces' in his work *ad extra*."[53] In God's work *ad intra* and *ad extra*, the hypostatic character of the Son is elective, and thereby communicative and

---

48. Barth, *CD* III.1, 51.

49. Narcisse, O.P., *Les raisons de Dieu*, 523: "La problématique de la convenance est bien un essai de scruter le pourquoi de la Sagesse divine."

50. Edwards, "Miscellanies," no. 777, *WJE* 18:428.

51. For example, notice the use of διά subsequent to Col. 1:16, as well as in 1 Cor. 8:6 and Jn 1:3.

52. Cf. Goodwin, *Works* 4:454-76.

53. John Webster, "Trinity and Creation," in *God Without Measure: Working Papers in Christian Theology*, Vol. 1: God and the Works of God (New York: T&T Clark, 2016), 97.

declarative. The full compass of God's works groups around the incarnation of the Son because the mutual glorification of the Father and Son in each other is the communicative telos of any created order. "When the Son of God becomes man, the Father prolongs the eternal generation into the outside world, utters His infinite Word from the interior to the exterior, and by this very utterance gains the greatest glory which He can attain in his external works."[54] In scriptural idiom: Θεὸν οὐδεὶς ἑώρακεν πώποτε· μονογενὴς θεὸς ὁ ὢν εἰς τὸν κόλπον τοῦ πατρὸς ἐκεῖνος ἐξηγήσατο, no one has ever seen God, the unique and beloved God, who is in the bosom of the Father, he has made him known (Jn 1:18). In keeping with the axiom *opera Dei ad extra sunt indivisa*, one must also be clear that the works of the Father and Son (and Spirit) remain undivided qua *nature*. There exists a unified operation—not cooperation—in the Father's sending of the Son by/in the Spirit and the Son's being sent by/in the Spirit. Even still, this neither disqualifies nor annuls what is hypostatically unique to each person in their work, whether *ad intra* or *ad extra*. In fact, the triune economy invites us by faith to "appropriate" what is distinct to each person.[55] Per the doctrine of appropriations, we might say thus: (1) qua Father, the Father sends the Son to declare the fullness of God as beheld in the Son (cf. Jn 5:19-29; 2 Cor. 4:6); (2) qua Son, the Son desires to present the fullness ("name") of the Father (cf. Jn 14:13; Jn 17); qua Holy Spirit, the Spirit desires to make available the Father-Son relation (cf. Jn 16:12-15; Gal. 4:6).[56] This is how they act; or, better still, this is their one activity. "Every word

---

54. Scheeben, *Mysteries of Christianity*, 423.

55. Cf. Tanner, *Christ the Key*, 174.

56. Importantly, "Jesus repräsentiert nicht den Vater, er *präsentiert* ihn" ["Jesus does not represent the Father, he presents him."] Klaus Scholtissek, *In ihm sein und bleiben. Die Sprache der Immanenz in den johanneischen Schriften* (Freiburg: Herder, 2000), 256. See also Scholtissek's larger discussion of the Father-Son(-Spirit) "Immanenz-Aussagen" and "Einheits-Aussagen" in John's Gospel such that these immanence-unity statements "interpret" Father-Son(-Spirit) relations in John's gospel, and this well beyond functional representation and authorized sending. Conclusively: "Der Vater als 'Gegenüber' des Sohnes bestimmt den Sohn ganz und gar, so daß er selbst in seinem Sohn und durch ihn zu Wort kommt, und so daß der Sohn selbst ganz im Vater eingeborgen ist" ["The Father as 'counterpart' of the Son totally determines the Son so that he himself speaks in his Son and through him, and so that the Son himself is entirely hidden in the Father."] (379). Grant Macaskill, in his study on union with Christ, too recognizes the centrality of immanent divine "presence": "the grounds for the presence of divine glory with human beings is the relationship between the Father and Son who mediates that presence by the Spirit." *Union with Christ in the New Testament* (Oxford: Oxford University Press, 2013), 266. For Macaskill, divine presence is intimately related to the images of "temple" (both in the OT and NT) and subsequently the "body" of Christ. See also Jörg Frey, "Jesus as the Image of God in the Gospel of John," in *The Glory of the Crucified One: Christology and Theology in the Gospel of John*, trans. Wayne Coppins and Christoph Heilig (Waco, TX: Baylor University Press, 2018), 285–312.

from the Father is surely through the Son and in the Spirit. And every work or miracle is through the Son and in the Spirit as well. It is carried out, however, as from the Father ... The nature of the Father is active, and it shines out beautifully in the Son."[57]

In saying that God loves human creatures only in God's self—that is, in the Son—I am merely reiterating a fundamental point: creatures cannot compel God's self-sufficient love, only receive it as an extension of the Father's love for the Son and the Son's love for the Father. Only derivatively do the missions of the Son and Spirit "open-up" the depths of God's triune life to creatures. More precisely, the election of the Son *ad extra* entails an adoptive elevation of human creatures into the Father-Son relationship. God the Father has predestined us for adoption as sons and daughters through Jesus Christ (Eph. 1:5). We are predestined in the Son's predestination. Uniquely, the Son's predestination just is the hypostatic union. The hypostatic union is nontransferable, and it exists as the perfect enactment of trinitarian life in creaturely form. Jesus Christ alone has this sort of life; Christ alone glorifies the Father perfectly as the Son's divine life distends into the creaturely sphere. Even still, God the Father had in the decree "his Christ present with him, and by him; and reckoned of us as members of him, and elected us as such."[58]

Herein lies the truest election of grace, over and above soteriological considerations. Adoption into the triune life is the end of the incarnation apart from consideration of sin, whereby human creatures are able to be united to Christ in his election as his spouse and body through the secret motion of the Holy Spirit, and, as such, are ushered into the presence of the Father in a manner analogous to Son's presence in and with the Father. Caution is required: human creatures only participate in the Son's election *ad extra*; they cannot and do not participate in his incommunicable relation as the Son of the Father. Ambrose notes the nontransferable distinction: *nos unum erimus, sed Pater et Filius unum sunt*, we shall be one, but the Father and Son are one (cf. Jn 17:23).[59] The "sovereign, supreme union between the three persons in the Godhead, peculiar and proper to themselves alone ... cannot be communicated to any mere creature."[60] Nevertheless, to be united with Christ means to be truly brought into the fullness of God as communicated in triune love (cf. Eph. 3:9).[61] "It seems by [the incarnation] to have been God's design to admit man as it were to the inmost fellowship with the

---

57. Cyril of Alexandria, *Commentary on John*, vol. 2, trans. David R. Maxwell and ed. Joel C. Elowsky (Downers Grove, IL: IVP Academic, 2015), 160 [Book 9, col. 429].

58. Goodwin, *Works* 4:362.

59. Ambrose, *De fide* 4.3.36 [37]. So Scholtissek: "Die ekklesiale Einheit, auf die hohepriesterliche Gebet Joh 17 zielt, hat ihr Maß in der *unio distinctionis* von Vater und Sohn." ["The ecclesial unity aimed at in the high priestly prayer of John 17 has its measurement as the *unio distinctionis* of Father and Son."] *In ihm sein und bleiben*, 376.

60. Goodwin, *Works* 4:362.

61. Cf. Scholtissek, *In ihm sein und bleiben*, 371–80.

deity ... The saints' enjoyment of Christ shall be like the Son's intimate enjoyment of the Father."[62] Following Matthias Scheeben, one may formulate a distinction here between mere adoption and supernatural adoption in Christ. The extrinsic conference of grace would certainly bestow an adoptive benefit of sorts, though it would not have a foundation in our nature and, as a result, fall short of bringing us into the higher, personal relationship between the Father and Son. So, Scheeben argues:

> By the Incarnation, however, we are in truth embodied in the person of God's Son and have become his members ... Because of Christ this sonship is no longer a mere adoptive sonship, since we receive it not as stranger, but as kinsfolk, as members of the only-Begotten Son, and can lay claim to it by right ... In literal truth, and not by simple analogy or resemblance, we call the Father of the Word our Father, and in actual fact He is such not by a purely analogous relationship, but by the very same relationship which makes Him the Father of Christ. He is our Father in somewhat the way that He is Father to the God-man in His humanity by the same relationship whereby He is Father of the eternal Word ... Because of this oneness we become like and conformable to Him in his glory.[63]

Eschatologically, adoptive union culminates in the beatific vision. Such a vision is not a purely intellectual (even if dynamic) vision of the divine essence (à la Thomas Aquinas); rather, it "consists mostly in beholding the glory of God in the face of Jesus Christ, either in his work or in his person as appearing in the glorified human nature."[64] That is, no human creature "sees" the divine essence apart from its subsistence among the persons, in particular the person of the Son. To see Christ is to see God; to see God the Son is to see God the Father. Beatitude, therefore, consists in beholding with unveiled faces the glory of God (the Father) in Christ in the Spirit as we gaze in stunned wonder at Christ's transfigured and ascended state, wherein his human nature shines like the sun from its union with his divinity (cf. Mt. 17:1-8). Most stunningly, the resurrected and embodied Son says, "See my hands and my feet, that I myself am. Touch me and see" (Lk. 24:39); and so "fear not" (Rev. 1:17).

Thinking Supralapsarianism and the Felix Culpa

One final thread remains. In unpacking the lineaments of various supralapsarian schemes—Edwards included—the reflex to integrate nature and grace, creation and redemption around one unitive end was uncovered. Though Reformed supralapsarians navigate this thicket in different manners, the refusal to carve

---

62. Edwards, "Miscellanies," no. 741, *WJE* 18:367.
63. Scheeben, *The Mysteries of Christianity*, 383.
64. Edwards, "Miscellanies," no. 1137, *WJE* 20:515.

up the orders of creation and redemption into discrete spheres with discrete ends was clear enough. Theologians as wide ranging as Goodwin, Edwards, Barth, and Bavinck resist any manner of "Plan A-Plan B" thinking. When this path is pursued, however, one must also provide some account of the Fall. In recent theological and supralapsarian reflections, one reflex has been to downplay the magnitude of the Fall, sin, and therefore the cross, in the supralapsarian framing of the incarnation, especially as it relates to any species of *felix culpa* thinking. Edwin van Driel is painstakingly clear on this point: "Supralapsarians … should explore the meaning of the incarnation, the presence of God among us, as an excellent good in and of itself, and not take refuge in a doctrine of sin to beef up incarnation's meaning. We do not need the bad to enjoy Christ."[65] When worked out with an eye to the death of Christ, van Driel is again clear and consistent in his thinking: "Because our relationship to Christ is not based on sin, we will also not have to permanently remember our sin or Christ's sacrifice."[66] The claim is certainly arresting, though van Driel's overall point is to foreground the incarnation and death of Christ as God's consistent acts of love and faithfulness, as opposed to solutions to problems.

On this score, I want to suggest a version of the *felix culpa* argument that resonates with van Driel's supralapsarian instincts while resisting some of his stronger eschatological claims about "forgetting" sin and the cross. In order to do so, I will first specify—in conversation with Eleonore Stump—the version of the *felix culpa* I have in mind. To refresh, the term *felix culpa* is taken from the Easter *Exsultet*: "O truly necessary sin of Adam, which was blotted out by the death of Christ! / O happy fault (*felix culpa*), that merited to possess such and so great a Redeemer!" On Stump's reading, the central claim of the *felix culpa* is this: "The post-Fall world and the [individual] lives of those in grace in this world are somehow better, more glorious, more of triumph for the Creator, than the world and those lives would have been had there been no Fall."[67] This view does not imply, however, anything whatsoever about the intrinsic value of suffering or that one should seek suffering voluntarily or that the "bad" is necessary for the "good." For Stump, the comparative "better" fixes upon openness to the depths of God's love in Christ and the ability to mirror that love through union with Christ, and so fulfill the image of God to some maximal degree. As witnessed in Stump's interpretation of the *felix culpa*, one need not take the *felix culpa* to mean that incarnation is contingent upon the

---

65. Edwin van Driel, *Incarnation Anyway*, 131.

66. Edwin van Driel, "'To Know Nothing Except Jesus Christ, and Him Crucified': Supralapsarian Theology and a Theology of the Cross," 379.

67. Eleonore Stump, *The Image of God: The Problem of Evil and the Problem of Mourning* (Oxford: Oxford University Press, 2022), 11. I will leave aside here the various distinctions made by Stump between a defense and a theodicy, as well as the problem of mourning as conceptualized in possible and actual worlds and the interconnected concerns of narrative and atonement.

Fall, only that a "supralapsarian" world with a Fall is somehow more glorious than one without a Fall.

Utilizing portions of Stump's framing of the *felix culpa*, I now want to incorporate insights from Edwards's theological reasoning. Recall, Edwards insists that the Fall is "a great occasion for the manifestation of the fullness of God's heart. In the creatures' unworthiness and misery is [an] extraordinary occasion for opening the treasury of infinite riches and fullness of the divine nature."[68] When fleshed out, Edwards's emphasis falls upon the perception of the beauty of divine love—its depth, as it were. For human creatures qua creature to perceive—to taste and see—the inner life of love that exists among the triune persons, they must be allowed to receive its depths, to experience its contours from the inside, and to know that the love of God in Christ alone sustains them. Redemption is not, on this interpretation, first and foremost about a solution to the problem of sin (though the death and resurrection and ascension of Christ does truly secure our restoration and reconciliation), but about the faithfulness and fullness of God's love for human creatures, even and especially in a world of sin and sinners. Christ is not "greater" or "more lovely" because of his atoning work, but human creatures are "brought in" so as to plumb the infinite expanse that is the fullness of the Son's love as given and returned to the Father in the motion of the Holy Spirit. Divine love, in other words, just looks like this. Eschatologically, the realities of sin and its adjuncts—shame and guilt—are neither a reason for mourning nor loss. Like the resurrected wounds of Christ, as Robert Jenson so eloquently put it, our wounds will neither "heal nor fester."[69] They will become icons of the Son's love.

Concluding Theological Postscript

Supralapsarianism should be conceived of as a theological shorthand for the christological conditioning of God's decree as it arises out of the plenitude of God's self-sufficient life as Trinity. In employing the language of supralapsarianism, I sought to specify the integration of nature and grace, creation and redemption around the incarnate Son as the telos of the world's organism. As such, the central mystery of supralapsarianism is the God-man, Jesus Christ, and the blessed adoption of human creatures into the trinitarian life of love through union with the Son as engendered by the Holy Spirit: "And because you are sons, God has sent the Spirit of his Son into our hearts, crying, "Abba! Father!" So you are no longer a slave, but a son, and if a son, then an heir through God" (Gal. 4:6-7).

---

68. Edwards, "Approaching the End of God's Grand Design" (December 1744), *WJE* 25:119.

69. Jenson, *Systematic Theology, Vol. 1*, 200.

BIBLIOGRAPHY

Unpublished Primary Sources (Jonathan Edwards)

Edwards, Jonathan. Sermon 534. Heb. 9:15-16 (Jan. 4, 1740). Edited by R. Craig Woods. Unpublished and edited MS provided by Kenneth Minkema, Director of the Jonathan Edwards Center at Yale University. The edited transcription is published as follows: P534. In *The Works of Jonathan Edwards Online*. Vol. 55, *Sermons, Series II, January–June 1740*, edited by Jonathan Edwards Center. New Haven, CT: Jonathan Edwards Center at Yale University. http://edwards.yale.edu/.

Edwards, Jonathan. Sermon 699. Heb. 2:7-8 (Mar. 1743). Box 11, Folder 816, Beinecke Rare Book and Manuscript Library, Yale University. Transcription provided by Kenneth Minkema, Director of the Jonathan Edwards Center at Yale University.

Edwards, Jonathan. Sermon 819. Gal. 3:13-14 (Apr. 1746). Edited by Tom Koontz. Unpublished and edited MS provided by Kenneth Minkema, Director of the Jonathan Edwards Center at Yale University. Original MS at Andover Newton Theological School.

Published Primary Sources (Jonathan Edwards)

Edwards, Jonathan. *Previously Unpublished Sermons of Jonathan Edwards*. Vol. 1, *The Blessing of God*, edited by Michael D. McMullen. Nashville, TN: Broadman and Holman, 2003.

Edwards, Jonathan. *Previously Unpublished Sermons of Jonathan Edwards*. Vol. 2, *The Glory and Honor of God*, edited by Michael D. McMullen. Nashville, TN: Broadman and Holman, 2004.

Edwards, Jonathan. *Sermons by Jonathan Edwards on the Epistle to the Galatians*, edited by Kenneth P. Minkema, Adriaan C. Neele, and Allen M. Stanton. Eugene, OR: Cascade Books, 2019.

Edwards, Jonathan. *The Works of Jonathan Edwards*. Vol. 1, *Freedom of the Will*, edited by Paul Ramsey. New Haven, CT: Yale University Press, 1957.

Edwards, Jonathan. *The Works of Jonathan Edwards*. Vol. 2, *Religious Affections*, edited by John E. Smith. New Haven, CT: Yale University Press, 1959.

Edwards, Jonathan. *The Works of Jonathan Edwards*. Vol. 3, *Original Sin*, edited by Clyde A. Holbrook. New Haven, CT: Yale University Press, 1970.

Edwards, Jonathan. *The Works of Jonathan Edwards*. Vol. 6, *Scientific and Philosophical Writings*, edited by Wallace E. Anderson. New Haven, CT: Yale University Press, 1980.

Edwards, Jonathan. *The Works of Jonathan Edwards*. Vol. 8, *Ethical Writings*, edited by Paul Ramsey. New Haven, CT: Yale University Press, 1989.

Edwards, Jonathan. *The Works of Jonathan Edwards*. Vol. 9, *A History of the Work of Redemption*, edited and transcribed by John F. Wilson. New Haven, CT: Yale University Press, 1989.

Edwards, Jonathan. *The Works of Jonathan Edwards*. Vol. 10, *Sermons and Discourses, 1720–1723*, edited by Wilson H. Kimnach. New Haven, CT: Yale University Press, 1992.

Edwards, Jonathan. *The Works of Jonathan Edwards*. Vol. 13, *The "Miscellanies," Entry Nos. a-z, aa-zz, 1–500*, edited by Thomas A. Schafer. New Haven, CT: Yale University Press, 1994.

Edwards, Jonathan. *The Works of Jonathan Edwards*. Vol. 15, *Notes on Scripture*, edited by Stephen J. Stein. New Haven, CT: Yale University Press, 1998.

Edwards, Jonathan. *The Works of Jonathan Edwards*. Vol. 17, *Sermons and Discourses, 1730–1733*, edited by Mark Valeri. New Haven, CT: Yale University Press, 1999.

Edwards, Jonathan. *The Works of Jonathan Edwards*. Vol. 18, *The "Miscellanies," 501–832*, edited by Ava Chamberlain. New Haven, CT: Yale University Press, 2000.

Edwards, Jonathan. *The Works of Jonathan Edwards*. Vol. 19, *Sermons and Discourses, 1734–1738*, edited by M. X. Lesser. New Haven, CT: Yale University Press, 2001.

Edwards, Jonathan. *The Works of Jonathan Edwards*. Vol. 20, *The "Miscellanies," 833–1152*, edited by Amy Plantinga Pauw. New Haven, CT: Yale University Press, 2002.

Edwards, Jonathan. *The Works of Jonathan Edwards*. Vol. 21, *Writings on the Trinity, Grace, and Faith*, edited by Sang Hyun Lee. New Haven, CT: Yale University Press, 2002.

Edwards, Jonathan. *The Works of Jonathan Edwards*. Vol. 23, *The "Miscellanies," 1153–1360*, edited by Douglas A. Sweeney. New Haven, CT: Yale University Press, 2004.

Edwards, Jonathan. *The Works of Jonathan Edwards*. Vol. 24, *The Blank Bible*, edited by Stephen J. Stein. New Haven, CT: Yale University Press, 2006.

Edwards, Jonathan. *The Works of Jonathan Edwards*. Vol. 25, *Sermons and Discourses, 1743–1758*, edited by Wilson H. Kimnach. New Haven, CT: Yale University Press, 2006.

Edwards, Jonathan. *The Works of Jonathan Edwards Online*. Vol. 27, *"Controversies" Notebook*, edited by Jonathan Edwards Center. New Haven, CT: Jonathan Edwards Center at Yale University. http://edwards.yale.edu/.

Edwards, Jonathan. *The Works of Jonathan Edwards Online*. Vol. 31, *"History of Redemption" Notebooks*, edited by Jonathan Edwards Center. New Haven, CT: Jonathan Edwards Center at Yale University. http://edwards.yale.edu/.

Edwards, Jonathan. *The Works of Jonathan Edwards Online*. Vol. 39, *Church and Pastoral Documents*, edited by Jonathan Edwards Center. New Haven, CT: Jonathan Edwards Center at Yale University. http://edwards.yale.edu/.

Edwards, Jonathan. *The Works of Jonathan Edwards Online*. Vol. 42, *Sermons, Series II, 1723–1727*, edited by Jonathan Edwards Center. New Haven, CT: Jonathan Edwards Center at Yale University. http://edwards.yale.edu/.

Edwards, Jonathan. *The Works of Jonathan Edwards Online*. Vol. 45, *Sermons, Series II, 1729–1731*, edited by Jonathan Edwards Center. New Haven, CT: Jonathan Edwards Center at Yale University. http://edwards.yale.edu/.

Edwards, Jonathan. *The Works of Jonathan Edwards Online*. Vol. 47, *Sermons, Series II, 1731–1732*, edited by Jonathan Edwards Center. New Haven, CT: Jonathan Edwards Center at Yale University. http://edwards.yale.edu/.

Edwards, Jonathan. *The Works of Jonathan Edwards Online*. Vol. 48, *Sermons, Series II, 1733*, edited by Jonathan Edwards Center. New Haven, CT: Jonathan Edwards Center at Yale University. http://edwards.yale.edu/.

Edwards, Jonathan. *The Works of Jonathan Edwards Online*. Vol. 49, *Sermons, Series II, 1734*, edited by Jonathan Edwards Center. New Haven, CT: Jonathan Edwards Center at Yale University. http://edwards.yale.edu/.

Edwards, Jonathan. *The Works of Jonathan Edwards Online*. Vol. 50, *Sermons, Series II, 1735*, edited by Jonathan Edwards Center. New Haven, CT: Jonathan Edwards Center at Yale University. http://edwards.yale.edu/.
Edwards, Jonathan. *The Works of Jonathan Edwards Online*. Vol. 51, *Sermons, Series II, 1736*, edited by Jonathan Edwards Center. New Haven, CT: Jonathan Edwards Center at Yale University. http://edwards.yale.edu/.
Edwards, Jonathan. *The Works of Jonathan Edwards Online*. Vol. 53, *Sermons, Series II, 1738, and Undated, 1734-1738*, edited by Jonathan Edwards Center. New Haven, CT: Jonathan Edwards Center at Yale University. http://edwards.yale.edu/.
Edwards, Jonathan. *The Works of Jonathan Edwards Online*. Vol. 55, *Sermons, Series II, January-June 1740*, edited by Jonathan Edwards Center. New Haven, CT: Jonathan Edwards Center at Yale University. http://edwards.yale.edu/.
Edwards, Jonathan. *The Works of President Edwards*. IV vols. New York: Leavitt & Allen, 1857.

Published Primary Sources (Other)

Anselm, *Why God Became Man*. In *Anselm of Canterbury: Major Works*, edited by Brian Davies and G. R. Evans, 260–356. Oxford: Oxford University Press, 1998.
Asselt, Willem J. van, Michael D. Bell, Gert van den Brink, and Rein Ferwerda, eds. *Scholastic Discourse: Johannes Maccovius (1588-1644) on Theological and Philosophical Distinctions and Rules*. Apeldoorn: Instituut voor Reformatieonderzoek, 2009.
Barth, Karl. *Church Dogmatics*. Edited by G. W. Bromiley and T. F. Torrance. 4 vols in 13 pts. Edinburgh: T&T Clark, 1936–77.
Barth, Karl. *Der Römerbrief 1922* (Zweite Fassung). Edited by Cornelis van der Kooi and Katja. Section II, Vol. 47 of *Gesamtausgabe*. Zurich: TVZ, 2010.
Barth, Karl. *Gottes Gnadenwahl*. Theologische Existenz heute, Heft 47. München: Chr. Kaiser Verlag, 1936.
Barth, Karl. *Göttingen Dogmatics: Instruction in the Christian Religion*. Vol. 1. Edited by Hannelotte Reiffen. Translated by Geoffrey W. Bromiley. Grand Rapids, MI: Wm. B. Eerdmans, 1991.
Bavinck, Herman. *Christian Worldview*. Edited and translated by Nathaniel Gray Sutanto, James Eglinton, and Cory C. Brock. Wheaton, IL: Crossway, 2019.
Bavinck, Herman. *Reformed Dogmatics*. Edited by John Bolt. Translated by John Vriend. 4 vols. Grand Rapids, MI: Baker Academic, 2003–8.
Belt, Hank van den, ed. *Synopsis Purioris Theologiae: Latin and English Translation*. Translated by Riemer A. Faber. Vol. 2 of *Synopsis Purioris Theologiae: Latin and English Translation*, edited by Andreas J. Beck, William den Boer, and Riemer A. Faber. Studies in Medieval and Reformation Traditions 204. Leiden: Brill, 2016.
Boston, Thomas. *The Whole Works of the Late Thomas Boston of Ettrick*. Edited by Rev. Samuel McMillan. 12 vols. Aberdeen: George and Robert King, 1848-58.
Bower, John R, ed. *The Westminster Confession of Faith: A Critical Text and Introduction*. Grand Rapids, MI: Reformation Heritage Books, 2020.
Calvin, John. *Institutes of the Christian Religion*. Edited by John T. McNeill. Translated by Ford Lewis Battles. 2 vols. Louisville, KY: Westminster John Knox Press, 2006.

Cyril of Alexandria. *Commentary on John*. Translated by David R. Maxwell. Edited by Joel C. Elowsky. 2 vols. Ancient Christian Texts, eds. Thomas Oden and Gerald Bray. Downers Grove, IL: IVP Academic, 2015.

Goodwin, Thomas. *The Works of Thomas Goodwin*. 12 vols. Edinburgh: James Nichol, 1861–6. Reprint, Lafayette, IN: Sovereign Grace Publishers, 2000.

Heidegger, Johann. *The Concise Marrow of Theology*. Translated by Casey Carmichael. Grand Rapids, MI: Reformation Heritage Books, 2019.

Hodge, Charles. *Systematic Theology*. 3 vols. 1871. Reprint, Grand Rapids, MI: Wm. B. Eerdmans, 1977.

Kierkegaard, Søren. *Sickness unto Death: A Christian Psychological Exposition for Upbuilding and Awakening*. Edited and translated by Howard V. Hong and Edna H. Hong. Princeton, NJ: Princeton University Press, 1980.

Mastricht, Petrus van. *Theoretico-practica theologia: qua, per singular capita theologica, pars exegetica, dogmatica, elenchtica et practica, perpetua successione conjugantur*. Ed. nova, priori multo emendatior et plus quam tertia parte auctior. Utrecht: Thomae Appels, 1699.

Mastricht, Petrus van. *Theoretical-Practical Theology*. Vol. 3, *The Works of God and the Fall of Man*, edited by Joel Beeke and translated by Todd Rester. Grand Rapids, MI: Reformation Heritage Books, 2021.

Owen, John. *Christologia*. Vol. 1 of *The Works of John Owen*, edited by William H. Goold. Edinburgh: Banner of Truth, 1965.

Perkins, William. *The Manner and Order of Predestination*. Vol. 6 of *The Works of William Perkins*, edited by Joel R. Beeke and Greg A. Salazar. Grand Rapids, MI: Reformation Heritage Books, 2018.

The Salmanticenses (Discalced Carmelites of Salamanca). *On the Motive of the Incarnation*. Translated with introduction by Dylan Schrader. Early Modern Catholic Sources 1. Washington, DC: The Catholic University of America Press, 2019.

Schleiermacher, Friedrich. *On the Doctrine of Election, with Special Reference to the Aphorisms of Dr. Bretschneider*. Translated by Iain G. Nicol and Allen G. Jorgensen. Louisville, KY: Westminster John Knox, 2012.

Shedd, William G. T. *Dogmatic Theology*. Vol. 1. New York: Charles Scribner's Sons, 1888.

Thomas Aquinas. *Scriptum super libros Sententiarum* (Books I–II). Edited by P. Mandonnet. 2 vols. Paris: P. Lethielleux, 1929.

Thomas Aquinas. *Summa Theologiae*. Edited by John Mortensen and Enrique Alarcón. Translated by Fr. Laurence Shapcote, O.P. Vols 13–20 of *Latin/English Edition of the Works of St. Thomas Aquinas*. Lander, WY: The Aquinas Institute, 2012.

Turretin, Francis. *Institutio theologiae elencticae*. 2nd edition. Geneva: Samuel de Tournes, 1688.

Turretin, Francis. *Institutes of Elenctic Theology*. Edited by James T. Dennison. Translated by George Musgrave Giger. 3 vols. Phillipsburg, NJ: P&R Publishing, 1992.

Twisse, William. *A Treatise of Mr. Cottons, Clearing Certaine Doubts Concerning Predestination. Together with an Examination Thereof*. London: J. D. for Samuel Creek, 1648.

Twisse, William. *Vindiciae gratiae, potestatis ac providentiae Dei: hoc est Ad examen libelli Perkinsiani de praedestinationis modo et ordine, institutum a Jacobo Arminio, responsio scholastica, tribus libris absoluta*. 2nd edition. Amsterdam: Joannes Janssonius, 1648.

Warfield, Benjamin B. *Studies in Theology*. Vol. 9 of *The Works of Benjamin B. Warfield*. Grand Rapids, MI: Baker Books, 2003.

Secondary Sources

Adams, Marilyn McCord. *Christ and Horrors: The Coherence of Christology*. Cambridge: Cambridge University Press, 2006.
Anatolios, Khaled. *Deification through the Cross: An Eastern Theology of Salvation*. Grand Rapids, MI: Wm. B. Eerdmans, 2020.
Anatolios, Khaled. "Divine *Disponibilité*: The Hypostatic Ethos of the Holy Spirit." *Pro Ecclesia* 12, no. 3 (Summer 2003): 287–308.
Anatolios, Khaled. *Retrieving Nicaea: The Meaning and Development of Trinitarian Doctrine*. Grand Rapids, MI: Baker Academic, 2011.
Allen, Michael. "Jonathan Edwards and the Lapsarian Debate." *Scottish Journal of Theology* 62, no. 3 (2009): 299–315.
Allen, Michael. "Reformed Retrieval." In *Theologies of Retrieval: An Exploration and Appraisal*, edited by Darren Sarisky, 67–79. New York: T&T Clark, 2017.
Allen, Michael, and Scott Swain. *Reformed Catholicity: The Promise of Retrieval for Theology and Biblical Interpretation*. Grand Rapids, MI: Baker Academic, 2015.
Asselt, Willem J. van. *Introduction to Reformed Scholasticism*. Translated by Albert Gootjes. Grand Rapids, MI: Reformation Heritage Books, 2011.
Barnes, Corey. "Necessary, Fitting, or Possible: The Shape of Scholastic Christology." *Nova et Vetera*, Eng. edition. 10, no. 3 (2012): 657–88.
Beach, J. Mark. *Christ and the Covenant: Francis Turretin's Federal Theology as a Defense of the Doctrine of Grace*. Göttingen: Vandenhoeck & Ruprecht, 2007.
Beeke, Joel. *Debated Issues in Sovereign Predestination: Early Lutheran Predestination, Calvinian Reprobation, and Variations in Genevan Lapsarianism*. Göttingen: Vandenhoeck & Ruprecht, 2017.
Bell, Michael Daniel. "*PROPTER POTESTATEM, SCIENTIAM, AC BENEPLACITUM DEI*: The Doctrine of the Object of Predestination in the Theology of Johannes Maccovius." PhD Diss., Westminster Theological Seminary, 1986. ProQuest (8619234).
Berkouwer, G. C. *Divine Election*. Translated by Hugo Bekker. Grand Rapids, MI: Wm. B. Eerdmans, 1960.
Berkouwer, G. C. *The Triumph of Grace in the Theology of Karl Barth: An Introduction and Critical Appraisal*. Translated by Harry R. Boer. Grand Rapids, MI: Wm. B. Eerdman, 1956.
Boer, William den. *God's Twofold Love: The Theology of Jacob Arminius (1559–1609)*. Göttingen: Vandenhoeck & Ruprecht, 2010.
Boersma, Hans. *Seeing God: The Beatific Vision in the Christian Tradition*. Grand Rapids, MI: Wm. B. Eerdmans, 2018.
Bogue, Carl. *Jonathan Edwards and the Covenant of Grace*. New Preface. The Jonathan Edwards Classic Studies Series. Eugene, OR: Wipf & Stock, 2008. First published 1975 by Mack Publishing Company.
Bombaro, John. *Jonathan Edwards's Vision of Reality: The Relationship of God to the World, Redemption History, and the Reprobate*. Eugene, OR: Pickwick Publications, 2012.
Bush, Michael David. "Jesus Christ in the Theology of Jonathan Edwards." PhD Diss., Princeton Theological Seminary, 2003. ProQuest (3093899).
Brown, Paul Edwards. "The Principle of the Covenant in the Theology of Thomas Goodwin." PhD Diss., Drew University, 1950. ProQuest (8807394).
Caldwell III, Robert W. *Communion in the Spirit: The Holy Spirit as the Bond of Union in the Theology of Jonathan Edwards*. Colorado Springs, CO: Paternoster, 2006.

Carter, Jonathan M. *Thomas Goodwin on Union with Christ: The Indwelling of the Spirit, Participation in Christ and the Defence of Reformed Soteriology*. London: T&T Clark, 2022.

Cassidy, James. *God's Time for Us: Barth's Reconciliation of Eternity and Time in Jesus Christ*. Bellingham, WA: Lexham Press, 2016.

Clark, R. Scott. "Christ and Covenant: Federal Theology in Orthodoxy." In *A Companion to Reformed Orthodoxy*, edited by Herman J. Selderhuis, 403–28. Boston: Brill, 2013.

Colwell, John. *Actuality and Provisionality: Eternity and Election in Theology of Karl Barth*. Eugene, OR: Wipf and Stock, 2011. First published 1989 by Rutherford House Books.

Como, David. "Puritans, Predestination, and the Construction of Orthodoxy in Early Seventeenth-Century England." In *Conformity and Orthodoxy in the English Church, c. 1560-1660*. Corrected edition, edited by Peter Lake and Michael Questier, 64–87. Woodbridge: Boydell Press, 2000.

Courtenay, William J. *Capacity and Volition: A History of the Distinction of Absolute and Ordained Power*. Bergamo: Lubrina, 1990.

Crisp, Oliver. "How 'Occasional' was Edwards's Occasionalism?" In *Jonathan Edwards: Philosophical Theologian*, edited by Paul Helm and Oliver D. Crisp, 61–77. Burlington, VT: Ashgate, 2003.

Crisp, Oliver. "Incarnation without the Fall." *Journal of Reformed Theology* 10, no. 3 (2016): 215–33.

Crisp, Oliver. *Jonathan Edwards and the Metaphysics of Sin*. Burlington, VT: Ashgate, 2005.

Crisp, Oliver. *Jonathan Edwards on God and Creation*. New York: Oxford University Press, 2012.

Crisp, Oliver. "Jonathan Edwards on God's Relation to Creation." *Jonathan Edwards Studies* 8, no. 1 (2018): 2–16.

Crisp, Oliver, and Kyle Strobel. *Jonathan Edwards: An Introduction to His Thought*. Grand Rapids, MI: Eerdmans, 2018.

Dempsey, Michael, ed. *Trinity and Election in Contemporary Theology*. Grand Rapids, MI: Wm. B. Eerdmans, 2011.

Dijk, Klas. *De strijd over Infra- en Supralapsarisme in de Gereformeerde Kerken van Nederland*. Kampen: J. H. Kok, 1912.

Driel, Edwin Chr. van. *Incarnation Anyway: Arguments for a Supralapsarian Christology*. Oxford: Oxford University Press, 2008.

Driel, Edwin Chr. van. "Sharing in Nature or Encountering a Person: A Tale of Two Different Supralapsarian Strategies." *Scottish Journal of Theology* 75, no. 3 (August 2022): 193–206.

Driel, Edwin Chr. van. "'To Know Nothing Except Jesus Christ, and Him Crucified': Supralapsarian Theology and a Theology of the Cross." In *The Wisdom and Foolishness of God: First Corinthians 1-2 in Theological Exploration*, edited by Christophe Chalamet and Hans-Christoph Askani, 359–82. Minneapolis, MN: Fortress Press, 2015.

Driel, Edwin Chr. van. "'Too Lowly to Reach God without a Mediator': John Calvin's Supralapsarian Eschatological Narrative." *Modern Theology* 33, no. 2 (April 2017): 275–92.

Duby, Steven. "Divine Immutability, Divine Action and the God–World Relation." *International Journal of Systematic Theology* 19, no. 2 (April 2017): 144–62.

Duby, Steven. *Divine Simplicity: A Dogmatic Account*. New York: Bloomsbury, T&T Clark, 2016.

Duby, Steven. "Election, Actuality, and Divine Freedom: Thomas Aquinas, Bruce McCormack, and Reformed Orthodoxy in Dialogue." *Modern Theology* 32, no. 3 (July 2016): 325–40.

Duby, Steven. *God in Himself: Scripture, Metaphysics, and the Task of Christian Theology.* Downers Grove, IL: IVP Academic, 2019.

Echeverria, Eduardo J. *Divine Election: A Catholic Orientation in Dogmatic and Ecumenical Perspective.* Eugene, OR: Pickwick Publications, 2016.

Eglinton, James. *Trinity and Organism: Towards a New Reading of Herman Bavinck's Organic Motif.* London: Bloomsbury T&T Clark, 2012.

Ellis, Brannon. "The Eternal Decree in the Incarnate Son: Robert Rollock on the Relationship between Christ and Election." In *Reformed Orthodoxy in Scotland: Essays on Scottish Theology 1560–1775*, edited by Aaron Clay Denlinger, 45–66. New York: Bloomsbury T&T Clark, 2016.

Fesko, J. V. *Diversity within the Reformed Tradition: Supra- and Infralapsarianism in Calvin, Dort, and Westminster.* Greenville, SC: Reformed Academic Press, 2001.

Fesko, J. V. *The Covenant of Redemption: Origins, Development, and Reception.* Göttingen: Vandenhoeck & Ruprecht, 2016.

Fesko, J. V. *The Covenant of Works: The Origins, Development, and Reception of the Doctrine.* Oxford: Oxford University Press, 2020.

Fisher, George. *History of Christian Doctrine.* Edinburgh: T&T Clark, 1896.

Fisk, Philip John. *Jonathan Edwards's Turn from the Classic-Reformed Tradition of Freedom of the Will.* Göttingen: Vandenhoeck & Ruprecht, 2016.

Foster, Frank. *A Genetic History of the New England Theology.* Chicago: University of Chicago Press, 1907.

Frey, Jörg. "Jesus as the Image of God in the Gospel of John." In *The Glory of the Crucified One: Christology and Theology in the Gospel of John*, 285–312. Translated by Wayne Coppins and Christoph Heilig. Waco, TX: Baylor University Press, 2018.

Fry, J. R. "The Grace of Election in the Writings of Thomas Goodwin." PhD Diss., University of Durham, 1971. ProQuest (U374473).

Gallaher, Brandon. *Freedom and Necessity in Modern Trinitarian Theology.* Oxford: Oxford University Press, 2016.

Gelber, Hester Goodenough. *It Could Have Been Otherwise: Contingency and Necessity in Dominican Theology at Oxford, 1300–1350.* Leiden: Brill, 2004.

Gerstner, John. *The Rational Biblical Theology of Jonathan Edwards.* Vol. 2. Powhatan, VA: Berea Publications, 1992.

Gibson, David. *Reading the Decree: Exegesis, Election and Christology in Calvin and Barth.* New York: Bloomsbury T&T Clark, 2009.

Griffiths, Paul. *Decreation.* Waco, TX: Baylor University Press, 2014.

Griswold, Daniel. *Triune Eternality: God's Relation to Time in the Theology of Karl Barth.* Minneapolis, MN: Fortress Press, 2015.

Gockel, Matthias. *Barth and Schleiermacher on the Doctrine of Election: A Systematic-Theological Comparison.* Oxford: Oxford University Press, 2006.

Goudriaan, Aza, and Fred van Lieburg, eds. *Revisiting the Synod of Dordt (1618–1619).* Leiden: Brill, 2011.

Hamilton, S. Mark. *A Treatise on Jonathan Edwards: Continuous Creation and Christology.* n.p.: JESociety Press, 2017.

Hamilton, S. Mark. "Jonathan Edwards on the Election of Christ." *Neue Zeitschrift für Systematische Theologie und Religionsphilosophie* 58, no. 4 (2016): 525–48.

Hart, David Bentley. *Beauty of the Infinite: The Aesthetics of Christian Truth*. Grand Rapids, MI: Wm. B. Eerdmans, 2003.

Hastings, W. Ross. *Jonathan Edwards and the Life of God: Toward an Evangelical Theology of Participation*. Minneapolis, MN: Fortress Press, 2015.

Hattrell, Simon, ed. *Election, Barth, and the French Connection: How Pierre Maury Gave a "Decisive Impetus" to Karl Barth's Doctrine of Election*. Eugene, OR: Pickwick Publications, 2016.

Hegel, G. W. F. *Georg Wilhelm Friedrich Hegel: Encyclopedia of the Philosophical Sciences in Basic Outline*, Part 1: The Science of Logic. Edited and translated by Klaus Brinkmann and Daniel O. Dahlstrom. Cambridge: Cambridge University Press, 2010.

Heppe, Heinrich. *Reformed Dogmatics*. Edited by Ernst Bizer. Translated by G. T. Thomson. London: George Allen and Unwin, 1950.

Herzer, Mark A. "Adam's Reward: Heaven or Earth?" In *Drawn into Controversie: Reformed Theological Diversity and Debates within Seventeenth-Century British Puritanism*, edited by Michael A. G. Haykin and Mark Jones, 162–82. Göttingen: Vandenhoeck & Ruprecht, 2011.

Hick, John. *Evil and the God of Love*. New York: Harper & Row, 1966.

Hoehner, Paul James. "The Covenantal Theology of Jonathan Edwards." PhD Diss., University of Virginia, 2018. Now published as *The Covenant Theology of Jonathan Edwards: Law, Gospel, and Evangelical Obedience*. Eugene, OR: Pickwick Publications, 2021.

Holmes, Stephen. *God of Grace and God of Glory: An Account of the Theology of Jonathan Edwards*. Grand Rapids, MI: Wm. B. Eerdmans, 2001.

Holmes, Stephen. "The Justice of Hell and the Display of God's Glory in the Thought of Jonathan Edwards." *Pro Ecclesia* IX, no. 4 (2000): 389–403.

Horton, Michael S. "Covenant." In *The Oxford Handbook of Reformed Theology*, edited by Michael Allen and Scott Swain, 433–45. Oxford: Oxford University Press, 2020.

Horton, Michael S. *Lord and Servant: A Covenant Christology*. Louisville, KY: Westminster John Knox, 2005.

Horton, Michael S. *The Christian Faith: A Systematic Theology for Pilgrims on the Way*. Grand Rapids, MI: Zondervan, 2011.

Horton, Michael S. "Thomas Goodwin and the Puritan Doctrine of Assurance: Continuity and Discontinuity in the Reformed Tradition, 1600–1680." PhD Diss., University of Coventry, 1998. ProQuest (U103023).

Houck, Daniel. *Aquinas, Original Sin, and the Challenge of Evolution*. Cambridge: Cambridge University Press, 2020.

Hunsinger, George. "*Mysterium Trinitatis*: Karl's Barth's Conception of Eternity." In *Disruptive Grace: Studies in the Theology of Karl Barth*, 186–209. Grand Rapids, MI: Eerdmans, 2000.

Hunter, Justus H. *If Adam Had Not Sinned: The Reason for the Incarnation from Anselm to Scotus*. Washington, DC: Catholic University of America Press, 2020.

Irby, Joe Ben. "Changing Concepts of the Doctrine of Predestination in American Reformed Theology." ThD Diss., Union Theological Seminary in Virginia, 1975.

Janowski, J. Christine. "Gnadenwahl." In *Barth Handbuch*, edited by Michael Beintker, 321–8. Tübingen: Mohr Siebeck, 2016.

Jenson, Robert. *America's Theologian: A Recommendation of Jonathan Edwards*. Oxford: Oxford University Press, 1988.

Jenson, Robert. *Systematic Theology*. Vol. 1, *The Triune God*. New York: Oxford University Press, 1997.

Jones, Mark. "The 'Old' Covenant." In *Drawn into Controversie: Reformed Theological Diversity and Debates within Seventeenth-Century British Puritanism*, edited by Michael A. G. Haykin and Mark Jones, 183–203. Göttingen: Vandenhoeck & Ruprecht, 2011.

Jones, Mark. "Thomas Goodwin's Supralapsarian Christology." In *A Puritan Theology: Doctrine for Life*, edited by Joel R. Beeke and Mark Jones, 149–59. Grand Rapids, MI: Reformation Heritage Books, 2012.

Jones, Mark. *Why Heaven Kissed Earth: The Christology of the Puritan Reformed Orthodox Theologian, Thomas Goodwin (1600–1680)*. Göttingen: Vandenhoeck & Ruprecht, 2010.

Kearney, John. "Jonathan Edwards's Account of Adam's First Sin." *Scottish Bulletin of Theology* 15, no. 2 (Autumn 1997): 127–41.

Knijff, Cornelis van der, and Willem van Vlastuin. "The Development in Jonathan Edwards' Covenant View." *Jonathan Edwards Studies* 3, no. 2 (2013): 269–81.

Krötke, Wolf. "Erwählungslehre." In *Barth Handbuch*, edited by Michael Beintker, 221–6. Tübingen: Mohr Siebeck, 2016.

Krötke, Wolf. *Sin and Nothingness in the Theology of Karl Barth*. Translated and edited by Philip G. Ziegler and Christina-Maria Bammel. Studies in Reformed Theology and History 10. Princeton: Princeton Theological Seminary, 2005.

Kvanvig, Jonathan. "Jonathan Edwards on Hell." In *Jonathan Edwards: Philosophical Theologian*, edited by Paul Helm and Oliver D. Crisp, 1–11. Burlington, VT: Ashgate, 2003.

Kvanvig, Jonathan. *The Problem of Hell*. New York: Oxford University Press, 1993.

Lee, Sang Eun. *Karl Barth und Isaak August Dorner: eine Untersuchung zu Barths Rezeption der Theologie Dorners*. Frankfurt: Peter Lang, 2014.

Lee, Sang Hyun. "God's Relation to the World." In *The Princeton Companion to Jonathan Edwards*, edited by Sang Hyun Lee, 59–71. Princeton: Princeton University Press, 2005.

Lee, Sang Hyun. *The Philosophical Theology of Jonathan Edwards*. Expanded edition. Princeton: Princeton University Press, 2003.

Legge, Dominic, O.P. *The Trinitarian Christology of Thomas Aquinas*. Oxford: Oxford University Press, 2017.

Levering, Matthew. *Predestination: Biblical and Theological Paths*. New York: Oxford University Press, 2011.

Lindsay, Mark R. *God Has Chosen: The Doctrine of Election through Christian History*. Downers Grove, IL: IVP Academic, 2020.

Macaskill, Grant. *Union with Christ in the New Testament*. Oxford: Oxford University Press, 2013.

McClymond, Michael. "Creation in Jonathan Edwards." PhD Diss., University of Chicago, 1992.

McClymond, Michael. *Encounters with God: An Approach to the Theology of Jonathan Edwards*. Oxford: Oxford University Press, 1998.

McClymond, Michael, and Gerald McDermott. *The Theology of Jonathan Edwards*. Oxford: Oxford University Press, 2012.

McCormack, Bruce. *Karl Barth's Critically Realistic Dialectical Theology: Its Genesis and Development 1909–1936*. Oxford: Clarendon Press, 1995.

McDonald, Suzanne. *Re-imaging Election: Divine Election as Representing God to Others and Others to God*. Grand Rapids, MI: Wm. B. Eerdmans, 2010.

McKelvey, Robert. "Eternal Justification." In *Drawn into Controversie: Reformed Theological Diversity and Debates within Seventeenth-Century British Puritanism*, edited by Michael A. G. Haykin and Mark Jones, 223–62. Göttingen: Vandenhoeck & Ruprecht, 2011.

Muller, Richard A. *A Dictionary of Latin and Greek Theological Terms: Drawn Principally from Protestant Scholastic Sources*. 2nd edition. Grand Rapids, MI: Baker Academic, 2017.

Muller, Richard A. *Christ and the Decree: Christology and Predestination in Reformed Theology from Calvin to Perkins*. Grand Rapids, MI: Baker Academic, 2008.

Muller, Richard A. *Divine Will and Human Choice: Freedom, Contingency, and Necessity in Early Modern Reformed Thought*. Grand Rapids, MI: Baker Academic, 2017.

Muller, Richard A. "Giving Direction to Theology: The Scholastic Dimension." *Journal of Evangelical Theological Society* 28, no. 2 (1985): 183–93.

Muller, Richard A. *God, Creation, and Providence in the Thought of Jacob Arminius: Sources Directions of Scholastic Protestantism in the Era of Early Orthodoxy*. Grand Rapids, MI: Baker Book House, 1991.

Muller, Richard A. "The Covenant of Works and the Stability of the Divine Law in Seventeenth-Century Reformed Orthodoxy: A Study in the Theology of Herman Witsius and Wilhelmus à Brakel." In *After Calvin: Studies in the Development of a Theological Tradition*, 175–89. New York: Oxford University Press, 2003.

Muller, Richard A. "Toward the *Pactum Salutis*: Locating the Origins of a Concept." *Mid-America Journal of Theology* 18 (2007): 11–65.

Narcisse, Gilbert, O.P. *Les raisons de Dieu: Argument de convenance et esthétique théologique selon saint Thomas d'Aquin et Hans Urs von Balthasar*. Fribourg: Éditions Universitaires, 1997.

Neele, Adriaan C. *Petrus van Mastricht (1630–1706): Reformed Orthodoxy: Method and Piety*. Leiden: Brill, 2009.

Nevin, John Williamson. "*Cur Deus Homo*?" In *The Incarnate Word: Selected Writings on Christology*, edited by William B. Evans, 113–35. Vol. 4 of Mercersburg Theology Study Series. Eugene, OR: Wipf & Stock, 2014.

O'Neill, Taylor Patrick. *Grace, Predestination, and the Permission of Sin: A Thomistic Analysis*. Washington, DC: The Catholic University of America Press, 2019.

Pannenberg, Wolfhart. *Systematic Theology*. Vol. 2. Translated by Geoffrey Bromiley. Grand Rapids, MI: Wm. B. Eerdmans Publishing, 1994.

Pass, Bruce R. *The Heart of Dogmatics: Christology and Christocentrism in Herman Bavinck*. Göttingen: Vandenhoeck & Ruprecht, 2020.

Pauw, Amy Plantinga. *The Supreme Harmony of All: The Trinitarian Theology of Jonathan Edwards*. Grand Rapids, MI: Wm. B. Eerdmans Publishing Co., 2002.

Pauw, Amy Plantinga. "Where Theologians Fear to Tread." *Modern Theology* 16, no. 1 (January 2000): 39–59.

Rehnman, Sebastian. "Is the Narrative of Redemptive History Trichotomous or Dichotomous? A Problem for Federal Theology." *Nederlands archief voor kergeschiedenis* 80 (2000): 296–308.

Rouwendal, Pieter. "The Doctrine of Predestination in Reformed Orthodoxy." In *A Companion to Reformed Orthodoxy*, edited by Herman Selderhuis, 553–90. Boston: Brill, 2013.

Rowe, William. *Can God Be Free?* Oxford: Clarendon Press, 2004.

Ryu, Gilson. *The Federal Theology of Jonathan Edwards: An Exegetical Perspective*. St. Bellingham, WA: Lexham Academic, 2021.

Sairsingh, Krister. "Jonathan Edwards and the Idea of Divine Glory: The Trinitarian Foundation of Edwards' Theology and Its Ecclesial Import." PhD Diss., Harvard University, 1986. ProQuest (8620575).
Salladin, James R. *Jonathan Edwards and Deification: Reconciling Theosis and the Reformed Tradition*. Downers Grove, IL: IVP Academic, 2022.
Sarisky, Darren. "Tradition II: Thinking with Historical Texts—Reflections on Theologies of Retrieval." In *Theologies of Retrieval: An Exploration and Appraisal*, edited by Darren Sarisky, 193–209. New York: T&T Clark, 2017.
Schafer, Thomas. "Jonathan Edwards's Conception of the Church." *Church History* 24, no. 1 (March 1955): 51–66.
Scheeben, Matthias Joseph. *The Mysteries of Christianity*. Translated by Cyril Vollert, S.J. St. Louis, MO: B. Herder Book Co., 1946.
Scholl, Brian. "The Excellency of Minds: Jonathan Edwards's Theological Style." PhD Diss., University of Virginia, 2008. ProQuest (3300265).
Scholtissek, Klaus. *In ihm sein und bleiben: Die Sprache der Immanenz in den johanneischen Schriften*. Freiburg: Herder, 2000.
Schrader, Dylan. *A Thomistic Christocentrism: Recovering the Carmelites of Salamanca on the Logic of the Incarnation*. Washington, DC: Catholic University of America Press, 2021.
Schultz, Walter J. *Jonathan Edwards' Concerning the End for Which God Created the World: Exposition, Analysis, and Philosophical Implications*. Göttingen: Vandenhoeck & Ruprecht, 2020.
Schwöbel, Christoph. "God as Conversation: Reflections on a Theological Ontology of Communicative Relations." In *Theology and Conversation: Towards a Relational Theology*, edited by J. Haers and P. De Mey, 43–67. Leuven: Leuven University Press, 2003.
Selderhuis, Herman. "Die Dordrechter Canones, 1619." In *Reformierte Bekenntnisschriften*, Band 3/2, 1605-75, [1. Teil. 1605–45], edited by Ebehard Busch, Torrance Kirby, Andreas Mühling, and Herman Selderhuis, 87–93. Neukirchen-Vluyn: Neukirchener Theologie, 2015.
Selderhuis, Herman. "Introduction to the Synod of Dordt (1618–1619)." In *Acta et Documenta Syndodi Nationalis Dordrechtanae (1618–1619)*, vol. 1, Acta of the Synod of Dordt, edited by Donald Sinnema, Christian Moser, and Herman Selderhuis; in collaboration with Janika Bischof, Johanna Roelevink, and Fred van Lieburg, xv–xxxii. Göttingen: Vandehoeck & Ruprecht, 2015.
Sinnema, Donald. "Introduction" to *Acta et Documenta Syndodi Nationalis Dordrechtanae (1618–1619)*, vol. II/2, Early Sessions of the Synod of Dordt, edited by Christian Moser, Herman J. Selderhuis, Donald W. Sinnema, and Johanna Roelevin, xxi–xxviii. Göttingen: Vandehoeck & Ruprecht, 2018.
Sinnema, Donald. "The issue of reprobation at the Synod of Dordt (1618–1619) in light of the history of the doctrine." PhD Diss. University of St. Michael's College, Toronto, 1985. ProQuest (NL28124).
Sonderegger, Katherine. *Systematic Theology*. Vol. 1, *The Doctrine of God*. Minneapolis, Fortress Press, 2015.
Stanglin, Keith D. *Arminius on the Assurance of Salvation: The Context, Roots, and Shape of the Leiden Debate, 1603–1609*. Leiden: Brill, 2007.
Stanglin, Keith D., and Thomas H. McCall. *Jacob Arminius: Theologian of Grace*. New York: Oxford University Press, 2012.

Storms, Sam. *Tragedy in Eden: Original Sin in the Theology of Jonathan Edwards*. Lanham, MD: University Press of America, 1985.

Strobel, Kyle. *Jonathan Edwards's Theology: A Reinterpretation*. London: Bloomsbury T&T Clark, 2014.

Strobel, Kyle. "Theology in the Gaze of the Father: Retrieving Jonathan Edwards's Trinitarian Aesthetics." In *Advancing Trinitarian Theology: Explorations in Constructive Dogmatics*, edited by Oliver Crisp and Fred Sanders, 147–70. Grand Rapids, MI: Zondervan, 2014.

Stump, Eleonore. *The Image of God: The Problem of Evil and the Problem of Mourning*. Oxford: Oxford University Press, 2022.

Sutanto, Nathaniel Gray. "Organic Knowing: The Theological Epistemology of Herman Bavinck." PhD Diss., The University of Edinburgh, 2017. ProQuest (13833555). Now published as *God and Knowledge: Herman Bavinck's Theological Epistemology*. London: Bloomsbury T&T Clark, 2020.

Swain, Scott. "The Covenant of Redemption." In *Christian Dogmatics: Reformed Theology for the Church*, edited by Michael Allen and Scott Swain, 107–25. Grand Rapids, MI: Baker Academic, 2016.

Tan, Seng-Kong. *Fullness Received and Returned: Trinity and Participation in Jonathan Edwards*. Minneapolis, MN: Fortress Press, 2014.

Tan, Seng-Kong. "Jonathan Edwards's Dynamic Idealism and Cosmic Christology." In *Idealism and Christian Theology*, edited by Joshua Harris and S. Mark Hamilton, 177–96. Vol. 1 of *Idealism and Christianity*. New York: Bloomsbury Academic, 2016.

Tanner, Kathryn. *Christ the Key*. Cambridge: Cambridge University Press, 2010.

Thomas, John Newton. "Determinism in the Theological System of Jonathan Edwards." PhD Diss., The University of Edinburgh, 1937.

Thuesen, Peter J. *Predestination: The American Career of a Contentious Debate*. New York: Oxford University Press, 2009.

Tolsma, Marijke, Keith D. Stanglin, and Theodoor Marius van Leeuwen, eds. *Arminius, Arminianism, and Europe: Jacobus Arminius (1559/60–1609)*. Leiden: Brill, 2009.

Trueman, Carl. *The Claims of Truth: John Owen's Trinitarian Theology*. Carlisle: Paternoster Press, 1998.

Tseng, Shao Kai. *Karl Barth's Infralapsarian Theology: Origins and Development (1920–1953)*. Downers Grove, IL: IVP Academic, 2016.

Tseng, Shao Kai. "Karl Barth on Nothingness: A Christological-Predestinarian Defiance of Theodicy." *Sino-Christian Studies* 20 (2015): 35–64.

Tseng, Shao Kai. *Trinity and Election: The Christocentric Reorientation of Karl Barth's Speculative Theology, 1936–1942*. New York: T&T Clark, 2023.

Vale, Fellipe Do. "On Thomas Aquinas's Rejection of an 'Incarnation Anyway.'" *TheoLogica: An International Journal for Philosophy of Religion and Philosophical Theology* 3, no. 1 (2019): 144–64.

Velde, Dolf te. *The Doctrine of God in Reformed Orthodoxy, Karl Barth, and the Utrecht School: A Study in Method and Content*. Boston: Brill, 2013.

Venema, Cornelis P. "Covenant and Election in the Theology of Herman Bavinck." *Mid-America Journal of Theology* 19 (2008): 69–115.

Vetö, Miklos. *La pensée de Jonathan Edwards: avec une concordance des différentes editions de ses Œuvres*, nouvelle édition remaniée. Paris: L'Harmattan, 2007. Translated as *The Thought of Jonathan Edwards*. Translated by Philip Choinière-Shields. Eugene, OR: Wipf & Stock, 2021.

Webster, John. *Barth's Earlier Theology: Four Studies*. London: T&T Clark, 2005.

Webster, John. "Biblical Reasoning." In *Domain of the Word: Scripture and Theological Reasoning*, 115–32. New York: Bloomsbury T&T Clark, 2012.
Webster, John. "Christology, Theology, Economy. The Place of Christology in Systematic Theology." In *God Without Measure: Working Papers in Christian Theology*, 43–58. Vol. 1, *God and the Works of God*. New York: T&T Clark, 2016.
Webster, John. "Life in and of Himself." In *God Without Measure: Working Papers in Christian Theology*, 13–28. Vol. 1, *God and the Works of God*. New York: T&T Clark, 2016.
Webster, John. *Karl Barth*. 2nd edition. New York: Bloomsbury Continuum, 2004.
Webster, John. "*Non Ex Aequo*: God's Relation to Creatures." In *God Without Measure: Working Papers in Christian Theology*, 116–26. Vol. 1, *God and the Works of God*. New York: T&T Clark, 2016.
Webster, John. "Theologies of Retrieval." In *Oxford Handbook of Systematic Theology*, edited by John Webster, Kathryn Tanner, and Ian Torrance, 583–99. New York: Oxford University Press, 2007.
Webster, John. "Trinity and Creation." In *God Without Measure: Working Papers in Christian Theology*, 83–98. Vol. 1, *God and the Works of God*. New York: T&T Clark, 2016.
Weeks, John Stafford. "A Comparison of Calvin and Edwards on the Doctrine of Election." PhD Diss., University of Chicago, 1962.
Wessling, Jordan. *Divine Love: A Systematic Account of God's Love for Humanity*. Oxford: Oxford University Press, 2020.
Wilcoxen, Matthew. *Divine Humility: God's Morally Perfect Being*. Waco, TX: Baylor University Press, 2019.
Williams, Rowan. *Christ the Heart of Creation*. London: Bloomsbury Continuum, 2018.
Wittman, Tyler R. *God and Creation in the Theology of Thomas Aquinas and Karl Barth*. Cambridge: Cambridge University Press, 2019.
Wolterstorff, Nicholas. "Barth on Evil." *Faith and Philosophy* 13, no. 4 (1996): 584–608.
Woo, B. Hoon. *The Promise of the Trinity: The Covenant of Redemption in the Theologies of Witsius, Owen, Dickson, Goodwin, and Cocceius*. Göttingen: Vandenhoeck & Ruprecht, 2018.
Wüthrich, Matthias Dominique. *Gott und das Nichtige: eine Untersuchung zur Rede vom Nichtigen ausgehend von § 50 der Kirchlichen Dogmatik Karl Barths*. Zürich: Theologischer Verlag Zürich, 2006.
Yazawa, Reita. "Covenant of Redemption in the Theology of Jonathan Edwards: The Nexus between the Immanent and Economic Trinity." PhD Diss., Calvin Theological Seminary, 2013.
Ziegler, Philip G. *Militant Grace: The Apocalyptic Turn and the Future of Christian Theology*. Grand Rapids, MI: Baker Academic, 2019.

INDEX

Adams, Marilyn McCord 7 n.27
Adam's reward 129
actualism 83 n.179, 207
adoption 7, 47–8, 53, 176, 178, 183–4, 187, 194, 223
   as enabled by Christ 222
   into God's triune life 205, 214, 218, 222, 225
   priority over redemption 214
Allen, Michael 169 n.62
Allen, Michael and Scott Swain, *Reformed Catholicity* 2
Anatolios, Khaled 205, 217 n.40
angels
   confirmation of, the 132–3
   fall of, the 114–15
Anselm 131
apocalyptic theology 215–16
apophaticism 216–17
appropriations, doctrine of 102, 221
Arminius, Jacob 16, 25, 59
aseity, divine 216

Barth, Karl 2, 53, 198–200, 213
   actualism of 73
   on atonement 81
   on *Aufhebung, die* 69, 81 n.161
   on covenant and creation 79, 83–4, 117 n.123
   on *decretum absolutum* 70, 73, 75–6, 87
   on *felix culpa* 82–3
   on God's Yes and No 77–80, 82, 84
   Gottes Gnadenwahl 68–70
   on *homo labilis* 76, 78, 80, 82, 84
   on infralapsarianism 74–6
   integration, supralapsarian and christological 83–4, 86
   on natural theology 69, 72
   on *Nichtige, das* 78–84
   and Pierre Maury 68
   on purified supralapsarianism 76–8, 85–6
   and theological method 71 n.96
Bavinck, Herman 156, 163, 198, 209–10, 216, 224
   on asymmetry of election and rejection 60
   on Christ as organic center of decrees 66–8
   on election and incarnation 67–8
   on Fall, the 59, 61, 67, 210
   on *felix culpa* 61 n.30
   on infralapsarianism 58–9, 62–6
   on organicism and the decrees 63–5
   on supralapsarianism 60–6
beatific vision 210, 223 (*see also under* Edwards, Jonathan)
Bell, Michael D. 21–2, 40 n.134
Berkouwer, G. C. 61 n.29, 77 n.136, 78, 86
Bogue, Carl 121–2, 127, 141, 144
Bombaro, John 158

Carter, Jonathan 44 n.159
Christ
   and beatific vision 223
   as communicative medium 220–1
   and creation 117, 217, 220
   and divine ideas 160
   election of 108, 204, 222 (*see also under* Edwards, Jonathan)
   as end of the decree 110, 210
   for us 216
   as ground of election 110, 220
   as *incarnandus* 112, 153
   perception of 160
   and reprobation 216
   union with 111–12
Christology, supralapsarian 214–15, 217–18
   and Bavinck, Herman 68
   and counterfactuals 45, 48, 119, 207, 210, 218
   definition of 6–7

and Edwards, Jonathan (*see under* Edwards, Jonathan)
and Goodwin, Thomas 45–9
Clark, R. Scott 124
Colwell, John 83
convenientia. See fittingness
covenant 219
  of grace 123 (*see also under* Edwards, Jonathan)
  of redemption 123–4, 205, 210 (*see also under* Edwards, Jonathan)
  taken as marriage of Christ and church 141–3, 148–9
  of works 122–3, 205 (*see also under* Edwards, Jonathan)
    abrogation of covenant 127–8
    fulfillment by Christ 139
creation
  Christ and (*see under* Christ)
  as communication from the Son of God 104–5
  trinitarian logic of 103–4, 204–5, 217
Crisp, Oliver 95–6, 105 n.64, 107, 145–6, 187, 198, 211

decree, divine
  of the Fall 206, 210
  harmony of the 206
  in signo rationis 19–20, 209
  in Reformed theology 15–16
  trinitarian structure of 207, 213–14
Do Vale, Fellipe 107 n.71
dogmatics, definition of 1
donum superadditum 199
Duby, Steven 2 n.6, 71 n.96, 86, 218 n.43

Edwards, Jonathan 8
  on angels 113–15, 132–4
  on beatific vision, the 184–9
  on beauty 157–8
  on consent 176, 186, 190
    of Adam 125–6
    to Christ 193, 196–7
    metaphysics of 175
  on covenant,
    of grace 131, 140–7
    of redemption 134–47, 148–52
    taken as marriage 141–52
    of works 125–34, 138–40, 152–4

on crucifixion, the 178–80
on decree of reprobation 164–73
and determinism 9
on dissent 190–4
on divine ideas 100
End of Creation 93, 99–100, 104, 147, 150, 162
on election of Christ, the 117
  ad intra 97–8
  ad extra 99–108, 147–8, 167, 182–4
on ends, original and hypothetical 162–3
on excellency 158, 166
on Fall, the 154, 168, 173–6
and *felix culpa* 115 n.116, 131–2, 154, 156, 174–80, 186, 193, 198–9
Freedom of the Will 96, 159
on futurition of sin 161
on God's self-glorification 146
on harmony of decrees, the 156–61
on hell 189–93
on holiness, God's 166
on Holy Spirit, the 133, 137, 174, 182–4
hypostatic union, benefit of 131
on idealism 159
as infralapsarian 9
on image of God 173–4
interpretations of 9
lapsarian scheme of 195
metaphysics of justice in 166–7, 179
necessity of creation and 93–7, 100
on objects in the decree, the 171–2
on order of the decree, the 171–2
Original Sin 173
on perception 187–9, 192–4, 198
principle of proportionate regard in 167, 190, 192
and reprobation 168–73, 193–5
on Satan 114–15, 131
and Spirit-Christology 182–4
on spouse of Christ, the 111, 142–3, 146–8, 151
as supralapsarian 195–200
and supralapsarian Christology 108–16
on trinitarian relations 97–8, 166–7
on vindictive justice 165, 169, 177, 179, 187–98, 197–8, 208
Eglinton, James 63–4

election
    and creation in Christ 108, 204–5
    as creative communication 105, 148

Fall, the 154, 206, 210, 215
felix culpa 7, 61, 82–3, 115 n.116, 131–2, 154, 156, 174–80, 186, 193, 198–9, 223–5
Fisk, Philip 181 n.114
fittingness
    definition of 106–8
    of incarnation 204, 214, 219–20
    in theology of Jonathan Edwards 106–8, 117
Formula Consensus Helvetica 26 n.53

Gallaher, Brandon 179 n.102
Gibson, David 71 n.96
Gomarus, Franciscus 16
Goodwin, Thomas 86, 108–10, 115 n.112, 118–19, 124, 129, 142 n.111, 172, 174 n.79, 194, 196, 199–200, 203, 208, 224
    on Adam's reward 45 n.160
    on Christ and the decree (*see* Christology, supralapsarian)
    on election, acts of 49–51
    on Fall, the 50–1
    on glory of Christ's person, the 48
    on nature and grace 53
    on reprobation 49–51
    on super-creation grace 43–5
    on supernatural adoption in Christ 47
    and supralapsarianism 53–4
Griffiths, Paul 212 n.24

Hamilton, S. Mark 159 n.13
Hastings, W. Ross 184 n.137
Hegel, G. W. F. 69 n.97
hell
    and annihilation 212–13
    presence of Christ in 213
Hick, John 177
Hoehner, Paul 140
Holmes, Steven 119, 145–6, 189, 194
Holy Spirit, the 205
Houck, Daniel 174 n.79
hypostatic union 117, 148, 205
    as predestination of Christ 222

incarnation
    as act of communicative love 214
    in coordination with creation 220
    as greater end than redemption 205

Jones, Mark 42, 44, 49 n.186
Jenson, Robert 105, 109 n. 80, 109 n. 82, 135 n.76, 152–3, 207, 212, 225

Kierkegaard, Søren 192
Kvanvig, Jonathan 190 n.170

Lapsarian controversy, 16–18
Lee, Sang Hyun 94–6, 100
Legge, Dominic 102 n.51
Levering, Matthew 6, 8

Maccovius, Johannes 15 n.2, 38–40, 172
McClymond, Michael 167
McClymond, Michael and Gerald McDermott 115 n.116, 131
McDonald, Suzanne 5
Muller, Richard 4 n.17, 28

Narcisse, Gilbert 106 n.71, 107 n.73, 220
nature and grace 6, 218, 223–4
    as central to lapsarian debate 11, 21–2, 33, 41, 52, 203
    and supralapsarian integration 85–6
necessity 15 n.2
    as absolute (natural) in Trinity 97–8, 204, 214
    fittingness as (*see* fittingness)
    hypothetical 106
    of incarnation 113
    moral 96
Nevin, John Williamson 214

O'Neill, Taylor Patrick 8 n.29
Owen, John 1–2, 214 n.30, 215 n.32, 217 n.38

pactum salutis 49 n.186, 71 n.96 (*see also* covenant of redemption)
potentia absoluta 39, 107, 217
Pass, Bruce 63, 67
Pauw, Amy Plantinga 115 n.116, 133, 181
Perkins, William 16, 38–9
predestination 4

of Christ 112 (*see also* Christ)
  display of mercy and justice in 216
  scope of 203–4

Ramsey, Paul 146 n.127, 158
Remonstrants. *See* Arminius, Jacob
Reformed theology 16–17
  definition of 4 n.17
  and Jonathan Edwards 11, 210
  and predestination 4–5
reprobation 216, 218
ressourcement 3 n.15

Salladin, James 105 n.63
Salmanticenses, the 209–10
Sarisky, Darren 3–4
Schafer, Thomas 181
Scheeben, Matthias 54 n.207, 197 n.195, 223
Schleiermacher, F. D. E. 5, 215 n.33
Scholtissek, Klaus 221 n.56, 222 n.59
Schultz, Walter, 101 n.50
sin
  futurition of 161
  as punishment 212
Sonderegger, Katherine 160 n.20
Strobel, Kyle 182, 185
Stump, Eleanore 224–5
supralapsarianism, *desiderata* for 216–19
Sutanto, Nathaniel Gray 64
Synod of Dordrecht 16–17

Tan, Seng-Kong 101, 102 n.52, 103 n.57, 160
Tanner, Kathryn 174, 199
theological retrieval 2–4
Thomas Aquinas 101, 102 n.51, 134 n.74, 214, 223
Thomas, John Newton 198
Trinity
  and creation 217, 219 (*see also under* creation)
  and election 214–15
  and supralapsarianism 217–18
Tseng, Shao Kai 68–9, 80 n.155
Turretin, Francis 18, 54 n.208, 59 n.10, 75, 109 n.81, 173, 199–200, 203
  on Adam's reward 129
  and Amyraldianism 26
  on election of Christ, the 22–4

and infralapsarianism 52
  on object of predestination, the 19–22
  on order of decrees, the 24–7
  on orders of creation and redemption, the 20–2
  rejection of supralapsarianism in 20, 25, 31
  on sin 20–1
Twisse, William 38–41, 84, 163 n.36, 203, 215

van Driel, Edwin Chr. 81–3, 215 n.342, 224
van Mastricht, Petrus 84, 159, 172, 196, 203
  on distinction between damnation and reprobation, the 36
  on election, the logical acts of 32–3
  on election of Christ, the 32
  on futurition of sin, the 36–7
  on impulsive cause of predestination, the 29
  on means of predestination, the 29–30
  mediating position of 41–2
  on objects of predestination, the 31
  on order of predestination, the 38
  on reprobation, the logical acts of 33–7
  and supralapsarianism 29, 33, 38–42, 52, 84
Velde, Dolf te 71
Vetö, Miklos 104–5, 169 n.64, 192, 196–7
vindictive (vindicatory) justice. *See also under* Edwards, Jonathan
  Barth's critique of 73
  Bavinck's critique of 60, 65
  Mastricht, Petrus van on 29–30, 34, 37, 41, 52
  as problem in Edwards's theology 211–13
  Turretin, Francis on 26–7
  Twisse, William on 40–2

Warfield, B. B. 5 n.18
Webster, John 64 n.50, 217 n.39, 217 n.41, 218 n.42, 220 n.53
Westminster Confession of Faith 5, 8, 122–3, 180
Williams, Rowan 183
Wittman, Tyler 71 n.96
Woo, B. Hoon 42 n.142, 124
Wüthrich, Matthias 78

www.ingramcontent.com/pod-product-compliance
Lightning Source LLC
Chambersburg PA
CBHW051520230426
43668CB00012B/1673